THE TALMUD OF BABYLONIA

Program in Judaic Studies
Brown University
BROWN JUDAIC STUDIES
Edited by
Jacob Neusner,
Wendell S. Dietrich, Ernest S. Frerichs,
Alan Zuckerman

Project Editors (Project)

David Blumenthal, Emory University (Approaches to Medieval Judaism)
Ernest S. Frerichs, Brown University (Dissertations and Monographs)
Lenn Evan Goodman, University of Hawaii (Studies in Medieval Judaism)
William Scott Green, University of Rochester (Approaches to Ancient Judaism)
Ivan Marcus, Jewish Theological Seminary of Americas
(Texts and Studies in Medieval Judaism)
Marc L. Raphael, Ohio State University (Approaches to Judaism in Modern Times)
Jonathan Z. Smith, University of Chicago (Studia Philonica)

Number 74
THE TALMUD OF BABYLONIA
An American Translation
VI. Tractate Sukkah

translated by
Jacob Neusner

THE TALMUD OF BABYLONIA
An American Translation
VI. Tractate Sukkah

translated by
Jacob Neusner

Scholars Press
Chico, California

THE TALMUD OF BABYLONIA
An American Translation
VI. Tractate Sukkah

translated by
Jacob Neusner

© 1984
Brown University

Library of Congress Cataloging in Publication Data

Talmud. Sukkah. English.
  Tractate Sukkah.

  (The Talmud of Babylonia ; 6) (Brown Judaic studies ;
no. 74)
  Includes index.
  I. Neusner, Jacob, 1932– . II. Title. III. Series:
Talmud. English. 1984 ; 6. IV. Series: Brown Judaic
studies ; no. 74.
BM499.5.E4 1984 vol. 6   296.1'2505 s   84–14076
[BM506.S9E5]   [296.1'2505]
ISBN 0-89130-786-9 (alk. paper)
ISBN 0-89130-788-5 (pbk. : alk. paper)

Printed in the United States of America
on acid-free paper

In memory of

URIEL TAL

Tormented, great soul, he bore on himself the burdens of our age.
His learning lives on, a light to our encounter with the other.
What is lost is the self, the selfless, suffering man.
For that we mourn.

CONTENTS

PREFACE

This is the third tractate of the new American translation, but, of course, not the first tractate of the Talmud of Babylonia. The project, when completed, will consist of the following parts (number of folio pages in the original):

The several tractates will be issued when they become ready. The corps of translators hopes that the entire project will be complete by 1994, that is, within ten years of the date of the appearance of this tractate.

Tractates will be numbered by volume, then, if appearing in two or more fascicles, lettered, e.g., as follows:

THE TALMUD OF BABYLONIA. AN AMERICAN TRANSLATION

Vol. XXX.C then would contain the index for all three parts and also the reproduction of the text.

I expect to translate five tractates in all, this one and Arakhin, Berakhot, Sotah, and Sanhedrin. Translators for the other volumes already are at work.

To refer to passages of the Talmud, I have preserved my system of Mishnah-references. Thus in my translation of M. Sukkah, I followed the established system of using the first Arabic number to designate the chapter of the Mishnah, the second, the paragraph of the chapter as conventionally divided, e.g., in Albeck's edition, hence 1:1 stands for the first chapter and the first paragraph of M. Sukkah. I then proceeded to divide each paragraph into completed units of thought, whether whole sentences or parts of sentences, indicating what I conceived to be a complete thought by a letter. So 1:1A stands for the first completed thought of the first paragraph of the first chapter of the cited tractate. Now in the present work, I have marked the Mishnah-paragraphs so that they may be readily cross-referenced with my translation. To refer to the Talmudic materials, as is clear, I then use Roman numerals to signify what I believe to be a complete and whole unit of discourse of a given problem or topic, beginning to end, and then letters to mark the complete units of thought, as before. So 1:1.I.A stands for the first unit of thought of the first complete unit of discourse relevant to the first paragraph of the first chapter of the Mishnah-tractate at hand, and so throughout. The system makes possible easy reference to specific statements. I also have indicated where the folios begin and end, thus [2A], [2B], and so on throughout.

This is the second English translation of Babylonian Talmud tractate Sukkah. More than three decades ago Israel W. Slotki published <u>Sukkah. Translated into English with notes, glossary, and indices,</u> (London, 1948: The Soncino Press), part of a complete translation of the Talmud of Babylonia. I have consulted Slotki's excellent translation and notes on every page. Where I reproduce his language in solving a problem I could not otherwise work out, I indicate it by placing his name in parentheses.

In my own case I undertake this translation because I wish to ask those questions of the Talmud of Babylonia that I raised, for the Talmud of the Land of Israel, in my Talmud of the Land of Israel. 35. Introduction. Taxonomy (Chicago, 1983: University of Chicago Press). For that purpose I require access, in my own sort of analytical translation, to a suitable statistical sample of the whole. But I do not have to translate and then construct my analytical tables for all of the tractates all together. I plan to take approximately 10% of the whole, Berakhot, Sukkah, Sotah, Sanhedrin, and Arakhin, that is, 316 folios of the total of 2,964 folios of the Talmud of Babylonia. These come from all four divisions of the Mishnah served by Bavli, plus the opening tractate, Berakhot. Some are long, some are short. Since, overall, I have the impression that the same redactional techniques characterize every tractate, with a uniform rhetoric and shared mode of constructing units of discourse commonplace throughout, the sample at hand should suffice to allow for the kind of generalizations of a literary and redactional character that I hope to be able to make.

Other translators, covering the thirty-two tractates in the thirty-one volumes I shall not translate, as I said, are already at work. But once we have a theory of the character of the document as a whole, even before the fresh translation is complete, a further set of studies, parallel to my Judaism in Society: The Evidence of the Yerushalmi (Chicago, 1984: University of Chicago Press) and Judaism: The Evidence of the Mishnah (Chicago, 1981: University of Chicago Press), should become possible. Accordingly, the present exercise fits into the larger program of my step-by-step inquiry into the formation of Judaism. Let me now spell out precisely how the theory of translation governing the present project differs from that by which Rabbi Slotki and his fellow-translators determined how to carry out their work.

The classic and enduring texts of humanity undergo translation in age succeeding age. For each new generation takes up the task of confronting and making its own the intellectual heritage of civilization. An exception to that rule until the present day has been the sacred literature of the canon of Judaism. Excluding only the Hebrew Scriptures (Tanakh, "Old Testament"), no text originally in Hebrew or Aramaic of the Judaic canon reached a foreign language, except for Latin, before the nineteenth century. The reason is that, before modern times, Jews took for granted only they would wish to receive and revere the literary heritage of their people. They further assumed that all male, worthy Jews could learn to read them in the original Hebrew or Aramaic. Learned men translated into, not out of, Hebrew. The act of translation therefore drew a certain opprobrium. Serious scholars would not bother; self-respecting male Jews would master the original language anyhow.

In the later nineteenth century in Germany and France, and in the twentieth century in Britain and the USA, by contrast, numerous scholars have turned to the task of transmitting the heritage of Judaism to an audience of Western Jews of both genders, and a considerable reception among non-Jews and Jews awaited the results. The Mishnah reached most of the Western languages, the Babylonian Talmud came into German and twice into English (Rodkinson, Soncino), and the Palestinian Talmud into French at the end of the nineteenth century and English just now. Many (though by no means all) of the compilations and compositions of scriptural exegesis produced by the rabbis of late antiquity and medieval times ("midrashim") exist in German and English. By the end of this century, all of those classics of the canon of Judaism that were completed by the end of late antiquity will have come into the English (mainly, the American) language. The reason, as is clear, is that there is a sizable audience, both Jewish and gentile, and there also is a significant corps of competent and interested translators available to do the work. (In passing, we take note also that many of the documents at hand turn out to attract the interest of translators into modern, Israeli Hebrew as well.) The substantial interest in the labor of moving the old texts from one language and system of thought into another would surprise no one, except, as I said, those many generations of male Jews who took for granted translation was neither necessary nor valuable, in the untested theory that whoever cared knew Hebrew or should learn it.

Outside of the canon of writings at hand no one debates the question of whether a given text requires more than a single translation into a given language. Great scholars who also are poets undertake the successive retranslation of every great classic of world literature, whether philosophical or dramatic or poetic. Who can count the number of translations into English alone of the Hebrew Scriptures? It is a commonplace that through the work of serious translation great literary creations have come into being, in the case, for instance, of Homer, Plato, and Euripides. None therefore need wonder why someone would translate afresh a classic text of Judaism that already exists in the English language. What requires attention is only the issue of what the latter-day translator wishes to accomplish, that has been left undone by a predecessor.

In the present context, I see no fewer than four available theories of translation, any one of which enjoys its distinctive value. Let me spell them out, so as to place into context the newest effort to translate a classic text of Judaism into the American language. These may be briefly entitled a literary translation, a reference translation, a research translation, and a conversation-translation.

A literary translation aims at presenting in English not a literal and exact rendition of the text but an elegant and poetic one. It transmits main ideas, thoughts closely related to, but not in the exact language of, the original. Such a translation aims through the power of the contemporary idiom at winning to the gist of the text a sizable audience of lay readers. Success then means a large and understanding audience. The translator serves as a partner to the original author. My impression is that all efforts at translating poetry fall into this classification.

A reference translation, the opposite of the foregoing, provides a succinct and literal account of the original, with few notes of the character of more than brief references. The utility of such a translation is to facilitate quick reference to the original text. It will serve to guide the outsider to a given passage, but not to lead into the heart of matters someone who does not know the original language. Such a purpose, for the aesthetic side, is served by the literary translation.

For the substantive side of things, the research translation, the exact opposite of the reference translation, serves admirably. Such a translation draws together into one place every piece of information that appears to pertain to the passage at hand. Philological, historical, textual issues intervene into the text. The scholar, particularly one who works in an area other than that of the text at hand, finds in such a translation enormous assistance. The research translation further will address the issue of variant text-traditions of the text at hand, so that diverse manuscripts will come to testify to the original sense and wording of the passage.

Standing apart from the first three types of translation, the conversation-translation aims at one thing only, and that is, clear comprehension not only of the words but also of the sense of the classic text. By "talking the reader through" the text, clearly distinguishing language added by the translator from the original words of the text, the translator renders accessible the distinctive message and mode of thought of the ancient text. Who will want such a translation? The same sort of reader who responds to the literary sort of translation, but with a difference. The reader at hand wants access to not only the gist of discourse but the mode and medium. It is insufficient to such a reader to know what, in general, the text wishes to tell us. Such a reader wishes to know the message in relationship to the medium.

Let me now spell out my views of these available theories of translation and explain my preference for the fourth one in particular. The reference-translation I deem inadequate, because it is essentially useless, in leaving the text unexplained. The research-translation has merit; since it stands as a convenient source for whatever is relevant (and much that is not relevant) to the particular text subject to translation. But it is not a great deal more useful than the reference-translation for those whose principal interest is in what this text says and what it means. Only a reference-translation, putting down on paper only the corresponding words in the other language so that people may look things up and pick and choose what may be useful, justifies an essentially unadorned translation, a simple "rendition" from one language to the other. A research translation meant to raise and solve all the problems, philological and linguistic, textual and lexicographical, historical and theological, ranging here, there, and everywhere, with endless notes and a dazzling display of erudition -- such a translation seems to me of equally limited use. For someone opening it will find overwhelming the limitless ranges of erudite discourse and so lose sight of the issue at hand. That issue is the protracted and brilliant exercise in practical reason and applied logic which is the Babylonian Talmud at its most interesting, if also its most difficult.

Clearly, the criterion for evaluating a translation among the available types derives in the end from the audience at hand. For whom does one translate the document anyhow? It cannot be only for those able to make sense of the document in its original language. For them, a translation is merely another commentary. Lacking all canonical status, in the acutely theological and nervous atmosphere of the schools in which this particular document is studied, a translation enjoys no standing whatsoever. That does not mean it will not be used. The excellent efforts of the translators of the Babylonian Talmud into German, then into English, have hardly been neglected in the German- and English-speaking world in which the sacred writings of Judaism are studied. But it is foolish to contribute to a world with its own conventions and canonical exegesis a translation which that world claims not to need and forthrightly alleges it does not want. To that world a translation is not a commentary. It is an affront.

On the other hand, if the translator proposes to present the text "to whom it may concern," that is, to no one in particular, then the question arises of how much requires explanation. Here there can simply be no end to the matter. In the case of a document that assumes so vast a knowledge of the Hebrew Scriptures and the Mishnah as does the Talmud, even if one quotes the whole of a verse alluded to only by a word or two, should the translator then proceed to interpret that verse? Its context? Its meaning and use in the passage of the Talmud before us? Similarly, if the Talmud rests upon a pericope of the Mishnah that is not cited at all, should the translator merely allude to the passage and expect the reader to look it up? Should the translator cite the passage in full? And if so, how extensive an explanation is required?

As to the discourse of the Talmud itself, the translation, of course, constitutes a substantial judgment upon the meaning of the text. Where we put a period or a comma, or indicate the end of one major discourse and the start of another, how we break up the undifferentiated columns of words into paragraphs, the paragraphs into sentences, and the sentences into their individual, small units of cognition -- these decisions are conveyed in the very simple facts of how we present what we claim to be the meaning of the text. And yet, beyond that simple statement, it is clear, a fair amount of explanation is demanded. How much, or how little, must be explained is not self-evident, and probably will never be readily settled. It is invariably an exercise of judgment and taste. That is why, as I said, the translator has to find a balance between the requirements of intelligibility, indeed, to whom it may concern, on the one side, and the limited possibilities of full and ample presentation of a single text in a single book, on the other. Too much will overwhelm the reader, who will lose sight of the text, which is, after all, at the center of the translation. Too little will puzzle the reader, leaving the text translated but still inaccessible.

In order to show in a graphic way the different choices confronting a translator of Bavli, I set side by side the translation of Babylonian tractate Arakhin 2A-2B in, first, the version appearing in the great Soncino translation of the Babylonian Talmud produced, for the tractate at hand, by Leo Jung, and second, my version. In this way the difference in the theories governing how the work is to be done becomes vivid. Within the scheme I have laid forth, I should categorize Jung's (and the rest of the Soncino translations) as essentially a reference-translation. Mine, clearly, is meant to be a conversation-translation. In order to provide a full picture of how Jung explains what is not self-evidently clear in the text, further, I have included those of his footnotes which constitute more than mere references to other texts. The notes follow the extracts.

In order to make clear how I think my approach to translation differs, let me spell out a few of its salient traits. The single significant trait in what follows is the extensive use of square brackets to add to the flow of discourse those sources alluded to but not cited. The translation is richly augmented by understanding not made explicit and by rhetorical shifts and turns in no way indicated in the original Aramaic. To state the theory of translation of this document as simply as I can: Here I propose to talk my way through an account of what the document says -- not stated in square brackets but translated into fairly fluent American English -- and of what the document means. That is, both what we need to know to make sense of it, and also what we are supposed to conclude on the basis of what the document says and the facts added by me, are supplied. Translation here is a kind of extended conversation, an interchange within the document, with the document, and through the document, and, always, an urgent encounter with the reader.

If I had to make a guess as to what we have, I should imagine we deal with nothing more than brief notes, notations really, out of which a whole and complete discourse is supposed to be reconstructed by those essentially familiar with the (original) discourse. The Babylonian Talmud is a kind of abbreviated script, a set of cue cards drastically cut down to a minimum of words. But these metaphors are meant only to account for the theory of translation followed here, I mean the theory that out of the sherds and remnants of coherent speech we have to reconstruct and fully reconstitute the (original) coherent discourse, as best we can, whole sentences from key words, whole analyses from truncated allusions.

MISHNAH. [2a] All [persons] are fit to evaluate or to be made the subjects of valuation, are fit to vow [another's worth] or have their worth vowed: -- priests, Levites and [ordinary] Israelites, women and slaves. Persons of unknown sex and hermaphrodites are fit to vow [another's worth], or to have their worth vowed, and are fit to evaluate, but they are not fit to be made the subjects of valuation, for the subject of valuation may be only a person definitely either male or female. A deaf-mute, an imbecile, or a minor are fit to have their worth vowed or be made the subject of valuation, but they are not fit to make either a vow [of another's worth] or to evaluate, because they have no mind.

[2A]

A. All may pledge the Valuation [of others] and are subject to the pledge of Valuation [by others].

B. may vow [the worth of another] and are subject to the vow [of payment of their worth by another]:

C. priests   and   Levites   and Israelites, women and slaves.

D. A person of doubtful sexual traits and a person who exhibits traits of both sexes may vow [the worth of another] and are subject to the vow [of payment of their worth by another], may pledge the Valuation [of others], but are not subject to the pledge of Valuation by others,

E. for evaluated is only one who is certainly a male or certainly a female.

F. A deaf-mute, an imbecile, and a minor are subject to the vow [of payment of their worth by another], and are subject to the pledge of Valuation by others, but do not vow the worth, and do not pledge the Valuation, of others,

G. for they do not possess understanding.

GEMARA. What does ALL [PERSONS] ARE FIT TO EVALUATE mean to include? -- It is meant to include one close to manhood who must be examined.[1] What does [ALL[2] ARE] FIT TO BE MADE THE SUBJECTS OF VALUATION mean to include? -- It is meant to include a person disfigured, or one afflicted with boils. For one might have assumed that since Scripture says: A   vow... according   to   thy

I.   A. [When the framer explicitly refers to] all, [in framing the Mishnah-paragraph at hand, saying All pledge....,] what [classification of persons does he intend] to include, [seeing that in what follows C, he lists the available classifications of persons in any event, and, further, at D-G specifies categories of persons that are excluded. Accordingly, to what purpose does he add the encompassing language, all, at the outset?]

valuation,[4] that only such persons as are fit to be made the subjects of a vow [as regards their worth], are fit to be made subjects of a valuation, and that persons who are unfit to be made subjects of a vow [as regards their worth], are also unfit to be made subjects of a valuation, hence Scripture informs us: of persons.[4] i.e., no matter who they be.

[1]Mufla' from the root meaning, to make clear, to examine, hence 'one to be examined' as to the purpose for which he made the valuation. Above the age of thirteen such knowledge is taken for granted. Below the age of twelve it is assumed to be absent. During the period from twelve to thirteen the boy is to be subject to questioning. If the examination establishes his knowledge of the purpose of the dedication, his dedication is considered valid, and renders payment obligatory. Otherwise no significance is to be attached during that period to his utterance of the formula: Erek peloni' alay.

[2]The first word of the Mishnah ALL is assumed to apply to the four cases enumerated. This word does not seem necessary, the Mishnah might have stated e.g., Priests, Levites and Israelites are fit etc. The additional ALL hence is assumed by the questioner to have implied the inclusion of persons whom, without this inclusion, one might have excluded. Hence the series of questions establishing the identity of the persons included in each case. This discussion leads to the consideration of other passages throughout the Mishnah, in which the word 'all' occurs, and to an explanation of who is included in each statement.

B. It serves to include a male nearing puberty [who has not yet passed puberty. Such a one is subject to examination to determine whether he grasps the meaning of a vow, such as is under discussion. A child younger than the specified age, twelve years to thirteen, is assumed not to have such understanding, and one older is taken for granted to have it.]

C. [When the framer explicitly frames matters as all] are subject to the pledge of Valuation, what [classification of persons does he intend] to include?

D. It is to include a person who is disfigured or afflicted with a skin ailment.

E. [Why in any event should one imagine that persons of that classification would be omitted?] I might have supposed that, since it is written, "A vow... according to your Valuation" (Lev. 27:2), [with Scripture using as equivalent terms "vow" and "Valuation,"] the rule is that [only] those who possess an [instrinsic] worth [e.g., whoever would be purchased for a sum of money in the marketplace, hence excluding the disfigured persons under discussion, who are worthless] also would be subject to a vow of Valuation [at fixed price, such as Scripture specified]. On the other hand, [I might have supposed that] whoever does not possess an [intrinsic] worth also would not be subject to a vow of Valuation.

F. Accordingly, [the formulation of the Mishnah-passage at hand] tells us, [to the contrary, that a pledge of Valuation is not dependent upon represents an absolute charge and is not relative to the subject's market-value.]

G. [How does Scripture so signify? When the framer of Scripture refers at

[4]A person disfigured, or afflicted with boils, would fetch no price at all on the market place. In the expression A vow according to thy valuation, one might have inferred from this juxtaposition, that a certain fundamental agreement prevailed between cases of vow (of one's worth) and of valuation, and that therefore a person unfit to have his work vowed (because a vow was redeemable by payment of the market value, which did not exist in the case of a disfigured person) would be unfit to be made the subject of a valuation. But this inference is cancelled by another Biblical phrase, which indicates that what is required is but 'persons', independent of their physical condition: When a man shall clearly utter a vow of persons (ibid.).

Lev. 27:2 to] "persons," [the meaning is that a pledge of Valuation applies] to anyone at all.

What does [ALL PERSONS] ARE FIT TO VOW mean to include? -- [The phrase ALL] is needed only for [the clause] 'are fit to have their worth vowed'. What is to be included [in the phrase ALL] ARE FIT TO HAVE THEIR WORTH VOWED? Is it to include persons of unknown sex or hermaphrodites -- but they are expressly stated [in our Mishnah]! Again is it to include a deaf-mute, an imbecile and a minor -- they too are expressly stated! And if it is to include a person below the age of one month -- that too is expressly mentioned! And again if it is to include an idolator -- he too is expressly mentioned! -- In reality it is meant to include a person below the age of one month; and the Mishnah states it [by

H. [When the framer of the Mishnah, further, states that all] vow [the worth of another], what [classification of persons does he thereby intend] to include [seeing that at C we go over the same matter, specifying those who may make such a vow]?

I. It is necessary for him [to specify that all take such a vow to indicate that all also applies to] those concerning whom such a vow is taken.

J. [Therefore, when the framer specifies that all] are subject to a vow, what [classification of persons does he thereby intend] to include?

K. [Here matters are not so self-evident, for] if the intention is to include a person of doubtful sexual traits and a person who exhibits the traits of both sexes, both of those classifications

implication] and later on expressly mentions it.[3]

[3]By the redundant ALL, which obviously includes some person or persons, which but for this all-inclusive term, would have been excluded. The particular reason why this case rather than any other of the four here dealt with is included here Rashi finds in the fact that it is the only one concerning which a controversy exists (infra 5a), whence the statement here by implication is of importance in teaching that even the Rabbis who hold that one who is less than a month cannot be subject to evaluation, nevertheless agree that he can have his worth vowed.

are explicitly stated [in the formulation of the Mishnah-passage itself].

L. And if the intention is to include a deaf-mute, an imbecile, and a minor, these classifications also are explicitly stated. [So what can have been omitted in the explicit specification of the pertinent classifications, that the framer of the Mishnah-passage found it necessary to make use of such amplificatory language as all?]

M. If, furthermore, the intent was to include an infant less than a month old, that classification also is explicitly included [below].

N. If, furthermore, the intent was to include an idolator, that classification furthermore is explicitly included as well. [Accordingly, what classification of persons can possibly have been omitted in the framing of the Mishnah-passage at hand, that the author found it necessary to add the emphatic inclusionary are in mind?]

O. In point of fact, [the purpose of adding the emphatic language of inclusion] was to include an infant less than a month in age.

P. [The framer of the passage] taught [that such a category is included by using the word all] and then he went and stated the matter explicitly [to clearly indicate the inclusion of that category].

What does 'All persons are obliged to lay on hands' mean to include?[4] — It is meant to include the heir, and this against the view of R. Judah.[5] What does 'All persons can effect a substitute'[6] mean to include? -- That, too, means to include the heir, in contrast to the view of R. Judah. For it

II. A. [When at M. Men. 9:8, we find the formulation], All lay hands [on a beast to be slaughtered, that is, including not only the owner of the beast, who set it aside and consecrated it for the present sacrificial purpose, but also some other party], whom do we find included [by the inclusionary language, all]?

was taught: An heir must lay on hands, an heir can effect a substitute. R. Judah says: An heir does not lay on hands, and an heir cannot effect a substitute.

[4]The Gemara proceeds now to discuss all other cases in which a redundant 'all' is to convey some inclusion in the principle of other persons. The laying on of the hands on the head of the animal to be sacrificed conveyed the sense of ownership. It was a duty, hence a question arises in the case of several partners, or in the case of proxy.

[5]R. Judah denied this obligation to an heir. Lev. I, 3 reads: If he be a burnt offering...he shall lay his hand upon the head. This, R. Judah argues, expressly limits the duty of laying the hand to the man who offered it, not to his heir, who is freed from his obligation.

[6]Lev. XXVII, 10: He shall not alter it, nor change it, a good for a bad, or a bad for a good; and if he shall at all change beast for beast, then both it and that for which it is changed shall be holy. The dispute concerns only the case of an heir in respect of an offering dedicated by his father but all agree that an exchange made by anyone besides the original owner of the sacrifice would have no effect at all, the first animal remaining sacred, the second not being affected by the unauthorized attempt at exchange.

B. [It is used to indicate] the inclusion of the heir [of the owner of the beast who consecrated it and subsequently died. The heir of the deceased owner, may take his place vis à vis the beast, lay hands on the beast, and so derive benefit from the sacrifice of that beast, even though he did not originally designate it as holy].

C. And that inclusion does not accord with the position of R. Judah [who maintains that, since Scripture specifies at Lev. 1:3 that the person who has designated the beast as a holy sacrifice "shall lay hands on it," excluded are all other parties, who did not designate the beast as holy. Only the owner of the beast may lay hands, and no one else. In so formulating the rule by using the inclusionary language all, the framer of the passage has indicated that he rejects the position of Judah].

D. [And when, at M. Tem. 1:1, we find the formulation,] All effect an act of substitution [so consecrating the beast that is supposed to take the place of the originally consecrated beast, in line with Lev. 27:10, but leaving that originally consecrated beast in the status of consecration nonetheless], what category of person do we find included [by the use of such language]?

E. [Once more], the use of such language indicates the inclusion of the heir [of the owner of the beast, who originally consecrated it and died before sacrificing it, just as at B, above].

F. And that inclusion once more does not accord with the position of R. Judah [for Lev. 27:10 states, "He shall not alter it...," thus referring solely to the owner of the beast, and not to an heir or any other third party].

G. [Now the statements just given accord with] that which has been taught [in a tradition external to the Mishnah but deriving from authorities named in the Mishnah], as follows:

H. An heir lays hands [on a beast originally consecrated by the deceased], an heir effects an act of substitution [in regard to a beast originally consecrated by the deceased].

I. R. Judah says, "An heir does not lay on hands, an heir does not effect an act of substitution."

What is the reason of R. Judah's view? -- [Scripture says:] His offering,[1] i.e., but not his father's offering. And he infers the rule concerning the commencement of the dedication of the animal from the rule governing its end. Just as at the end of the dedication the heir does not lay on hands, thus also at the beginning[2] he cannot effect a substitute. And the Rabbis? -- [Scripture says redundantly:] And if he shall at all change -- that included the heir. And we infer the rule concerning the end of the dedication from the rule governing the commencement of the dedication. Just as at the beginning of the dedication the heir has power to effect a substitute, so at the end is he obliged to lay his hands on the animal's head.[3] But what do the Rabbis do with 'his offering'? -- [They interpret:] 'his offering', but not the offering of an idolator; 'his offering', but not the offering of his neighbour; 'his offering', i.e., to include all who have a share[4] in the ownership of a sacrifice in the duty to lay on hands. And R. Judah?[5] -- He does not hold that all who have a share in the ownership share the

J. What is the Scriptural basis for the position of R. Judah?

K. "His offering..." (Lev. 3:2, 7, 13: "He shall lay his hand upon the head of his offering") -- and not the offering that was set aside by his father.

L. From the rule governing the end of the process of consecration [the laying on of hands] [R. Judah further] derives the rule governing the beginning of the process of consecrating a beast [e.g., through an act of substitution, which indicates that a given beast is substituted for, therefore shares the status, of another beast that already has been consecrated. In this way the beast put forward as a substitution is itself deemed to be sanctified. Accordingly, a single principle governs both stages in the sacrificial process, the designation of the beast as holy and therefore to be sacrificed, e.g., through an act of substitution, and the laying on of hands just prior to the act of sacrificial slaughter itself. Just as the latter action may be performed solely by the owner of the beast, who derives benefit only when the owner of the beast carries it out, so is the rule for the former action.]

obligation of laying hands thereon; or, indeed, if he should hold so [2b] he would infer [the exclusion of] idolator and neighbour from one passage,[6] so that two more would remain redundant, from one of which he would ifer that 'his offering' means 'but not that of his father', and from the other that all who have a share in the ownership of a sacrifice are obliged to perform the laying on of hands. But what does R. Judah do with 'If he shall at all change'? -- He needs that to include woman,[7] for it was taught: Since all this chapter is couched in masculine gender, what brings us eventually to include woman? The text stated: 'If he shall at all change'[8] But [whence do] the Sages [infer this]? -- From the [redundant] 'And if'. And R. Judah? -- He does not interpret 'And if'.[9]

[1]Lev. II, 2, 7 and 13 in connection with the laying on of hands in the case of peace-offerings. V. Rash and Tosaf. a.l.

[2]First an animal is separated for the purpose of being offered on the altar. That is the commencement of its sanctification. At the end, just before the slaying of the animal, the owner lays his hand on its head. R. Judah infers from the regulations at the end, viz., the prohibition for anyone but the owner to lay hands on the head, the inefficacy of the change at the beginning, i.e., his intended exchange has no effect on the animal he wanted to substitute.

[3]The Sages infer from the redundant 'shall at all change' that even another may effect the substitute and argue from the beginning of the sanctification to the end, hence permit an heir to lay hands on the animal.

M. Accordingly, just as, at the end of the process of consecration, the heir does not lay on hands, so at the beginning of the process of consecration, an heir does not carry out an act of substitution.

N. And as to the position of rabbis [vis à vis Judah, who maintain that the heir may do so, how do they read Scripture in such wise as to derive their view?]

O. [Scripture states,] "And if changing, he shall change" (Lev. 27:10) [thus intensively using the same verb twice, with one usage understood to refer to the owner himself, the other usage to some closely related person].

P. [The use of the verbal intensive therefore is meant] to include the heir, and, as before, we derive the rule governing the conclusion of the sacrificial process [with the laying on of hands] from the rule governing the commencement of the sacrificial process [the designation of the beast as holy, by its substitution for an already-consecrated beast].

Q. Accordingly, just as, at the beginning of the process of consecration, the heir does carry out an act of substitution, so at the end of the process of consecration, the heir does lay on hands.

R. Now [given rabbis' reading of the relevant verses], how do these same rabbis deal with Scripture's three references to "his offering" [which in Judah's view makes explicit that only the owner of the beast lays hands on his beast, cf. Lev. 3:2,7,13]?

S. They require that specification of Scripture to lay down the rule that [an Israelite] lays hands on his sacrifice, but not on the sacrifice of an idolator, on

[4] The phrase 'his offering' occurs three times in Lev. III, viz., vv. 2, 7 and 13, and while two of these expressions have a limiting sense, one has an inclusive meaning. Just as 'his' implies ownership, so must anyone who has a claim to ownership lay his hands on the animal's head. Therefore, every member of a group who offer the animal together must perform the laying on of hands on the part of anyone who shares in it — for which an inclusive interpretation is necessary?

[6] The word 'his' could exclude both the fellow-Jew and the idolator, since the Scriptural 'his sacrifice' logically excludes both.

[7] That a woman can effect a substitute in her offering.

[8] Lit., 'if change he shall change' the emphasis is inclusive.

[9] He does not ascribe to that word the implications attributed to it by the Sages. About the limits of such interpretation and the basic suggestions implied in disputes thereon v. D. Hoffman, Leviticus I, 9f.

his sacrifice and not on the sacrifice of his fellow;

T. on his sacrifice, further, to include all those who own a share in the sacrificial animal, according to each the right to lay hands upon the beast [of which they are partners].

U. And as to R. Judah? He does not take the view that all those who own a share in the sacrificial animal have a right to.

V. Alternatively, [one may propose that] he does maintain the stated position [concerning the partners in a sacrificial animal].

W. [But] he derives the rule governing [2b] the idolator['s beast] and that of one's fellow from a single verse of Scripture [among the three verses that make explicit that one lays hands on his animal], leaving available for the demonstration of a quite separate proposition two [other] of these same [three] references.

X. [It follows, for Judah's position, that] one of these verses serves to indicate, "His offering" and not the offering of his father," and another of the available verses then serves to include [among those who indeed may lay hands on the sacrificial beast] all shareholders, according to each of them the right to lay hands on the beast held in common partnership.

Y. [Further exploring the thesis of Judah about the scriptural basis for his view, exactly] how does R. Judah interpret the intensive verb used at Lev. 27:10, "And if changing, he shall change"?

Z. He requires that usage to include the participation of the woman [in the process of substitution, so that if a woman makes a statement effecting an act of substitution, that statement is as valid as if a man had made it].

AA. That [view of his reading] is in accord with the following tradition assigned to Tannaitic authority:

BB. Since the entire formulation of the passage concerning an act of substitution speaks of the male, how in the end shall we include the female as well [so that an act of substitution of a woman is regarded as valid]?

CC. Scripture states, "And if changing, he shall change..." [The intensive language serves to include the woman.]

DD. And as to rabbis, [how do they prove the same position]?

EE. It is from the use of the inclusionary word, and if, in the phrase, "And if changing...."

GG. The usage, "And if...," in his view is not subject to exegesis at all [and yields no additional information about the role under discussion. Accordingly, in order to prove that a woman is involved in the process of substitution, as much as a man, Judah must refer solely to the intensive verb construction.]

What does 'All persons are obliged[5] to observe [the laws concerning] the booth' mean to include? -- That is meant to include a minor that no more needs his mother,[6] for we have learnt: A minor that no more needs his mother is obliged to observe the laws concerning the booth.

[5]The Gemara proceeds now to a systematic examination of all cases in which the word 'all' is used. Unless it can be proved that in each case that word includes something normally excluded, the argument, or rather the

III.   A. All are obligated [to carry out the religious duty of dwelling in] a tabernacle [on the Festival of Tabernacles].

B. [When the framer of the foregoing statement makes explicit use of the inclusionary language, all], what [classification of persons is] included, [that otherwise would have been omitted]?

C. It is to include a minor who does not depend upon his mother [but can take care of himself], in line with the following statement found in the Mishnah [M. Suk. 2:8:] A child who does not depend upon his mother is liable to [carry out the religious duty of dwelling in a] tabernacle.

first question posed on 2a will be invalidated.

[6]A child which (Suk. 28b) on awakening no more calls out 'Mother!' but attends to his needs, dresses himself, etc.

What does 'All are obliged to observe the law of the lulab'[8] mean to include? -- That includes a minor who knows how to shake the lulab, for we learnt: A minor who knows how to shake[9] the lulab is obliged to observe [the laws of] the lulab. What does 'All are obliged to observe the [law of] the fringes' include? -- That includes the minor who knows how to wrap himself, for it was taught: A minor who knows how to wrap himself [into the tallith][10] is obliged to observe the law of the fringes. What does 'All are obliged to observe the rules concerning the tefillin' include? -- That includes a minor who knows how to take care of the tefillin, for it was taught: If a minor knows how to take care of the tefillin,[11] his father buys tefillin for him.

[8]The palm-branch forming with citron, myrtle and willow, the cluster taken during the Feast of Tabernacles (v. Lev. XIII, 40) is every day waved in every direction to symbolize the omnipresence of God.

[9]The lulab is waved in the four main directions: south, north, west and east, and there are some details as to the position of the components of the cluster, which are known to the worshipper, so that he may follow the cantor's lead.

D. All are liable [to carry out the religious duty of taking up] the palm branch [enjoined at Lev. 23:40.

E. [When the framer of the foregoing statement makes explicit use of the inclusionary language, all] what [classification of persons is] included, [that otherwise would have been omitted]?

F. It is to include a minor who knows how to shake [the palm-branch, so, with proper intention, making appropriate use of the holy object].

G. That is in line with the following statement found in the Mishnah [M. Suk. 3:15:] A minor who knows how to shake [the palm branch with proper intention] is liable to [the religious duty of taking up] the palm branch.

H. All are liable [to carry out the religious duty of affixing] fringes [to the corners of garments].

I. [When the framer of the foregoing statement makes explicit use of the inclusionary language, all] what [classification of persons is] included, [that otherwise would have been omitted]?

J. It is to include a minor who knows how to cloak himself [in a garment, and so enters the obligation of affixing to said cloak the required fringes].

K. For it has been taught [at T. Hag. 1:2:] **A minor who knows how to cloak himself [in a garment] is liable to [affix to that garment the required show] fringes.**

L. All are liable [to carry out the religious duty of wearing] phylacteries.

M. [When the framer of the foregoing statement makes explicit use of the inclusionary language, all,] what [classification of persons is] included, [that otherwise would have been omitted]?

[10]The prayer shawl at the four corners of which the fringes are attached, and into which one wraps himself, 'in order to remember the commandments of the Lord'. The wrapping must be performed in a special manner, v. M.K. 24a.

[11]Commonly called phylacteries. The attachment, leather box and leather strap, each on left arm and forehead, containing the Shema' and other extracts from the Torah, originally worn all day, now only at the morning prayer.

What does 'All are obliged to appear' include[3] — It is meant to include one who is half[4] slave and half freedman. According, however, to Rabina, who holds that one who is half slave and half freed is free from the obligation to appear, [the word 'All'] is meant to include one who was lame[5] on the first day of the festival and became normal again on the second day. -- That would be right according to the view that all the days of the festival may make up for each other. But according to the view that they all are but making up for the first day, what will 'All' come to include?[6] -- It will include one blind in one of his eyes. This [answer] is not in accord with the following Tanna, for it was taught: Johanan b. Dahabai said in the name of R. Judah: One blind in one eye is free from the obligation to appear, for it is said:[7] Yir'eh-yera'eh [he shall see -- he shall appear] i.e., just as He is present to see [the comer], so shall He be seen, just as His sight is complete, so shall the sight of him who appears be intact.

N. It is to include a minor who knows how to take care of phylacteries [and therefore may be entrusted with them].

O. For it has been taught [at T. Hag. 1:2:] As to a minor who knows how to take care of phylacteries, his father purchases phylacteries for him.

IV.   A. All are obligated [on the occasion of a pilgrim festival to bring] an appearance-offering [to the Temple and to sacrifice it there in honor of the festival M. Hag. 1:1].

B. [When the framer of the foregoing statement makes explicit use of the inclusionary language, all,] what [classification of persons is] included, [that otherwise would have been omitted]?

C. It is to include a person who is half-slave and half-free. [Such a person is subject to the stated liability of bringing an appearance-offering. But a person who is wholly a slave is exempt from the stated requirement of making the pilgrimage and bringing the offering.]

D. But in the view of Rabina, who has made the statement that one who is half slave and half free [also] is exempt from the obligation of bringing an appearance-offering [in celebration of the pilgrim festival and in his view], what [classification of persons] is included [by the specification that all are subject to the stated obligation]?

[3]Ex. XXIII, 17: Three times in the year all thy males shall appear before the Lord God. The Scriptural text is all-inclusive, hence the Mishnaic 'All' must deal with a case which, but for its redundant 'all', one would have excluded from the obligation to appear.

[4]A full slave is free because 'before the Lord God' is interpreted to mean: only those who have but one Lord or Master, i.e., excluding the slave, who has a terrestrial master in addition to the Eternal Lord to serve. If owned by two masters, one of whom frees him, the slave becomes half freed, and stays half slave.

[5]The word regel in Hebrew may mean either 'foot' or 'festival' (on the three festivals the men 'footed' it to Jerusalem). Hence the inference that only those who could foot it normally are obliged to appear on these three festivals, which excludes a lame man.

[6]There are two views as to the statement of the Mishnah (Hag. 9a: One who has made no offering on the first day of the feast must make up, or has the opportunity to make up for it, throughout the other days of the festival), the first holding that each day has its own obligation; hence even if the worshipper was unfit on the first day of the festival, provided he is fit on the next, he is not exempt on the other days per se imposing the obligation, whilst the other considers only the first day imposing the obligation of an offering. Consequently, if he was disqualified on the first day, or free of that obligation, he would be exempt a complementary offering. The practical difference, in our case, would be this: One who on the

E. It is to include a person who is lame on the first day of the festival but is restored [to full activity] on the second day. [A lame person is exempt from the religious obligation of coming up to Jerusalem on the pilgrim festival, since he obviously cannot make the trip. If, however, as of the second day of the festival, the lame person should be healed, then, according to the formulation of the rule at hand, such a person would become obligated, retroactively, to bring the required appearance-offering, as of the first day.]

F. [The foregoing statement rests on the position that on the successive days of the festival, one has the option of meeting an obligation incurred but not met on the earlier day. Thus if one did not make the required appearance-offering on the first day, he is obligated for it but also may make up for it on the later days of the festival. The obligation for one day pertains to, but then may be made up, on the days following, thus, on day three for day two, on day four for day three, and the like. Accordingly, at E we maintain, first, that the person becomes obligated on the second day, and, second, that the obligation then is retroactive to the first. So he can make up what he owes. But the obligation to begin with likewise is retroactive. On day two he became obligated for an appearance-offering to cover day one. Accordingly, what we have just proposed] fully accords with the position of him who said that offerings made on] all [of the days of the festival] serve as a means of carrying out the obligations incurred on each one of them [as just now explained].

G. But in the view of him who

first day of the festival had been lame, hence not obliged to offer the festal sacrifices, would be free according to the second view, but according to the first, would be obliged to make the offering on one of the subsequent days of the festival.

[7]The massoretic text y-r-'-h may be accentuated to read either yir'eh (he will see) or yera'eh (he will be seen). The first reading applied to the Lord, the second to the Israelite appearing before Him, would be thus interpreted: Just as the Lord sees him 'with two eyes' i.e., with undisturbed vision, so shall the worshipper be one appearing with both eyes intact, i.e., with undiminished sight. For an alternative rendering v. Hag., Sonc. ed., p. 3. n. 3. Or, if you like, say this: In truth it is meant to include one who is half slave and half freed man, and if the view of Rabina should appear as the difficulty, this is no difficulty either; the first view is in accord with the former Mishnah, the second with the later Mishnah. For we learnt: One who is half slave and half freed man shall serve himself one day and his master the other -- thus Beth Hillel. Said Beth Shammai to them: You took care of the interests of his master, but you have done nothing [thereby] on his behalf. For he is unable to marry either a female slave or free woman. Shall he do without marriage? But the world was created only for propagation of the species, as it is said: He created it not a waste. He formed it to be inhabited. Rather, for the sake of the social welfare we force his master to set him free, and the slave writes out a document of indebtedness covering the other half of his value. Beth Hillel retracted and taught as Beth Shammai.

says that all of the days of the festival [may serve to make up only for an obligation] incurred on the first day [of the festival alone, so that, first, one does not incur an obligation on a later day of the festival affecting what one owes for an earlier day of the festival, and so that, second, if one is not obligated to bring an appearance-offering on the first day of the festival, he is not obligated to bring such an offering to all, what category of persons] is included [by use of the inclusionary language, all]?

H. It serves to include a person who is blind in one eye. [A person blind in both eyes is exempt from the appearance-offering on the pilgrim festival. One fully sighted, of course, is liable. The intermediate category then is dealt with in the stated formulation].

I. Now that view would not accord with the following teaching in the authority of sages of the Mishnah, as it has been taught:

J. Yohanan b. Dahabbai says in the name of R. Judah, "One who is blind in one eye is exempt from the religious duty of bringing an appearance-offering, for it is said, 'He will see... he will see...' (Ex. 23:14) [reading the scriptural language not as 'make an appearance,' but, with a shift in the vowels, 'will see,' cf. T. Hag. 1:1].

K. "[The proposed mode of reading the verse at hand yields the following consequence:] Just as one comes to see [the face of the Lord], so he comes to be seen. Just as one sees with two eyes, so one is seen with two eyes" [cf. T. Hag. 1:1F-H]. [The exegesis then excludes a person blind in one eye.]

L. If you prefer, [however, we may revert to the earlier proposal, and] state: Indeed, [the use of the inclusionary language 'all' is meant] to include a person who is half slave and half free.

M. And now as to the question you raised above [D], that that position would not accord with the opinion of Rabina, that indeed poses no problem.

N. [Why not?] The formulation at hand, [which prohibits the half-slave half-free man from bringing the necessary offering] is in line with the original formulation of the Mishnah-law [prior to the debate, cited presently, between the Houses of Shammai and Hillel]. The other formulation [which permits and hence requires the half-slave half-free person, in the intermediate status, to bring the appearance-offering] is in line with the posterior formulation of the Mishnah-law.

O. For we have learned [at M. Git. 4:5:]

P. "He who is half-slave and half-free works for his master one day and for himself one day," the words of the House of Hillel.

Q. Said to them the House of Shammai, "You have taken good care of his master, but of himself you have not taken care.

R. "To marry a slave-girl is not possible, for half of him after all is free [and free persons may marry only free persons.]

S. "[To marry] a free woman is not possible, for half of him after all is a slave [and slaves may marry only other slaves.]

T. "Shall he refrain?

U. "But was not the world made only for procreation, as it is said, 'He created it not a waste, he formed it to be inhabited' (Is. 45:18).

V. "But: For the good order of the world,

"they force his master to free him.

W. "And he [the slave] writes him a bond covering half his value."

X. And the House of Hillel reverted to teach in accord with the opinion of the House of Shammai. [Accordingly, the law prior to the reversion specified at X treated one who is half-slave and half-free as in a fixed category, and such a one would not bring an appearance-offering, since he was partially a slave. But after the reversion, one who was half-slave and half-free could leave that interstitial category easily and so would not be regarded as essentially a slave. Such a one then would be obligated to bring the appearance-offering, there being no permanent lord over him except for the Lord God.]

What does 'All are obliged to sound the shofar' mean to include? -- That includes a minor who has reached the age of training, for we learnt: One does not prevent a minor from blowing the shofar on the festival.[1]

[1] R.H. 32b. The source quoted does not seem to fit the inference made, for the answer postulates evidence that a minor is obliged to sound the shofar, whereas the reference quoted refers to the fact that one does not prevent a minor from sounding the horn, which allows for the possibility of his being neither obliged nor forbidden to sound it. There is a lacuna in the text which Tosaf. s.v. 'yn m^{c}kbyn supplies, from R.H. 33a, where such obligation is definitely stated.

V. A. All are obligated [to the religious duty of hearing] the sounding of the ram's horn [on the New Year, T.R.H. 4:1].

B. [When the framer of the passage makes use of the inclusionary language, all,] what [classification of persons does he thereby] include?

C. It is to include a minor who has reached the age [at which he is able to benefit from] instruction.

D. For we have learned [in a teaching attributed to the authority of Mishnah-sages:] They do not prevent a minor from sounding the ram's horn on the festival day.

'All are obliged to read the scroll. All are fit to read the scroll.' What are these meant to include? -- [3a] They are meant to include women, in accord with the view of R. Joshua b. Levi; for R. Joshua b. Levi said: Women are obliged to read the scroll because they too, had a part in that miracle.[1] What does 'All are obliged to arrange zimmun[2] mean to include? -- It means to include women and slaves, for it was taught: Women are under the obligation of zimmun amongst themselves, and slaves are under the obligation of zimmun amongst themselves. What does 'All may be joined to a zimmun' mean to include? -- That includes a minor who knows to Whom one pronounces a blessing. What does 'All defile by reason of their flux' include? -- That includes a child one day old, for it was taught: [It could have said,] When a man [hath an issue out of his flesh].' Why does the text state 'any man'? That is to include a child one day old, [teaching] that he defiles by reason of his flux; this is the view of R. Judah. R. Ishmael the son of R. Johanan b. Beroka says: [This inference] is not necessary, for behold, Scripture reads: And of them that have an issue whether it be a male or a female, i.e., once he is 'a male,' however minor or major, once she is 'a female,' whether minor or major. If so, why does the Torah use [the redundant phrase] 'any man'? The Torah speaks in the language of man.[3]

[1]V. Meg. 4a, Rashi and Tosaf. Either they too were included in Haman's decree of extinction, or their

VI.   A.   All are subject to the religious obligation of hearing the reading of the Scroll of Esther, [T. Meg. 2:7A-B].

B.   All are suitable to read the Scroll of Esther aloud [for the community, thereby fulfilling the religious obligation of all those who are present, M. Meg. 2:4].

C.   [When the framer of the passage makes use of the inclusionary language, all,] what [classification of persons does he thereby] include [3A]?

D.   It is to include women [who may read the Scroll of Esther aloud for the community and thereby carry out the obligation of all present to do so].

E.   This view accords with the position of R. Joshua b. Levi. For R. Joshua b. Levi said, "Women are liable [to the religious duty of] the reading of the Scroll of Esther, for they too were included in the miracle [of redemption from Israel's enemies, celebrated on Purim]."

VII.   A.   All are liable to the religious duty of saying Grace in public quorum [if they have eaten together. They thus may not say Grace after meals by themselves, if a quorum of three persons is present. In that circumstance a public recitation, involving a call to Grace, is required, T. Ber. 5:15.]

B.   [When the framer of the rule uses the inclusionary word, all,] what [classification of persons does he mean to] include?

C.   He means to include women and slaves.

D.   For it has been taught [in a teaching bearing the authority of Mishnah-teachers:] Women say Grace in public as a group [unto] themselves, and

merit, too, brought about the miracle of the deliverance.

[2]Ber. 45a: Three who ate together are under the obligation of zimmun, i.e. of saying grace together. Literally zimmun means appointing and may thus refer to the appointment to eat together, with the implied obligation to say grace together.

[3]The repetition of the word 'man' is redundant. 'Ish ish' means every man, any man.

slaves do likewise. [Accordingly, both classifications of persons are subject to the liability of saying a public Grace, should a quorum of appropriate persons be present].

VIII.   A.   All join in the public saying of Grace [responding to the call to say Grace].

B.   [When the framer of the ruler uses the cited inclusionary language,] what [classification of persons] does he mean to include?

C.   It is to include a minor who has knowledge on his own concerning Him to whom they say a blessing [in the Grace after meals].

D.   That is in line with what R. Nahman said, "He who knows to Whom they say a blessing [in the Grace after meals] -- they include such a one in the public call to say the Grace after meals."

IX.   A.   All are subject to becoming unclean by reason of the flux [specified at Lev. 15:1ff, M. Zab. 2:1].

B.   [When the framer of the rule uses the cited inclusionary language,] what [classification of persons does he mean to] include?

C.   It is to include an infant one day old [who, should he produce a flux, would   be   deemed   subject   to flux-uncleanness   under   appropriate circumstances. This form of genital uncleanness is not limited to an adult.]

D.   For it has been taught [in a teaching   bearing   the   authority   of Mishnah-sages:]   "'[When   any]   man [produces flux out of his flesh]' (Lev. 15:2).

E.   "Now why does the Author of Scripture state, 'When any man...' [so

indicating an inclusion of some category
beyond man]?

F. "It is to include even an infant
a day old, who thus is subject to the
uncleanness of flux," the words of R.
Judah.

G. R. Ishmael, the son of R.
Yohanan b. Beroqah, says, "It is hardly
necessary [to interpret Scripture in such
wise]. Lo, [Scripture] says, 'And any of
them who has an issue, whether it is male
or female' (Lev. 15:33).

H. "[The sense is], 'Male,'
meaning, whoever is male, whether minor
or adult. 'Female' [means], whoever is
female, whether minor or adult. [Both
categories, minor and adult, male and
female, fall within the classification of
those subject to uncleanness through
flux. Scripture is explicit in this matter,
without the necessity of interpreting the
language important in Judah's view.]

I. "If that is the case, then on
what account does [the Author of
Scripture] use the language, 'If any
man...'? [The Author of] the Torah made
use of the language of common speech
[and did not mean to provide occasions for
exegesis of minor details of formulation]."

Let me conclude by stating why I think the present approach improves upon the
former one. In my view the work of transmitting an ancient text to a new generation
should go on so long as new readers in successive ages come to the classic document. No
great text of antiquity has ever reached English only one time, and then for all time. As I
said, just as one generation after another has taken up the challenge of translating and
therefore interpreting Plato and Aristotle, Euripides and Herodotus, not to mention the
Hebrew Scriptures and the New Testament, so the classics of Judaism, the Mishnah, the
Tosefta, the several scriptural-exegetical compilations ("midrashim"), the Talmud of the
Land of Israel, and the Talmud of Babylonia demand renewed encounter in age succeeding
age. The reason is not solely the possibility that a better text, better lexicographical
aids, better interpretative commentaries, become available. In the case of Bavli, that

presently is certainly not the case. It is that a new generation simply raises a fresh set of questions and so wants a translation that addresses its concerns in particular.

In my case and in that of my colleagues at work on the other tractates of the Talmud of Babylonia, we come with all due respect for the achievements of our predecessors. If in any aspect we improve upon their work, the reason is that, to begin with, we build upon what they already have achieved. What we want to know, which the Soncino generation did not, is several things. First, how the materials of the Bavli fall into diverse genres; second, how the framers of the document arranged their discussion of the Mishnah; third, what sorts of materials, in addition to those serving as Mishnah-exegesis, they constructed or borrowed, and fourth, how they proposed to put the whole together.

In other words, apart from occasional improvements in the understanding of a passage, though we would not claim that that is common, our principal contribution lies in the more analytical character of our translation than that which came before. We do not present long columns of undifferentiated type, broken up merely by paragraphs. We distinguish from one another the large-scale and complete discussions of problems or topics. Within these large-scale discussions we distinguish one completed thought from another. In our remarks at the end of each of the discussions of a Mishnah-paragraph, we furthermore comment on the relationship to the Mishnah-paragraph at hand of the completed units of thought of the Bavli.

For the reader who does not know Hebrew and Aramaic at all, we add an enormous quantity of explanatory language, included in square brackets in the text, to make the text readable and accessible in its own terms. The footnotes of the Soncino translators simply do not lead a reader through the text. In most instances, the Soncino translators take for granted a fundamental comprehension of the text in Aramaic that, if widely present, would have rendered the work of translation superfluous to begin with. To put matters more bluntly, where the text is not self-evidently accessible, the Soncino translators do not seem to me to make it so. My principal contribution is to attempt to remedy this enormous failing in the otherwise superb work of those who attempted the work before now.

We readily add our hope that those who in a coming generation will undertake yet another translation will improve upon what we have done. So, in all, successive ages will call forth translators who aim at making clear and readily understood in the host-language what hithertofore has been puzzling and essentially incomprehensible (however elegantly worded). In all, therefore, we do not apologize to our predecessors in the on-going work of translating the great text at hand, while we also do not for one minute denigrate their contribution. We recognize the abiding value of what they did, and we hope that for another age we may improve upon what is now available.

It goes without saying, moreover, that as scholarship in the Bavli's Aramaic becomes accessible in dictionaries, as study of the text and exegesis of its meanings reaches still higher levels, and as a critical edition and commentary come to realization, translators will bring to the text at hand a still deeper grasp of its meanings than we do. We should label this translation "preliminary," if it were not so self-evident to us that any translation of the Talmud of Babylonia at this primitive stage in our knowledge must be preliminary. We work on translation before the completion of a critical text, a competent dictionary, and a reliable commentary drawing upon the exegetical achievements of all times. On that basis, any translation must be regarded as temporary and, at best, a mere expedient.

My graduate students of this period, Mr. Roger Brooks, Mr. Howard Eilberg-Schwartz, Mr. Paul Flesher, and Mrs. Judith Romney Wegner, divided up the first draft and corrected it against the original. They vastly facilitated the project, and I am grateful to them for taking time out from their own work to do mine. It is typical of them.

INTRODUCTION TO SUKKAH

This brief tractate does little more than supply further information about objects and rites defined to begin with by Scripture's commandments for the Festival, Mishnah's name for Sukkot, the feast of tabernacles. To be sure, some rites are known to Mishnah which will have surprised the priestly legislators who made up Leviticus and Numbers. But the authors of the Mishnah did not invent these rites, so far as the Mishnah's language and mode of discourse appear to suggest, but refer to them as data out of Israel's liturgical past. It follows that Sukkah would be incomprehensible without the frame of Scripture. Sukkah simply tells us what we need to know to do what, to begin with, Scripture requires. In all, the tractate serves as little more than a law-code on rather fundamental facts. We have now to consider the relevant verses:

Leviticus 23:33-43:

And the Lord said to Moses, "Say to the people of Israel, On the fifteenth day of this seventh month and for seven days is the feast of booths to the Lord. On the first day shall be a holy convocation; you shall do no laborious work. Seven days you shall present offerings by fire to the Lord; on the eighth day you shall hold a holy convocation and present an offering by fire to the Lord; it is a solemn assembly; you shall do no laborious work.

"These are the appointed feasts of the Lord, which you shall proclaim as times of holy convocation, for presenting to the Lord offerings by fire, burnt offerings and cereal offerings, sacrifices and drink offerings, each of its proper day; besides the sabbaths of the Lord, and besides your gifts, and besides all your votive offerings, and besides all your freewill offerings, which you give to the Lord.

"On the fifteenth day of the seventh month, when you have gathered in the produce of the land, you shall keep the feast of the Lord seven days; on the first day shall be a solemn rest and on the eighth day shall be a solemn rest. And you shall take on the first day the fruit of goodly trees, branches of palm trees, and boughs of leafy trees, and willows of the brook; and you shall rejoice before the Lord your God seven days. You shall keep it as a feast to the Lord seven days in the year; it is a statute for ever throughout your generations; you shall keep it in the seventh month. You shall dwell in booths for seven days; all that are native in Israel shall dwell in booths, that your generations may know that I made the people of Israel dwell in booths when I brought them out of the land of Egypt: I am the Lord your God."

Numbers 29:12-38:

"On the fifteenth day of the seventh month you shall have a holy convocation; you shall do no laborious work, and you shall keep a feast to the Lord seven days; and you shall offer a burnt offering, an offering by fire, a pleasing odor to the Lord, thirteen young bulls, two rams, fourteen male lambs a year old; they shall be without blemish; and their cereal offering of fine flour mixed with oil, three tenths of an ephah for each of the thirteen bulls, two tents for each of the two rams, and a tenth for each of the fourteen lambs; also one male goat for a sin offering, besides the continual burnt offering, its cereal offering and its drink offering.

"On the second day twelve young bulls, two rams, fourteen male lambs a year old without blemish, with the cereal offering and the drink offering for the bulls, for the rams, and for the lambs, by number, according to the ordinance; also one male goat for a sin offering, besides the continual burnt offering and its cereal offering, and their drink offerings.

"On the third day eleven bulls, two rams, fourteen male lambs a year old without blemish, with the cereal offering and the drink offerings for the bulls, for the rams, and for the lambs, by number, according to the ordinance; also one male goat for a sin offering, besides the continual burnt offering and its cereal offering and its drink offering.

"On the fourth day ten bulls, two rams, fourteen male lambs a year old without blemish, with the cereal offering and the drink offerings for the bulls, for the rams, and for the lambs, by number, according to the ordinance; also one male goat for a sin offering, besides the continual burnt offering, its cereal offering and its drink offering.

"On the fifth day nine bulls, two rams, fourteen male lambs a year old without blemish, with the cereal offering and the drink offerings for the bulls, for the rams, and for the lambs, by number, according to the ordinance; also one male goat for a sin offering; besides the continual burnt offerings and its cereal offering and its drink offering.

"On the sixth day eight bulls, two rams, fourteen male lambs a year old without blemish, with the cereal offering and the drink offerings for the bulls, for the rams, and for the lambs, by number, according to the ordinance; also one male goat for a sin offering; besides the continual burnt offering, its cereal offering, and its drink offerings.

"On the seventh day seven bulls, two rams, fourteen male lambs a year old without blemish, with the cereal offering and the drink offerings for the bulls, for the rams, and for the lambs, by number, according to the ordinance; also one male goat for a sin offering; besides the continual burnt offering, its cereal offering, and its drink offering.

"On the eighth day you shall have a solemn assembly: you shall do no laborious work, but you shall offer a burnt offering, an offering by fire, a pleasing odor to the

Lord: one bull, one ram, seven male lambs a year old without blemish, and the cereal offering and the drink offerings for the bull, for the ram, and for the lambs, by number, according to the ordinance; also one male goat for a sin offering; besides the continual burnt offering and its cereal offering and its drink offering."

Deuteronomy 16:13-15:

"You shall keep the feast of booths seven days, when you make your ingathering from your threshing floor and your wine press; you shall rejoice in your feast, you and your son and your daughter, your manservant and your maidservant, the Levite, the sojourner, the fatherless, and the widow who are within your towns. For seven days you shall keep the feast to the Lord your God at the place which the Lord will choose; because the Lord your God will bless you in all your produce and in all the work of your hands, so that you will be altogether joyful."

Let us now turn to the layout of the tractate:

I. The appurtenances of the Festival: Sukkah, Lulab. 1:1-3:15

    A.   The sukkah and its roofing. 1:1-2:3

        1:1   A sukkah taller than twenty cubits is invalid. Other points of invalidation.

        1:2   He who makes a sukkah under a tree is as if he made it in his house.

        1:3   A sheet spread over a sukkah invalidates it.

        1:4   A vine, gourd, or ivy trained over a sukkah, and then covered with sukkah-roofing, the sukkah is invalid.

        1:5   Bundles of straw, wood, or brush are not to be used for sukkah-roofing.

        1:6   They make sukkah-roofing with boards, so Judah. Meir prohibits.

        1:7   Boards as sukkah-roofing, continued.

        1:8   Spits or side-pieces of a bed as sukkah-roofing.

        1:9   He who suspends the sides of the sukkah.

        1:10   If a roof was damaged and one covered the hole with sukkah-roofing.

        1:11   He who makes his sukkah in the shape of a cone (without a roof).

        2:1   He who sleeps under a bed in a sukkah has not fulfilled his obligation.

        2:2   He who props up his sukkah with the legs of a bed.

        2:3   He who makes his sukkah on top of a wagon or a boat.

    B.   The obligation to dwell in the sukkah. 2:4-9

        2:4-6 Those exempt from dwelling in the sukkah. Eating in the sukkah.

        2:7   He who can eat in the sukkah but cannot sit there.

2:8   Women, slaves, and minors are exempt from the religious require-
         ments of dwelling in a sukkah.

2:9   All seven days a person treats his sukkah as his regular dwelling and
         his house as his sometimes dwelling.

C.   The lulab and etrog. 3:1-15

3:1   A stolen or dried up palm branch is invalid.

3:2   A stolen or dried up myrtle branch is invalid.

3:3   A stolen or dried up willow branch is invalid.

3:4   How many myrtle-branches, willow-branches, and palm-branches are
         required.

3:5-7   A stolen or dried up etrog [citron] is invalid. Suitable and unsuitable
         etrogs.

3:8   They bind up the lulab (palm-branch, willow-branch, and myr-
         tle-branch) with its own species.

3:9   Waving the lulab in the liturgy: At what point in the Hallel-psalms.

3:10   Reciting the Hallel-psalms.

3:11   Reciting the Hallel-psalms.

3:12   Carrying the lulab in the Temple and in the provinces.

3:13   Carrying the lulab on the Sabbath.

3:14   Special problems relating to the foregoing.

3:15   Special problems relating to the foregoing.

II. The rites and offerings of the Festival. 4:1-5:8

A.   The Festival rites carried out on various days of the Festival. 4:1-5:4

4:1   The lulab and willow-branch are for six or seven days, the Hal-
         lel-psalms and rejoicing (eating meat) for eight, dwelling in the
         sukkah and the water-libation for seven, flute-playing for five or six
         days.

4:2   The lulab is for seven days: how so?

4:3   The willow-branch is for seven days: how so?

4:4   The lulab on the Sabbath: how so?

4:5-7   The willow-branch rite: how so?

4:8   The Hallel-psalms and rejoicing are for eight days: how so?

4:9-10   The water-libation: how so?

5:1   The playing of the flute: how so?

5:2-4   The celebration of bet hasho'ebah.

B.   The offerings. 5:5-8

5:5   Sounding the shofar in the Temple rite. They sound no fewer than
          twenty-one notes in the Temple and no more than forty-eight.

5:6-8   The priestly-courses and the offerings of animals on the eight days of
          the Festival.

The plan for the tractate could not be more straight-forward. The framers have taken a
special interest in the matter of dwelling in the sukkah -- that is, a topic subjected to
rather slight definition in Scripture itself and particularly relevant to the observance of
the festival outside of the Temple. The tractate gives rules for the building of the
sukkah, with special reference to the roofing which defines its valid state. Logically, the
next question is the use of the sukkah, that is "dwelling" therein. The requirement to
make use of a lulab and etrog next forms the bridge from the sukkah to the liturgy of the
festival (I.C. to II). For it is here that the lulab and etrog, first, are defined and, second,
have their use specified. The rites and offerings of the festival form the final point of
interest.

As is the Mishnah's way, the effort of unit II is to draw together and present as a
comprehensive generalization a range of diverse rites. This exercise in organization is
successfully effected at II.A. II.B closes the tractate with further information relevant to
the cult. The sequence of topics -- (1) sukkah, (2) lulab and etrog + Hallel-psalms, (3)
liturgy of the Festival in general -- cannot have been other than what it is, because of the
integral relationship, in just this order, of lulab-etrog-Hallel-liturgy. It follows that the
tractate is tight and logical, leaving no doubt of the highly disciplined character of the
program and exegetical and redactional plan of the men who framed it.

I consulted Israel W. Slotki, Sukkah. Translated into English, with notes, glossary
and indices (London, 1948: Soncino). Where I have used one of Slotki's formulations, I
have added his name, within the translation, in square brackets. I have copied some of his
footnotes verbatim, always indicating that the contribution is his. In addition I consulted
his translation on nearly every passage and always benefited from his excellent work.

CHAPTER ONE
BAVLI SUKKAH CHAPTER ONE

1:1 A-F

A.   A sukkah which is taller than twenty cubits is invalid.

B.   R. Judah declares it valid.

C.   And one which is not ten handbreadths high,

D.   one which does not have three walls,

E.   or one, the light of which is greater than the shade of which,

F.   is invalid.

I.

A.   We have learned in the Mishnah at another passage: The crossbeam above an alley-entry which is higher than twenty cubits [is invalid, and one therefore] should diminish it [making it lower]. R. Judah says, "It is not necessary to do so" [M. Er. 1:1A-B].

B.   What differentiates the case of the sukkah, in which instance the rule is formulated in the language of unfitness [without remedy], from the case of the alley-way, in which instance the framer of the Mishnah has specified the remedy [for an improper arrangement]?

C.   Since [the religious requirement of building] a sukkah derives [from the authority] of the Torah, the framer of the passage uses the language, "unfit," while, since the arrangement creating an artificial alley-way derives from the authority of rabbis, the framer of the passage has taught the remedy [namely, diminishing the height of the crossbar].

D.   If you prefer, I shall propose a different solution:

E.   Even in matters deriving from the authority of the Torah one may well teach the required remedy. But in the case of the sukkah, with its numerous rules, the framer of the passage has simply framed matters in terms of unfitness. In the case of the alley-way, without numerous rules and regulations, the framer of the passage taught the remedy [for an improper arrangement].

II.

A.   What is the scriptural source for the rule [that the sukkah may not be taller than twenty cubits]?

B.   Said Rabbah, "It is because [Scripture] has stated, 'So that your coming generations may know that I made the children of Israel dwell in sukkot' (Lev. 23:43).

C.   "[If the roof is] up to twenty cubits, someone will know that he is dwelling in a sukkah. If it is higher than twenty cubits, one will not know that he is dwelling in a sukkah, because [the roof] will be out of [the ordinary line of] sight."

D. R. Zira said, "The proof derives from here: 'And there shall be a booth [sukkah] for a shadow in the daytime from the heat' (Is. 4:6).

E. "[If the roof is] up to twenty cubits, someone will sit in the shadow of the [roof of the] sukkah. If it is higher than twenty cubits, one will not sit in the shadow of the [roof of the] sukkah [since the shadow will be cast by the walls entirely], but rather, in the shadow of the walls."

F. Said to him Abayye, "But if someone made his sukkah in a glen between two hills [where there is no sun], would you maintain that in such a case it is not a valid sukkah? [Surely not!]"

G. He said to him, "In that case, if one removes the two mountains there will be shade deriving from the roof of the sukkah, but here, if you remove the walls of the sukkah, there will not be any shadow cast by the sukkah at all."

H. And Raba said, "The proof derives from here: 'You shall dwell in sukkot for seven days' (Lev. 23:42), is what the Torah has said. For all seven days, go out of your permanent dwelling and stay in a temporary dwelling.

I. "Now [if the roof is] twenty cubits high, someone will make the sukkah a merely temporary dwelling. If it is higher than that, someone will not make the sukkah a temporary dwelling but a permanent one." [Slotki, p. 2, n. 13: Such a high structure requires firm foundations and walls, and these give it the characteristic of a permanent abode.]

J. Said to him Abayye, "But if so, if one has made the walls of his sukkah out of iron and then made a sukkah-roofing on them, would it be the case that this would not be a valid sukkah? [It certainly is a valid sukkah.]"

K. He said to him, "This is what I was saying to you: If the roof is up to twenty cubits in height, which is the sort of house that a person makes his temporary dwelling, if he makes it his permanent dwelling, he [nevertheless] carries out his obligation. But if the roof is higher than twenty cubits, which is the sort of house a man makes a permanent dwelling, if one makes it a temporary dwelling, he has not carried out his obligation."

L. [2B] [We now review the proofs of Rabbah, Zira, and Raba, and ask what is at fault that all parties do not concur on any one of the three proposed proof-texts.] All parties do not concur with the proof of Rabbah, for his proof-text depends upon the knowledge of the coming generations.

M. All parties do not concur with the proof-text of R. Zira, for the proof-text he cites refers to the days of the Messiah.

N. But R. Zira [would respond], "If so, the verse should make use of the language of a canopy: 'A canopy will serve for a shade in the daytime.' Why does the verse say, 'A sukkah shall serve for a shade in the daytime'? It serves to make two points [one concerning the proper height of a sukkah, the other concerning matters in the messianic age]."

O.   Likewise as to the proof-text adduced by Raba, all parties do not concur, on account
     of the question raised by Abayye.

III.

A.   [With reference to the proof-texts adduced in unit II we turn to the dispute at M.
     1:1A-B]: In accord with what authority is the following statement: R. Josiah said
     Raba said, "The dispute [of the Mishnah at M. 1:1A-B] treats a case in which the
     walls of the sukkah do not touch the sukkah-roof. But if the walls do touch the
     sukkah-roof, then even though the roof is higher than twenty cubits, the sukkah is
     valid.

B.   In accord with whose view? It accords with Rabbah, who has said, "The reason is
     that the roof [if higher] will be out of sight. But since the walls touch the suk-
     kah-roofing, the sukkah-roofing is not out of sight. [The eye will be led up the walls
     to the sukkah-roofing, which forms a single visual image with the walls.]"

C.   In accord with whose view is the following statement that R. Huna made in the
     name of Rab: "The dispute concerns a case in which the roof is only four cubits by
     four cubits in area. But if it is larger than four cubits by four cubits in area, then
     even if the roofing is higher than twenty cubits, the sukkah is valid."

D.   In accord with whom? It accords with the view of R. Zira, who has said, "It is
     because of the need to cast a proper shadow." Now since there is ample space in the
     sukkah-roofing, the shadow of the sukkah [will be suitable even though the roof is
     higher than twenty cubits].

E.   In accord with which authority is the following statement which R. Hanan bar
     Rabbah made in the name of Rab: "The dispute concerns a case in which the sukkah
     can hold only someone's head, the greater part of his body, and his table, then even
     if the roof is taller than twenty cubits, the sukkah will be valid"?

F.   In accord with whom? In accord with none of them [since even if the sukkah can
     hold more than one's head, etc., the stated reasons still pertain.]

G.   Now R. Josiah surely differs from R. Huna and R. Hanan bar Rabbah, for they define
     a minimum measure for the extent [of the sukkah], while he does not do so.

H.   But may we maintain that R. Huna and R. Hanan bar Rabbah differ as to what
     renders the sukkah valid?

I.   The proposed theory will be as follows: one party maintains that what renders the
     sukkah valid is the four cubits of sukkah-roofing, and the other holds that what
     renders the sukkah valid is the capacity to contain the head, the greater part of the
     body, and the table [of a resident].

J.   No, that theory is not valid. All parties concur that what renders a sukkah valid is
     the capacity to hold the head, the greater part of one's body, and the table. But in
     the present case, this is the point of difference:

K.   One party holds that at issue in the Mishnah's dispute is a case of a sukkah which
     indeed holds one's head, the greater part of one's body, and his table. But if [a
     sukkah] holds more than one's head, the greater part of one's body, and his table, all
     parties concur that a sukkah with a roof above twenty cubits remains valid.

L. The other party [Judah, M. 1:1B] maintains the view that at issue in the Mishnah's dispute is a case of a sukkah from a size which suffices to hold one's head, the greater part of one's body, and his table, to a size of four cubits. But if the sukkah is larger than four cubits, all parties concur that the sukkah is valid.

IV.

A. [The specification of the cited authorities, III A, C, E, on the minimum requirements of the sukkah, now comes under discussion in its own terms.] The following objection was raised:

B. A Sukkah which is taller than twenty cubits is invalid.

C. R. Judah declares it valid [M. 1:1A-B], even up to forty or fifty cubits.

D. Said R. Judah, "M'SH B: The sukkah of Helene in Lud was twenty cubits tall, and sages went in and out, when visiting her, and not one of them said a thing."

E. They said to him, "It was because she is a woman, and a woman is not liable to keep the commandment of sitting in a sukkah."

F. He said to them, "Now did she not have seven sons [who are disciples of sages, and all of them were dwelling in that same sukkah!"] [T. Suk. 1:1A-E].

G. "And furthermore, everything she ever did was done in accord with the instruction of sages."

H. Now what need do I have for this additional reason: "Furthermore, everything she ever did was done in accord with the instructions of sages"?

I. This is the sense of what he said to them: "Now, if you say that the sons were minors, and minors are exempt from the religious duty of dwelling in the sukkah, since she had seven sons, it is not possible that among them was not a single one who no longer needed his mother's tending [and so would be required to dwell on his own in the sukkah]."

J. "And if, further, you should maintain that a minor who no longer needs his mother's tending is subject to the law only on the authority of rabbis, and that woman paid no attention to rules that rested only on the authority of the rabbis, come and note the following: 'And furthermore, everything she ever did was done in accord with the instructions of sages'."

K. [We now revert to the issue with which we began, namely, the comparison of the story at hand to the reasons adduced by the authorities at unit III:] Now with references to one who said, the dispute applies to a case in which the walls of the sukkah do not touch the sukkah-roofing, would a queen dwell in a sukkah, the walls of which do not touch the sukkah-roofing?

L. [3A] [Indeed so! The reason is that] the space makes possible good ventilation.

M. But in the view of the one who has said that the dispute pertains to a small sukkah, would a queen ever dwell in a small sukkah?

N. Said Rabbah bar R. Ada, "At issue in the dispute is solely a case of a sukkah which is made with many small cubbies."

O. But would a queen take up residence in a sukkah that was subdivided into many small cubbies?

P. Said R. Ashi, "At issue is only [a large sukkah which had] such recesses."

Q. "Rabbis take the view that the queen's sons were dwelling in a sukkah of absolutely valid traits, while she dwelled in the recesses on account of modesty [i.e., not showing her face among the men], and it was on that account that rabbis said nothing to her [about her dwelling in what was, in fact, an invalid part of the sukkah]."

R. "And R. Judah maintains the position that her sons were dwelling along with her [in the cubbyholes of the sukkah], and even so, the rabbis did not criticize what she was doing [which proves that the small cubbies of the sukkah were valid]."

V.

A. Said R. Samuel bar Isaac, "The law is that a valid sukkah must be able to contain a person's head, the greater part of his body, and his table."

B. Said R. Abba to him, "In accord with which party is this rule? Does it concur with the view of the house of Shammai [at M. 2:7: He whose head and the greater part of whose body are in the sukkah, but whose table is in the house -- the House of Shammai declare invalid. And the House of Hillel declare valid]."

C. He said to him, "Then in accord with whose opinion [might one allege that this is decided]?"

D. There are those who report [the matter in the following terms:]

E. Said R. Abba, "And who says [that the law is as] you [have stated]?"

F. He said to him, "It is in accord with the House of Shammai, and do not move from that view."

G. R. Nahman bar Isaac objected [to the thesis of Abba, B]: "How [do we know that] the House of Shammai and the House of Hillel debate about a small sukkah, [so that the conclusion drawn at A, B would follow, in line with M. 2:7]? Perhaps the dispute concerns a large sukkah.

H. "It would then involve the case of one who sat at the entrance of the shadowed [part of the large sukkah], with his table in his house.

I. "The House of Shammai then maintain that we rule by decree [that such an arrangement is unacceptable], lest the person be drawn [into the house] after his table.

J. "The House of Hillel take the view that we make no such decree.

K. "From a close reading of the language of the Mishnah itself the same conclusion may be drawn, for it has been taught: He whose head and the greater part of whose body are in the sukkah, but whose table is in the house -- the House of Shammai declare invalid. And the House of Hillel declare valid [M. 2:7].

L. "Now if matters were [as you say, that is, if the dispute involved a small sukkah, then the framer of the Mishnah should have used the language,] '... holds or does not hold... [one's head, the greater part of the body, etc.].'"

M. Now do they really not dispute concerning the validity of a small sukkah?

N. And has it not been taught on Tannaite authority: [A sukkah that holds one's head, the greater part of his body, and his table is valid. Rabbi says, "It is valid only if it is at least four cubits by four cubits."

O. And it has further been taught on Tannaite authority: Rabbi says, "Any sukkah that is not at least four cubits by four cubits is invalid."

P. And sages say, "Even if it holds only his head, and the greater part of his body, it is valid."

Q. Now note that there is no reference to one's table at all!

R. The cited [teachings on Tannaite authority] present inconsistencies among themselves, so would it not follow that one of them represents the view of the House of Shammai and the other the view of the House of Hillel? [At issue then is the validity of a small sukkah.]

S. Said Mar Zutra, "The Mishnah-paragraph before us also [supports the same view]. Take note that a close reading sustains it: The House of Shammai declare invalid, and the House of Hillel declare valid.

T. "Now if [at issue were a large sukkah, used in an improper manner, such as was proposed above,] then it should read, 'The House of Shammai say, "The user has not carried out his obligation,: and the House of Hillel say, "The user has carried out his obligation."' [At issue would be not the character of the sukkah but the use made of it by the owner.]"

U. But there is yet a problem, [since the language at hand is,] He whose head... [etc., as Nahman bar Isaac noted earlier, Gff.].

V. It must follow that there is a dispute on two matters, a dispute first about a small sukkah, second, about a large sukkah. The passage then presents a lacuna, and this is its proper wording:

W. He whose head and the greater part of whose body were in the sukkah, but whose table was in the house --

X. the House of Shammai say, "He has not carried out his obligation."

Y. And the House of Hillel say, "He has carried out his obligation."

Z. And he whose sukkah is able to contain only his head and the greater part of his body alone --

AA. the House of Shammai declare [the sukkah] invalid.

BB. And the House of Hillel declare it valid.

VI.

A. [Reverting to the discussion of Rabbis' opinion, V N, above:] Who stands behind the following teaching, which our rabbis have taught on Tannaite authority:

B. A building that is not at least four cubits by four cubits [is not truly a "house," and so] is exempt from the requirement of placing a mezuzah and of building a parapet [Deut. 22:8], does not contract uncleanness through a nega [Lev. 14:34], is not permanently assigned to the ownership of a purchaser in line with the rules governing the transfer of real property in a walled city [Lev. 25:29]; on its account those who are in the battle line do not return from battle [if they have not used the house a requisite period of time, Deut. 20:5]; people do not provide an erub-meal for it [symbolically to create joint ownership among the houses in a given courtyard so as to permit carrying within the entire courtyard in the theory that the whole constitutes a single property] or a <u>shittuf</u>-meal for it [so as symbolically to create joint ownership among the courtyards of a single alley-way, for the same purpose as above]; people do not leave an <u>erub</u>-meal in such a house [so as to make it the locus of the symbolic joint meal]; [3B] they do not make of it an extension [outpost] between two towns [regarding such a building as a house equally location in two distinct towns, with the result that the two towns are regarded as one, so that people may walk on the Sabbath from one to the other]; and brothers or partners may not partition it [since it is too small].

C.   [Since, in all of the cited matters, Scripture speaks of a house, and Rabbi has said that a <u>sukkah</u> is valid only if it is four cubits by four cubits,] may one say that the cited catalogue represents the views of Rabbi and not those of the rabbis [who would regard a building of smaller size as falling into the category of a house]?

D.   You may say that the catalogue represents the views even of the rabbis.

E.   They take the views stated there only with reference to a <u>sukkah</u>, which may serve as a random dwelling [not as a permanent house, and hence may be smaller than the normal proportions that would define a house]. But in respect to the definition of a house, which must be able to serve as a permanent dwelling, even rabbis would concur that if a building is four cubits by four cubits, it constitutes a suitable dwelling for people, and if not, it does not constitute a suitable dwelling for people.

F.   [Proceeding to the analysis of the passage cited above, B, we move forward:] A master has said, "It is exempt from the requirement of placing a <u>mezuzah</u> and building a parapet, does not contract uncleanness through a <u>nega</u>, is not permanently assigned to the ownership of a purchaser in line with the rules governing the transfer of real property in a walled city; on its account those who are in the battle line do not return from battle."

G.   What is the [scriptural] basis for that view?

H.   The reason is that in all of these instances, Scripture makes reference to a house. [In no case among those listed is a building of such modest size regarded as a house.]

I.   "People do not provide an <u>erub</u> meal for it or a <u>shittuf</u>-meal for it; people do not leave an <u>erub</u>-meal in such a house."

J.   What is the reason for that view?

K.   It will not serve as [an ordinary] dwelling.

L.   [But if that is the operative consideration, then, while] people may not place the <u>erub</u>-meal there for the purpose of joining houses into a single courtyard, a <u>shittuf</u>-meal might well be placed there [since it joins not houses but entire courtyards that open out into a single alley-way. The consideration of whether or not it is a house does not apply.]

M.   What is the reason [for such a position]? It is that the building at hand is no worse than a courtyard in an alley-way [and falls into that same category]. For we have learned in a teaching on Tannaite authority: The <u>erub</u>-meals that serve courtyards are placed in a courtyard, and the <u>shittuf</u>-meals serving alleyways are located in alley-ways.

N. And we reflected on that teaching as follows: "Erub-meals serving courtyards are to be placed in a courtyard." And have we not learned in the Mishnah: He who places his erub in a gate-house, portico, or gallery -- it is not a valid erub. And he who lives there [in the gate-house, portico, or gallery, and who does not share in the erub] does not prohibit [another from carrying objects in the courtyard] [M. Er. 8:4A-B]. [Hence these are not regarded as houses in the courtyard for the purposes of the erub-meal.]

O. Accordingly, I must interpret the cited statement [M] as follows: Erub-meals serving courtyards must be placed in a house located in the courtyard, and shittuf-meals serving alleyways must be located in a courtyard in that alley-way.

P. The matter at hand then [the house less than four cubits by four cubits] is no less [a case] than the courtyard in an alley-way [as proposed just now].

Q. "They do not make of it an extension between two towns:" for it is not treated even as equivalent to a watchtower. Why not? Watchtowers [however modest] serve their purpose, but this serves no purpose.

R. "And brothers or partners may not partition it:" What is the reason? Because it is not in area four cubits by four cubits.

S. But if it were of such an area, would they be able to partition it?

T. And have we not learned in the Mishnah: People may not divide up a courtyard unless there will be four cubits for one resident and four for another [after the partition] [M. B.B. 1:6]?

U. Rather, read the matter simply as follows: The law of partition does not apply [to such a house] as it does to a courtyard.

V. For R. Huna has said, "A courtyard is [wholly] divided up in accord with its entry-ways."

W. And R. Hisda said, "One assigns four cubits to each entry way, and they partition the remainder equally."

X. The stated rules apply to a house, which one plans to keep standing. In such a case one assigns a courtyard [space to such a house]. But as to this building, which is going to be demolished, we do not assign it courtyard-space.

VII.

A. [If a sukkah] was taller than twenty cubits and one attempted to diminish its height by placing on the ground blankets and pillows, that does not constitute a valid act of diminution [4A], and that is so even though the owner declared the objects to be abandoned [and null, of no value whatsoever] so far as all parties are concerned.

B. The reason is that his intention in the matter is null when measured against the prevailing view of all other people [who will nonetheless regard the blankets and pillows not as abandoned but as objects of value].

C. If he did so with straw and nullified [its value], this does indeed constitute an act of valid diminution, and all the more so if he did it with dirt and nullified [its value].

D. As to the use of straw which the man is not planning to remove later on, and as to dirt of indeterminate condition, there is a dispute between R. Yose and rabbis.

E. For we have learned in the Mishnah: A house which one wholly filled with dirt or pebbles and which one abandoned is regarded as abandoned [M. Oh. 15:7].

F. That is the case if one has abandoned the house. If one did not abandon the house, that is not the case.

G. And in this regard there is a Tannaite teaching:

H. R. Yose says, "Straw which one is not destined to remove, lo, it is in the category of ordinary dirt and is regarded as abandoned and dirt which one is destined to remove, lo, it is in the category of ordinary straw and is not regarded as abandoned [T. Oh. 15:5B] [= D].

VIII.

A. [If a sukkah] was higher than twenty cubits, but palm leaves were hanging down within the twenty cubits, if the shade that they cast is greater than the sunlight they let through, the sukkah is valid, and if not, it is invalid.

B. [If a sukkah] was ten handbreadths high, and palm leaves were hanging down into the space of ten handbreadths,

C. Abayye considered ruling that if the shade that they cast is greater than the sunlight they let through, the sukkah is valid, and if not, it is invalid.

D. [But] Raba said to him, "This really would be a disgraceful sort of dwelling, and no one would live in such a disgraceful dwelling [so the sukkah would be invalid to begin with]."

E. [If] it was higher than twenty cubits, but the owner built a ledge in it across the entire front of the middle [of the three] walls of the sukkah, and [the ledge] has sufficient space to constitute a valid sukkah, it is a valid sukkah.

F. [If the owner] built the ledge on the side wall, if from the edge of the ledge to the [opposite] wall of the sukkah is a space of four cubits [or more], the sukkah is invalid. If the space from the ledge to the wall is less than four cubits, it is a valid sukkah. [Slotki: It is valid because the roof above the area between the ledge and the opposite wall is regarded as a continuation of that wall which thus serves as a third wall for the ledge.]

G. What inference [does the framer of this case] wish to provide for us? Is it that we invoke the principle of the "curved wall"? [Slotki]?

H. But we have learned on Tannaite authority: As to a house which is lacking [the middle of its flat roof], and the owner put sukkah-roofing over that empty area, if from the wall to the sukkah-roofing is a distance of four cubits, the area is invalid [to serve as a sukkah].

I. Lo, if the distance is less than that, it is valid. [Accordingly, the principle yielded by the case at hand is not fresh, since it is readily derived from an available teaching.]

J. [No, it was necessary to make the principle explicit in the present case.] What might you have said? In that [available] case, it is valid because [each side] is suitable to serve as a wall [Slotki: it is not higher than the permitted maximum], but here, [where the sukkah is higher than twenty cubits] so that the wall is not suitable to serve as a wall for a sukkah, I might have held that it was not a suitable arrangement.

K.   Thus the framer of the case informs us that that is not a consideration.

L.   [If a sukkah] was taller than twenty cubits, and the owner built a ledge in the middle of the sukkah, if from the edge of the ledge to the wall is a space of four cubits in all directions, the area is invalid to serve as a sukkah. But if it is less than that space, it is valid.

M.   What principle does the framer of the case wish to tell us? Is it that we invoke the principle of the "curved wall"? This is the same [case as the one just reviewed].

N.   [No, it was necessary to specify the matter.] What might you have imagined? We invoke the principle of the "curved wall" in the case of a [wall in a] single direction, but we do not invoke that principle in all four directions.

O.   Thus the framer informs us that that is not the case. [We invoke the principle for all four directions.]

P.   [If a sukkah] was lower than ten handbreadths, and one made a hole in the ground of the sukkah so as to fill out the sukkah ['s requisite space, from ground to roof] up to ten handbreadths, if from the edge of the hole to the wall there is a distance of three or more handbreadths, the sukkah is invalid. If the distance is less than this, [4B] it is valid.

Q.   What differentiates the other case, in which you have maintained that the maximum distance may be four cubits, from the present case, in which the maximum acceptable difference is less than three handbreadths?

R.   In the earlier case, in which there is a wall, a distance of as much as four cubits will suffice. Here, where the owner has to make a wall, if the distance from the hole to the wall is three handbreadths or less, it is acceptable, and if not, it is not acceptable.

S.   If a sukkah was higher than twenty cubits, and the owner built in the sukkah a pillar ten handbreadths in height, with sufficient space [four cubits by four cubits] to constitute a valid sukkah,

T.   Abayye considered invoking the principle that the partitions [formed for the sides of the pillar] are [imaginarily] projected upward [Slotki, p. 13, n. 1: As far as the ceiling, and that, since the sides are no less than ten handbreadths high and the distance between the top of the pillar and the roof is less than twenty cubits, the pillar constitutes a valid sukkah].

U.   Raba, however, said to him, "To invoke that principle we require partitions that can be recognized, and that condition is not met here."

IX.

A.   Our rabbis have taught on Tannaite authority:

B.   If a person drove four posts into the ground and spread sukkah-roofing on them,

C.   R. Jacob declares the arrangement a valid sukkah.

D.   And sages declare it invalid.

E.   Said R. Huna, "The dispute concerns an arrangement made at the edge of a roof. R. Jacob takes the view that we invoke the principle that the walls extend upward, and rabbis maintain that we do not invoke that rule.

F.   "But if one erected such a contraption in the middle of the roof, all parties concur that the arrangement is invalid [since the sukkah has no walls]."

G.   R. Nahman said, "If one erected the arrangement in the middle of the roof, there is a dispute."

H.   The following question troubled [the later exegetes of the passage]: Is it true that there is a dispute in the case of such an arrangement built at the middle of the roof, but if it were located on the edge of the roof, all parties would concur that it is valid [in Nahman's view of the matter]? Or is it true that whether the arrangement is in this area [the middle of the roof] or in that [the edge of the roof] [in Nahman's view] there is a dispute?

I.   The question stands unanswered.

J.   The following objection was raised:

K.   If someone drove four poles into the ground and arranged sukkah-roofing on them,

L.   R. Jacob declares [the contraption to be a] valid [sukkah].

M.   And sages declare it invalid.

N.   Now lo, the ground is equivalent to the middle of the roof, and yet R. Jacob declares it valid.

O.   That would constitute a refutation of the theory [F] of R. Huna [on what is at issue], would it not? It indeed constitutes a refutation.

P.   Furthermore, there is a dispute as to such a contraption's being located at the middle of the roof, but if it is located at the edge of the roof, all parties concur that it is valid.

Q.   Now may I propose that this too constitutes a refutation of R. Huna in both matters?

R.   [No, not at all]. R. Huna may reply to you that the dispute pertains to such a contraption in the middle of the roof, and the same rule applies to one constructed at the edge of the roof.

S.   And as to the fact that there is a dispute concerning such an arrangement in the middle of the roof, it serves to tell you just how far R. Jacob is prepared to go. For even if we deal with such an arrangement in the middle of the roof, [Jacob] even in such a case would declare it to be valid.

T.   Our rabbis have taught on Tannaite authority:

U.   If someone dug four [round] poles into the ground and put sukkah-roofing on them,

V.   R. Jacob says, "[To determine whether we have valid walls,] we take a perspective such that, if one should cut the pole and plane it, what would result would be a beam with a handbreadth of space on one side and a handbreadth of space on the other. Then the poles are judged to form a rectangular corner piece [and so to constitute a double wall with each surface regarded as a wall unto itself], and if not, they are not required in that way." [If there are two walls, one in each direction, to be imputed to the pillar, we have an adequate sukkah.]

W.   For R. Jacob says, "The measure for the assessment of a rectangular corner piece in
      the case of a sukkah is a handbreadth."

X.   And sages say, "The appropriate measure is only if two [of the nearby walls] are
      fully articulated walls in accord with the law pertaining to them. In that case, then
      the third wall of the sukkah may be even so small as a handbreadth [in depth]. [So
      sages reject Jacob's view that we invoke the principle that the estimate, if met,
      would yield two valid walls for the sukkah, one on each side of the pillar. Sages
      insist on two fully valid walls, and here there is none.]

X.

A.   And one [a sukkah] which is not ten handbreadths high [M. 1:1C]:

B.   How do we know [from Scripture] that that is the rule?

C.   It has been stated [on Amoraic authority]:

D.   Rab, R. Hanina, R. Yohanan, and R. Habiba repeated --

E.   -- in the whole of the Division of Appointed Times, in any case in which this set
      appears together, the name of R. Jonathan may be substituted for the name of R.
      Yohanan --

F.   "The ark was nine handbreadths high, and the ark cover one more, thus, ten in all.

G.   "And it is written, 'And there I will meet with you and I will speak with you from
      above the ark-cover' (Ex. 25:22)."

H.   [5A] [And it has been taught on Tannaite authority:

I.   "R. Yose says, 'The Presence of God never came down, and Moses and Elijah never
      went upward to the height, for it is said, "The heavens are the heavens of God, and
      the earth he has given to the children of men" (Ps. 115:16).'" [Slotki, p. 15, n. 4:
      Now since the Shechinah descended as low as the ark-cover it may be concluded that
      the boundary of the earth is at that level, viz., ten handbreadths from the ground.
      Consequently a wall whose height is less than ten handbreadths cannot be regarded
      as a valid wall.]

J.   But did the Presence of God never come down to the earth? And has it not been
      written, "And the Lord came down upon Mount Sinai" (Ex. 19:20)?

K.   It was only to the space above ten handbreadths over the mountain.

L.   And is it not written, "And his feet shall stand in that day upon the Mount of Olives"
      (Zech. 14:4)?

M.   It will still be above ten handbreadths [from the ground].

N.   And did Moses and Elijah not go upward? And has it not been written, "And Moses
      went up to God" (Ex. 19:3)?

O.   It was ten handbreadths below [the height].

P.   And has it not been written, "And Elijah went up by a whirlwind into heaven" (2 Kgs.
      2:11)?

Q.   It was ten handbreadths below [the height].

R.   And has it not been written, "He seizes hold of the face of his throne and he spreads
      his cloud upon him" (Job 26:9)? And in this connection R. Tanhum said, "This

teaches that the All-Mighty spread over him some of the splendor of his Presence and his cloud."

S. This was nonetheless lower than ten handbreadths [from the height].

T. Nonetheless, it is written, "He seizes hold of the face of his throne"!

U. The throne was lowered down until it was ten handbreadths below the height, at which point he laid hold of it.

XI.

A. [Reverting to the main point, X G, above], now there is no difficulty in showing that the ark was nine handbreadths high, for it has been written, "And they shall make an ark of acacia wood, two cubits and a half shall be the length of it, and a cubit and a half the breadth of it, and a cubit and a half the height of it (Ex. 25:10) [and a cubit is six handbreadths, so a cubit and a half will be nine].

B. But how do we know that the ark-cover was a handbreadth in height?

C. It accords with what R. Hanina taught on Tannaite authority, "For all of the utensils that Moses made, the Torah defined the measure of their length, breadth, and height.

D. "In the case of the ark-cover, while the Torah specified its length and its breadth, it did not specify the dimensions of its height.

E. "Go and derive an analogy from the dimensions of the smallest of all of the utensils.

F. "For it has been said, 'And you shall make it a border of a handbreadth round about' (Ex. 25:25).

G. "Just as that is a handbreadth in height, so in the present case, the utensil is to be a handbreadth in height."

H. But should we not derive the measurement from the utensils themselves?

I. If you hold onto a great deal, you hold nothing, but if you hold onto a little, you will hold onto it. [Slotki, p. 16, n. 5: The lesser is included in the greater, but the greater is not included in the lesser. The selection of the lesser is therefore the safer course.]

J. Then let us derive the measurement from the dimensions of the plate [Ex. 28:36, still smaller than a handbreadth]!

K. For it has been taught on Tannaite authority:

L. The plate was like a gold plate, two fingerbreadths broad and stretching from ear to ear, and on it were inscribed two thin lines with a Y and H above, and "Holy" and an L below [yielding, from right to left, Holy to the Lord]."

M. And R. Eliezer b. R. Yose said, "I saw it in Rome, and on it was written, 'Holy to the Lord,' on a single line."

N. [It follows that the measurement of the plate is less than a handbreadth in height. Why not derive the measurement of the ark-cover from that analogy?] We form an analogy from one utensil to another, but we do not form an analogy from an ornament for a utensil.

O. And why not derive the measurement of the ark-cover from the analogy of the crown [of gold around the ark, Ex. 25:11]?

P.   For in that connection a master has stated, "The crown was the smallest possible size."

Q.   We establish an analogy between one utensil and another, but not between a utensil and an appurtenance to a utensil.

R.   But the border also served as an appurtenance to a utensil.

S.   The border was below [the top of] the table [Slotki, p. 17, n. 2: Joining its legs together and forming part of the structure].

T.   That answer suffices for the one who maintains that the border was beneath the top of the table. But in the view of the one who maintains that the border was above it, what is there to say? For the object at hand served only as an appurtenance to a utensil.

U.   Rather, we draw an analogy from an object to which the Torah has assigned a measure for another object to which the Torah has assigned a measure, but neither the plate or the crown should provide evidence, since in neither case did the Torah assign fixed measurements to them.

V.   R. Huna said, "[We derive proof on the height of the ark-cover] from the verse that follows: 'Upon the face of the ark-cover on the east' (Lev. 16:14).

W.   "And 'face' must be at least a handbreadth."

X.   But might I propose that [the face] would be like the face [5B] of Bar Yokhani [a very large bird]?

Y.   [No,] if you hold onto a great deal, you hold nothing, but if you hold onto a little, you will hold onto it [as at I, above].

Z.   But I might propose that [the face] would be like that of a siparta [-bird] which is very small.

AA. Said R. Aha bar Jacob, "R. Huna [derives the lesson] from the use of the word 'face' in two passages, [applying by analogy the meaning imputed in one case to that appropriate in the other].

BB. "Here it is written, 'Upon the face of the ark cover' (Lev. 16:14).

CC. "And elsewhere it is written, 'From the face of Isaac his father' (Gen. 27:30). [A human face in the latter case is meant, hence a handbreadth in size, and the same dimension then applies in the former case]."

DD. But why not derive the lesson from the use of "face" with reference to the one above [God].

EE. For it is written, "As one sees the face of God, and you were pleased with me" (Gen. 33:10).

FF. [No,] if you hold onto a great deal, you hold onto nothing, but if you hold onto a little, you will hold onto it.

GG. Then how about deriving the besought dimension from the case of the cherub, for it is written, "Toward the face of the ark-cover shall the faces of the cherubim be" (Ex. 25:20)?

HH. Said R. Aha bar Jacob, "We have learned that the faces of cherubs are not less than a handbreadth."

II.   R. Huna, for his part, also derived the same lesson from here.

JJ.   And what is a cherub (KRWB)?

KK.   Said R. Abbahu, "Like a child [KRBY'], for so in Babylonia they call a child a 'rabei.'"

LL.   Said to him Abayye, "But [if you hold the face of a cherub was a handbreadth] how do you deal with that which is written, 'The first face was the face of the cherub, and the second face the face of a man' (Ez. 10:14)? So is the face of a cherub the same as the face of a man?"

MM.   One face is large, the other small.

XII.

A.   And how [do you know] that the contained space [of the sukkah] not counting the covering is to be ten handbreadths? Perhaps that measurement encompasses the covering. [In that case, the sukkah from the roofing to the ground may be less than ten handbreadths, and only inclusive of the roofing from the top, must it be ten handbreadths in height.]

B.   The rule derives from the eternal house.

C.   For it is written, "And the house which King Solomon built for the Lord was threescore cubits long, twenty cubits broad, and thirty cubits high" (1 Kgs. 6:2).

D.   And it is written, "The height of the one cherub was ten cubits, and so was that of the other cherub" (2 Kgs. 6:26).

E.   And it has been taught on Tannaite authority:

F.   Just as we find in the eternal house that the cherubs were a third of the height of the house, so also in the case of the tabernacle [standing on the ark, inclusive of the ark and ark cover (Slotki, p. 18, n. 15)] they were a third of its height.

G.   Now how high was the tabernacle? It was ten cubits, for it is written, "Ten cubits shall be the length of a board" (Ex. 26:16).

H.   How much is that? Sixty handbreadths. If you take a third, what do you have? Twenty handbreadths. Then take off the ten for the ark and the ark-covering, and you are left with ten [the measure of the height of the sukkah].

I.   And it is written, "And the cherubim shall spread out their wings on high, covering the ark-cover with their wings" (Ex. 25:20).

J.   The All-Merciful thus regards [the wings] above ten handbreadths "roofing" [such as serves for a sukkah]. [Q.E.D.].

K.   How do we know that their wings rose above their heads? Perhaps they were at the same level with their heads [Slotki, p. 19, n. 1: In which case, the hollow space between the wings and the ark-cover was only ten handbreadths minus the thickness of the wings].

L.   Said R. Aha bar Jacob, "'Above' is what is written."

M.   And might I say that they were very high?

N.   Is it written, "Above and upward"? [The sense of the language would not support the notion that they were raised up very high.]

O. [The proof just now given] affords no problems to the view of R. Meir, who has taken the position that all of the cubits were intermediate [normal] [with six handbreadths in a cubit, as stated above, X F].

P. But in the view of R. Judah, who has said that the cubit-measure used in the building was six handbreadths, but that used for utensils was only five handbreadths, what is there to be said?

Q. How high were the ark and the ark-covering? Eight and a half, leaving eleven and a half handbreadths. [The ark was a cubit and a half, hence seven and a half handbreadths by Judah's measure, and the ark-cover one handbreadth. That will leave, between the ark-cover and the wings of the cherubim, eleven and a half handbreadths.]

R. Shall I then say that [in Judah's view] the sukkah is valid only if it is eleven and a half handbreadths in height? [Surely not!]

S. But R. Judah derived [the required measure, ten] on the basis of received law [transmitted orally, and not on the basis of exegesis of Scripture].

T. For R. Hiyya bar Ashi said Rab [said], "The [laws covering] measurements [of minimal quantities], of interpositions and partitions constitute law revealed to Moses at Sinai."

U. [But to the contrary] the laws governing minimal quantities derive from the Torah ['s written rules, not from revelation orally transmitted], for it has been written, "A land of wheat and barley, vines, fig-trees, and pomegranates, a land of olive trees and honey" (Deut. 8:8).

V. And [in regard to the cited verse] R. Hanina said, "This entire verse is stated with reference to the provision of minimum measures [for various purposes, thus:]

W. "'Wheat' serves to make reference to a house afflicted with nega, as we have learned in the Mishnah:

X. "He who entered a house afflicted with a nega, with his garments slung over his shoulder and his sandals and rings in his hands -- he and they are unclean forthwith. [6A] If he was dressed in his garments with his sandals on his feet and his rings on his fingers, he is unclean forthwith. But they are clean until he will remain for a time sufficient to eat a piece of bread -- a piece of bread of wheat and not a piece of bread of barley, reclining and eating it with condiment [M. Neg. 13:9].

Y. "'Barley;' as we have learned in the Mishnah: A barley-grain's bulk of a bone [of a corpse] imparts uncleanness if someone touches or carries it, but not if someone overshadows it' [M. Oh. 2:3].

Z. "'Vines:' That reference provides the measurement of a fourth-log of wine, constituted that minimum measure for which a Nazir becomes culpable [since he may not drink wine].

AA. "'Fig-trees:' That reference provides the measurement of a minimum volume for which one becomes liable if he removes something on the Sabbath from one domain to another:

BB.   "'Pomegranate:' As we have learned in the Mishnah: <u>Any utensil [made of wood]</u>
      <u>belonging to a householder [becomes useless and therefore no longer susceptible to</u>
      <u>uncleanness] if in it there is a crack [or hole] the size of a pomegranate [so there is</u>
      <u>a hole that renders the utensil no longer a receptacle at all] [M. Kel. 17:1].</u>

CC.   "'A land of olive-trees:' A land all of whose minimal measures are the equivalent of
      the bulk of an olive."

DD.   Do you really mean to say that <u>all</u> of the minimum measures are of the size of an
      olive? Lo, there are [to the contrary] those others that we already have catalogued!

EE.   Rather, I should say, "...most of whose minimal measures are the equivalent of the
      bulk of an olive."

FF.   "'Honey:' This refers to the size of a large date. [On the Day of Atonement one
      who eats food the bulk of a large date becomes liable for violating the prohibition
      against eating, while if one eats food less than that bulk, he is not culpable]."

GG.   [Reverting to the point at which we started, U], it follows that [the minimum
      measures] derive from the Torah [and not from laws revealed to Moses at Sinai and
      handed on orally]!

HH.   Do you take the position that the stated measures are actually written down in the
      Torah? Rather, they are laws [handed on orally], and Scripture then provided
      general support [for the same measurements. But from Scripture one could not
      derive the measurements just now catalogued].

II.   And the rules of interposition in fact derive from the Torah [vs. T], for it is written,
      "And he shall wash his body in water" (Lev. 14:9).

JJ.   This indicates that there should be nothing to interpose between him and the water.

KK.   [No, there is an aspect of the rules that derives from oral transmission], for, when
      the orally-transmitted law serves a purpose, it is as to the interposition of one's
      hair, in accord with the formulation of Rabbah bar bar Hana.

LL.   For Rabbah bar bar Hana said, "A single knotted hair interposes [between the flesh
      and the water], while three do not interpose. As to the effect of two, I do not know
      the law."

MM.   The interposition of one's hair also is a matter of law deriving from the Torah [and
      not from an orally-transmitted law].

NN.   For it has been written, "And he shall wash [+ accusative particle] his body in water"
      (Lev. 14:9).

OO.   [The use of the] accusative principle serves to indicate that at issue is what is
      attached to his body, that is, the hair.

PP.   [Reverting to the original claim, then] when there is a matter of law [orally
      transmitted, in connection with interposition], it is in accord with that which R.
      Isaac said.

QQ.   For R. Isaac said, "[6B] As matter of law deriving from the Torah, if most [of one's
      hair is covered with mud, each hair knotted singly (Slotki)], and the person pays
      attention to it, then the matted hair serves to interpose, but if he does not pay

attention to it, then it does not interpose. And [sages] furthermore have made a decree concerning a case in which most of the hair is matted with mud but the person does <u>not</u> pay attention to it [indicating that in such a case, the hair interposes, even though the person pays it no mind], on account of a case in which most of the hair is matted with mud and the person does pay attention to it,

RR. "as well as concerning a case in which the small part [of one's hair is matted with mud] and the person does pay attention to it [in which case, the hair interposes, though it is not the bulk of the person's hair], on account of the case in which the bulk of the hair is matted with mud and the person pays attention to it."

SS. And why not let sages make a decree concerning a case in which the smaller part of one's hair is matted with mud, and the person does not pay attention to it, on account of the case in which the smaller part of one's hair is matted with mud and the person does pay attention to it?

TT. Or [let the decree be made on account of the rule governing the case in which] the greater part of one's hair is matted with mud, but one pays no attention to it?

UU. That very matter is subject to an [arbitrary] decree, and should we then go and impose yet another decree [applying a strict law to a matter which to begin with is subject to a decree [on our part? Such would be altogether too strict].

VV. "As to the laws of partitions [T]:" they are those to which we have already made reference [concerning the height of the <u>sukkah</u>].

WW. That view accords well with the position of R. Judah [S, who does not claim the measurements derive from Scripture], but as to the view of R. Meir, what is to be said?

XX. As to the point at which a law [transmitted orally] is needed, it concerns the principles of [the legal fictions involving] extension [Slotki, p. 22, n. 7: a partition that does not reach the ground or the ceiling may in certain conditions be deemed to touch the ground or the ceiling, respectively], junction [Slotki, p. 22, n. 8: small interstices, of less than three handbreadths, are disregarded, and the wall is deemed to be a solid whole], and the curved wall [Slotki, p. 22, n. 9: If a portion of the roof of a <u>sukkah</u> consists of materials that are legally unfit for the purpose, the <u>sukkah</u> may nevertheless be valid if that portion is adjacent to any of its walls and terminates within a distance of four cubits from that wall. That portion of the roof together with the wall it adjoins are regarded as one curved wall; and the space under the remainder of the roof consisting of suitable materials may be used as a proper <u>sukkah</u>].

<u>XIII.</u>

A. <u>One which does not have three walls [M. Suk. 1:1D]:</u>

B. Our rabbis have taught on Tannaite authority:

C. Two [of the walls must be] in accord with the law applying to them, but the third may be even a handbreadth.

D. And R. Simeon says, "Three must be in accord with the law applying to them, but the fourth may be even a handbreadth.

E.   What is at issue between them?

F.   Rabbis take the view that the traditional text [Slotki] is authoritative [without regard to the vowels placed with the consonants] while R. Simeon holds that the traditional mode of reading the text [inclusive of reference to the vowels] is authoritative.

G.   The rabbis take the view that the traditional text is authoritative [without regard to the vowels], and sukkot two times [read without the vowel indicating the plural] while sukkot is written only once with the consonantal vowel indicating the plural, yielding four allusions in all [one, one, two]. You take off one needed for itself [teaching the fact that one must dwell in a sukkah], leaving three, that refer to the walls: two to be built in accord with the law applying to them, and the law transmitted orally comes along and reduces the requirement affecting the third wall, leaving it [suitable even if it is only] at a handbreadth.

H.   R. Simeon holds that the traditional mode of reading the text is authoritative, and since the word sukkot is written three times, there are six available references in all.

I.   You take off one verse of Scripture for itself [covering the fact that one has to make a sukkah], and you are left with four, three to be built in accord with the law governing them, and the law transmitted orally comes along and reduces the requirement affecting the third wall, leaving it at a handbreadth.

J.   If you want, I shall explain the cited disputed [B-D] differently, conceding that all parties concur that the traditional mode of reading the text is authoritative.

K.   Then in the present instance on what point do they differ?

L.   One authority takes the view that the fact that the sukkah must be covered with sukkah-roofing requires a proof-text, and the other authority maintains that the fact that the sukkah must be covered with sukkah-roofing does not require a proof-text.

M.   If you wish, I may concede that all parties concur that the traditional text is authoritative [and not the traditional mode of reading it].

N.   Then in the present instance on what point do they differ?

O.   One authority takes the view that when the law handed on orally comes along, it serves the purpose of lowering the requirements at hand, and the other authority holds that when the law transmitted orally comes along, it serves to add to what is required [Slotki, p. 23, n. 12: Scripture teaches us the necessity of three walls and tradition adds a fourth].

P.   If you wish, I may concede that all parties concur that the law handed on orally serves to lower the requirements at hand, and, further, that the traditional text is authoritative.

Q.   And in the present case, what is at issue between the contending parties?

R.   At issue is whether or not one imposes an exegesis upon the first occurrence of a word [in a given series in which the same word is repeated, as in the case of the several uses of the work sukkot].

S.   One authority takes the view that we impose a secondary exegetical meaning upon a word on the first occasion of its appearance [not as we read it above], and the other authority holds that we do not impose a secondary exegetical meaning upon a word on the first occasion of its appearance [just as we did not impose such a meaning above].

T.   R. Mattenah said, "The scriptural basis for the view of R. Simeon derives from the following verse: 'And there shall be a sukkah for a shadow in the day time from the heat, and for a refuge for a cover from storm and from rain' (Is. 4:6). [This can be provided only by four walls]."

XIV.

A.   Now as to the wall that may be only a handbreadth [of the three or of the four, as indicated just now], where does the builder set it?

B.   Said Rab, "He sets it at right angles to one of the projecting walls [Slotki]."

C.   R. Kahana and R. Asi said to Rab, [7A] "Let him set it in a slanting position [not at right angles]."

D.   Rab remained silent.

E.   It has been stated also upon Amoraic authority:

F.   Said Samuel in the name of Levi, "One sets it at right angles to one of the projecting walls."

G.   And so too is it taught in the house of study: One sets it at right angles to one of the projecting walls."

H.   R. Simeon, and some say, R. Joshua b. Levi said, "One makes the projecting wall a handbreadth measured loosely and sets it up within three handbreadths of the wall, for whatever stands within three handbreadths of the wall is held to be joined to the wall." [Slotki, p. 24, n. 5: The total width now being four handbreadths and the prescribed minimum size of a sukkah wall being seven handbreadths, the wall constitutes the greater part of a valid sukkah wall.]

I.   Said R. Judah, "A sukkah that is made like an open alley-way is suitable, and as to the wall a handbreadth in size, one may place it in any position that he wants.

J.   R. Simeon, and some say, R. Joshua b. Levi said, "One makes a strip of four handbreadths and a bit more and sets it up within three handbreadths of the wall, for whatever stands within three handbreadths of the wall is held to be joined to the wall."

K.   Now what differentiates the former case, in which you have held that what is sufficient is a handbreadth loosely measured, from the present case, in which you have said that what is required is a strip of four handbreadths [which would be considerably larger]?

L.   In that other case, in which there are two walls that accord with the law governing the matter, it is sufficient to have a wall that is, in addition, merely a handful measured loosely. But here [where we have a sukkah in the shape of an alley-way [that is, open at the two ends], where there are not two clearly differentiated walls, if there is (in addition) a strip of four handbreadths, it is acceptable, and if not, it is not acceptable.

M. Said Raba, "Such an arrangement is acceptable only if it is in the form of a doorway." [Slotki, p. 25, n. 2: "It is not enough to attach one board of the width of four handbreadths to one of the walls (of the sukkah in the shape of an alley), but two posts each half a handbreadth in width must be attached to each opposite wall with a cross-beam joining them." This forms a recognizable house, not just an alley-way."]

N. There are those who say that Raba said, "And [a sukkah lacking a required wall] also is valid if it is in the shape of a doorway."

O. There is yet another version that has Raba say, "It must also have the shape of a doorway." [Slotki, p. 25, n. 5: One of the posts on which the cross-beam lies must be a full handbreadth wide.]

P. R. Ashi found R. Kahana making [a sukkah using a wall the size of] a handbreadth loosely measured, and making it in the shape of a doorway.

Q. He said to him, "Does not the master accord with the view of Raba, for Raba said, 'It also is valid if it is in the shape of a doorway'?"

R. He said to him, "I have taken a position in accord with a different version of what Raba said, for R. Raba said, 'It must also have the shape of a doorway.'"

XV.

A. "Two having the dimensions in accord with the law governing them" [= XIII B]:

B. Said Raba, "And so is the rule concerning [definition of a private domain for purposes of permitting carrying] on the Sabbath. [There must be three walls, two ordinary, one fictional. If such a sukkah is erected by the door of one's home, on the Sabbath he may carry from the sukkah to the house.]

C. "[Why so?] Since the [fictional] wall is regarded as a wall for the purposes of the sukkah, it serves also for the purposes of [establishing private domain for carrying on] the Sabbath."

D. Abayye objected [to the reasoning of C], "Do we invoke the argument [of analogy represented by the phrase beginning], 'since'?

E. "And has it not been taught on Tannaite authority: 'The rules covering a wall for the purpose of building a sukkah are equivalent to the walls covering [partitions to indicate a private domain for purposes of carrying on] the Sabbath [e.g., a sukkah attached to a door to permit carrying on the Sabbath], so long as between one reed [wall-marker] and the next is no space exceeding three handbreadths. But there is a further rule pertaining to [partitions for] the [sukkah built in connection with carrying on the] Sabbath that does not pertain to the sukkah, for [a domain constituted by a sukkah and so partitioned off for carrying on the Sabbath does not constitute a] permitted [domain] unless the standing part of the wall is greater than the breaches [in that same wall], a rule that does not apply to the sukkah [constructed solely in observance of the Festival].'

F. "Now is not the sense of the language, 'a further rule for sukkah in connection with the Sabbath' that we do not invoke [the argument of analogy beginning with the word] 'since'?"

G. [Raba replied], "No, the language indicating that 'a further rule applies to the Sabbath' refers to the Sabbath in general [and indicates that, overall, a valid wall is required, but not to] sukkah constructed to permit carrying on the Sabbath."

H. "If so, the framer of the passage should then have framed matters to indicate that the requirements governing a sukkah in general are more stringent than the requirements relating to the sukkah that is used [to permit carrying] on the Sabbath, for the sukkah in general requires [for the fictional, defective wall] a breadth of a handbreadth measured loosely, while the sukkah in regard to [carrying on] the Sabbath does not require such a measurement, but suffices with a mere side-post.

I. "For you [Raba] are the one who has maintained that if one has spread sukkah-roofing over an alley-way which is marked off by a side-post, it is a valid arrangement."

J. "It was not necessary at all to make such specification [concerning the imposition of a more strict rule]. [Why not?] If we invoke the argument beginning with the word 'since,' with the effect of applying the role governing the less strict case [the sukkah] to the more strict case [the Sabbath], we should surely invoke the same argument to apply the rule governing the more strict case to the less strict one [with the result that the side-post which is suitable to serve for purposes of the Sabbath is acceptable also with regard to the sukkah]."

K. [Reverting to the earlier] body [of discourse]: Said Raba, [7B], "If one has spread sukkah-roofing over an alley-way that is marked off by a side post, it is a valid [arrangement]."

L. And Raba said, "If one has placed sukkah-roofing on top of boards placed around wells, it is a valid arrangement." [A well which by definition constitutes private domain, located in a public domain, may not be used for its water, since one would have to transport the water on the Sabbath from the private domain of the well to public domain round about. To solve this problem, four corner-pieces will be placed around the well. These indicate that the enclosed space is private domain, and the water may be taken and used within that space without violating the law against carrying from one domain to the other.]

M. And it was necessary [to make explicit the law about placing sukkah-roofing over an alley-way marked off by a side-post, the law on sukkah-roofing on the upright boards around a well, and the law that, since a wall the size of a handbreadth is acceptable for a sukkah, it also is acceptable as a valid wall to mark off private domain for carrying on the Sabbath].

N. For had we heard the rule only about the alleyways, we should have assumed that the reason is that there are two perfectly valid walls [so the arrangement is acceptable], but in regard to the corner-boards around a well, in which case there are not two valid walls at all, I might have said that such an arrangement was not acceptable.

O. If we had learned the rule governing the acceptability of sukkah-roofing placed over the corner-posts around a well, I might have assumed that the reason that such an

arrangement is acceptable is that there are four walls, but if one spread sukkah-roofing over an alley-way, in which there are not four walls [even symbolically],
I might have ruled that that would not be acceptable.

P.   If we had heard the rule in these two cases, I might have supposed that where we
     invoke for the less strict case the rule pertaining to the more strict case, that poses
     no problems, but I might have supposed that we do not invoke the rule governing the
     less strict case for judging the more strict case.

Q.   Accordingly, it was necessary to make explicit all three rules.

XVI.

A.   Or one, the light of which is greater than the shade of which, is invalid [M. 1:1E-F]:

B.   Our rabbis have taught on Tannaite authority:

C.   [When] the light [of the sukkah] is more than the shadow on account of [inadequate]
     sukkah-roofing, [the sukkah is invalid],

D.   but not when the greater light is on account of the character of] the walls [which
     may not be opaque and so may permit light to fall into the hut].

E.   R. Josiah says, "Also on account of the character of the walls."

F.   Said R. Yemar bar Shelamayah in the name of Abayye, "What is the scriptural
     reason for the view of R. Josiah? It is because it is written, 'And you shall cover
     the ark with the veil' (Ex. 26:33).

G.   "The veil constitutes a partition, and the All-Merciful has referred to it with the
     word used for sukkah-roofing.

H.   "Therefore [the partition and not only the roof constitutes an aspect of the
     sukkah-roofing], and we require the partition to be similar to the sukkah-roofing
     [and opaque]."

I.   And rabbis [who take the contrary view]?

J.   They take the word, "You shall cover" [which uses the root of the word for
     sukkah-roofing] to mean that at the top the veil should bend so as to appear like
     roofing.

XVII.

A.   Said Abayye, "Rabbi, R. Josiah, R. Judah, R. Simeon, Rabban Gamaliel, the House of
     Shammai, R. Eliezer, and 'others' all take the view that the sukkah must serve as a
     permanent [not only temporary] dwelling."

B.   Rabbi: As it has been taught on Tannaite authority:

C.   Rabbi says, "Any sukkah which is not of the area of four cubits by four cubits is
     invalid." [A space of less than that is insufficient for a dwelling for a human being.]

D.   R. Josiah: As we have just now indicated [since he requires fully filled-in walls].

E.   R. Judah: As we have learned in the Mishnah: A sukkah which is taller than twenty
     cubits is invalid. R. Judah declares it valid [M. 1:1A-B] [since it can serve as a
     permanent dwelling].

F.   R. Simeon: As it has been taught on Tannaite authority:

G.   Two in accord with the law applying to them, and a third [wall] even a handbreadth.
     R. Simeon says, "Three walls in accord with the law applying to them, and the fourth

even a handbreadth [since without three solid walls, the hut cannot be considered a permanent dwelling]."

H.   Rabban Gamaliel: As it has been taught on Tannaite authority:

I.   He who makes his sukkah on top of a wagon or on top of on the deck of a ship -- Rabban Gamaliel declares it invalid, and R. Aqiba declares it valid. [The former holds that on moving vehicles there cannot be a permanent residence.]

J.   The House of Shammai: As we have learned in the Mishnah: He whose head and the greater part of whose body are in the sukkah, but whose table is in the house -- the House of Shammai declare the sukkah invalid, and the House of Hillel declare it valid [M. Suk. 2:7].

K.   R. Eliezer: As we have learned in the Mishnah: He who makes his sukkah in the shape of a cone or who learned it up against a wall -- R. Eliezer declares it invalid, because it has no roof, and sages declare it valid [M. Suk. 1:11A-D].

L.   "Others": As it has been taught on Tannaite authority:

M.   Others say, "A sukkah make like a dovecote [round-shaped (Slotki)] is invalid, since it does not have corners."

XVIII.

A.   Said R. Yohanan, "A sukkah that is shaped like a furnace [round shaped (=XVII M)], if in its circumference is enough space so that twenty-four men can sit around it, is valid, and if not, it is invalid."

B.   In accord with whom does R. Yohanan rule?

C.   He accords with the view of Rabbi, who has said, "Any sukkah that is not four cubits by four cubits is invalid [XVII C]."

D.   But since a man occupies the space of a cubit, and since [in rabbinical mathematics, $Pi = 3$ so that] any circumference of three handbreadths has a diameter of a handbreadth, should it not be sufficient [if the sukkah in the shape of a circle] can seat only twelve [and not twenty-four]? [Why then A's measurement?]

E.   [8A] The view [that $Pi = 3$] applies to a circle, but in the case of a square a greater perimeter is necessary.

F.   But by how much is a square greater than a circle [inscribed therein]? It is greater by a quarter.

G.   Then should it not be sufficient [if the sukkah in the shape of a circle] can seat only sixteen [and not twenty-four]?

H.   That would be the case for a circle that is inscribed in a square, but in the case of a square inscribed in a circle, more would be required on account of the projection of the corners. [Slotki, p. 29, n. 11: The circumferences of the sukkah must therefore be large enough to contain a square of four cubits.]

I.   But if the side of a square is a cubit, its diagonal is approximately one and two fifths cubits [Slotki]. Should not the circumference be seventeen cubits less a fifth? [Slotki, p. 29, n. 13: The diagonal of the square being equal to $(4 + 4 \times 2/5 = 5\ 3/5$ths cubits, and Pi being approximately equivalent to three, a circumference of $3/5\ 3/5$ cubits = $16\ 4/5$ cubits ought to suffice.]

J.   [Yohanan] did not give a precise figure.

K.   While we may take the view that, where the difference is minor, one does not give a precise figure, do we say so [in the present case] when the difference is considerable?

L.   Said Mar Qashisha, son of R. Hisda, to R. Ashi, "Do you maintain that a man occupies the space of an entire cubit? Three men can sit in the space of two cubits. How much is then [required for twenty four men]? Sixteen [would be enough]. So we require sixteen and four fifths, and [Yohanan] did not give an exact [but only an approximate] figure.

M.   While we may take the view that one does not give an exact figure when it yields a strict ruling, do we maintain that one does not give an exact figure when it would yield a lenient ruling?

N.   Said R. Assi to R. Ashi, "In point of fact a person occupies the space of a cubit. But R. Yohanan did not take account of the space occupied by persons at all." [Slotki, p. 30, n. 2: The men are considered as sitting around the circumference of the sukkah they themselves forming a circumference of twenty-four cubits, equivalent to the space occupied by twenty-four men, with a diameter of eight cubits. But the inner circumference formed by the sukkah is smaller, since its diameter is eight minus two, the space occupied lengthways by the legs of two men, one sitting at each end, is six cubits.] How many [cubits] would [the circumference of the sukkah] then require? Eighteen [Slotki, p. 30, n. 4: Since a diameter of six cubits has a circumference of eighteen cubits], though sixteen and four fifths cubits would be enough.

O.   That is the sense of the statement that he did not give a precise figure, and here it is to impose a strict ruling [Slotki, p. 30, n. 5: instead of a circumference of 16 4/5, one of eighteen cubits is prescribed, while the difference in the diameter (6-5 3/5 = 2/5) is even less.]

P.   Rabbis of Caesarea, and some say, the judges of Caesarea, say, "In the case of a circle inscribed in a square, the circumference is a quarter [less than the perimeter of the square], [8B] and in the case of a square inscribed in a circle, the circumference is a half [of the circumscribed square]. [Slotki, p. 30, n. 8: Thus if a circumference is twenty-four cubits, the figure given by R. Johanan, the circumscribed square has a perimeter of 24 + 24/3 = 32 cubits, while the inscribed square has a perimeter of approximately 32/2 = 16 cubits, the measurements prescribed by Rabbi.]

Q.   But that is not the case, for lo, we notice that they are not that much [larger]. [It is not correct to claim that the perimeter of the circumscribed square is twice the perimeter of the inscribed square and that the circumference of the circle is therefore bigger than the latter by half of its perimeter (Slotki).]

XIX.

A.   Said R. Levi in the name of R. Meir, "Two sukkot built for a potter, one inside the other [in the inner one, the potter works, in the outer, he shows his pots] —

B.   "the inner one is not in the status of a sukkah and is liable to the requirement of
      having a mezuzah, while the outer one is in the status of a sukkah and is exempt
      from the requirement of having a mezuzah."

C.   And why so? Let the outer one be regarded as the gatehouse for the inner one and
      be liable to the requirement of having a mezuzah?

D.   It is on account of the impermanence [of both sukkot]. [The inner sukkah is fragile
      and of insufficient standing to be assigned a gatehouse.]

XX.

A.   Our rabbis have taught on Tannaite authority:

B.   A sukkah built for gentiles, women, cattle, and or Samaritans falls into the category
      of a sukkah on all accounts [and is] valid, so long as it has sukkah-roofing in accord
      with the law applying to it.

C.   What is the sense of "in accord with the law applying to it"?

D.   Said R. Hisda, "And the rule applies on condition that [the one who put on the
      sukkah-roofing] did so in order to create shade appropriate to a sukkah."

E.   What is included by the language, "on all accounts"?

F.   It is to encompass booths built for shepherds, watchmen, city guards, and keepers of
      orchards [given in mnemonic].

G.   For our rabbis have taught on Tannaite authority:

H.   A sukkah built for shepherds, a sukkah built for guards [for crops], a sukkah built for
      city guards, and a sukkah built for keepers of orchards on all accounts falls into the
      category of a sukkah [and is] valid, so long as it has sukkah-roofing in accord with
      the law applying to it.

I.   What is the sense of "in accord with the law applying to it"?

J.   Said R. Hisda, "And the rule applies on condition that [the one who put on the
      sukkah-roofing] did so in order to create shade appropriate to a sukkah."

K.   What is included by the language "on all accounts"?

L.   It is to encompass booths built for gentiles, women, cattle, or Samaritans.

M.   The Tannaite authority [who encompasses the listed items under the phrase, "on all
      accounts"] regards as having a stronger claim to acceptability the sukkahs built for
      gentiles, women, cattle, or Samaritans, because they are permanent in character,
      and he therefore repeated the language, "on all accounts" to encompass a sukkah
      built for shepherds, watchmen, city guards, and keepers of orchards, none of which
      sorts of sukkah is of a permanent character.

N.   The Tannaite authority who phrased matters in terms of a sukkah built for
      shepherds, watchmen, city guards, and keepers of orchards regards those sorts of
      sukkah as having a stronger claim of acceptability because they are built for
      categories that are obligated [to keep the religious requirement of dwelling in a
      sukkah], and he therefore repeated the language, "on all accounts" to encompass a
      sukkah built for gentiles, women, cattle, or Samaritans, not categories obligated [to
      keep the religious requirement of dwelling in a sukkah].

The protracted Talmud serving M. 1:1A-F not only works its way through the Mishnah-paragraph but systematically expands the law applicable to that paragraph by seeking out pertinent principles in parallel or contrasting cases of law. When a unit of discourse abandons the theme or principle connected to the Mishnah-paragraph, it is to take up a secondary matter introduced by a unit of discourse that has focused on that theme or principle. Unit I begins with an analysis of the word-choice at hand. At the same time it introduces an important point, namely, the comparison between the sukkah and a contraption erected also on a temporary basis and for symbolic purposes. That is a symbolic gateway, that transforms an alley-entry into a gateway for a courtyard and so alters the status of the alley and the courtyards that open on to it and turns them into a single domain. As one domain, they are open for carrying on the Sabbath, at which time people may not carry objects from one domain, e.g., private, to another, e.g., public. That comparison is repeatedly invoked. Units II and III then move from language to scriptural sources for the law. Unit IV then stands in the same relationship to unit III, and so too unit V. Unit VI reverts to an issue of unit V. So the entire discussion -- II-VI -- flows out of the exegetical requirements of the opening lines of the Mishnah-paragraph. But the designated unit-divisions seem to me to mark of discussions that can have stood originally by themselves. Unit VII then reverts to the original topic, the requisite height of the sukkah. It deals with a fresh problem, namely, artificially diminishing or increasing the height of the sukkah by alterations to the inside of the hut. One may raise the floor to diminish the height or lower the floor to increase it. Unit VIII pursues the same interest. It further introduces principles distinct from the Mishnah's rules but imposed upon the interpretation of those rules or the amplification of pertinent cases. This important exercise in secondary expansion of a rather simple rule through the introduction of fresh and rather engaging principles -- "curved wall," fictional extension of walls upward of downward and the like -- then proceeds in its own terms. Unit IX is continuous in its thematic interest with unit VIII. Unit X reverts to the Mishnah-paragraph, now M. 1:1C, and asks the question usually raised at the outset about the scriptural authority behind the Mishnah's rule. This leads us into a rather sizable digression on scriptural exegesis, with special interest in establishing the analogy between utensils in the Temple and dimensions pertinent to the sukkah. The underlying conception, that what the Israelite does on cultic occasions in the home responds to what is done in the cult in the Temple, is familiar. Units XI and XII pursue the same line of thought. Then unit XIII reverts once more to the Mishnahs rule, M. 1:1D. Now we take up the issue of the walls of the sukkah. These must be three, in rabbis' view, and four in Simeon's. Each party concedes that one of the requisite walls may be merely symbolic. The biblical source for the required number of walls forms the first object of inquiry. Unit XIV then takes up the symbolic wall. Unit XV reverts to a statement on Tannaite authority given in unit XIII. Subject to close study is a somewhat complicated notion. There are diverse kinds of sukkah-buildings. One, we know, is a sukkah erected to carry out the religious duty of the Festival. But a person may build a sukkah, also, to extend the enclosed and private area of his home. If he places such a sukkah by the door, the area in which it is permitted to carry objects -- private domain -- covers not only the space of the house but also the space of the sukkah. That sukkah, erected in connection with Sabbath-observance, is compared to the sukkah erected for purposes of keeping the Festival. The issue is appropriate here, since the matter concerns the character of the walls of the sukkah built for Sabbath-observance. Unit XVI then returns to the Mishnah-paragraph. Unit XVIII moves back from the Mishnah's statements and deals with the general principle, taken by some parties, that the sukkah must bear the qualities of a permanent dwelling. That issue intersects with our Mishnah paragraph in connection with Judah's and Simeon's views on the requirement that there be a roof of a certain height and four walls. But the construction as a whole stands independent of the Mishnah-paragraph and clearly was put together in its own terms. XVIII takes up XVII M. The mathematics at hand derive from Slotki's notes, as indicated. Units XIX and XX evidently are miscellaneous -- the only such units of discourse in the entire massive construction. I cannot point to a more thorough or satisfying sequence of Talmudic units of discourse, in which the Mishnah's statements are amplified, then the amplifications themselves worked out on their own. The whole is thorough, beautifully articulated, and cogent until the very end.

1:1 G-N

G.   [9A] A superannuated sukkah --

H.   The House of Shammai declare it invalid.

I.   And the House of Hillel declare it valid.

J.   And what exactly is a superannuated sukkah?

K.   Any which one made thirty days [of more] before the Festival [of Sukkot].

L.   But if one made it for the sake of the Festival,

M.   even at the beginning of the year,

N.   it is valid.

I.

A.   What is the scriptural basis for the position of the House of Shammai?

B.   Scripture has said, "The festival of Sukkot, for seven days for the Lord" (Lev. 23:34).

C.   [Since the statement thus indicates that sukkah must be "for the Lord,"] the sense is that we require the sukkah to be built solely for the sake of observance of the Festival.

D.   And the House of Hillel?

E.   They require that statement of Scripture [to stand behind the position of] R. Sheshet.

F.   For R. Sheshet has said in the name of R. Aqiba, "How do we know that, as to the wood used for building a sukkah, it is forbidden [for use for any other purpose] all seven days of the festival?

G.   "Scripture states, 'The festival of Sukkot, for seven days for the Lord' (Lev. 23:34). [This indicates that, for the entire period, what is devoted to observance of the festival must be used only for that purpose.]"

H.   And it has been taught on Tannaite authority:

I.   R. Judah b. Beterah says, "Just as the dedication to Heaven takes hold of the animal set aside for the festal offering [so that that animal may not be slaughtered for any other purpose but celebration of the festival], so the dedication to Heaven takes hold of whatever is used for the sukkah [with the same result].

J.   "As it is said, 'The festival of Sukkot, for seven days for the Lord' (Lev. 23:34). The meaning is, 'Just as the animal set aside for the festal offering is to be only for the Lord, so whatever is used for the sukkah likewise is to be only for the Lord.'"

K.   Now does not the House of Shammai also require the stated proof for the present proposition?

L.   That indeed is the case.

M.   But then what is the scriptural basis for the view of the House of Shammai?

N.   Another verse of Scripture states, "You shall make the festival of Sukkot for seven days" (Deut. 16:13) -- a sukkah that is made for the sake of the festival is what we require.

O.   And the House of Hillel?

P.   They require the force of that proof-text to indicate that one may construct a sukkah on the intermediate days of the festival of Sukkot.

Q.   And the House of Shammai?

R.   They take the view of R. Eliezer who has said, "People may not make a sukkah [to begin with] on the intermediate days of a festival of Sukkot."

II.

A.   But does the House of Hillel [M. 1:1G, I] not concur with the view of R. Judah stated in the name of Rab?

B.   For R. Judah said Rab said, "If one made show-fringes out of the hanging web or woof of a woven garment, or out of sewing threads, the fringes are not valid. If he made them out of tuft [attached for that purpose to a garment], the fringes are valid. [Attaching the tuft to the garment was for the purpose of making the show-fringes, while simply drawing out an available thread and twisting it would not constitute purposefully making show-fringes.]" [How, then, can the House of Hillel accept as valid a sukkah that is not constructed for the purpose of observing the festival, in line with the principle expressed in Rab's statement?]

C.   "Now when I [Judah] repeated this statement before Samuel, he said to me, 'Also show-fringes made from tufts are invalid.'

D.   "'For we require an act of weaving of the show-fringes that is done for its own sake [and in the present case, there is no such act].'"

E.   Here too should we not require a sukkah that is made for its own sake [and not accept one constructed without the observance of the festival in mind]?

F.   The case [of the fringes] is different, for Scripture has said, "You shall make twisted cords for yourself" (Deut. 22:12).

G.   "For yourself" -- to carry out your obligation.

H.   But here too it is said, "The festival of Sukkot you shall make for yourself" (Deut. 16:13) --

I.   [Thus:] "For yourself" -- to carry out your obligation!

J.   That verse [serves to prove a different proposition entirely, namely] to serve to exclude [the use of a sukkah] that has been stolen. [The sukkah one uses must be legally owned.]

K.   But in the matter of show-fringes, surely the same usage then should serve the same purpose, namely, to exclude stolen show-fringes!

L.   In that other context, a separate verse of Scripture is available, namely, "And you shall make for them" (Num. 15:38) -- out of what belongs to them.

Unit I clarifies the source of the law, and unit II introduces a separate, but related consideration. The exegesis of the Mishnah's rule in relationship to scriptural proof-text is thorough.

1:2

A.   [9B] He who makes his sukkah under a tree is as if he made it in [his] house.

B.   A sukkah on top of a sukkah --

C.   the one on top is valid.

D.   And the one on the bottom is invalid.

E.   R. Judah says, "If there are no residents in the top one, the bottom one is valid."

I.

A.   Said Raba, "[The statement at M. 1:2A] has been made only with regard to a tree whose branches produce more shade than light. But if the light [under the tree] is greater than the shadow, [in which case, the sukkah's own sukkah-roofing produces the shadow in the sukkah], the sukkah is valid.

B.   "How [do I know this to be true]? Since it is taught, It is as if he made it in his house [M. 1:2A]. Now what need do I have to formulate matters in this way, namely, It is as if he made it in his house? Let the framer of the passage state merely, 'It is invalid'!

C.   "In framing matters as he did, the author of the passage has informed us that the tree is comparable to a house. Just as a house produces more shade than light, so if a tree produces more shade than light [and thus is like a house, the sukkah built in the shade would be invalid, but, if not, it would be valid.]"

D. But even if the shade produced by a tree is greater than the light that the branches let through, what difference does it make?

E. Lo, we have a case in which invalid <u>sukkah</u>-roofing [namely, the branches of the tree, which are yet attached through the trunk to the ground] is joined together with valid <u>sukkah</u>-roofing [namely, branches of trees that have been detached from the ground], [and such a mixture is invalid.]

F. Said R. Papa, "We deal with a case in which the owner has intertwined [the invalid and the valid branches. In this case, if the valid branches outnumber the invalid ones, the arrangement is valid.]"

G. If we deal with a case in which the owner has intertwined the valid and invalid branches, what purpose was there in making the ruling explicit? [The point is self-evident and hardly requires specification.]

H. What might you have maintained? We should make a decree in prohibiting a case in which the owner intertwined valid and invalid <u>sukkah</u>-roofings on account of a case in which one has not done so. So the framer of the passage informs us that we make no such decree.

I. But we have learned exactly that principle on Tannaite authority: <u>If one trained a vine, gourd, or ivy over it and then spread sukkah-roofing on one of these, it is invalid. But if the sukkah-roofing exceeded them, or if the cut the vines down, it is valid</u> [M. 1:4A-D]. [How do we gain the same principle?]

J. Now how can we imagine such a case? If I say that we deal with a case in which the owner did not intertwine the valid and in a valid <u>sukkah</u>-roof, lo, we deal with a case in which invalid <u>sukkah</u>-roofing is joined together with valid <u>sukkah</u>-roofing.

K. So is it not a case in which one did intertwine them?

L. And it bears the implication that we make no such decree [as we proposed]. [So why repeat the same law here?]

M. [We repeat the same principle to make this point:] One might have taken the view that [the joining of the two sorts of roofings would be permitted] only after the fact, but not to begin with.

N. Now we are told that even to begin with, it is allowed [so long as the two materials are interwoven].

II.

A. <u>A sukkah on top of a sukkah</u> [M. 1:2B]:

B. Our rabbis have taught on Tannaite authority:

C. "You shall dwell in Sukkot" (Lev. 23:42) -- and not in a <u>sukkah</u> which is underneath another <u>sukkah</u>, nor in a <u>sukkah</u> that is underneath a tree, and not in a <u>sukkah</u> which is in a house.

D. [On the contrary, perhaps the use of the plural, "<u>sukkot</u>"] bears two meanings [one of which would be to permit exactly the kind of setting rejected at C]?

E. Said R. Nahman bar Isaac, "It is written without the mark of the plural, thus, 'in a <u>sukkah</u>' [so excluding all but the accepted mode of locating the <u>sukkah</u>]."

III.

A. Said R. Jeremiah, "There are cases in which both [the upper and the lower] sukkah will be valid, cases in which both of them will be invalid, cases in which the one on the bottom will be invalid and the one on the top valid, and cases in which the one on the bottom will be invalid and the one on the top valid.

B. "What would be an instance in which both of them would be valid? It would be an instance in which the one on the bottom had more light than shade, but the one on the top had more shade than light [so was valid], and the one on the top [had its roofing] within twenty cubits of the ground [so forming a single sukkah out of the two].

C. "What would be an instance in which both of them would be invalid? It would be a case in which both of them had sukkah-roofing that produced more shade than light, and the [sukkah-roofing of the] one on the top was stood more than twenty cubits above the ground. [In this case, both are, independent of one another, invalid.]

D. "What would be an instance in which the one on the bottom is invalid and the one on the top valid? [10A] It would be a case in which the one on the bottom produced more shade than light, and the one on the top produced more light than shade, and [the sukkah-roofing of both of them] stood within twenty cubits [of the ground].

E. "And what would be a case in which the one on the top was valid and the one on the bottom invalid? It would be a case in which for both of them the shade produced by the roof was greater than the light let through, and the one [sukkah-roofing of the] one on the top was within twenty cubits of the ground."

F. These rulings are self-evident [and why was it necessary to state them]?

G. It was necessary to make explicit the case in which the one on the bottom was valid and the one on the top was invalid. What might one have falsely supposed? We should make a decree [against such an arrangement] lest the invalid sukkah-roofing join together with the valid sukkah-roofing.

H. Accordingly, we are informed that we make no such decree.

IV.

A. And how much space would there be between one sukkah and the other so that the lower sukkah would be invalid [as a sukkah beneath a sukkah]?

B. Said R. Huna, "A handbreadth. [If the space between the upper sukkah-roofing and the lower sukkah-roofing is less than a handbreadth, the two sets of roofing are regarded as one. [Then we do not have a case of one sukkah beneath another sukkah at all.]"

C. [Huna continues,] "For so we find that the handbreadth is the standard measure in connection with cases of overshadowing of corpse-uncleanness, for we have learned in the Mishnah: A handbreadth of space by a handbreadth at the height of a handbreadth brings uncleanness [should it be left open in a partition between corpse matter in one otherwise closed room and another such room] or interposes against the passage of the same uncleanness [if such a space is closed off], but a space less than a handbreadth in height neither brings uncleanness [if open] nor interposes [if closed] [M. Oh. 3:7]. [The operative measure is a handbreadth. If the roof is higher than that distance, it is deemed a separate roof, and if it is lower, it is deemed part of the contained space]."

D. R. Hisda and Rabbah bar R. Huna say, "Four [handbreadths], for we do not find a contained space taken into account if it is less than four handbreadths."

E. And Samuel said, "Ten."

F. What is the reason for the view of Samuel? The requisite measure for rendering the sukkah valid [ten handbreadths above the ground] also operates to render it invalid.

G. Just as the requisite measure of height is ten handbreadths, so the distance that will invalidate likewise is ten handbreadths.

H. [Arguing to the contrary conclusion on the basis of the same principle as F:] We have learned in the Mishnah: R. Judah says, "If there are no residents in the top one, the bottom one is valid" [M. 1:2E].

I. What is the sense of "...no residents..."?

J. If it is in concrete terms, that is, if the issue is that there really are no occupants, is this the governing criterion? [It is a random fact.]

K. But rather is not the sense of there being no residents to mean, any [upper] sukkah which is not suitable for a dwelling [would leave the lower sukkah valid]?

L. What would be an example of such a case? One which was not ten handbreadths in height.

M. Would this then bear the implication that, in the view of the first [anonymous] authority [vis à vis Judah], even one which is not suitable for dwelling [would leave the lower sukkah] invalid? [This would then refute Samuel's position, above].

N. When R. Dimi came, he said, "In the West they say, If the lower [sukkah's roof] cannot hold the weight of the pillows and blankets of the upper one, the lower one is valid. [The upper sukkah then is not sufficiently strong. Its floor, the roof of the lower sukkah, cannot carry the weight.]"

O. Does this then bear the implication that the first of the two authorities takes the view that even if the [lower sukkah] is not suitable to bear [the weight of the upper, the lower one] is invalid?

P. At issue between [Judah and the first authority] is the case of a [lower] sukkah, the floor-roof of which can bear the weight of the upper sukkah only with difficulty.

The point is that the roof of the sukkah must be exposed to the firmament and not covered, A, in large part by the boughs of the tree. D follows the same principle, now with reference to a sukkah covered by another. Judah's view is that, without residents, the upper sukkah does not constitute a dwelling, thus excluding A's consideration. Unit I then clarifies M. 1:2A. But the real interest is the notion that if invalid and valid forms of sukkah-roofing are intertwined, with a greater portion of valid, the whole is valid. That principle, not demanded by the Mishnah's rule, does clarify that rule. Unit II proceeds to the scriptural basis for M. 1:2B. Unit III focuses upon that same rule, making a point that the Talmud's anonymous voice itself calls self-evident. Unit IV clarifies a

secondary question — the relationship of the two sukkah-constructions, upper and lower —
but in so doing also invokes M. 1:2E. There is a slight intricacy in the argument on
Samuel's principle, IV F, which I have not reproduced; Slotki's notes (p. 38, ns. 8-13) may
be consulted with profit (as always).

1:3

A.   [If] one spread a sheet on top of [a sukkah] on account of the hot sun,

B.   or underneath [the cover of boughs] on account of droppings [of the
      branches or leaves of the bough-cover],

C.   or [if] he spread [a sheet] over a four-post bed [in a sukkah],

D.   it is invalid [for dwelling or sleeping and so for fulfilling one's obligation
      to dwell in the sukkah].

E.   But he spreads it over the frame of a two-poster bed.

I.

A.   Said R. Hisda, "The stated condition pertains only to doing so on account of
      droppings of the branches [M. 1:3B]. But if it was to adorn [the sukkah] it is valid."

B.   That fact is self-evident. After all, in the Mishnah we have learned, ...on account of
      the droppings of the branches!

C.   What might you have said? That would be the rule even if the intent was to beautify
      the sukkah. The reason that the framer of the Mishnah-passage has specified, On
      account of the droppings of the branches, was simply that that is the ordinary way
      things happen.

D.   So we are informed [that that is not the case].

E.   May we propose that the following supports the thesis just now advanced:

F.   If one put up a proper sukkah-roofing and then decorated [the sukkah] with
      embroidered hangings and sheets and [in T.'s version:] [If] one hung up in it nuts,
      peaches, pomegranates, bunches of grapes, and wreaths of ears of corn, it is valid.

G.   [But] one should not eat of any of these, [10B] even on the last day of the Festival.

H.   But if one made a stipulation concerning them that he would eat of them on the
      Festival, it is permitted to do so [T. Suk. 1:7G-I]. [The passage refers to em-
      broidered sheets and treats them as valid adornment, in line with Hisda's view.]

I.   But perhaps [the framer of the passage assumes that the sheets are put up] along the
      sides [and so there is no bearing upon Hisda's claim.]

II.

A.   It has been taught on Amoraic authority:

B.   Things put up to decorate the sukkah do not diminish the height of the sukkah.

C.   Said R. Ashi, "But if put up at the side, they do diminish the height of the sukkah."

D.   Minyamin, the servant of R. Ashi, soaked his short in water and spread it out on the
      sukkah [to cool it off].

E.   Said to him R. Ashi, "Take it down, so that people will not reach the conclusion that one may make sukkah-roofing out of something that is susceptible to uncleanness."

F.   [The slave answered,] "But lo, people will see that it is wet [and so used for air-conditioning. Why then take it into account?]"

G.   [He replied,] "My instruction to you is for when it dries off."

III.

A.   It has been stated on Amoraic authority:

B.   Decorations for a sukkah which are four handbreadths higher than the roof --

C.   R. Nahman said, "Such an arrangement is valid."

D.   R. Hisda and Rabbah bar R. Huna say, "It is invalid."

E.   R. Hisda and Rabbah bar R. Huna happened by the house of the exilarch. R. Nahman [the major domo of the exilarch] put them up in a sukkah, the decorations of which were four handbreadths higher than the roof. They remained silent and said nothing to him.

F.   He said to them, "Have our rabbis reversed themselves from their original teaching?"

G.   They said to him, "We are agents for the commission of a religious obligation and so are exempt from the further religious duty of dwelling in a valid sukkah. [So it does not matter to us that your sukkah is invalid.]"

IV.

A.   Said R. Judah said Samuel, "It is permitted to sleep in a canopied bed in a sukkah, even though the canopy forms a roof [vs. M. 1:3C], so long as it is not ten hand-breadths high."

B.   Come and take note [of a contrary teaching]: He who sleeps in a canopied bed in a sukkah has not carried out his obligation [to dwell in a sukkah, since the roof of the canopied bed interposes between the person and the sukkah-roofing].

C.   [That poses no objection to the stated thesis, for] in that case, with what sort of a bed do we deal? With one the canopy of which is ten handbreadths high [and so forms a roof unto itself].

D.   They objected: He who sleeps under a bed in a sukkah has not fulfilled his obligation [M. 2:1A]. [Would that not contradict Samuel's rule?]

E.   Samuel interpreted the rule to speak of a bed that is ten handbreadths high.

F.   Come and take note: Or if he spread a sheet over a four-post bed in a sukkah -- it is invalid [M. 1:3C].

G.   In that case, also, it is one that is ten handbreadths high.

H.   But lo, that is not precisely what has been taught, for it has been stated on Tannaite authority:

I.   [The word used at M. 1:3E] speaks of a two-post bed, and [the word used at M. 1:3C] speaks of a four-post bed.

J.   If [then] one spread a sheet over a four-post bed, it is invalid. If he spread it over a two post bed, it is valid, so long as the posts are not more than ten handbreadths high over the bed.

K.   This then bears the implication that, in the case of a four-post bed, even though the posts are not ten handbreadths high [it is invalid].

L.   The case of the four-post bed is to be differentiated, because the posts are firmly set in the ground.

M.   But there is [the parallel case of] one sukkah on top of another sukkah, in which case the posts are firmly set in the ground, and yet Samuel took the view that that trait which would validate such an arrangement serves also to invalidate it [Slotki, p. 41, n. 3: which shows that even a permanent structure cannot be valid unless it is ten handbreadths high].

N.   I may then explain [how to differentiate the rulings] as follows: In that case [of one sukkah on top of another], in which case at issue is the invalidation of the sukkah, the criterion [of invalidation] is ten handbreadths. Here, where at issue is [not the status of the space in the sukkah unaffected but only] the making of a tent [by spreading a sheet over the canopy of the bed], even though the height is less than ten handbreadths, the canopy also constitutes a tent.

V.

A.   Said R. Tahalipa bar Abimi said Samuel, "He who sleeps naked in a canopied bed pokes his head out of the canopy and recites the Shema. [He may not do so if he is naked. If he pokes his head out, then his body is deemed to be covered by the canopy, and the man then may say the Shema and is not regarded as naked but as clothed.]"

B.   They objected: "He who sleeps naked in a canopied bed may not poke his head out from under the canopy and recite the Shema."

C.   In the latter case, with what sort of arrangement do we deal? With a bed more than ten handbreadths high. [Here we have a room, not a garment].

D.   That view is quite reasonable, for since at the end of the cited passage, it is said, "Lo, to what may the case be compared? To someone who stands naked in a house, who mad may not poke his head out the window and recite the Shema," the implication is [just as I have proposed.

E.   [11A] But as to a house, even though it is not ten handbreadths high, since it is firmly attached to the ground, it is in the status of a tent, for it is not of lesser status than the frame of a four-post bed.

F.   Some present another version [of the foregoing, as follows:]

G.   R. Judah said Samuel said, "It is permitted to sleep in a sukkah in a bed constructed for newly weds, even though it is ten handbreadths high, for it has no roof [but rather a sloping cover above the bed]."

H.   This objection was raised: He who sleeps in a sukkah in a canopied bed has not carried out his obligation [to sleep under sukkah-roofing].

I.   In this case with what sort of a situation do we deal? With one that has a roof [and this is different from a canopy].

J.   Come and take note of the following: [The word used at M. 1:3E] speaks of a two-post bed, and [the word used at M. 1:3C] speaks of a four-post bed. If one spread a sheet over a four-post bed, it is invalid. If he spread it over a two-post bed, it is valid, so long as the posts are not more than ten handbreadths high over the bed [IV I-J]. This then bears the implication that, if the <u>posts</u> rise ten hand-breadths over the bed, the arrangement is invalid and that is the case even though over the bed is no roof-like canopy.

K. The case of the two-post bed is to be differentiated, because the posts are firmly affixed to the ground.

L. If the criterion is that they are firmly affixed to the ground, then why are they not in the category of the four-post bed [in which case the arrangement is not to be allowed in a <u>sukkah</u>]?

M. When compared to a four-post bed, the posts are not deemed firmly affixed to the ground, but when compared to a bed for newly weds, they are. [Slotki, p. 42, n. 6: They cause... invalidity where they are ten handbreadths high even if they have no roof, while a canopied bed that has no roof causes no invalidity even where it is ten handbreadths high.]

VI.

A. Rabbah bar R. Huna expounded [the law as follows: "It is permitted to sleep in a <u>sukkah</u> in a bed with a canopy, even though the canopy is in the form of a roof [and] even though it is higher than ten handbreadths [thus constituting an arrangement of a <u>sukkah</u> within a <u>sukkah</u>]."

B. In accord with whose view is this statement made? It conforms to the principle of R. Judah, who has said that a tent built at random [and not for permanent use] does not serve to nullify the validity of a permanently constructed tent. [The <u>sukkah</u> falls into the latter category, the bed into the former.]

C. We have learned in the Mishnah: <u>Said R. Judah, "We had the practice of sleeping under the bed before the elders, and they said nothing at all to us" [M. 2:1B].</u> [This would then sustain the thesis that Judah's principle is represented by Rabbah's statement of the law].

D. Why not state simply, "The law is in accord with R. Judah" [instead of citing the precedent that he adduces in behalf of his view]?

E. If the text had said simply, "The law is in accord with R. Judah," I might have supposed that that is the case for a bed, which has been set up, after all, for people to sleep on top of it. [If they sleep underneath, that constitutes abnormal use.] But in the case of a bed with a canopy, which is set up for people to sleep within it, I might have said that that is not the rule. [In the later latter case, we really do have one <u>sukkah</u> constructed inside of another.]

F. So we are informed that the operative criterion for R. Judah's view is that a tent built at random [and not for permanent use] does not serve to nullify the validity of a permanently constructed tent. And, in this regard, there is no difference between a bed and a canopied bed.

If a four-post bed, located in the sukkah, is covered over, it is not suitable as a place for sleeping in the sukkah, deemed to be like a sukkah in a house. But a two-post covered over has a sloping roof, which does not enter the category of a roof annulling the effects of the sukkah-roofing. The Talmud begins with analysis of the implications of the Mishnah's language, unit I attending to M. 1:3B. Unit II is inserted because it deals with decorations in a sukkah, important in the discussion of unit I. Unit III carries forward the same point of interest. Unit IV then reverts to the Mishnah, now to M. 1:3C, E, the contrast between two types of beds, explained just now. This leads to the secondary discussion at units V, VI. So the Talmud forms around the principal clauses of the Mishnah, and then extends its discussion to secondary matters generated by its original inquiry.

1:4

A. [If] one trained a vine, gourd, or ivy over it and then spread sukkah-roofing on [one of these], it is invalid.

B. But if the sukkah-roofing exceeded them,

C. or if he cut them [the vines] down,

D. it is valid.

E. This is the general rule:

F. Whatever is susceptible to uncleanness and does not grown from the ground -- they do not make sukkah-roofing with it.

G. And whatever is not susceptible to uncleanness, but does grow from the ground [and has been cut off] -- they do make sukkah-roofing with it.

I.

A. R. Joseph was in session before R. Huma, and he said, "...or if he cut the vines down, it is valid [M. 1:4C-D]. And [in this connection, he continued], Rab said, 'It is necessary to shake [the vines loose [after cutting them down, so that the sukkah-roofing is constructed by deliberate action and so that the materials at hand are actually validated by such action. Merely cutting the vines from the ground by itself does not constitute an act of deliberate validation.]'"

B. Said R. Huna to him, "Lo, it is Samuel who made that statement."

C. R. Joseph turned away and said to him, "Did I tell you that Samuel did not say it? I told you that Rab said it, and Samuel said it [too]."

D. Said R. Huna to him, "This is what I was saying to you, that Samuel is the one who said it, and not Rab.

E. "For Rab treats the arrangement as valid [without a deliberate act of shaking the vines]."

II.

A. This is comparable to the case of R. Amram, an exceptionally pious man, who hung show-fringes to the aprons of the women of his household.

B. He tied them on, but he did not cut off the ends of the threads. [Slotki, p. 44, n. 4: He folded on thread four times and attached it to the garment. But subsequently cutting it he made of it the eight requisite threads.]

C. He came before R. Hiyya bar Ashi [to ask whether this procedure was valid, that is, (Slotki) whether the mere cutting of the long thread constitutes the making of the fringes.] He said to him, "This is what Rab said: 'One simply cuts them off [as explained] and they will be valid."

D. It follows, therefore, that merely cutting off [the threads and so accomplishing a deliberate act of validation] constitutes the requisite act of making them. Here too the mere act of cutting off [the vines from the ground for use of sukkah-roofing, without shaking them and so accomplishing a deliberate act of validation] likewise constitutes the requisite act of making them.

E. But in fact is it the view of Samuel that merely cutting off [the threads or the vines, without a deliberate act of manufacture] constitutes the act of making them?

F. And lo, Samuel taught in the name of R. Hiyya, "If one threaded a string through two corners at once, and only then cut apart the ends of the string, the show-fringes are valid."

G. Does this not mean that one tied them and only afterward cut them [as Rab would find sufficient]?

H. No, he cut the threads and afterward tied them.

I. If he cut them and afterward tied them, what purpose is there in so stating [since everyone knows that would be a valid procedure]?

J. What might you have maintained? [11B] That we require someone to insert the threads in one corner at a time [Slotki] and that procedure has not been followed [so it is not valid]. So we are informed [that that consideration is not operative].

K. This objection was raised: If one hung [threads of the show-fringes] and did not cut off the ends, the arrangement is invalid.

L. Does this not mean that the arrangement remain permanently invalid [even if one did so later on], in which case it is a refutation of Rab's view?

M. [Hardly, for] Rab may say to you, "What is the meaning of 'invalid'? The arrangement is invalid until the threads are cut."

N. And Samuel would maintain that that arrangement remains permanently invalid.

O. And so did Levi say, "It is permanently invalid," and so did R. Mattenah say Samuel said, "It is permanently invalid."

P. Said R. Mattenah, "The case took place in connection with me, and I came before Mar Samuel and he said to me, 'The arrangement is permanently invalid.'"

Q. This objection was raised: [If] one inserted [the threads of the show-fringes] and afterward cut off the ends of the threads, [the arrangement is] invalid.

R. And in regard to a sukkah it has been taught on Tannaite authority: "You shall make..." (Deut. 16:13) -- and not use something already made.

S. On the basis of the foregoing exegesis, they have said: If one trained a vine, gourd, or ivy over [the sukkah] and then spread sukkah-roofing on one of these, it is invalid [M. 1:4A].

T. Now with what sort of case do we deal [in the foregoing exegesis]? If we say that it is a case in which the householder did not cut the vines off from the ground, what need is there to invoke, as the reason, the consideration of the exegesis: "'You shall make...' -- and not use something already made"?

U. One may derive the invalidating cause from the simple fact that the vines are attached to the ground [and that by itself is the sufficient reason].

V. Now, it must follow, we deal with a case in which the householder has cut off the vines, and it has been taught that the arrangement nonetheless is invalid.

W. It must then follow that we do not rule that merely cutting the [threads or the vines] constitutes the proper act of making them [without any further intervention of a deliberate act of validation], and that would constitute ample refutation of Rab's view of the matter.

X. [Hardly!] Rab may say to you, "With what sort of case do we deal here? It is with a case in which he pulled the branches up [without wholly severing the bark], in which case the act of actually making [the vines into sukkah-roofing] is not to be discerned.

Y. Nonetheless, we have a case in which one has inserted the threads and only afterward cut off the ends, and that does indeed present a problem to the view of Rab.

Z. May I propose that the present dispute [on whether merely cutting the vines, without shaking them or otherwise deliberately changing their condition, constitutes an act of validation] runs along the lines of a dispute of Tannas, which is as follows: [If, on the festival day, one] violated the law and gathered [berries of a myrtle that is attached to the lulab], [the myrtle remains] invalid," the words of R. Simeon b. Yehosedeq.

AA. And sages declare it valid. [At issue is whether the myrtle conforms to the law that it must have more leaves than berries. On the festival itself, one may not remove berries to validate the myrtle. On the week day one may do so.]

BB. [We shall now explain the relevance of the present case to the one we have just examined.] Now in considering this matter, it was assumed that all parties concurred that the elements joined for the lulab must be tied together. The rule governing the making of the lulab, furthermore, was derived by analogy from the sukkah, in which case it is written, "You shall make..." (Deut. 16:13) -- and not use something already made.

CC. Now [in line with the stated premises], is this not what is at issue? Namely, the one who declares the arrangement valid takes the view that in connection with the making of the sukkah, we hold that merely cutting off the vines constitutes an the act of making them [valid for use as sukkah-roofing]. In respect to the preparation of the lulab, we also take the view that merely collecting the myrtle [without further actions in connection with it, e.g., removing excess berries] constitutes the valid act of preparing it.

DD. The one who holds that the arrangement is invalid then takes the position that we do not rule in connection with the sukkah that the mere act of cutting off the vines constitutes an adequate act of preparing the vines to serve as <u>sukkah</u>-roofing.

EE. Likewise in connection with the <u>lulab</u>, we also do not rule that the mere act of collecting the myrtle does not constitute an act of validation.

FF. No, [that theory of matters does not hold]. All parties concur that, in connection with the <u>sukkah</u>, we do <u>not</u> rule that the act of cutting down the vines constitutes a sufficient act of preparing the vines to serve as <u>sukkah</u>-ruling.

GG. Then what is at issue here is whether, to begin with, we derive the rules governing the <u>lulab</u> from the case of the <u>sukkah</u> at all.

HH. The one who declares the arrangement valid takes the view that we simply do not derive the rules governing the <u>lulab</u> from the case of the <u>sukkah</u>.

II. The one who declares the arrangement invalid takes the position that we do derive the rules governing the <u>lulab</u> from the case of the <u>sukkah</u>.

JJ. If you wish, I may propose a different explanation. If we take the view that all of the parts of the <u>lulab</u> have to be joined. All parties furthermore concur that we do derive the rules governing the making of the <u>lulab</u> from those having to do with the making of the <u>sukkah</u>.

KK. But here at issue is the following: One party holds that it is necessary to join the parts of the <u>lulab</u> together. The other party holds that it is not necessary to join the parts of the <u>lulab</u> together. [Simeon takes the position that the <u>lulab</u> must be tied together. This is done before the festival. But it was not done before the festival. Taking the berries off during the festival does not do any good. The <u>lulab</u> already had been made and invalidly made. Sages differ and hence declare the removal of the berries to be valid, even though it was done later on. Why? The <u>lulab</u> itself is suitable even if its parts are not bound together prior to the festival.]

LL. The dispute, then, follows along lines of what is under dispute in the following disagreement among Tannaite authorities, for it has been taught on Tannaite authority:

MM. **A lulab [made up of a palm branch, willow branch, and myrtle branch] whether bound up or not bound up, is valid.**

NN. **R. Judah says, "One which is bound up is valid, and one which is not bound up is invalid"** [T. Suk. 2:10A-B].

OO. What is the scriptural basis for the view of R. Judah?

PP. He derives the meaning of the word "take" [used in connection with the <u>lulab</u>] from the use of the word "take" used in connection with the hyssop-bundle.

QQ. There it is written, "And you shall take a bundle of hyssop" (Ex. 12:22), and here it is written, "And you shall take on the first day..." (Lev. 23:40).

RR. Just as, in that other instance, it must be taken as a bundle, so here too it must be taken as a bundle.

SS. And rabbis do not derive the meaning of the "taking" used in the present connection from the analogy supplied by the meaning of the word "take" used in that other connection.

TT. In accord with what authority is the following teaching on Tannaite authority:

UU. The proper performance of the religious duty in regard to the lulab is to bind the species together, but if one has not done so, it is valid.

VV. Now this cannot be in accord with R. Judah, for if one has not bound the species together, why should the arrangement be valid?

WW. And it can hardly accord with rabbis [vis à vis Judah], for why should it be an element of the religious duty [to do so at all, if they say one need not do so]?

XX. Indeed, the statement accords with rabbis, since it is written "This is my God and I will glorify him" (Ex. 15:2), which means one should be glorified before him through carrying out religious duties [in an especially felicitous manner, but if one does not do things exactly in that way, the action remains valid].

III.

A. This is the general rule: Whatever is susceptible to uncleanness, etc. [M. 1:4F-G]:

B. What is the scriptural basis for this rule?

C. Said R. Simeon b. Laqish, "Scripture has stated, 'And a mist went up from the earth' (Gen. 2:6).

D. "Just as mist is something which is not susceptible to uncleanness and grows from the ground, so a sukkah must be made of some thing which does not receive uncleanness and grows from the ground."

E. That explanation is suitable to the person who holds that the sukkah in which Israel dwelled in the wilderness was clouds of glory.

F. But in the view of him who holds that the sukkah was the genuine article which the Israelites actually made for themselves [and not an analogy to clouds of glory], what sort of proof may one bring?

G. The problem at hand accords with that which has been taught on Tannaite authority:

H. "'For I made the children of Israel dwell in sukkot' (Lev. 23:43), meaning in clouds of glory," the words of R. Eliezer.

I. R. Aqiba says, "They were actually sukkot that people made for themselves."

J. Now [as just noted] the stated proof poses no problems to the view of R. Eliezer, but as to the position of R. Aqiba, what is there to say?

IV.

A. When R. Dimi came, [he said that] R. Yohanan said, "Scripture has stated, 'The festal offering of Sukkot you shall prepare' (Deut. 16:13).

B. "The sukkah thus is compared to the festal offering [brought as an animal sacrifice on the festival day].

C. "Just as the festal offering is something that does not receive uncleanness [animals fed from what grows from the ground are, in Yohanan's view, as if they too grow from the ground] and also grows from the ground [as just now explained], so the sukkah must be made of something which does not receive uncleanness and grows from the ground."

D. [12A] But what if you wish to propose a further analogy, just as the festal offering is of an animate being, so the sukkah must be made of an animate being?

V.

A.   When Rabin came, he said that R. Yohanan said, "Scripture has stated, 'After you
       have gathered in from your threshing floor and from your winepress...' (Deut.
       16:13). Scripture speaks of what is left on the threshing floor and the dregs of the
       wine press. [These grow from the ground and are not susceptible to uncleanness, so
       too the sukkah-roofing, of which the verse at hand speaks, must conform to the
       same traits.]'"

B.   And may I say that Scripture speaks of the threshing floor itself and the wine press
       itself? [Perhaps somehow the sukkah must be composed of these objects?]

C.   Said R. Zira, "Here it is written, 'Wine press,' and it is hardly possible to make use
       of a wine-press for sukkah-roofing!"

D.   To this explanation R. Jeremiah objected, "And might I speculate that what is
       required is use of congealed wine which comes from Senir, like fig cakes? [Perhaps
       the sense of Scripture is that that is what must be used for sukkah-roofing!]'"

E.   Said R. Zira, "We had a valid proposition in hand, but R. Jeremiah came along and
       threw an ax at it [and smashed it]!'"

F.   R. Ashi said, "'From your threshing floor' and not the threshing floor itself, 'from
       your wine press' and not the wine press itself [is to be the source of materials used
       for sukkah-roofing]."

G.   R. Hisda said, "Proof for the desired proposition derives from here: 'Go forth to the
       mountain and collect olive branches, branches of wild olive, myrtle branches, palm
       branches, and branches of thick trees' (Neh. 8:15). [All of these are not susceptible
       to uncleanness and grow from the ground, and, in context, are specified for use as
       sukkah-roofing]."

H.   Myrtle branches fall into the category of branches of thick trees [of Lev. 23:40.
       Why specify the same species twice]?

I.   Said R. Hisda, "The wild myrtle is for the sukkah-roofing, and the branches of thick
       trees for the lulab."

       The sukkah-roofing must now grow from the ground, M. 1:4F-G, which explains A,
C. The consideration of uncleanness is not operative here. The Talmud's elaborate
discussion, units I-II, accomplishes two things. First, it raises the question of the
procedure to be followed in connection with M. 1:4C. Second, it introduces the underlying
principle at issue, whether the mere act of cutting down the vines also serves to render
them suitable for the specific purpose of use as sukkah-roofing, or whether some distinct
act of designation, thus preparation, is required. The former view is worked out in unit I.
Unit II then produces a striking analogy, in which a quite different case -- making strings
into show-fringes -- is shown to invoke upon the same principle, namely, whether a mere
act of destruction -- cutting the vines, severing the string -- suffices, or whether a
clearcut deed of deliberate and positive validation also is required. It is clear that the
issue of show-fringes need not involve the matter of the vines for sukkah-roofing, but unit
II makes a strong case that the two cases must be worked out in tandem. Units III-V then
present the familiar exercise of locating scriptural proof for a mishnaic proposition.

1:5

A. Bundles of straw, wood, or brush --

B. they do not make a sukkah-roofing with them.

C. But any of them which one untied is valid.

D. And all of them are valid [as is] for use for the sides [of the sukkah].

I.

A. Said R. Jacob, "I heard from R. Yohanan two [explanations], one for the rule at hand, and the other for the rule that follows:

B. "He who hollowed out a space in a haystack to make a sukkah therein -- it is no sukkah [M. 1:8D-E].

C. "[The reason for] one [of the rulings] is on account of a [precautionary] decree [on account of the possibility of a person's using a sukkah as a] store-house.

D. "[The reason for] the other [of the rulings] is on account of the exegesis, "'You shall make" (Deut. 16:13) -- and not make use of what is ready-made.'

E. "Now I do not know which of the two rulings [of the Mishnah at hand] is on account of the consideration of not using the sukkah as a store-house, and which one of them is on account of the exegesis, "'You shall make" -- and not from what is ready-made."'

F. Said R. Jeremiah, "Let us see [how we may work matters out on the basis of a further ruling in Yohanan's name].

G. "For R. Hiyya bar Abba said R. Yohanan said, 'On what account did they rule: Bundles of straw, wood, or brush -- they do not make a sukkah-roofing with them [M. 1:5A-B]?

H. "'[It is because] there are times that a person will come in from the field in the evening, with his bundle [of produce] on his back, and he might just push it up and leave it on top of his sukkah, so as to allow the produce to dry. Then he will reconsider the matter and determine to make use of [the bundles] for sukkah-roofing. Yet the Torah has said, "You will make" (Deut. 16:13) -- and not from what is ready-made.'

I. "Now since the rule at hand is on account of a precautionary decree [lest the farmer use the sukkah] as a store-house [in the scenario just now described, it must follow that] the other ruling [about hollowing out a haystake and turning it into a sukkah] is on the count of the exegesis of 'You shall make' -- and not what is ready-made."

J. And R. Jacob? [What left him in doubt as to Yohanan's explanations for the two rulings, since, after all, the teaching cited by Hiyya bar Abba was available?]

K. In point of fact, he had not heard the tradition [in Yohanan's name] made available by R. Hiyya bar Abba.

L. Said R. Ashi, "[Can we really say that the operative consideration in the ruling about] bundles of straw, wood, or brush is only on account of the precautionary decree [against using the sukkah as a] storehouse, but there is no consideration at all of the exegesis, "'You shall make for yourself" -- and not from what is ready-made'?

M.   "And [as to the ruling concerning] hollowing out a space in a haystack, [may we say that the operative consideration is only] on account of the exegesis, "'You shall make for yourself" -- and not from what is ready-made,' while the criterion based on the precautionary decree [against using the sukkah as a] store-house is not operative? [Surely each of the two rulings is susceptible to both of the available explanations!]"

N.   [Then how can we explain the position of] R. Yohanan, [who invokes only a single consideration for each case]?

O.   [Yohanan] may say to you, "In the present case, in which it is taught in the Mishnah, They do not make a sukkah-roofing with them [M. 1:5B], [that prohibition applies] to begin with, [12B], in which case they do not make the sukkah-roofing on account of a precautionary decree against [using the sukkah for a] store-house.

P.   "But as to the rule as the Torah would have it, it would be a valid procedure. [Rabbi's decree against it, making the law more strict than the Torah requires, is in point of fact applicable only to begin with. But if one has actually done so, then after the fact, the procedure is acceptable].

Q.   "And in that other case [hollowing out a hole in a haystack for use as a sukkah], in which case the Mishnah is phrased, It is no sukkah [at all] then, even after the fact, on the authority of the law of the Torah, it also does not constitute a valid sukkah."

II.

A.   Said R. Judah said Rab, "If one made sukkah-roofing with male arrow-shaft [which are inserted into the arrow-head], it is valid [because the wood is regarded as unprepared, and a flat piece of wood not subjected to a process of manufacture is not susceptible to uncleanness].

B.   "If he did so with female ones, it is invalid [because the female shafts have a bored hole, into which the arrow-head is inserted, and so have been subjected to a process of manufacture. As is clear, a hole is bored into an end, and an arrow-head inserted into it. So there is a valid receptable in the wood, with the result that the wood then is susceptible to uncleanness]."

C.   With male... it is valid: That is self-evident.

D.   What might you have said? Let us make a precautionary decree against using the male [unbored] ones on account of the female [bored] ones.

E.   So we are informed that that is not the case.

F.   With female... it is invalid: That too is self-evident.

G.   What might you have said? A receptacle that is made to be filled up [e.g., with the arrow-head] is not in the category of a valid receptacle [and so the shaft would remain insusceptible, since the hole that has been made in fact will not remain unfilled].

H.   So we are informed that that is not the case.

III.

A.   Said Rabbah bar bar Hana said R. Yohanan, "If one made a sukkah-roofing of processed stalks of flax, it is invalid. If he made it of unprocessed stalks of flax, it is valid [T. Suk. 1:5]. [The latter are not susceptible to uncleanness, the former are.]

B. "But I do not know the status of stalks of flax in an intermediate stage of preparation [Slotki].

C. "And as to those in an intermediate stage of preparation, I also do not know [Slotki:] whether if it has been pounded and not corded it is regarded as in an intermediate stage, but if it has been soaked and not pounded, it is regarded as being in its natural stage, or, perhaps, even if it has been soaked but not pounded, it is also regarded as being in an intermediate stage."

IV.

A. Said R. Judah, "As to licorice-wood and wormwood, they make sukkah-roofing with them."

B. Abayye said, "They make sukkah-roofing with licorice wood but not with wormwood."

C. What is the operative consideration?

D. Since [13A] they stink, a person might leave them and abandon [the sukkah].

E. Said R. Hanan bar Raba, "People may make sukkah-roofing with a certain species of thorns and one of prickly shrubs."

F. Abayye said, "People may make sukkah-roofing with the species of thorns but not that of prickly shrubs.

G. "What is the reason for this distinction?

H. "Since the leaves [of the latter] fall off [and scratch people below], people will go and abandon the sukkah."

V.

A. Said R. Giddal said Raba, "People may make sukkah-roofing with the forked portion of a palm tree. Even though they form a bundle, since it is formed in nature ["at the hands of Heaven"], it is not regarded as a bundle [which in line with M. 1:5A-B would be forbidden]. [Furthermore], even though a person may go back and make them into a bundle, rejoining [something that originally was joined] is not regarded as forming a bundle."

B. Said R. Hisda said Rabina bar Shila, "People may make a sukkah-roofing with forked reeds. Even though they form a bundle, since it is formed in nature, it is not regarded as a bundle. [Furthermore], even though a person may go back and make them into a bundle, rejoining [something that originally was joined] is not regarded as forming a bundle."

C. It has been taught on Tannaite authority along these same lines:

D. People may make sukkah-roofing with reeds and forked reeds.

E. As to reeds, that is self-evident! [Why specify what everyone knows?]

F. The passage should be repeated as follows: People may make sukkah-roofing with [Slotki:] reeds of the forked variety.

G. And R. Hisda said Rabina bar Shila said, "With bitter herbs of the marsh a person carries out his obligation on Passover to eat bitter herbs."

H. This objection was raised: "Hyssop" -- but not Greek hyssop, stibium hyssop, wild hyssop, Roman hyssop, or any kind of hyssop that has a distinctive name [M. Par.

11:7]. [This would exclude from consideration bitter herbs of the marsh, which have a distinctive name.]

I.   Said Abayye, "In the case of anything that had a name that was changed prior to the giving of the Torah, [if] then the Torah came along and made particular mention of such a species, [such a species] assuredly falls into the category of something that has a special name. But as to the item under discussion, the name was not changed prior to the giving of the Torah at all." [Slotki: "Whatever had different names prior to the Giving of the Law, and yet the Torah makes specific mention of the general name only obviously (the intention is to exclude such of the species which) have special names; but the former did not have different names before the Giving of the Law at all.]

J.   Raba said, "As to the item or under discussion, the common name is simply 'bitter herb,' [which would then qualify], and they are called 'marsh herbs' because that happens to be where they are found."

VI.

A.   Said R. Hisda, "Joining something to itself does not fall into the category of a bundle. Joining three distinct items together does put the whole into the category of a bundle. As to joining two distinct objects together, there is a dispute of R. Yose and rabbis, for we have learned in the Mishnah:

B.   "The religious requirement concerning the hyssop is that it have three separate stalks, and on them three buds.... R. Yose says, 'The religious requirement of the hyssop is that it have three stalks on which are three buds. Its remnants are two, and its stumps of any size at all' [M. Par. 11:9A-B, I-K].

C.   "Now it is assumed [from Yose's perspective] that since the remnants are two, to begin with two are required. The reason that three are specified is to indicate that the religious requirement [optimally carried out] involves three. [But a bundle is constituted by two items.]

D.   "Since R. Yose takes the view that the religious requirement [optimally carried out] involves three, it follows that in the view of rabbis, three are absolutely necessary. [Slotki, p. 53, n. 13: Thus we see that according to R. Yose, two can constitute a bunch or joining, whereas according to the rabbis three are required.]"

E.   But has it not been taught on Tannaite authority: R. Yose says, "As to a hyssop, if in the first instance it has two stalks and its remnant one, it is unfit [T. Par. 12:1F].

F.   "It is valid only if to being with it has three and its remnants two."

G.   Then reverse the attributions. In R. Yose's view, three are absolutely necessary, and in rabbi's view, three are required only for the optimal carrying out of the religious duty, [but two suffice in fact]. [Then a bundle is two.]

H.   And has it not been taught on Tannaite authority:

I.   As to the hyssop, to begin with it must have two stalks, and its remnants [after use] must consist of at least one, in which case it is valid. It is invalid only if both to begin with and in its remnant it consists of only one stalk.

J.   If its remnant is only one stalk, it is invalid.

K.   But can you then say that a remnant of one stalk is invalid?

L.   Lo, you have just said that a remnant of one stalk is valid!

M.   [13B] Rather I should state the matter as follows: [It is valid] only if to begin with it contains the number that would leave it valid even in its remnant [that is to say,] a single stalk. [Slotki, p. 54, n. 3: Thus it has been shown that the number of three stalks mentioned supra in the name of the rabbis refers only to what is expected for the most proper observance of the commandment. If the number is to be insisted upon as indispensable this last cited baraitha could agree neither with R. Yose nor with the rabbis.]

VII.

A.   Maremar expounded, "As to [reeds tied into bundles which are on sale in] Sura, people may make sukkah-roofing with them. Even though they are bound together. The reason is that [the reed-seller] bound them together only in order to make an accurate count [of what he is selling, and the reeds do not have to be bound together for any substantive purpose. They will certainly be unbound before they are used]."

B.   Said R. Abba, "As to cone-shaped bundles of bulrushes, once one has unbound the top knots, they are suitable for use as sukkah-roofing."

C.   But lo, they are bound on the bottom?

D.   Said R. Pappa, "[We deal with a case in which] he has already loosened them."

E.   R. Huna son of R. Joshua [said], "Even if you say that one has not loosened them, in the case of any bundle that is not made so as to permit carrying, [what is bundled up] is not in the category of a bundle at all."

VIII.

A.   Said R. Abba said Samuel, "As to those vegetables about which it is specified that [by eating them] a person may carry out his obligation [to eat bitter herbs] on Passover, all have the capacity to bring uncleanness [as a Tent, should they overshadow both something susceptible to uncleanness and a corpse]; they do not interpose against uncleanness [as a vertical partition]; they invalidate [sukkah-roofing] if they are used in a sukkah as does an open air space. [That is, just as open space in sukkah-roofing invalidates the sukkah, so do the named vegetables. It is as if they are simply not present.]"

B.   What is the reason?

C.   Since they wither and then crumble and fall, it is as if they were not there to begin with.

IX.

A.   And R. Abba said R. Huna said, "He who cuts grapes for the vat does not render the stalks of the grapes susceptible to uncleanness. [When one cuts grapes for pressing, the stalks attached to the grapes serve no useful purpose. As something useless, they are not susceptible to uncleanness. If one had to use the stalks for some purpose, e.g., to lift the produce, then the stalks would be susceptible to uncleanness.]"

B. R. Menassia bar Gada said R. Huna said, "He who cuts [grain] for sukkah-roofing does not render the stalks of the grain susceptible to uncleanness." [Here too, the stalks serve no purpose in relationship to the grain that is attached to them.]

C. He who states the ruling with regard to cutting stalks all the more so would take that same position in respect to cutting grapes, for one would not want the stalks for the grapes, which[, after all,] are going to absorb the wine.

D. He who states the view regarding cutting grapes will maintain that the stalks of the grapes are not subject to uncleanness [since they are not wanted]. But as to cutting stalks of grain for sukkah-roofing, the stalks will be susceptible to uncleanness. [Why?] For the man surely wants to make use of the stalks for sukkah-roofing so that the grain will not be scattered. [Without the stalks he could not use the grain for the sukkah-roofing at all.]

E. May we say that the view of R. Menassia bar Gada [B] runs parallel to what is under dispute among Tannaite authorities, for it has been taught on Tannaite authority:

F. Boughs of fig-trees holding figs, vines holding grapes, stalks holding ears of corn, palm-branches holding dates -- in the case of all of them, if the inedible part is more than the edible produce, it is valid [for use in sukkah-roofing], and if not, it is invalid.

G. Others say, "Only if the straw is more than both the stalk and the food [put together] [may they be used. The stalk is susceptible to uncleanness, since it is useful.]"

H. Now is it not in the following principle that there is a dispute:

I. One party holds that the stalks are susceptible to uncleanness [and fall into the category of the edible produce and therefore are not suitable for sukkah-roofing unless the inedible part is more than both the stalks and the edible produce], and the other party maintains that the stalks are not susceptible to uncleanness [and so do not enter the same category as the edible produce at all].

J. In the view of R. Menassia bar Gada, does one have to concede that at issue is a principle subject to Tannaite dispute?

L. R. Menassia may reply to you that all parties concur in the principle that he who cuts stalks of grain for sukkah-roofing does not impart susceptibility to uncleanness to the stalks.

M. Here what is at issue? It is a case in which people began to cut the grain intending the harvest for food and then changed their minds and intended the harvest to serve for sukkah-roofing instead. [In that case we have a dispute on the status of the stalks, such as is at issue between "others" and the anonymous ruling. Others hold that the stalk is susceptible to uncleanness as much as the produce, on the principle the change of mind makes no difference. The anomymous ruling is that, since the purpose for which the harvest has been carried out has no bearing upon the use of the stalks in connection with the attached fruit, the stalks fall into the category of useless vegetation and are not susceptible to uncleanness and so may be used for sukkah-roofing.]

N. If the people harvested the crop for food, what is the reason of the [anonymous] rabbis [who do not take account of the status of the stalks and do not regard them as susceptible to uncleanness]?

O. If you should say that rabbis take the view that, since the farmer has changed his mind in their regard and determined to make use of them for sukkah-roofing, what he originally planned to do is null [and of no effect], [that argument cannot stand].

P. For is there a consideration of the nullification of one's original intention when it comes to such a matter [that is, can a mere change of mind affect the status of something as to its susceptibility to uncleanness at all]?

Q. Have we not learned in the Mishnah: All utensils [14A] descend through the effects of human intention into the status of susceptibility to uncleanness but do not ascend from that status unless there is a concrete deed [to carry out the intention of the owner]. A concrete deed may nullify the effect of another concrete deed as well as of the owner's [mere] intention, but a mere change of mind and intention does not nullify the effect either of a concrete deed [with a contrary effect] or even another intention [not confirmed by a concrete deed] [M. Kel. 25:9].

R. Now should you maintain the proposition that the stated rule pertains only to utensils, which are matters of some consequence, but as to stalks of fruit, which serve only what is needful in connection with eating, the rule is that by mere intention they become susceptible to uncleanness, and by mere intention they may be made insusceptible to uncleanness, have we not learned a Mishnah-passage that bears the contrary implication?

S. For we have learned in the Mishnah: The stalks of all produce that is harvested in the threshing floor are insusceptible to uncleanness [since by bringing the produce to the threshing floor, the owner has indicated that he sees no use in the stalks. The previous susceptibility of the stalks thus if nullified by the act of the owner in bringing the produce as a whole to the threshing floor. His mere intention would have had no effect at all.] [M. Uqs. 1:5].

T. Now in the view of him who says that the meaning of "brought to the threshing floor" is simply that the farmer has unloosed the bundles, there is no problem. [Loosening the stalks indicates that the farmer does not have the intention of using the stalks. The mere intention then has the effect of nullifying the previous susceptibility to uncleanness that had affected the stalks, and no concrete action, e.g., at the threshing floor, is required.]

U. But in the view of him who has said that the language of "bringing to the threshing floor" means just that [and is not figurative], what is there to say? [Mere intention, not accompanied by a concrete deed, is not effective.]

V. In the aforecited dispute [concerning the anonymous authority and "others"] we deal with a case in which the farmer actually brought the produce to the threshing floor.

W. If that is the case, what is the reason for the opinion of "others" [who regard the stalks of the produce as susceptible to uncleanness despite the action of the farmer in bringing the produce to the threshing floor? By the farmer's action, should the stalks not have been signified as insusceptible to uncleanness?]

X.   They maintain the view of R. Yose [in the Mishnah-passage just now cited, for] we have learned [in that same Mishnah-paragraph]:

Y.   R. Yose declares [the stalks still] susceptible to uncleanness [even though the farmer has brought the grain to the threshing floor and so indicated that he does not want the stalks any more].

Z.   [But what makes the analogy between the case cited above and the law in M. Uqs. 1:5 so self-evident, so that the matter rule of the one case is deemed applicable to the other?] Why compare them?

AA.   There [in the case of threshing at the threshing floor the reasoning of R. Yose accords with the view of R. Simeon b. Laqish.

BB.   For R. Simeon b. Laqish said, "Since [if the produce has the stalks affixed,] it is more suitable to be turned over with a pitch fork [the stalks remain useful to the farmer, even at the threshing floor]."

CC.   But in the case under discussion here [where one cuts ears for use in the sukkah] what use do the stalks have [that anyone should regard them as useful and so susceptible to uncleanness, as do "others"]?

DD.   They remain useful [Slotki:] to seize hold of them by their haulms when he takes [the sukkah roof] to pieces. [So later on they will be useful, and hence they retain their original susceptibility to uncleanness.]

X.

A.   [Reverting to the] body [of the aforecited passage:]

B.   All stalks of produce which one threshed in the threshing floor are insusceptible to uncleanness.

C.   R. Yose declares them susceptible to uncleanness [M. Uqs. 1:5A-B].

D.   What is the meaning of "threshed in the threshing floor"?

E.   R. Yohanan said, "It means actually threshing them in the threshing floor."

F.   R. Eleazar says, "It means simply unloosening the bundles [of produce, wherever]."

G.   Now with respect to the view of R. Eleazar, who has said that the language, "[Threshing them at the threshing floor]" is [figurative and means only] unloosened the bundles, that is why R. Yose [nonetheless] declares the stalks to be susceptible to uncleanness [since a concrete action in connection with the stalks has not taken place].

H.   But as to R. Yohanan, who has said that one has actually brought the produce to the threshing floor, what basis is there for R. Yose to continue to regard the stalks as susceptible to uncleanness [seeing that the farmer has shown he does not want them any more]?

I.   Said R. Simeon b. Laqish, "Since they remain suitable [for more easily] turning them over with a pitchfork [they are still wanted]."

XI.

A.   Said R. Eleazar, "Why are the prayers of the righteous compared to a pitchfork?

B.   "It is to tell you that just as the pitchfork turns over the grain in the threshing floor moving it from one place to another,

C.   "so the prayers of the righteous move the mind of the Holy One blessed be he, from
      the measure of vindictiveness to the measure of mercy."

Used when bound up, the bundles look not like roofing but like a storage-area. The
bundles in any case may serve as sides or side-posts. Unit I provides a discussion for M.
1:5A-B, a rather complex composition. Unit II proceeds to make its own point about other
sorts of materials used, or not used, for sukkah-roofing. Unit III pursues the same
interest, which works its way through units IV and V. Unit VI takes up the secondary
theme of what does, and does not, constitute a bundle, clarifying M. 1:5A only in a very
general way. Unit VII makes the same sort of contribution. I take it unit VIII is included
because of the appearance, in its catalogue, of use for materials for sukkah-roofing. Unit
IX, with its appended supplements at X and XI, raises a very interesting question. It has
to do with the status of the stalks of pieces of fruit as regards uncleanness. The basic
principle is that if we regard them as useful, they also are susceptible, but if they are held
to be useless, they are insusceptible. This is worked out with exceptional sophistication
throughout, and I see no problems in following either the arguments or the relevance of
the cases adduced In evidence. Units IX-XI ignore the Mishnah-paragraph.

                                        1:6

A.   "They make sukkah-roofing with boards," the words of R. Judah.
B.   And R. Meir prohibits doing so.
C.   [If] one put on top of it a board which is four handbreadths broad, it is
      valid,
D.   so long as one not sleep underneath [that particular board].

I.
A.   Said Rab, "The dispute [at M. 1:6A-B] deals with boards of four handbreadths, for R.
      Meir affirms the precautionary decree [against using such boards, lest they form] a
      roof, while R. Judah does not affirm that precautionary decree.
B.   "But as to boards that are not four handbreadths, all parties concur that use of such
      boards in sukkah-roofing is valid."
C.   And Samuel said, "The dispute concerns boards that are not four handbreadths. But
      if they are four handbreadths, all parties concur that [a sukkah with roofing made up
      of such boards] is invalid."
D.   "If they are less than four" suggests that even if they are less than three, [there is
      an issue]. But in such a case they are merely reeds [and all parties concur they are
      valid]:
E.   Said R. Pappa, "This is the sense of what [Samuel] said: 'If they are four hand-
      breadths broad, all parties concur that [sukkah-roofing made of them] is invalid. If
      they are less than three [handbreadths in breadth] all parties concur that [the
      sukkah-roofing] is valid.'

F.   "Why so? Because there are merely reeds.

G.   "Where there is a dispute [in Samuel's view] it is in the case of boards that are from three to four handbreadths. One party maintains the position that, since they do not encompass a space that would serve as a distinguishable 'place' [or house, that is, four cubits by four cubits], we make no precautionary decree against using such boards], and the other party takes the view that since in this case we cannot invoke the legal fiction that we regard small interstices in a wall, of less than three handbreadths, as though they were filled in and part of the wall [for by definition we deal with boards larger than that size], we do make such a precautionary decree.' [Slotki, p. 59, n. 15: Even if each plank were to be regarded as a mere air space. (The cited fiction) applies only to an air space of less than three handbreadths in width.]

H.   We have learned in the Mishnah: If one put on top of it a board which is four handbreadths broad, it is valid, so long as one not sleep underneath that particular board [M. 1:6C-D].

I.   Now with regard to the view of Samuel, who maintains that there is no dispute in the case of a board less than four handbreadths there is a dispute. If there is a space of four handbreadths in the board, all parties concur that the sukkah-roofing is invalid. Now there is no problem. That is exactly why one should not sleep under such a board.

J.   But in the view of Rab, who holds that where there are four handbreadths in the board, there is a dispute, but if the board is less than four handbreadths, [there is no dispute], for all parties concur that sukkah-roofing is valid, -- in the view of R. Judah, why should someone not sleep under that board at all?

K.   [The reply is simple.] Do you maintain the view that the statement of the Mishnah accords with the position of all parties? The concluding clause accords only with the view of R. Meir.

L.   Two sheets join together [to form four handbreadths and so render sukkah-roofing invalid], [14B] while two boards do not join together [to be regarded as covering more space than can be completely opaque in the sukkah-roofing]. R. Meir says, "Also boards fall into the same category as sheets."

M.   Now in the theory of Samuel, who has said that where there is not a space of four handbreadths, we have a dispute, but if the boards are four handbreadths, all parties concur [that the sukkah-roofing made with them is] invalid, [there is no problem]. What in the cited rule is the meaning of "join together"? It is to "join together to form the form invalidating breadth of four handbreadths."

N.   But in the view of Rab, who has said that where there is a space of four handbreadths in the boards, there is a dispute, but if the breadth of the boards is less than four handbreadths, all parties concur [that the sukkah-roofing made with such boards is] valid, what sort of case [can we deal with in the cited passage]?

O.   If the boards are four handbreadths, why is there an issue of "joining together" at all? If they are not four handbreadths, what difference does it make? They are in the status of mere reeds [which are valid, and no issue of joining together can be evoked to begin with]!

P.   We deal, in point of fact, with boards that are four handbreadths. And what is the consideration as to their joining together? It is joining together to form four cubits on a given side [Slotki, p. 60, n. 7: of the sukkah, where invalid covering does not invalidate the sukkah unless it covers four cubits of space].

Q.   Another version of the same matter:

R.   Now in the theory of Samuel, who has said that where there is not a space of four handbreadths, there is a dispute, but if the boards are four handbreadths, all parties concur [that sukkah-roofing made of such boards] is invalid, what is the sense of "joining together"?

S.   It means "joining together to form the four cubits [of invalid roofing that would render the sukkah-roofing unacceptable if located] at the side."

T.   And in the view of Rab, so far as R. Meir is concerned, what would be the sense of "joining together"? It would be joining together to constitute the four cubits [that would invalidate the roofing if located] at the side.

U.   But as to the view of R. Judah, who has said that even if the boards are four handbreadths in breadth, [the sukkah-roofing] is valid, what [in Rab's view] is the sense of "not joining together"? We deal with mere reeds [and the issue of joining together is not relevant to mere reeds]!

V.   Since the language of "joining together" is assigned to the position of R. Meir, the language of "not joining together" is assigned to R. Judah [even though, from his viewpoint, it is not an issue to begin with].

W.   There is a teaching on Tannaite authority in accord with the position of Rab, and there is a similar teaching in accord with the view of Samuel [as to what is at issue here].

X.   For it has been taught on Tannaite authority in accord with the view of Rab:

Y.   If one has made a sukkah-roofing with boards of cedar, not four handbreadths in breadth, all parties concur that the sukkah-roofing is valid.

Z.   If they are four handbreadths in breadth, R. Meir declares [the roofing] invalid, and R. Judah declares it valid.

AA.   Said R. Judah, "There was the precedent that, in the time of danger, we brought boards of four handbreadths, and we made sukkah-roofing on the balcony and sat down under that roofing [to observe the requirement of sitting in a sukkah, without tipping the Romans off to what we were doing]."

BB.   They said to him, "There is no proof from what people did in the time of danger" [cf. T. Suk. 1:7D-E].

CC.   It was taught on Tannaite authority in accord with the view of Samuel:

DD.   If one made a sukkah roofing out of cedar boards that are four handbreadths, all parties concur that the sukkah is invalid.

EE.   If the boards were not four handbreadths,

FF.   R. Meir declares [the roofing] invalid, and R. Judah declares it valid.

GG. But R. Meir concurs that if there is a space between one board and the next of a breadth of a board, one may put laths between the boards, and the sukkah-roofing will be valid.

HH. R. Judah concedes that if one put on the roofing a board of four handbreadths, the sukkah-roofing is valid, but people may not sleep underneath that board.

II. And if someone slept underneath that board, he will not have fulfilled his obligation.

II.

A. It has been stated on Amoraite authority:

B. If one turned the boards on their sides,

C. R. Huna said, "The roofing nonetheless is invalid.

D. R. Hisda and Rabbah bar R. Huna said, "It is valid."

E. R. Nahman happened to come to Sura. He came up to visit R. Hisda and Rabbah bar R. Huna. They said to him, "If the householder turned the boards on their sides, what is the law?"

F. He said to them, "It is invalid, since they then fall into the category of metal spits." [Slotki, p. 61, n. 15: Since a plank of four handbreadths is invalid, as is any metal object, in whatever position it is placed it is still invalid.]

G. Said R. Huna to them, "Did I not tell you to rule as I do?"

H. They said to him, "Did the master give us a reason for his ruling, when he did not concur in his opinion?"

I. He said to them, "And did you ask me for a reason, which I did not then give you?"

J. May we adduce in support of [Nahman's] view the following statement:

K. [If the sukkah] cannot hold a person's head and the greater part of his body and his table,

L. or if a hole was made in it sufficient for a kid to hump in head first,

M. or if someone put on the roof [of the sukkah] a board four handbreadths broad, even though he did not actually insert into [the sukkah-roofing] more than three handbreadths of the extent of the board,

N. [the sukkah-roofing] is invalid.

O. Now is this [M] not a case in which one turned the board on its side [so that only three handbreadths of the board affected the sukkah roofing? The roofing then is invalid, as Nahman has claimed].

P. No, that is not support for Nahman's position. For with what sort of case do we deal? With one in which the owner placed the broad board at the entrance of the sukkah, so that three handbreadths of the extent of the board are inside [the sukkah, within the roofing] and one handbreadth is outside.

Q. In such a case we invoke the analogy of a lath that protrudes from the sukkah, and in the case of any lath that protrudes from the sukkah, the lath is adjudged as if it is fully within the category of the sukkah. [The result is that the handbreadth of the board that is outside of the sukkah is regarded as if it were inside the sukkah and the four together are not valid for use in sukkah-roofing. Nahman cannot derive support from the law at hand.]

Boards are analogous to normal roofing material for a house, M. 1:6B. C-D form a compromise. A single board may be used, but with the stated functional restriction. Unit I presents a beautifully articulated dispute between Rab and Samuel, clarifying the basic issues of the Mishnah-paragraph. Unit II then raises a secondary issue. The protracted discussion at hand is sustained and cogent.

1:7

A.   [15A] A timber-roofing which had no plastering --

B.   R. Judah says, "The House of Shammai say, 'One loosens it and removes one [board] between each two.'

C.   "And the House of Hillel say, 'One either loosens it or removes one [board] from between each two.'"

D.   R. Meir says, "One removes one from between each two, and does not loosen [the others at all]."

I.

A.   Now [if we ask for the principle behind the rulings at hand, we] assuredly [find no difficulty in accounting for the position of the House of Hillel.] Their ruling derives from the exegesis, "'You shall make' (Deut. 13:16) -- and not from what is ready-made. [On that count one cannot use what is at hand as a house.]"

B.   [Since one must do a specific deed in connection with the sukkah], if one loosens the boards, he carries out a deed, [and] if he removes one board between each two, he carries out a deed. [So either procedure suffices.]

C.   But as to the House of Shammai, what is the principle behind their view?

D.   If the operative criterion is on the count of "'You shall make' (Deut. 13:16) -- and not from what is ready-made," then it should suffice if the householder does one of the two deeds.

E.   If the operative criterion is on the count of a precautionary decree [against using boards for sukkah-roofing lest they appear to form] a roof, then it should suffice if the householder simply removes one of every two boards. [Why require loosening all the boards and also removing one out of every two?]

F.   Indeed, the operative criterion is the precautionary decree [to avoid the appearance of using an ordinary] roof, and this is what the House of Shammai wish to say: "Even though the householder loosens the boards, if he also removes one out of every two, it is valid, and if not, it is not valid."

G.   If that is the case, then let me cite the concluding part of the same paragraph:

H.   R. Meir says, "One removes one from between each two [boards] and does not [have to] loosen the others at all" (M. 1:7D).

I.   R. Meir says precisely what the House of Shammai says [in accord with the foregoing thesis on the sense of the position of the House of Shammai]. [How is this possible?]

J. This is the sense of [Meir's] position: The House of Shammai and the House of Hillel did not dispute about this matter at all. [Both Houses concur that one has to remove one board from between two others.]

K. What, then, does the passage at hand propose to tell us?

L. Is it that R. Meir invokes the precautionary decree on account of the possibility [that the sukkah-roofing will constitute] a roof, and R. Judah does not invoke the consideration of that precautionary decree? But even in that matter both parties already have stated their dispute, for we have learned:

M. "They make sukkah-roofing with boards," the words of R. Judah. And R. Meir prohibits doing so [M. 1:6A-B].

N. [Distinguishing M. 1:6's case from M. 1:7's and so validating the proposed solution,] said R. Hiyya bar Abba said R. Yohanan, "The former of the two paragraphs deals with planed boards, and it was on account of making a precautionary decree against the use of utensils [that are susceptible to uncleanness and so invalid for suk-kah-roofing] that [the Mishnah-passage] rules [as it does]. [Planed boards are not susceptible, since they are flat, and flat wooden objects are insusceptible. But they may serve a purpose and, seeing that, people in their confusion may assume that other utensils also may be used as sukkah-roofing.]"

O. But there is what R. Judah said Rab said, "If one made sukkah-roofing of male arrow-shafts, the roofing is valid. If he did so with female ones [having a recep-table] it is invalid." And [we see] no one made a precautionary decree against using male ones on account of the possibility of using female ones. Here too there should be no precautionary decree against using planed boards on account of the possible use, on that account, of other such utensils [for sukkah-roofing].

P. Accordingly, there is no choice but to concede that, in the former of the two Mishnah-paragraphs, there is a dispute on the count of whether or not there is a precautionary decree on account of [the consideration of using an ordinary] roof [for sukkah-roofing], and in the latter of the two clauses, there is a dispute about the same matter.

Q. [If so], why should the two authorities have disputed about the same principle on two separate occasions?

R. The latter of the two paragraphs represents the view of R. Judah, who [as it were] says to R. Meir, "Why have you made a prohibition against the use of boards on account of a precautionary decree to take account of the possibility of their forming an [ordinary] roof? That thesis belongs to the House of Shammai, who maintain [that we] do [make such a precautionary decree.] But the House of Hillel make no such precautionary decree."

S. [And to this claim], R. Meir would then reply, "The House of Shammai and the House of Hillel had no such dispute."

T. That view of matters poses no problems to Rab, who has said [above M. 1:6 I] that the dispute [of M. 1:6] concerns boards that are four handbreadths. In that case, R. Meir maintains that a precautionary decree does apply, and R. Judah maintains that it does not.

U.   But in the view of Samuel, who has said that the dispute deals even with boards that
      are not four handbreadths, while if they are four handbreadths, all parties concur
      that such boards are simply invalid, as to the latter of the two Mishnah-paragraphs,
      what can possibly be subject to dispute? [Samuel's thesis eliminates the possibility
      of a dispute on the question we have alleged is at issue.]

V.   They dispute about nullifying the effects of a roof. [If we have a roof that has
      served in an ordinary way, are we able to nullify that fact and so transform it into a
      sukkah-roofing, and, if so, how do we do it?]

W.   One authority [Judah] takes the view that one nullifies [the former status of the
      roofing] in the specified manner, and the other authority [Meir] takes the view that
      one cannot nullify [the effects of the former status of the roof] in the specified
      manner.

In this secondary development of M. 1:6, Judah now assigns his view, that boards
may be used, to both Houses and explains how they make it possible even to use a roof
composed of boards. The Shammaites remove every other board and loosen the remaining
ones. The Hillelites do either. Now Meir takes up the position of M. 1:6C-D; boards not
forming a continuous covering are valid. The Talmud is continuous with that serving at M.
1:6, yet clearly focuses upon M. 1:7. The sustained argument is truly impressive.

1:8

A.   He who makes a roof for his sukkah out of spits or with the side-pieces
      of a bed --

B.   if there is a space between them equivalent to their own breadth,

C.   [the sukkah] is valid.

D.   He who hollowed out a space in a haystack to make a sukkah therein --

E.   it is no sukkah.

I.

A.   May we say that the Mishnah-paragraph [at M. 1:8A-C] constitutes a refutation of
      the position of R. Huna, son of R. Joshua?

B.   For it has been taught on Amoraic authority:

C.   [In the case of a fence erected on a temporary basis by a caravan so as to form a
      distinct domain to permit carrying on the Sabbath,] if there is a breach in the
      perimeter that is as long as a standing portion [of the perimeter of the fence, so
      that the fence consists of a standing part, a breach, a standing part, another breach,
      and so on, and the breaches are as long in distance as the parts of the perimeter
      filled in by a standing partition of some sort,]

D.   R. Papa said, "[The fence] is permitted [so as to allow for carrying in the enclosed
      area.]"

E. And R. Huna, son of R. Joshua, said, "It is forbidden." [Slotki, p. 65, n. 11: Now since in the circumstances mentioned a partition is invalid, in the case of the Sabbath why is the roof valid in that of Sukkah?] [That is to say, since we do not invoke the principle that the empty spaces are considered as if they were filled for purposes of forming a partition for the Sabbath, why do we not recognize that same fact? The empty spaces for the sukkah also should not be considered as if they were filled, with the consequence that, for the purposes of sukkah-roofing, the arrangement should be valid, there being adequate open space between one spit or side-piece and the next.]

F. R. Huna, son of R. Joshua, may reply to you, "What is the sense of equivalent to their own breadth? [It is that through the empty space, a lath the exact breadth of one of the laths in use] may easily pass through and come out [so that the required empty space between spit and spit or board and board must be somewhat broader than the mere breadth of the spit or the board itself]."

G. [15B] But lo, one cannot measure matters so exactly [to know, as just now proposed, whether or not the space between the boards is larger than the boards themselves].

H. Said R. Ammi, "We deal with a case in which the householder makes them larger. [That is, M. 1:8A-C speaks of a case in which the space is not exactly equivalent but somewhat larger than the breadth of the boards.]"

I. Raba said, "Even if you say we deal with a case in which the householder did not make the spaces larger, [the arrangement would be valid]. How so? If [the boards or spits] were arranged as web, he puts the valid sukkah-roofing on as woof, or, if the boards were set as woof, he puts the valid sukkah-roofing on as the web." [Slotki, p. 65, n. 16: The valid covering is placed crosswise to the invalid, and, therefore, always exceeds it in volume.]

II.

A. Or with the sidepieces of a bed [M. 1:8A]:

B. May I say that the Mishnah-passage supports the position of R. Ammi bar Tibiomi?

C. For R. Ammi bar Tibiomi said, "If one made sukkah-roofing with worn-out garments, the roofing is invalid." [We cannot use boards which once served as valid utensils, not because they are susceptible any longer to uncleanness, for they are not, since they have ceased to serve their valid function. Rather, merely because they once were susceptible, they remain invalid for use in sukkah-roofing. The same consideration is operative in Ammi's statement on worn-out garments. They once were susceptible. Since they are now mere rags and useless, they are no longer susceptible. Nonetheless, they may not be used.]

D. [No, we may not reach that conclusion. For matters are] in accord with what R. Hanan said Rabbi said, "[At issue at M. Kel. 18:9's reference to side-pieces of a bed is a case involving] the long board and two legs, or the short board and two legs [of a bed]. Here too we deal with the long board and two legs or the short board and two legs. [In line with Rabbi's view at M. Kel. 18:9, these constitute a valid utensil. That is why there is a problem in using them in sukkah-roofing. So Ammi may not derive support for his view of matters at all. That is, it is not that the materials at hand once constituted valid utensils. Under discussion is something that still constitutes a valid utensil.]

E. In what context was the statement of R. Hanan in Rabbi's name made? It was in the following, which we learned in the Mishnah:

F. [16A] "A bed is rendered susceptible to uncleanness only when it is bound together [fully assembled] and is rendered insusceptible only when wholly bound together," the words of R. Eliezer. And sages say, "It is rendered unclean in pieces and may be made clean in pieces" [M. Kel. 18:9C-D]. [Eliezer: The processes of contamination and purification affect the bed only when it is all in one piece. When the parts are separate from one another, there is no consideration of uncleanness.]

G. What are these parts [to which reference has just now been made]?

H. Said R. Hanan said Rabbi, "The long board and two legs, or the short board and two legs."

I. For what would such a contraption be suitable?

J. To put up against a wall for use as a seat or for tying with ropes [to form a couch].

III.

A. [Returning to the] body [of the statement above], R. Ammi bar Tibiomi said, "If one made sukkah-roofing with worn-out garments, the roofing is invalid."

B. What sorts of rags fall into the status of worn-out garments?

C. Said Abayye, "Rags which are not at least three fingerbreadths by three fingerbreadths, which are not suitable for use either by poor people or by rich people."

D. It has been taught on Tannaite authority in accord with the view of R. Ammi bar Tibiomi:

E. As to a reed-mat of rushes or straw, even though the remnants are diminished [to less than the minimum measurement at which they are susceptible to uncleanness], they may not be used for sukkah-roofing.

F. As to a mat of reeds, a large one [ordinarily used as a covering] may serve for sukkah-roofing, and a small one [which may constitute a utensil] may not serve as sukkah-roofing.

G. R. Eliezer says, "Even a small one is susceptible to uncleanness, so people may not use it for sukkah-roofing" [cf. T. Suk. 1:10E-G].

IV.

A. He who hollowed out a space in a haystack [M. 1:8D]:

B. Said R. Huna, "The stated rule applies only to a case in which there is no empty space a handbreadth in height by seven handbreadths [square], but if there is a handbreadth in height and seven handbreadths square, it is suitable to serve as a sukkah." [If the farmer left an empty space of such a size, then the farmer has so constructed the hollow to begin with so that the top part should serve as sukkah-roofing for the empty space beneath. Then he has made a sukkah to begin with. If the space is less than the stated dimensions, by contrast, the roofing is made only as a result of the post-facto hollowing out of the space within. That is not a sukkah constructed for purposes of keeping the holiday.

C. It has been taught to the same effect on Tannaite authority:

D. He who hollows out a space in a haystack so as to make a <u>sukkah</u> for himself -- lo, this constitutes a valid <u>sukkah.</u>

E. Yet lo, have we not learned to repeat the passage in the following formulation: It is <u>not</u> a valid <u>sukkah</u>?

F. [There is then a contradiction between the two passages, and would that contradiction] not yield an inference in support of the claim of R. Huna [that there are conditions in which such a hollowed out space is valid, just as there are conditions in which it is not]?

G. It does indeed yield that inference.

H. There are those who present the cited passage as an objection:

I. We have learned: <u>He who hollowed out a space in a haystack to make a sukkah therein -- it is no sukkah</u> [M. 1:8D-E].

J. And lo, it has been taught on Tannaite authority: It is a valid <u>sukkah!</u>

K. Said R. Huna, "There is no contradiction between the two passages. In the one case [in which it is valid], it is a space a handbreadth high by seven squared handbreadths, and in the other case [in which it is not a valid arrangement] it is where there is no empty space a handbreadth in height by seven squared handbreadths."

A-C go over the ground of M. 1:7D. The <u>sukkah</u> of D-E has not been constructed with the Festival in mind (M. 1:1L-N); or it appears to be a storehouse. In any case, D-E are a misplaced, miscellaneous item. Unit I brings the present passage into confrontation with its exact opposite, concerning the fence erected for creating a distinct domain. The same principle applies in both cases, namely, the fictive filling in of small gaps in a fence, roofing, or partition. If we do not fill in such a gap in one case, we ought not to think the principle applies in the other. On that basis, the issue is worked out, and, as usual, the correct solution is to propose a distinction between the one case and the other. Unit II carries on the same exercise of bringing law in one topic to bear upon law in some other, and this is done by invoking the shared principle applicable to both. Unit III then reverts to the explication of the law as it applies to the <u>sukkah</u> in particular. Unit IV then completes the analysis of the Mishnah-passage specifying limitations to the invalidity of the arrangement specified in the Mishnah; this further explains the underlying principle.

1:9A-G

A. <u>He who suspends the sides from above to below --</u>

B. <u>if the [the partitions] are three [or more] handbreadths above the ground,</u>

C. <u>[the sukkah] is invalid.</u>

D. <u>[If he builds the sides] from the ground upward,</u>

E. <u>if [they are] ten handbreadths above the ground,</u>

F. <u>[the sukkah] is valid.</u>

G.   R. Yosé says, "Just as [the required height] from below to above [when
      the wall is built up from the ground] is ten handbreadths, "so [the
      required height] from above to below [when the wall is suspended from
      above toward the ground] is ten handbreadths [even though the bottom is
      not within three handbreadths of the ground]. [The operative criterion is
      the height of the partitions.]"

I.

A.   What is at issue? One authority maintains the view that a suspended partition
      validates [the sukkah], and the other authority holds that a suspended partition does
      not validate [the sukkah, in which case it must lie within three handbreadths above
      the ground. If the lower side is within three handbreadths of the ground, we invoke
      the legal fiction that it is connected to or resting on the ground. If the distance is
      greater, we cannot do so.]

B.   We have learned there:

C.   A cistern which is between two courtyards --

D.   they do not draw water from it on the Sabbath, unless they made for it a partition
      ten handbreadths high, whether it is above, beneath, or within its rim.

E.   Rabban Simeon b. Gamaliel says [16B], "The House of Shammai say, 'Below.' And
      the House of Hillel say, 'Above.'"

F.   Said R. Judah, "The partition should not be expected to be more powerful than the
      wall which is between them" [M. Er. 8:6]. [Since the cistern is located beneath a
      wall dividing two courtyards, it is in the domain of neither, so people may not draw
      water from it. The theory of the anonymous rule is that a partition must be placed
      in the cistern itself, so as to distinguish the shares of the two courtyards, respec-
      tively. The partition may be above the water in the cistern, below its surface, or at
      the rim of the cistern, not touching the water-surface. Simeon b. Gamaliel has a
      Houses' dispute on this matter. Judah rejects the entire conception. If the partition
      is a suitable division, so too is the wall between the two courtyards, so there is no
      need for a partition at all.]

G.   Said Rabbah bar bar Hana said R. Yohanan, "R. Judah accords with the principle of
      R. Yose, who has said that a suspended partition validates [the sukkah, as a proper
      wall]."

H.   But that is not the case at all. R. Judah does not accord with the principle of R.
      Yose, and R. Yose does not accord with the principle of R. Judah.

I.   R. Judah does not accord with the principle of R. Yose: R. Judah's ruling pertains
      only to the case of creating a common domain out of courtyards, authority for which
      derives only from the rabbis. But in the present case, in which a sukkah is involved,
      authority for which derives from the Torah, he would not invoke the stated
      principle. [So there is a clear distinction between the one case and the other].

J.   And R. Yose does not concur with the principle of R. Judah. R. Yose rules here as
      he does in the case of the sukkah, because it is a religious duty carried out by an act

of commission. But in the case of the Sabbath, which is subject to a prohibition the violation of which is penalized by stoning he would not invoke that same principle, [since he sees the latter case as more stringent than the former].

K. Now if you raise the objection, Then as to the precedent in the case of Sepphoris [cited presently, in which a suspended partition was regarded as acceptable in the case of the Sabbath], in accord with which of the two authorities was that ruling made? For it could not conform with the principle of R. Yose.

L. Rather, it was on the instruction of R. Ishmael, the son of R. Yose.

M. What was that precedent? When R. Dimi came, he said, "One time the people [of a courtyard, not preparing the erub to unite their property] forget and did not bring the scroll of the Torah on the eve of the Sabbath [Friday]. The next day [the Sabbath itself] they spread out sheets on top of pillars and carried the scroll of the Torah, and they read in it. [The scroll of the Torah was in one of the houses of the courtyard in which the synagogue was located. The people forgot to prepare the fictive collective meal which would have made the house of the courtyard along with the courtyard into a single domain. Their solution is as described, and in that way the people created a single domain.]

N. Did they really spread out the sheets? How did they bring [the sheets] on the Sabbath [to the pillars]?

O. Rather, they found sheets [where they were lying] and spread them out, and brought the scroll of the Torah and read in it. [The objection thus is worked out. Since Ishmael was resident-authority in Sepphoris, the ruling accorded with his principle, not Yose's.]

II.

A. Said R. Hisda said Abimi, "A matting somewhat more than four handbreadths [in length] validates a sukkah as a partition."

B. What does one do with it?

C. He suspends it in the middle [of the space between the roofing and the ground, less than three handbreadths from the bottom, less than three handbreadths from the top, since whatever lies within three handbreadths is treated as if it extends the requisite distance [by fictive extension].

D. That is perfectly self-evident.

E. [Nonetheless, it was necessary to make it explicit, for] what might you have said? We invoke the principle of fictive extension for one side [of a partition], but we do not do so for both sides. So we are informed that that is not the case, [and we invoke the fictive extension for both sides.]

F. An objection was raised on the basis of the following teaching: A matting seven handbreadths and a bit more validates the partition in the case of a sukkah. [Hence one a bit more than four would not, since we invoke the fictive extension only for one, not for both sides.]

G. When that statement was made on Tannaite authority, it was made with reference to a very tall sukkah, [that is, one taller than ten handbreadths in height. The mat

then is suspended from the roof and comes within three handbreadths of the ground
and so forms a wall ten handbreadths high on the principle of fictive extension.]

H.   What then did the statement serve to tell us?

I.   That one suspends walls from top to bottom, in accord with the principle of R. Yose
[at M. 1:9G].

III.

A.   Said R. Ammi, "A board a bit wider than four handbreadths serves to validate as a
wall in the case of a <u>sukkah</u>."

B.   [The householder] places it less than three handbreadths from the [existing] wall,
since whatever is less than three handbreadths from the wall is deemed, by fictive
extension, to be attached to the wall [and so the wall of seven handbreadths is
fictively obtained].

C.   What does this teaching tell us [that we should not otherwise have known]?

D.   Lo, it informs us that the minimum extent of a short <u>sukkah</u> is seven handbreadths.

M. 1:9D-F merely restate M. 1:1C, and they are inserted only to pave the way for
Yose's argument, G. He permits the wall to be suspended, on the principle of fictive
extension. Unit I introduces the mirror-ruling to the one at hand, that at M. Er. 8:6, and
asks about the positions of the authorities of each Mishnah-paragraph on the ruling in the
contrary passage. Units II and III then illustrate the law given at our Mishnah-paragraph,
showing us how it applies.

1:9H - 1:10

H.   <u>[17A] [If] one sets the sukkah-roofing three handbreadths from the walls</u>
<u>[of the sukkah], [the sukkah] is invalid.</u>

M. 1:9

A.   <u>A house, [the roof of] which was damaged, and on [the gaps in the roof of</u>
<u>which] one put sukkah-roofing --</u>

B.   <u>if the distance from the wall to the sukkah-roofing is four cubits, it is</u>
<u>invalid [as a sukkah].</u>

C.   <u>And so too, [is the rule for] a courtyard which is surrounded by a</u>
<u>peristyle.</u>

D.   <u>A large sukkah, [the roofing of which] they surrounded with some sort of</u>
<u>material with which they do not make sukkah-roofing --</u>

E.   <u>if there was a space of four cubits below it,</u>

F.   <u>it is invalid [as a sukkah].</u>

M. 1:10

I.

A.   What need do I have for all of these rulings [M. 1:9H, 1:10A-C, D-F]?

B.   If I had in hand only the ruling concerning a house, the roof of which was damaged, I might have supposed that, since the walls of the house were made for use in the house [and designated not as partitions for a sukkah], [the rule applies there]. But as to a courtyard which is surrounded by a peristyle, in which case the partitions were not made for use by the peristyle, I might have said the law does not apply. So it was necessary to make the rule explicit for both cases.

C.   Had I furthermore known only these two rulings, I might have supposed that in these cases, valid sukkah-roofing was used [so I invoke the notion that the intervening space is fictively deemed filled up]. But in the case of a large sukkah, which was surrounded by something with which people do not make sukkah-roofing, since the roofing involved is invalid, I might have said that we do not invoke [the principle of fictively filled up open space].

D.   So it was necessary to make all three rulings explicit.

II.

A.   Said Rabbah, "I came upon the rabbis of the household of Rab [teaching in Rab's tradition, at Sura] in session and saying, 'An unfilled gap of airspace invalidates a sukkah if it is three handbreadths wide, [and] invalid sukkah-roofing invalidates a sukkah if it is four handbreadths.'

B.   "Now I said to them, 'How do you know that an unfilled gap of airspace invalidates a sukkah at a measure of three handbreadths?

C.   "'It is because we have learned, If one sets the sukkah-roofing three handbreadths from the walls of the sukkah, the sukkah is invalid [M. 1:9H].

D.   "'As to invalid sukkah-roofing, however, it should invalidate only at a measure of four cubits [not handbreadths!], for we have learned: A house, the roof of which was damaged, and on the gaps of the roof of which one put sukkah-roofing — if the distance from the wall to the sukkah-roofing is four cubits, it is invalid as a sukkah [M. 1:10A-B].'

E.   "And they said to me, 'But this represents an exception. For both Rab and Samuel have said that [with reference to M. 1:10A-B], [the reason that putting suk-kah-roofing on the damaged roof] is on account of the fictive theory of the curved wall, which reaches [the exposed roof. That is to say, we imagine that the walls distant from the exposed portion of the roof are curved so as to reach the exposed portion and so form a partition for the sukkah-roofing placed at the exposed part of the roof].'

F.   "And I said to them, 'What would the law be in the case of the use of invalid sukkah-roofing less than four handbreadths in area, and an unfilled gap of airspace less than three handbreadths? It most certainly would be valid.

G.   "'If, then, one filled the space with spits, what would be the rule?

H.   "'It would be invalid. [The spits are invalid because they are susceptible to uncleanness and so may not be used for sukkah-roofing. Now, filling the space with them, the man has spread more than four handbreadths of invalid roofing. But when the space was open to the air, the sukkah-roofing was valid.]

I. "'Now should not an open gap of airspace, which invalidates at a measure of three handbreadths, be equivalent to invalid sukkah-roofing, which invalidates at a measure of four handbreadths? [So the air space here would invalidate the sukkah-roofing even if it is less than three handbreadths.]'

J. "And they said to me, 'If so, then in accord with your reasoning, which maintains that invalid sukkah-roofing renders the sukkah invalid only if it covers a space of four cubits, what would the law be in the case of invalid roofing less than four cubits and a gap of open airspace less than three? Would this not be a valid sukkah? Yet if one filled the gaps with spits, what would be the rule? It would be invalid.

K. "'Now should not the open gap of airspace, which invalidates the sukkah at a measure of three handbreadths, be in the same category as sukkah-roofing, which, if it is invalid, invalidates the sukkah if it covers an area of four cubits? [So the same argument applies to Rabbah's position, mutatis mutandis!]'

L. "And I said to them, 'How now! [The two cases are hardly comparable.] Now in my view -- and I take the position that the requirement is [at least] four cubits [of invalid sukkah-roofing will serve to invalidate the sukkah] [17B] because there is a fixed measurement [dictated by revelation on the minimum size of a sukkah, which is four cubits] -- in the present case there is not a standard measure of valid area. Here [in the case at hand] there is no standard measurement. Since the requisite sizes are not the same for the two dimensions [that is to say, invalid sukkah-covering has one measure, invalid gaps of air space in the roofing are subject to a different measure], the two dimensions [of invalid space] simply do not join together [to invalidate the entire sukkah].

M. "'But in your view -- and you take the position that [the requisite measures do not derive from revealed tradition but merely from] the principle of division [that is to say, the minimum size of a distinct place is four handbreadths, and if there are four handbreadths of an invalid roofing or four handbreadths of no roofing at all, the net effect is the same, that is, the invalidation of the sukkah], -- what difference does it make whether the [sukkah is subject to division into spaces invalidly covered on account of] invalid roofing or on account of a gap in the air space? [That is how I distinguish my reductio ad absurdum of your position, and your doing the same to mine.]'"

N. Said Abayye to him, "And in the view of the master [Rabbah], granted that the minimum measurements applying for each purpose are not equivalent in the case of a large sukkah, in a small sukkah are they not equivalent to one another? [Surely they are]!" [Slotki, p. 73, n. 6: A sukkah of minimum size, i.e., of seven hand-breadths square, is invalid if there are either three handbreadths of invalid covering or of air space; why then should not the two combine?]

O. He said to him, "In that case [of the small sukkah] the operative consideration is not that the applicable measurements are the same, but that to begin with, [if the parts of the roof are covered with invalid roofing or with no roofing at all, in either case] the minimum size of valid sukkah-roofing is not available. [The standard requisite measure is different for each category, and they cannot combine, even though they produce the same effect.]"

P. And is it the case that when requisite measures for diverse dimensions are not the same, then areas that are invalid [on distinct counts] do not join together? [Slotki: Do we not then combine standards when they are unequal?]

Q. And we have learned in the Mishnah: Cloth [of wool or flax] is subject to uncleanness if it is at least three by three handbreadths square... sacking -- four by four, leather -- five by five, a mat -- six by six [M. Kel. 27:2]. [These dimensions indicate the smallest size of a given piece of material that people will find useful, hence that is susceptible to uncleanness. We shall now see that, if we have invalid cloth of less than the requisite measure and invalid sacking of less than requisite measure, the two join together to form the requisite measure of susceptible material, in accord with the minimum size applying to the second, the larger, of the two materials.]

R. In that connection it was taught on Tannaite authority: Cloth joins together with sacking, sacking with leather, leather with matting. [And yet, we see, each is subject to its own minimum dimensions.]

S. In that case, the operative consideration is made explicit, for R. Simeon has said, "What is the reason? Since all of them are subject to the same mode of uncleanness, namely, that imparted when a person subject to uncleanness as a zab sits on any of them. [Hence, the different sorts of materials join together because the same mode of transfer of uncleanness pertains to all of them.]"

T. For we have learned in the Mishnah: He who cuts off from any of these items [susceptible to the uncleanness imparts as explained] a square handbreadth [the minimum size of fabric used for sitting,] the patch which is cut off is susceptible to uncleanness [from the prescribed mode of uncleanness] [M. Kel. 27:4A-B].

U. For what use is a piece of material a handbreadth squared?

V. R. Simeon b. Laqish said in the name of R. Yannai, "It can be made into a patch for the saddle of an ass."

III.

A. In Sura, that is how they presented the preceding teaching [Rab's view that four handbreadths of invalid roofing renders a sukkah useless]. In Nehardea they taught it in another way entirely. [This is what follows]. Here we see that Samuel, not Rab, is the one who says that under some conditions the requisite measure of invalid area is a more stringent area of four handbreadths, not four cubits. Both Rab and Samuel take the same view, but the authority behind that view has to be determined. Samuel's school, in Nehadrea transmits the matter differently, as we shall now see.]

B. Said R. Judah said Samuel, "If there is invalid sukkah-roofing in the middle of the roof of a sukkah, it invalidates the sukkah if it is four handbreadths, while if it is located at the side of the roofing, it invalidates [only] if it is four cubits in breadth [a much more considerable measure may then be invalid without invalidating the sukkah]."

C.   And Rab said, "Whether it is on the side or in the middle, the requisite measure is four cubits."

D.   [We now repeat the exercise of M. 1:6 I for this new issue.] We have learned in the Mishnah: If one put on top of sukkah-roofing a board which is four handbreadths broad, it is valid [so long as one not sleep underneath that particular board] [M. 1:6C-D].

E.   Now the cited passage surely poses no problems for Rab, who has said that, whether the invalid sukkah-roofing is in the middle or at the side [of the sukkah-roof], the invalidating measure is four cubits. On that account the board is valid [since the invalid portion, comprised by the board, is only four handbreadths].

F.   But in the view of Samuel, who has said that if the invalid roofing is in the middle of the sukkah-roof, the measure defining the area that will invalidate the roof is four handbreadths, why should the board be valid? [Surely we have four handbreadths of invalid roofing!]

G.   [In Samuel's behalf, we reply:] Here with what sort of case do we deal? With a board placed at the side [of the sukkah-roof, not in the middle].

H.   Come and take note: Two sheets join together [to form four handbreadths and so render sukkah-roofing invalid], while two boards do not join together [to be regarded as covering more space than can be completely opaque in the sukkah-roofing]. R. Meir says, "Also boards fall into the same category as sheets" [cf. M. 1:6 I L].

I.   Now in accord with the version of matters that has Rab say, "Whether at the middle or at the side, the invalidating measure is four cubits," what would be the sense of "join together"? It would mean, "Join together to make up the four cubits [of invalidating roofing, wherever it is located]."

J.   But in accord with that version of matters that has Rab say, "If the invalidating sukkah-roofing is at the center, the minimum measure of invalid roofing [that will disqualify the sukkah is four handbreadths," what sort of case can be in mind [in the cited dispute]?

K.   If the area of invalid roofing adds up to four handbreadths, why raise the issue of joining together at all? And if the invalid area is less than four handbreadths, they add up to nothing more than reeds! [Reeds are valid, and if the boards are less than four handbreadths, they are nothing more than reeds. So what is at issue?]

L.   In any event we deal with a case in which the boards are four handbreadths, and what is the sense of "join together"? It means that they join together to form the requisite measure of four cubits that will invalidate the sukkah-roofing if the improper area is located at the side of the sukkah-roof.

M.   Come and take note of the following [M. 1:6 I DD ff.]:

N.   If one has made a sukkah-roofing with boards of cedar which are four handbreadths broad, all parties concur that the sukkah-roofing is invalid.

O. If they are not four handbreadths, R. Meir declares the roofing invalid, and R. Judah declares it valid.

P. [18A] And R. Meir concedes that if, between one board and the next, there is a space of a breadth of a board, one may put laths between the boards, and the sukkah-roofing will be valid.

Q. Now in the view of him who has said that the invalidating measure of improper sukkah-roofing, whether it is located at the side or in the middle of the sukkah-roof, is four cubits, we can understand why the sukkah will be valid [since the boards are not four cubits wide].

R. But in the view of the one who has said that if the invalid portion of the roof in the middle if is four handbreadths, then why should the arrangement here be valid?

S. Said R. Huna, son of R. Joshua, "Here we deal with a sukkah which is of a measure of only eight cubits exactly. Now the householder places a board and a lath, a board and a lath, a board and a lath, on the one side, and a board and a lath, a board and a lath, a board and a lath, on the other side. In this arrangement, therefore, there are two laths in the middle." [Slotki, p. 76, n. 1: Eight cubits equal four-eight handbreadths which are duly covered by the six planks (six times four is twenty-four handbreadths), and the latter which also total six times four is twenty-four handbreadths, but the alternation of planks and laths is as follows (P is plank, L is lath): PLPLPLLPLPLP. The eight handbreadths in the middle represented by LL constitute a valid sukkah, the next being regarded as continuations of the walls, since on any side they are less than four cubits in extent.]"

IV.

A. Said Abayye, "An open airspace in the roofing of a sukkah of three handbreadths in a large sukkah, which one has cut down, whether with reeds or spits, is validly diminished [so that the sukkah-roofing is now valid].

B. "In the case of a small sukkah, if this is done with reeds, it constitutes a valid act of diminution of the open space, but if this was done with spits, this does not constitute a valid diminution of the open space." [Slotki, p. 76, n. 6: Because the airspace and the spits, which together extend along three handbreadths, cannot be regarded as a valid part of the roof, and the sukkah (being of the minimum size) is thus reduced to less than the prescribed minimum.]"

C. This rule [that a gap of less than three handbreadths does not invalidate sukkah-roofing, A] applies when the gap is at the side, but if it is located in the middle of the sukkah-roofing, it is the rule is subject to dispute between R. Aha and Rabina.

D. One of them said, "We invoke the principle of fictive extension of a valid area of covering -- the walls of the sukkah -- to an invalid area when the invalid area is located in the middle of the roof."

E. The other has said, "We do not invoke the principle of the fictive extension when the open area is in the middle of the sukkah-roofing."

F. What is the reason behind the view of him who has said that we do invoke the principle of the fictive extension of the walls even to the middle of the sukkah-roofing?

G.   As it has been taught on Tannaite authority:

H.   A beam which projects from one wall and does not reach the other wall, and so too in the case of two beams, one which projects from one wall and the other which projects from the other wall but do not reach one another, if the distance between them is less than three handbreadths, one does not have to bring another beam [and place it on top of them to complete a fictive doorway], but if it is three handbreadths, one has to bring another beam and place it on top of them to complete the covering] [T. Er. 1:6]. [This supports the view that we do invoke the principle of the fictive extension of the beams if the space between them is less than three handbreadths. In the case at hand, also, we invoke that same principle.]

I.   And the other party [who denies that, in the matter of the sukkah, we invoke the fictive extension]?

J.   The case of the beams is different [from the matter of the sukkah, and we impose a lenient ruling by invoking the principle of fictive extension, because, in the case of the beams, we deal with an arrangement which to begin with] derives from the authority of rabbis [and so allows for a more lenient application of the law. By the law of the Torah one could carry objects in the area to be joined by the cross-beam even without the erection of the cross-beam signifying that the area affected by it is a single domain. Rabbis imposed the requirement of creating the single domain.]

K.   What is the basis for the position of the one who maintains that we do not invoke the principle of fictive extension when the gap is located in the middle of the sukkah-roofing?

L.   As we have learned in the Mishnah:

M.   A hatchway which is in the midst of the house in the roof, open to the air, and there is in it an open space of a square handbreadth -- uncleanness is in the house under the roof, not under the hatchway -- that which is lying on the ground directly below the hatchway is clean. Uncleanness is directly below the hatchway -- the house is clean [M. Oh. 10:1A].

N.   If there is not a square handbreadth of open space in the hatchway -- uncleanness is in the house -- that which is directly under the hatchway is clean. Uncleanness is directly under the hatchway -- the house is clean [unaffected by the corpse-matter] [M. Oh. 10:2A]. [M. Oh. 10:1 thus shows that the space of the hatchway is not regarded as fictively covered by the roof. If we were to invoke the principle of fictive extension of the roof, then we should have to rule that the hatchway, a handbreadth square, is fictively covered as well, and so the roof is treated as extended over the corpse-matter located underneath the hatchway, with the result that, under all circumstances, everything under the roof, including what is under the hatchway, is unclean. Why? We have a common roof over all.]

O.   And the other party? [How does he account for the failure to invoke the principle of fictive extension?]

P.   The laws of transmitting uncleanness form a distinct category [and do not follow the principles effective for the sukkah], for that is how the tradition has been learned.

V.

A. [With reference to M. 1:10A], R. Judah bar Ilai expounded, "A house, the roof of which was damaged, and on the gaps in the roof of which one put sukkah-roofing --

B. "it is a valid arrangement."

C. R. Ishmael, son of R. Yose, said before him, "Master, amplify [this ruling]. This is how father [Yose] spelled it out: 'If it is a space of four cubits [between the gap and the walls of the house], it will remain invalid, but if it is less than four cubits, it is valid' [just as at M. 1:10B]."

D. R. Judah b. Ilai expounded, "A certain kind of fish is permitted."

E. R. Ishmael, son of R. Yose, said before him, "Master, amplify [this ruling]. This is how father [Yose] amplified it out: 'If it comes from such and such a place, it is forbidden, but if it comes from such and such a place, it is permitted.'"

F. That is in line with what Abayye said, "A certain kind of fish which comes from the Bab river is permitted."

G. What is the reason? If you say that the water flows swiftly there, and in the case of an unclean fish, because it has no backbone, it cannot survive a swift current.

H. [and if you say that the reason is that] the water is salty, and since the unclean fish has no scales, it cannot survive in salt water, lo, we see that that sort of fish does survive in salt water.

I. So the operative consideration must be that there is a lot of mud in the water and unclean fish do not breed in it.

J. Said Rabina, "These days, when the Ethan and the Gamda rivers flow into it [so there is clear water, no mud], it is forbidden."

VI.

A. It has been stated on Amoraic authority:

B. If one put sukkah-roofing over a peristyle [covered hall in front of a house] which has door-frames, the arrangement forms a valid sukkah.

C. If it had no door frames,

D. Abayye said, "It is valid."

E. Raba said, "It is invalid."

F. Abayye said, "It is valid. [18B] We invoke the fictive principle that the edge of the roof descends and closes off [the sides and so forms a valid partition on the sides of the peristyle]."

G. Raba said, "It is invalid. We do not invoke the fictive principle that the edge of the roof descends and closes off [the sides]."

H. Said Raba to Abayye, "In accord with your position, holding that the edge of the roof of the peristyle is seen fictively to descend and close off the sides [forming a valid partition-wall for the sukkah], would you say that is the case even if the middle wall is taken away? [What is one built a sukkah with only two opposed sides? Do we invoke the principle that the roofing fictively descends to form the missing partitions? Surely not! (cf. Slotki, p. 78, n. 9)]."

I.   He said to him, "In that case I concede your point, because such a construction is
        tantamount to an alley-way which is open at both ends. [We could not regard it as a
        valid sukkah, even if it were covered over on the top with sukkah-roofing.]"

J.   May we propose that Abayye and Raba differ on the same matter as is at issue
        between Rab and Samuel?

K.   For it has been taught on Tannaite authority:

L.   If there was a peristyle in a field [with a roof but no walls],

M.   Rab said, "[On the Sabbath] it is permitted to carry about the entire area [as a
        single, enclosed domain], for we maintain the view that the end of the roof fictively
        descends and closes off the sides, [so completing a properly enclosed domain]."

N.   And Samuel said, "One may on the Sabbath carry in that area only within [the
        ordinarily permitted space of] four cubits [which in any event one may utilize for
        carrying in the public domain. We do not have a private domain in the present case,
        for] we do not invoke the principle that the edge of the roof fictively descends and
        closes off the area [so forming a private domain]." [It would now appear as though
        Abayye concurs with Rab, and Raba with Samuel.]

O.   In regard to the position of Samuel, all parties concur [including Abayye]. [19A]
        Where there is a dispute, it is in regard to the position of Rab.

P.   Abayye accords with the principle of Rab, and [Raba will distinguish his position in
        regard to the peristyle used as a sukkah from the one applying to the framework
        located in the middle of a field.]

Q.   Raba will say to you, "Rab spoke of a case only in which there are partitions
        attached to the peristyle. But here, in which there are no partitions affixed to the
        peristyle, he would not [make such a ruling]. [The edge of the roof of the peristyle
        is fictively held to descend for the purposes of carrying on the Sabbath]."

R.   We have learned in the Mishnah: And so too is the rule for a courtyard which is
        surrounded by a peristyle [M. 1:10C].

S.   Why should that be the case? May we not invoke the rule that the edge of the roof
        fictively descends and closes off the sides?

T.   Raba interpreted the matter in accord with Abayye's view that [Slotki:] this is a
        case where one made the beams level. [Slotki, p. 79, n. 13: The beams of the
        sukkah-covering were not placed over the exedra [peristyle] roof, so that the edge of
        the latter was visible within the sukkah but on a level with it.]

VII.

A.   In Sura that is how they presented the preceding teaching [concerning the opinions
        of Abayye and Raba].

B.   In Pumbedita this is how they framed matters:

C.   If one put sukkah-roofing over a peristyle which has no door-frames, all parties
        concur that it is invalid.

D.   If it had door-frames,

E.   Abayye said, "It is a valid arrangement."

F.   Raba said, "It is invalid."

G.　Abayye said, "It is valid, because we invoke the principle of fictive descent [so that the roof is deemed to descend and form the requisite partitions].

H.　Raba said, "It is invalid, because we do not invoke the principle of fictive descent [of the roof to form the requisite partitions]."

I.　The decided law accords with the former [VI] of the two versions.

VIII.

A.　R. Ashi came upon R. Kahana, who was placing sukkah-roofing on a peristyle which had no door-frames.

B.　He said to him, "Does not the master concur with that which Raba said, 'If it has door-frames, it is valid, if it did not have door-frames, it is invalid'?"

C.　He pointed out to him [Slotki:] that a door-frame was visible within though level on the outside, or visible from without, though level from within. [Slotki, p. 80, n. 7: The peristyle had a door-frame no less than a handbreadthwide which commenced at the corner of the sukkah and extended outside the sukkah, being visible only from without.]

D.　For it has been taught on Amoraic authority:

E.　If [a side-post, placed at the edge of an alley to form a fictive gateway to permit the courtyards of the entire alley-way to be regarded as a single domain for purposes of carrying on the Sabbath] was visible from outside but was level on the inside, it is regarded as a valid side post.

F.　And the side-post is in the same category as a door frame.

IX.

A.　It has been taught on Tannaite authority:

B.　A lath which protrudes from a sukkah is regarded as equivalent to the sukkah [so that, if one sits under such a lath, he carries out his obligation to sit in the sukkah itself].

C.　What is a concrete case of a lath that protrudes from a sukkah?

D.　Said Ulla, "We deal with reeds that protrude from the back of the sukkah."

E.　But lo, [to form a valid sukkah], we require [not only roofing but] three partitions!

F.　We deal with a case in which there are such partitions.

G.　But we require also [a covered area that constitutes a] validly covered [roof] [so how can the mere lath suffice]?

H.　We deal with such a case.

I.　And lo, we require a case in which the shade cast by the sukkah-roofing is more than the light let through by it.

J.　We deal with such a case.

K.　If so, what in the world does the cited statement tell us [that we otherwise would not know? We have a totally valid sukkah anyhow.]

L.　What might you have said? Since the laths were placed for the purpose of filling up a roof for the inside of the sukkah, and were not prepared for the purpose of covering space outside of the sukkah, I might have said that such an arrangement is in any case invalid, [since it is contrary to the intent, for the laths, of the householder].

M. Accordingly, we are informed that that is not the rule.

N. Both Rabbah and R. Joseph say, "Here [at B] we speak of reeds that protrude in front of a sukkah [with three sides] and run along the front of one of the sukkah-walls.

O. What might you have said? In such a case we do not have the requisite area of sukkah-roofing that renders a sukkah valid.

P. So we are informed that we do not invoke that consideration here.

Q. Rabbah bar bar Hana said R. Yohanan [said], "The ruling was necessitated only to deal with a case of a sukkah, in the greater part of which the shade cast by the sukkah-roofing was more than the light let through it, and the smaller part of which was such that the light let through by the sukkah-roofing was greater than the shade cast by it.

R. "What might you have said? Let the sukkah be treated as invalid in that part of it in which the light was greater than the shade.

S. "So we are informed that that is not the case."

T. [If this is how we interpret the statement at hand, then] what can be the sense of "protruding"?

U. "Protruding from the status of that which validates the sukkah [namely, the requisite trait of having more shade than light cast by the sukkah-roofing]."

V. R. Oshaia said, "The ruling at hand was necessitated only to deal with a sukkah-roofing that is unfit, which covered an area of less than three handbreadths of a small sukkah [one less than seven handbreadths in all].

W. "What in such a case is meant by 'protruding'?

X. "'Protruding' from the status of being a sukkah at all!"

Y. R. Hoshaia objected, "Why not regard the invalid roofing as no more worthy of consideration than a gap in the sukkah-roofing. Will a gap in the sukkah roofing of less than three handbreadths in a small sukkah invalidate the sukkah? [Surely not! Then why make such a statement at all?]"

Z. Said R. Abba to him, "In the former case [of invalid roofing] the improperly covered roof joins together with the properly covered roof, so people may sleep under that space [and so carry out their obligation], while in the latter case [the gap in the covering], the uncovered space joins together with covered space, but people may not sleep under that uncovered space."

AA. But can there be a case in which an invalid area joins together with a valid area, and yet the invalid area itself remains invalid [such as Abba has just now posited]?

BB. Said R. Isaac b. Eliashab, "This is indeed the case. [19B] Mud that is sufficiently diluted to flow will prove the case. For it joins together [with valid water in an immersion pool] to form the requisite volume of forty seahs of water, yet a person who immerses in such a pool [with the requisite volume of liquid, but inadequate contents] does not gain credit for his act of immersion [and remains unclean, while the volume of the pool by itself is valid]. [That would be a perfectly parallel case]."

M. 1:9H is independent. The sukkah-roofing must be close to the wall and not suspended in the center of the ceiling. M. 1:10A-B restate the point of M. 1:9H, but with a different measurement in the case in which there is roofing, not empty space, in the gap. At C we have a roof extending more than four cubits from the walls on the sides of the courtyard, and open space in the center. If the center is provided with sukkah-roofing up to within four cubits of the existing roof, it is valid. If, D-E, between the walls of the sukkah and the valid roofing, there are four cubits of invalid roofing, it is invalid. The sizable Talmud at hand pursues its own interests and intersects mainly for using the Mishnah-paragraph for illustrative purposes. Unit I, for its part, starts with a familiar exercise of proving that the Mishnah does not repeat itself, the only word-for-word exegesis. Unit II asks an independent question, namely, the comparison between two sorts of invalid space in sukkah-roofing, one, a gap, the other, a filling of invalid materials. Each is supposedly subject to a distinct minimum measure for invalidating the suk-kah-roofing. Unit III provides a second version of the same dispute, and this, as we see, provides a mirror-image of the discussion at M. 1:6. It seems to me the person who has made up these protracted discussions had a rather sophisticated and comprehensive notion of how he wished to pursue the issue at hand. To the Mishnah-paragraph, the entire discussion is tangential. Its principle is important in its own right. Unit IV is continuous with the foregoing. At unit V we revert to the Mishnah-paragraph, now to M. 1:10A. We see that this passage has been constructed around its own framework -- Ishmael's sayings in his father's name -- and not around our Mishnah-passage. Unit VI raises a theoretical question but is inserted because it relates to M. 1:10C. But the issue is the theory of the law, not the amplification of the case of the peristyle. Unit VII is continuous with the foregoing. Unit VIII provides an illustration of the same matter. Unit IX does not seem to me to contribute in any way to the amplification of the rule of the Mishnah-paragraph. As a composition it hangs together on its own.

1:11 A-D

A.   He who makes his sukkah in the shape of a cone or who leaned it up against a wall --

B.   R. Eliezer declares it invalid,

C.   because it has no roof.

D.   And sages declare it valid,

I.

A.   It has been taught on Tannaite authority:

B.   R. Eliezer concedes that if one raised [the sukkah] a handbreadth above the ground or moved it a handbreadth away from the wall [as the case may be], it is a valid sukkah. [Now we have a roof, constituted either by the raised sukkah or by the space between the sukkah and the wall, with the open air space deemed fictively filled in, as we recall] [T. Suk. 1:10B-D].

C.   What is the reason behind rabbis' ruling?

D.   The inclining wall of the tent is deemed to fall into the category of a tent.

II.

A.   Abayye came upon R. Joseph, who was sleeping in a <u>sukkah</u> in a bridal bed [with curtains that sloped down from a point, not forming a roof]. He said to him, "In accord with whose opinion do you do so? [You clearly regard it as all right to sleep in a <u>sukkah</u> in a covered bed. Presumably this is because you do not regard the canopy as intervening and forming a roof between the bed and the <u>sukkah</u>-roofing.] Is this in accord with R. Eliezer [who does not regard a sloping roof as a roof at all]? Have you then abandoned the [majority] view of rabbis and acted in accord with R. Eliezer [a minority]?"

B.   He said to him, "There is a <u>baraita</u> [a Tannaite teaching alternative to the version now in the Mishnah] that has matters reversed: 'R. Eliezer declares [the arrangement] valid, and sages declare it invalid.'"

C.   He said to him, "Do you then abandon the version of the Mishnah and act in accord with the alternative version of a <u>baraita</u> [of lesser reliability]?

D.   He said to him, "The version of the Mishnah in any case stands for the viewpoint only of an individual, for it has been taught on Tannaite authority:

E.   "He who makes his sukkah in the shape of a cone or who leaned it up against a wall --

F.   "R. Nathan says <u>R. Eliezer declares it invalid, because it has no roof, and sages declare it valid.</u>'"

The Talmud's two units provide an amplification of the rule at hand (I) and then a set of secondary versions of the same matter (II), which, by the way, provide good examples of what is at issue.

1:11 E-J

E.   <u>A large reed-mat,</u>

F.   <u>[if] one made it for lying, it is susceptible to uncleanness, and [so] they do not make sukkah-roofing out of it.</u>

G.   <u>[If one made it] for sukkah-roofing, they make sukkah-roofing out of it, and it is not susceptible to uncleanness.</u>

H.   <u>R. Eliezer says, "All the same are a small one and a large one:</u>

I.   <u>"[if] one made it for lying, it is susceptible to uncleanness, and they do not make sukkah-roofing out of it.</u>

J.   <u>"[If one made it for] sukkah-roofing, they do make sukkah-roofing out of it, and it is not susceptible to uncleanness."</u>

I.

A.   Now there is a contradiction in the body of the formulation of the law.

B.   You have said: If one made [the mat] for lying, it is susceptible to uncleanness and
      they do not make sukkah-roofing out of it [M. 1:11F].

C.   The operative consideration therefore is that one has made it for use for lying. Lo,
      if it was made without further indication of its intended use, it is assumed to be
      meant to serve for sukkah-roofing.

D.   But then the framer of the passage states: If one made it for sukkah-roofing, they
      make sukkah-roofing out of it, and it is not susceptible to uncleanness [M. 1:11G].

E.   The operative consideration therefore is that one has made it for sukkah-roofing.
      Lo, if it was made without further indication of its intended use, it is meant to serve
      for lying.

F.   Lo, there is no internal contradiction at all. In one case, we speak of a large mat, in
      the other of a small mat.

G.   R. Eliezer says, "All the same are a small one and a large one: If one made it for
      lying, it is susceptible to uncleanness, and they do not make sukkah-roofing out of
      it" [M. 1:11H-I].

H.   The operative consideration therefore is that one has made it for use for lying. Lo,
      if it was made without further indication of its intended use, it is meant to serve for
      sukkah-roofing.

I.   Then I point to the concluding part of his statement: If one made it for suk-
      kah-roofing, they do make sukkah-roofing out of it, and it is not susceptible to
      uncleanness [M. 1:11J].

J.   The operative consideration therefore is that one has made it for sukkah-roofing.
      Lo, if it was made without further indication of its intended use, it is meant to serve
      for lying.

K.   Rather, said Raba, "In the case of a large mat, all parties concur that one made
      without further indication as to its intended use is meant for sukkah-roofing.

L.   "Where there is a dispute, it concerns a small mat. The anonymous Tannaite
      authority, [whose opinion appears] first, takes the position that a small mat made
      without indication as to its intended use is for lying, and R. Eliezer takes the view
      that such a mat also may serve for sukkah roofing.

M.   "[20A] This then is the sense of the passage: 'As to a large reed-mat, if one made it
      for lying, it is susceptible to uncleanness and so they do not make sukkah-roofing out
      of it.

N.   "The operative consideration is that one has made it for lying. Lo, one made
      without clear indication as to its intended use is as if one has made it for suk-
      kah-roofing, and so people may use it for sukkah-roofing.

O.   "R. Eliezer comes along to contribute the view [concurring with the foregoing] that
      all the same is the rule for the large mat and for the small one. If it was made
      without further indication as to its intended use, it is valid for sukkah-roofing."

P.   Said Abayye to him, "If that were so, when we take note of the language at hand: R.
      Eliezer says, 'All the same are a small one and a large one' [M. 1:11H].

Q.   "But within the stated theory, it should read, 'All the same is the rule for (1) a large
      one and (2) a small one, [for that order of wording is dictated by the theory of
      Eliezer's intended point given just now].

R.   "And furthermore, where there is a dispute [in the formulated Mishnah as we have
      it] it is in the case of a large mat that the matter is stated, and R. Eliezer adopts
      the more stringent ruling.

S.   "For it has been taught on Tannaite authority: 'In the case of a reed mat, with a
      large one, people may make <u>sukkah</u>-roofing out of it'" [Slotki, p. 85, n. 6: From
      which it follows that if a large mat was made without specific purpose it is regarded
      as made for a covering according to the first Tanna, while according to R. Eliezer it
      is regarded as made for lying upon]."

T.   Rather, said R. Pappa, "In the case of a small mat all parties concur that if it is
      made without indication as to its intended use, it is meant for lying.

U.   "Where there is a dispute, it concerns a large mat.

V.   "The first authority takes the position that a large mat made without further
      indication as to its purpose is meant for <u>sukkah</u>-roofing, and R. Eliezer maintains
      that a large mat made without further indication as to its intended roof may serve,
      as well, for lying.

W.   "And what is the sense of the phrasing, <u>If one made it for lying</u>? This is the sense of
      the passage: 'If it is made without further specification as to the purpose of making
      it, it may serve also for lying, unless one prepared it for use as <u>sukkah</u>-roofing.'
      [Slotki, p. 85, n. 9: The statement of the first Tanna is thus explained as before,
      that the first clause refers to a large mat, as was explicitly stated, while the latter
      clause refers to a small mat, the meaning being that if the mat was a small one,
      that was made specifically for a covering it may be used as a <u>sukkah</u>-covering, while
      ordinarily it is assumed to be intended for lying upon. To this R. Eliezer objected:
      A large mat also is subject to the same law as a small one, that if made for no
      specific purpose it is deemed to have been made for lying upon, is susceptible to
      ritual uncleanness and may not be used as a <u>sukkah</u>-covering, but if it was expressly
      made to serve as a covering it may be used as a <u>sukkah</u>-covering and is not
      susceptible to uncleanness.]'

<u>II.</u>

A.   Our rabbis have taught on Tannaite authority:

B.   A reed made mat of wicker or of straw.

C.   [if it is] large, they do use it for sukkah-roofing.

D.   [If it is small], they do not use it for sukkah-roofing [M. 1:11E-G].

E.   And one made of reeds or of helaf --

F.   [if it is] large, they use it for sukkah-roofing.

G.   [If it is] woven, they do not use it for sukkah-roofing.

H.   R. Ishmael b. R. Yose said in the name of his father, "Even one which is woven do
      they use for sukkah-roofing."

I.   And so did R. Dosa rule in accord with his opinion [T. Suk. 1:10E-L].

III.

A. There we have learned on Tannaite authority:

B. "All rush mats are susceptible only to corpse uncleanness [and not to midras-un-cleanness]," the words of R. Dosa.

C. And sages say, "To midras-uncleanness" [M. Ed. 3:4A-B]. [Midras-uncleanness affects what is used for lying or sitting.]

D. To midras-uncleanness but not to corpse-uncleanness?

E. And lo, we have learned on Tannaite authority: Whatever is susceptible to midras-uncleanness is susceptible to corpse-uncleanness [M. Nid. 6:3].

F. Then I should say [for C], "Also to midras-uncleanness."

G. What are rush-mats?

H. Said R. Abimi bar Hammedrui, "Marzublé."

I. What are marzumblé?

J. Said R. Abba, "[Slotki:] Bags filled with foliage."

K. R. Simeon b. Laqish said, "Actual rush-mats."

L. And R. Simeon b. Laqish is consistent with views expressed elsewhere, for R. Simeon b. Laqish said, "Lo, I am atonement for R. Hiyya and his sons, for in the beginning, when the Torah was forgotten in Israel, Ezra came up from Babylonia and placed it on solid foundations. When it was once more forgotten, Hillel the Babylonian came up and placed it on solid foundations. When it was forgotten yet again, R. Hiyya and his sons came up and placed it again on solid foundations.

M. "And so did R. Hiyya and his sons say, 'R. Dosa and sages did not dispute concerning reed mats made in Usha, [20B] which [they concur] are susceptible to uncleanness, nor concerning those of Tiberias, [concurring] that they are not susceptible to uncleanness.

N. "'Concerning what sort of mats did they differ? Concerning those that come from other places. One authority [who holds that they are not used for sitting and so are not susceptible to midras-uncleanness] takes the view that, since no one sits on them, they fall into the category of those of Tiberias, and the other maintains that since, from time to time, people do sit on them, they fall into the category of the mats made in Usha.'"

O. A master has stated, "'All rush mats are susceptible to corpse-uncleanness [alone], 'the words of R. Dosa."

P[. But has it not been taught on Tannaite authority: "And so did R. Dosa rule in accordance with his opinion"? [T. Suk. 1:10 I] [The reference is to Yose's view that the mats under discussion may be used for sukkah-roofing, cf. above, II H. It must follow that the mats are not susceptible.]

Q. There is no contradiction at hand. In the one case, the mat has a rim, in the other it has no rim. [The latter cannot be used for sitting but only for sukkah-roofing and does not fall into the category of a utensil.]

R. An objection was raised from the following teaching: "Mats made of bamboo, reed grass, sacking, and goat's hair are susceptible [only] to corpse-uncleanness," the words of R. Dosa.

S.   And sages say, "Also to <u>midras</u>-uncleanness [since they may be used for sitting]."

T.   Now with regard to him who the one who has said that [under discussion] are "bags filled with foliage," there is no problem, for those made of bamboo and of reed grass serve for baling produce, while those of sacking and goat's hair may serve for [Slotki:] haversacks or baskets.

U.   But in the view of him who has said that [under discussion] are actual mats, while there is no difficulty with reference to those of sacking and goat's hair, which they may serve for curtains or sieves, what can one do with those of bamboo or reed-grass?

V.   They may serve for brewing vats' [covers].

W.   There are those who state the foregoing as follows: Now with regard to the one who maintains that at issue [in the cited passage] are actual mats, those of bamboo and reed grass serve full well for brewing vats, and those of sacking and goat's hair serve for curtains or for sieves.

X.   But in the view of him who has said that under discussion are bags filled with foliage, while there is no problem with respect to those of sacking and goat's hair, which serve for haversacks and baskets, respectively, what use is there for those made of bamboo and reed grass?

Y.   They may be used for baling fruit.

Z.   It has been taught on Tannaite authority.

AA.   Said R. Hananiah, "When I went down to the Exile, I found an old man, who said to me, 'They make <u>sukkah</u>-roofing with reed mats.'

BB.   "When I came to R. Joshua, my father's brother, he accepted his opinion."

CC.   Said R. Hisda, "That is the case if it has no rim."

DD.   Said Ulla, "As to the reed mats of the people of Mahoza, were it not for their 'wall,' [rim], people could make <u>sukkah</u>-roofing of them."

EE.   It has been taught on Tannaite authority along these same lines:

FF.   People may make <u>sukkah</u>-roofing with reed mats, but if they have a wall [rim], people may not make <u>sukkah</u>-roofing with them.

Complementing M. 1:4F-G, the dispute of M. 1:11E-G <u>vs</u>. H-J is on Eliezer's view that one's intention for the mat, not the dimensions of the mat, is definitive of its character. E-G insist not one's plan for using the mat but one's act in making it is definitive. Unit I subjects the formulation of the Mishnah to a close reading, which allows reference to secondary considerations. Unit II is cited not only to complement the Mishnah but also to set the stage for unit III, which alludes directly to II I. Unit III amplifies the matter of mats, such as at M. 1:11E. At the same time the issues of M. 1:11E-J -- the consideration for what is susceptible to uncleanness -- are worked out. So the entire construction is devoted to the exegesis of the Mishnah-paragraph.

2:1

A. He who sleeps under a bed in a sukkah has not fulfilled his obligation.

B. Said R. Judah, "We had the practice of sleeping under the bed before the elders, and they said nothing at all to us."

C. Said R. Simeon, "M^CSH B: Tabi, Rabban Gamaliel's slave, slept under the bed.

D. "And Rabban Gamaliel said to the elders, 'Do you see Tabi, my slave -- he is a disciple of a sage, so he knows that slaves are exempt from keeping the commandment of dwelling in the sukkah. That is why he is sleeping under the bed.'

E. "Thus we learned that he who sleeps under bed has not fulfilled his obligation."

I.

A. But lo, [how can the bed be deemed to constitute a tent within the sukkah and so to intervene between a person sleeping under it and the sukkah-roofing, when the bed is not] ten handbreadths high?

B. Samuel interpreted [the rule to speak] of a bed that is ten handbreadths high.

II.

A. We have learned in the following passage of the Mishnah:

B. All the same is the hole dug by water or reptiles or which salt-petre has eaten through, and so a row of stones, and so [a hollow space formed by] a pile of beams: all these constitute Tents and interpose before uncleanness, [preventing its egress or entry if they are a cubic handbreadth in area].

C. R. Judah says, "Any Tent which is not made by man is no Tent." [But he agrees concerning the power to constitute an overshadowing Tent imputed to clefts and overhanging rocks] [M. Oh. 3:7V-Y].

D. What is the scriptural basis for the view of R. Judah?

E. [21A] He derives the meaning of the word "tent" from its use in connection with the tabernacle in the wilderness.

F. Here it is written, "This is the Torah. As to a man, when he dies in a tent" (Num. 19:14).

G. And elsewhere it is written, "And he spread the tent over the tabernacle" (Ex. 40:19).

H. Just as, in that later passage, the tent qualifies only if it is made by man, so here, it qualifies only if it is made by man.

I.   And as to rabbis [of B. (M. Oh. 3:7), why do they not reach the same conclusion]? They regard the recurrence of the word "tent" to serve to encompass [tents deriving both from human and from natural action].

J.   [Now we come to the point of the foregoing citation.] Is it then the case that R. Judah takes the position that any tent which is not made by man is no Tent?

K.   The following objection was raised from a pertinent passage of the Mishnah:

L.   There were courtyards in Jerusalem, built on rock, and under them was a hollow, which served as a protection against a grave in the depths. And they bring pregnant women, who give birth there, and who raise their sons there. And they bring oxen, and on them are wooden saddles, and the youngsters sit on top of them, with cups of stone in their hands. When they reached the Siloam, they descended and filled them, mounted and sat on top of them. R. Yose says, "From his place did he let down and fill the cup without descending" [M. Par. 3:2].

M.   And in this connection it has been taught on Tannaite authority: R. Judah says, "They did not make use of wooden saddles but rather of oxen [with broad bellies]" [T. Par. 3:2G].

N.   Now oxen constitute [for the purpose of the law at hand] a Tent [since they clearly serve to interpose between the children riding them and any grave in the depths over which they may ride,] yet [they are] a Tent not made by man, and lo, it has been taught on Tannaite authority. R. Judah says, "They did not make use of wooden saddles but rather of oxen"!

O.   When R. Dimi came, he said R. Eleazar [said], "R. Judah concurs concerning a [Tent] that is of the size of a fist [that is, larger than a handbreadth. Even though a tent of such size is not made by man, it nonetheless constitutes a valid tent.]" [That would then harmonize the two passages. In the case in which Judah does not regard a hole as a tent, as at M. 3:7V-W's hole dug by water or insects, it is because it is a small hole not made by man. In the case where he does, it is because it is a big one.]

P.   So too it has been taught on Tannaite authority:

Q.   R. Judah concurs in the case of clefts and overhanging rocks [M. Oh. 3:7Y].

R.   Yet there is the case of the wooden saddles, which are many times the size of a fist [and so should be regarded as adequate to serve as Tents to intervene against the effects of a grave in the depths], and yet in that regard, it has been taught:

S.   R. Judah says, "They did not bring wooden saddles but rather oxen" [T. Par. 3:2G]. [So the oxen served instead of wooden saddles, which should surely be large enough.]

T.   Said Abayye, "[His sense is that] they did not have to bring wooden saddles [because they could make do merely with the oxen, contrary to the story told in the Mishnah's version]."

U.   Raba said, "They did not bring wooden saddles at all, for, since a child is thoughtless, he might poke out his head or one of his limbs and contract corpse-uncleanness [21B] from a grave in the depths."

V.   It has been taught on Tannaite authority in accord with the view of Raba:

W.   R. Judah says, "They did not bring wooden saddles at all, for, since a child is
      thoughtless, he might poke out his head or one of his limbs and contract corpse-un-
      cleanness from a grave in the depths. Rather, they bring Egyptian oxen, which have
      broad bellies, and the children sit on top of them, with cups of stone in their hands.
      When they reached the Siloam, they descended and filled them, mounted and sat on
      top of them."

X.   [Now reverting to the Mishnah-passage at hand, we ask:] Lo, a bed is any number of
      fists in height, and yet we have learned in the Mishnah: Said R. Judah, "We had the
      practice of sleeping under the bed before the elders..." [M. Suk. 2:1B]. [So a bed is
      no tent but it should be regarded as one in line with the foregoing.]

Y.   A bed is different [from the case at hand], because it is made [so that someone can
      sleep] on top of it. [Sleeping underneath it then changes the normal practice and is
      not taken into account. The bed used in an unusual way does not constitute a tent.]

Z.   But oxen also are used [to be sat upon], [so that is no proper distinction between the
      two cases, which contradict one another].

AA.   When Rabin came, he said R. Eleazar [said], "The oxen are different, for they serve
      as protection against the sun for shepherds in the hot season, and against rain in the
      rainy season [so it would be usual to sit underneath, not only on top of, an ox, unlike
      the case of a bed.]"

BB.   If that is the argument, then the same may be said of the bed, which covers up
      [serves as a tent over] shoes and sandals that are placed underneath it.

CC.   Rather, said Raba, "The case of oxen is different, since their bellies serve to afford
      shelter for their intestines [so forming a tent beneath], as it is written, 'You have
      clothed me with skin and flesh and covered me with bones and sinews' (Job 10:11).
      [Slotki, p. 92, n. 8: "Covered" implies "shelter," "tent."]

DD.   If, on the other hand, you prefer, I may propose [a different explanation for Judah's
      view that it is all right to sleep under a bed in a tent namely], R. Judah is consistent
      with his position stated elsewhere.

EE.   For he has said that, for a sukkah, we require a permanent dwelling, while a bed
      provides at best only a temporary dwelling. Since a sukkah is a permanent Tent, a
      temporary Tent, namely, the bed, cannot come along and invalidate a permanent
      tent.

FF.   And lo, it is R. Simeon who has also said, "A sukkah is to be a permanent dwelling,
      but, [nonetheless, Simeon maintains at M. 2:1C-E] that a temporary tent -- a bed --
      may indeed come along and invalidate a permanent tent.

GG.   This is what is at issue between the two [at M. 2:1]:

HH.   One authority [Simeon] takes the view that a temporary Tent does come along and
      invalidate a permanent Tent, and the other master [Judah] takes the position that a
      temporary Tent may not come along and invalidate a permanent Tent.

III.

A.   Said R. Simeon, "M'SH B: Tabi, Rabban Gamaliel's slave..." [M. 2:1C]:

B.   It has been taught on Tannaitic Authority: said R. Simeon, "From the day to day remarks of Rabban Gamaliel we learned two lessons.

C.   "We learned that slaves are exempt from the religious requirement of dwelling in a sukkah.

D.   "And we learned that he who sleeps under a bed has not fulfilled his obligation" [M. 2:1E].

E.   And should one not say, "From the teachings of Rabban Gamaliel" [rather than "from the day-to-day remarks..."]?

F.   In phrasing matters as he did, he tells us a tangential lesson.

G.   What he says is in accord with that which Rab Aha bar Adda [said] -- and some say that Rab Aha bar Adda said Rab Hamnuna said Rab said, "How do we know that even the day-to-day remarks of disciples of sages require close study?

H.   "As it is said, 'And whose leaf does not wither' (Ps. 1:3)." [Slotki, p. 93, n. 3: The righteous man is compared to the tree and his casual talk to the leaf.]

M. 2:1A's theory, in line with M. 1:2's, is that the bed constitutes a tent within the sukkah. One has thus not slept in the sukkah -- under its roofing -- but under the tent constituted by the bed. The dispute, B, C-E, then consists of contradictory precedents. Unit I provides a minor clarification of the passage at hand. Unit II investigates the position of Judah on what constitutes a valid tent. The issue is pertinent, since the Mishnah-rule will not accept as valid a sukkah -- that is, a tent -- inside of another one, and yet, we see, Judah allows sleeping under a bed. The pertinent passages are nicely harmonized. Unit III moves on to Simeon's statement, in contradiction to Judah's. So the three units proceed in order from M. 2:1A, to M. 2:1B, to M. 2:1C-E.

2:2 A-B

A.   He who props his sukkah up with the legs of a bed -- it is valid.

B.   R. Judah says, "If it cannot stand on its own, it is invalid."

I.

A.   What is the reason for the view of R. Judah [at M. 2:2B]?

B.   There was a dispute on this matter between R. Zira and R. Abba bar Mammel.

C.   One said, "It is because [if the sukkah cannot stand on its own], it does not enjoy permanence."

D.   The other said, "It is because one thereby holds up the sukkah with something that is susceptible to uncleanness [if he leans it against a wall]."

E.   What is the practical difference between the two positions?

F.   It would be the case of someone who knocked iron stakes into the ground and spread sukkah-roofing over them."

G.   In the view of him who has said that the reason is that the sukkah lacks permanence, lo, in this case there really is permanence.

H.   In the view of him who has said that it is because one holds up the sukkah with something that is susceptible to uncleanness, lo, in this case one indeed holds up the sukkah with something that is susceptible to uncleanness. [So the former would validate the arrangement, the latter would invalidate it, both doing so in Judah's name.]

I.   Said Abayye, "What has just now been said applies only if one has leaned [the legs of a bed against a wall]. But if one spread sukkah roofing on the bed itself [so that the bed provides the walls, but the roof is supported on independent poles, which do not receive uncleanness], it is a valid arrangement.

J.   "What is the operative consideration?

K.   "In the view of him who has said that the reason is that the former arrangement lacks permanence, lo, here there is permanence.

L.   "In the view of him who has said that the operative consideration is that one holds up the sukkah with something that receives uncleanness, lo, [as just now defined], here the householder does not set up the sukkah with something that receives uncleanness."

The Talmud does a first rate job of both explaining the position of Judah and also explaining the implications of the adduced explanations.

2:2 C-H

C.   [22A] A sukkah [the roofing of which] is loosely put together,

D.   but the shade of which is greater than the light,

E.   is valid.

F.   The [sukkah] [the roofing of which] is tightly knit like that of a house,

G.   even though the stars cannot be seen from inside it,

H.   is valid.

I.

A.   What is the meaning of [a sukkah, the roofing of which is] loosely put together?

B.   Said Rab, "It is an impoverished sukkah."

C.   And Samuel said, "It is a sukkah in which one reed is above another, [so that the reeds are not on the same level]."

D.   Rab repeated [the opening clauses, C-E] as a single phrase, and Samuel repeated them as two phrases.

E.   Rab repeated it as a single phrase: "A sukkah, the roofing of which is loosely put together, [and] what is the meaning of loosely put together? Loosely put together, but the shade of which is greater than the light, is valid."

F.   Samuel repeated them as two phrases: "What is the meaning of loosely put together? And the passage provides two distinct rulings. A sukkah, the roof of which is loosely put together, is valid, and one, the shade of which is greater than its light, likewise is valid."

II.

A. Said Abayye, "The teaching [I. C, concerning a sukkah whose roof is made of reed that lie on different levels] applies only to a case in which there is not a [horizontal] gap between one reed and another of more than three handbreadths but if there is a gap between one and the next of more than three handbreadths, [the sukkah-roofing] is invalid."

B. Said Raba, "Even if there is a [horizontal] gap of more than three handbreadths between one reed and another, we do not rule [that the arrangement is invalid], unless [a section of the] roof is not a handbreadth [wide]. But if a reed is a handbreadth, the sukkah-roofing [arranged in this way] is in any case valid [even if it is three handbreadths higher than the lower reed]. [The reason is that we invoke the rule of fictively regarding the upper sections of the roof as] forced downward and treated as level [with the rest of the roof]." [Slotki, p. 94, n. 11: A legal fiction whereby a plane is regarded as though it were placed at a lower level. The section of the roof (i.e. a bunch of reeds) which is raised above the others is regarded as though it were lying on the same level as the lower ones. The necessity of a handbreadth of width is explained forthwith.]

C. Said Raba, "How do I know that when [the upper section of the roof] is a handbreadth, we invoke the fictive principle that it is forced downward and levelled, and that when [the upper section of thereof] is not a handbreadth, we do not invoke the fictive principle that the reed is forced downward and levelled?

D. "For we have learned in the following passage of the Mishnah:

E. "The beams, each a square handbreadth, of the house and of the upper room, on which there is no plaster, and which lie exactly in line with one another -- if uncleanness is under one of the lower ones, space under it is unclean. If uncleanness is between a lower and an upper beam, only the space between them is unclean. Uncleanness is on an upper one -- space directly above it up to the firmament is unclean. If the upper ones lay directly above and opposite the gaps between the lower ones, if uncleanness is under one of them, the space under all of them is unclean. If uncleanness is on top of them, the space directly above it up to the firmament is unclean [M. Oh. 12:5].

F. "In this regard it has been taught on Tannaite authority:

G. "Under what circumstances? When they have a square handbreadth [forming a tent] and between them is the space of a handbreadth. And if they do not have a square handbreadth between them, if uncleanness is located underneath one of them, [the space] underneath it is unclean. [The space] between the boards and on top of them is clean [cf. T. Ah. 13:7].

H. "It follows, therefore, that where there is a handbreadth [in one of the beams] we do invoke [the principle of fictively regarding the beam] as forced downward and treated as level [with the other beams], and where there is not a handbreadth [in one of the beams], we do not invoke [the principle of fictively regarding the beam] as forced downward and treated as level [with the other beams]."

I.   That indeed does prove [Raba's case].

J.   R. Kahana was in session and cited this tradition [of Raba about the requisite breadth of the bunch of reeds or beam]. Said R. Ashi to R. Kahana, "And is it the case that, wherever there is not a handbreadth [in the dimensions of the reed or beam], we do not invoke [the principle of fictively regarding the beam] as forced downward and treated as level [with the other beams or reeds]?

K.   "And has it not been taught on Tannaite authority:

L.   "In the case of a beam projecting from one wall [of an alley way toward the other, which we wish to regard as forming a cross beam for purposes of forming a fictive gateway to close off the alleyway and treat it as a single domain for purposes of carrying on the Sabbath], which does not reach the opposite wall,

M.   "and so too two beams, one protruding from one wall and the other protruding from the other wall, which do not touch one another --

N.   "[if there is a distance of] less than three [handbreadths between them], one does not have to bring another [beam to close off the space].

O.   "[If there is a space] of three [handbreadths between them], one does have to bring another [beam to close off the space].

P.   "Rabban Simeon b. Gamaliel says, '[22B] If it is less than four handbreadths, one does not have to bring another [beam]. If it is four handbreadths [or more], one does not have to bring another [beam].

Q.   "So in the case of two beams which run parallel to one another, and in the one there is not enough breadth to hold a half-brick, nor in the other enough breadth to hold a half brick,

R.   "if they can hold a half-brick placed breadthwise, [on their breadth of an entire handbreadth,] it is not necessary to bring another [beam], and if not, it is necessary to bring another [beam].

S.   "Rabban Simeon b. Gamaliel says, 'If they can hold a half brick placed lengthwise, over a distance of three handbreadths, it is not necessary to bring another [beam], and if not, it is necessary to bring another [beam].'

T.   "If one was above and one was below, R. Yose b. R. Judah says, 'They regard the lower one as if it goes upward, and the upper one as if it goes downward, on condition that the upper one not be more than twenty cubits from the ground, and the lower one not lower than ten handbreadths from the ground' [T. Er. 1:4-6, with different wording].

U.   "[What follows from the cited passage?] Lo, if both protruding beams lay within twenty cubits of the ground, we do invoke [the fictive principle that] the upper beam is regarded as forced down and levelled with the lower one, [and that is the case even though the distance between one beam and the other was more than three cubits], even though [in the beam] is not a handbreadth [contrary to Raba's view, H]."

V.   He said to him, "This is how to respond: And I invoke the rule on condition [now revising the language of T] that the upper one not be more than twenty cubits from the ground, and the lower one at least three handbreadths from the upper one.

W.   "Or, alternatively: On condition that the lower one not be within ten handbreadths of the ground but rather above ten handbreadths, and the upper one be within at least three handbreadths of it.

X.   "But [if they were] three handbreadths apart, if one of the beams is not a handbreadth, we do not invoke [the principle of fictively regarding the upper beam] as being forced down and levelled [with the lower one]."

III.

A.   But one, the shade of which is greater than the light, is valid [M. 2:2D-E]:

B.   But if the light and shade areas are equivalent, it is invalid.

C.   But lo, we have learned in the Mishnah of the earlier chapter: If the light is greater than the shade, it is invalid [M. Suk. 1:1E-F].

D.   That would indicate, therefore, that if they are equivalent, it is valid.

E.   There is no real contradiction, since the former [in which case, if the areas are of equal size, the sukkah is invalid] is when the sukkah is seen from above [that is, from the perspective of the roofing], the latter [in which the sukkah is valid], is when the sukkah is seen from below. [Slotki, p. 97, n. 5: If in the roof there is as much open as covered space, then it is invalid, since the sun appears on the floor in broader patches than the shade; if on the floor (below) there is as much sunshine as shade, it is evident that there is more of the roof covered than open. The idea is that the beams of the sun widen from the roof to the floor.]

F.   Said R. Pappa, "This is in line with what people say: 'What is the size of a zuz above becomes the size of an issar [a much larger coin] below.'"

IV.

A.   [The sukkah,] the roofing of which is tightly knit like that of a house... [M. 2:2F]:

B.   Our rabbis have taught on Tannaite authority:

C.   [The sukkah,] the roofing of which is tightly knit like that of a house, even though the stars cannot be seen from inside it, is valid [M. 2:2F-H]:

D.   If the rays of the sun cannot be seen through [the roofing],

E.   the House of Shammai declare it invalid.

F.   And the House of Hillel declare it valid.

So long, M. 2:2C-E, F-H, as the roofing conforms to the basic requirement, M. 1:1E, the sukkah is valid. Unit II is continuous with unit I, which begins with the exegesis of the language of the Mishnah, so the whole forms a protracted inquiry into the fundamental principles of the law, underlying both the passage at hand (as Samuel and Abayye explain it) and the quite distinct materials of tractate Erubin. The long citation of materials similar to what we find in the Tosefta is needed only for what occurs at the very end. Unit III compares the present passage to M. 1:1, and unit IV provides a minor clarification along the same lines as unit III, now in the names of earlier authorities.

2:3

A.   He who makes his sukkah on the top of a wagon or a boat -- it is valid.

B.   And they go up into it on the festival day.

C.   [If he made it] at the top of the tree or on a camel, it is valid.

D.   But they do not go up into it on the festival day.

E.   [If] two [sides of a sukkah] are [formed by] a tree, and one is made by man,

F.   or two are made by man and one is [formed by] a tree,

G.   it is valid.

H.   But they do not go up into it on the festival day.

I.   [If] three are made by man and one is [formed by] a tree, it is valid.

J.   And they do go up into it on the festival day.

K.   [23A] This is the governing principle: In the case of any [sukkah] in which the tree may be removed, and [the sukkah] can [still] stand by itself, it is valid.

L.   And they go up into it on the festival day.

I.

A.   In accord with which authority is the rule of the Mishnah-paragraph [M. 2:3A]?

B.   It accords with the view of R. Aqiba. For it has been taught on Tannaite authority:

C.   He who makes his sukkah on the deck of a ship --

D.   Rabban Gamaliel declares it invalid.

E.   And R. Aqiba declares it valid.

F.   There is a precedent involving Rabban Gamaliel and R. Aqiba, who were traveling on a boat. R. Aqiba went and made a sukkah on the deck of the ship. On the next day the wind blew and tore it away. Said to him Rabban Gamaliel, "Aqiba, where is your sukkah!"

II.

A.   Said Abayye, "All parties concur in a case in which a sukkah cannot withstand an ordinary land breeze, that such a sukkah is null.

B.   "If a sukkah can stand in an uncommon land breeze, all parties concur that it is a valid sukkah.

C.   "Where there is a dispute, it concerns a sukkah that can stand in a commonplace land breeze but cannot stand in a [supply:] commonplace sea breeze.

D.   "Rabban Gamaliel takes the view that a sukkah is meant to be a permanent dwelling, and since this one cannot stand in a commonplace sea breeze, it is null.

E.   "R. Aqiba takes the position that we require merely a temporary dwelling, and since this sukkah can withstand an ordinary land breeze [even though it cannot withstand a sea breeze], it is valid."

III.

A.   [If he made it at the top of a tree] or on a camel, it is valid [M. 2:3C]:

B.   In accord with which authority is the rule of the Mishnah-paragraph [at M. 2:3C]?

C.   It is R. Meir, for it has been taught on Tannaite authority:

D.   He who makes his sukkah on a beast --

E.   R. Meir declares [the sukkah] valid.

F.   And R. Judah declares it invalid.

G.   What is the scriptural basis for the view of R. Judah?

H.   Scripture has stated, "You shall keep the feast of Sukkot for seven days" (Deut. 16:13).

I.   A sukkah that is suitable for use for seven days is regarded as a sukkah.

J.   A sukkah that is not suitable for use for seven days is not regarded as a sukkah.

K.   And R. Meir? In his view, from the perspective of the law of the Torah, such a sukkah likewise may serve [even though it would not be ideal]. It is merely the rabbis who have made a precautionary decree against such a sukkah.

IV.

A.   If one made a beast as a wall for a sukkah, R. Meir declares it invalid.

B.   And R. Judah declares it valid.

C.   For R. Meir would say, "Of anything that is animate people may not make use either for the wall of a sukkah, the sidebeam for an alley [for use in fictively turning the alleyway into an enclosed space for common carrying on the Sabbath], boards around wells [for the same purpose], or a stone for covering a grave."

D.   In the name of R. Yose the Galilean they said, "Also they do not write on an animate creature a writ of divorce for a woman." [Cf. Unit VIII for exposition of this item.]

E.   What is the reason for the position of R. Meir [that an animate object may not serve as a wall for a sukkah]?

F.   Abayye said, "Lest the beast die [and deprive the sukkah of its services]."

G.   R. Zira said, "Lest the beast escape [with the same effect]."

H.   [In the case of a shackled elephant,] all parties concur [that the sukkah is valid], for, should it die, its carcass [nonetheless will form a wall of at least] ten handbreadths in height.

I.   Where there is a dispute, it concerns an elephant that is not shackled.

J.   From the viewpoint of him who has said, "... lest the beast die," we do not take account of that possibility, [since even in death the beast will continue to serve, as just now stated].

K.   From the viewpoint of him who has said, "We make a precautionary decree lest the beast escape," we surely should take account of the possibility that [the unshackled beast] will escape.

L.   But in the view of him who has said that the operative consideration is that the beast may die, should we not take account of the possibility that it may escape?

M.   Rather [revising H-K], in the case of an elephant that is not shackled, all parties concur [that the sukkah relying upon such an elephant for one of its walls would be invalid].

N.   Where there is a dispute, it concerns a beast [of commonplace size, not so large as an elephant], that is shackled.

O.   In the view of him who has said that the operative consideration is a precautionary decree, lest the beast die, here too we take account of that possibility.

P. In the view of him who has said that we make a precautionary decree lest the beast escape, we do not take account of that possibility [since the beast is properly shackled and cannot escape. Hence the wall remains firm.]

Q. But in the view of him who has said that the operative consideration is lest the beast escape, should we not take account of the possibility that it may die? [Surely that remains a consideration, even while the probability of escape is nil.]

R. Death is not so commonplace, [that we have to take that possibility into account in the case of the shackled beast.]

V.

A. But is there not too much open space between the animal's legs [so that the animal cannot form a valid wall]?

B. We deal with a case in which the space is stuffed with branches of palms and bay-trees.

C. But the animal might lie down [and crush the filling]?

D. We deal with a case in which the animal was suspended with ropes from above [!] [and will not lie down and crush the filling or diminish the height of the wall that it constitutes].

E. Now in the view of him who has said that we make a precautionary decree to take account of the possibility that the beast will die, [and that is why a sukkah with a wall formed by a beast is invalid], lo, one suspends the beast with ropes from above. [So why take account of the death of the beast? After all, being suspended, the carcass will still perform its service to the sukkah.]

F. There may be a case in which, when the beast is alive, it is set up three hand-breadths from the sukkah-roofing [hence in a valid position], but [23B], when the beast dies, its carcass will shrink, and that possibility will not have been taken into account by the owner [and so the sukkah will become invalid without the owner's knowledge].

VI.

A. Now did Abayye say [IV F] that it is R. Meir who takes account of the possibility of the beast's dying, and R. Judah who does not take account of such a possibility?

B. And have we not learned in the Mishnah:

C. An Israelite girl married to a priest whose husband went overseas eats priestly rations in the assumption that her husband is alive [M. Git. 3:3G-I].

D. Now the following objection was raised in this regard:

E. "Lo, here is your writ of divorce, to take effect one hour before I die," — the wife is forbidden to eat priestly rations forthwith [since we do not know when the husband will die].

F. [Now, in dealing with the contradiction between the cited passage of the Mishnah and the following statement,] said Abayye, "There is no contradiction. The one case represents the view of R. Meir, who does not take account of the possibility that the husband may die while overseas,] and the other case represents the view of R. Judah, who does take account of the possibility that the husband may die [suddenly].

G. For it has been taught on Tannaite authority:

H. He who purchases wine among Samaritans [in a situation in which he cannot separate tithes right away, but wishes to drink the wine], says, "Two logs out of one hundred which I shall separate, behold, these are made priestly rations, and the following ten logs are made first tithe, and the following nine logs are made second tithe." He regards the wine as unconsecrated produce and drinks it [M. Dem. 7:4, Sarason, Demai, p. 243], the words of R. Meir [T. Dem. 8:7AA].

I. [24A] R. Judah, R. Yose, and R. Simeon prohibited [doing so] [T. Dem. 8:7BB].

J. The attributions then should be reversed. R. Meir takes account of the possibility of death, and R. Judah does not take account of the possibility of death. [We reverse Abayye's attributions.]

K. For it has been taught on Tannaite authority:

L. If one made a beast into a wall for a sukkah,

M. R. Meir declares it invalid.

N. And R. Judah declares it valid.

O. Nonetheless, is there not a contradiction between what R. Meir says [concerning the conditional designation of tithes and priestly rations, in which case he disregards the possibility that some sort of accident — whether the breaking of the wineskin, which will make it impossible later on to do what the man now declares he will do, or whether the death of the man, which will have the same effect — will take place, and the matter of the use of the beast for a wall of a sukkah, in which case he takes full account of the possibility of some sort of disqualifying accident].

P. R. Meir may reply to you, "The accident of death is commonplace, [the accident of] the breaking of the wine skin is not commonplace. It is possible to hand it over to a watchman [to make sure that the wine remains available. But the case of the sukkah is different.]"

Q. [We proceed to address the same question to Judah.] There is a contradiction between what R. Judah says [concerning the conditional designation of tithes and the like, in which case he takes account of the possibility of an untoward accident, and the matter of the use of the beast for a wall for the sukkah, in which case he does not take account of the possibility of an accident].

R. The operative consideration for R. Judah's views [in the matter of the conditional designation of the tithes and priestly rations of wine in the wineskin] is not the matter of the possibility of an untoward accident, namely, the splitting of the wineskin [which will leave no wine available for the actual fulfillment of the man's original condition, but a quite separate principle]. Specifically, R. Judah does not concede the principle of post facto selection. [That is, some hold that we retrospectively apply the results of a selection made only later on in produce to be assigned to the several tithes. In Judah's view what one will do later on has no retroactive validity. That is why he prohibits the entire procedure.]

S. But does R. Judah not take account of the possibility of the splitting of the wineskin? [Is the only issue retrospective selection, which he denies?]

T. And lo, note what is taught on Tannaite authority at the end of the same passage:

U. They said to R. Meir, "Do you not concede that if his wineskin bursts after he has drunk the wine but before he has separated tithes from the remainder, he has drunk fully untithed produce?"

V. He said to them, "Only when it actually bursts. But we do not scruple from the outset, since this is not a common occurrence" [T. Dem. 8:7CC-DD, Sarason, Demai, p. 249].

W. Would this passage not present the implication, then, that R. Judah does take account of the possibility that the skin may break?

X. [Not really, for] in that case, it is R. Judah who is addressing R. Meir in this wise: "In my view, I maintain that we do not invoke the principle of retrospective selection [such as you would hold], but by your own reasoning, by which we do invoke the principle of retrospective selection, do you nonetheless not concur that, in any event, the wine skin may burst?"

Y. At that point, [Meir then] replied to him, "Only when it actually bursts..."

Z. But does R. Judah not take account of the possibility of untoward death?

AA. And lo, we have learned in the Mishnah:

BB. [Seven days before the Day of Atonement... they appoint another priest as the high priest's possible substitute, lest some cause of invalidation overtake him.] R. Judah says, "Also: they appoint another woman as a substitute for his wife, lest his wife die..." [M. Yoma 1:1D-E].

CC. [No, that poses no problem, for] it has been stated in this regard: Said R. Huna, son of R. Joshua, "Sages imposed a higher requirement on the [Day of] Atonement [and normally would not take account of the possibility of sudden death]."

VII.

A. Both the one who maintains that the operative consideration is that the beast might die, and the one who holds that the criterion is that the beast might flee, [will concur that,] viewed from the aspect of the law of the Torah, a beast constitutes a perfectly acceptable partition, and it is only rabbis who made a precautionary decree. [Accordingly, we now ask about the status of the issue at hand.]

B. If that is the case, then, in the view of R. Meir, the beast should impart uncleanness when it serves as a rolling stone to seal a grave. [Slotki, p. 102, n. 7: Since according to Pentateuchal law it is a valid partition, it ought to contract uncleanness, even if the rabbis decreed later that it is no valid partition. With regard to sukkah and the alley the rabbinical decree might well be upheld, since it restricts the law, but in the case of uncleanness, where it leads to a relaxation of the Pentateuchal law, the rabbinical decree must obviously be disregarded.]

C. Why, then, have we learned in the Mishnah:

D. [R. Judah declares that] An animate creature which is used to cover up the entrance of a tomb imparts uncleanness as a sealing-stone [M.'s text lacks "R. Judah declares"]. But R. Meir declares it insusceptible to uncleanness when used for that purpose [M. Er. 1:7D-E]. [Meir could not maintain that the uncleanness at hand is

pentateuchal in authority and must then hold that it is a decree of rabbis that is
involved.]

E.   Rather, said R. Aha bar Jacob, "R. Meir takes the view that any partition that
[Slotki:] is upheld by wind is no partition."

F.   There are those who report the matter as follows: Said R. Aha bar Jacob, "R. Meir
takes the view that any partition which is not made by human action is no partition."

G.   What is at issue between these two versions [of Meir's view]? At issue is a case in
which one set up [the wall] with an inflated wineskin.

H.   In the view of the one who holds that a partition that is upheld by wind is no
partition, lo, in this case we have a partition that is upheld by wind [and it is
unsuitable in Meir's view].

I.   In the view of one who holds that if it is not made by human action [it is no
partition,] [24B] lo, this one is made by human action."

VIII.

A.   A master has stated: "In the name of R. Yose the Galilean they said, 'Also they do
not write on it [i.e., an animate object] a bill of divorce for a woman.'" [See 2:3 IV
D.]

B.   What is the scriptural basis for the position of R. Yose the Galilean?

C.   It is in accord with that which has been taught on Tannaite authority:

D.   "[He will write her] a writ [of divorce]," (Deut. 24:1) --

E.   I know only that one may use a writ. How do I know that the law encompasses
anything?

F.   Scripture states, "He will <u>write</u> for her..." -- in any manner.

G.   If so, why does Scripture state, "A writ..."

H.   It is to indicate to you that just as a "writ" is something which is inanimate and does
not consume [produce], so anything that is inanimate and does not consume produce
[may be used, thus excluding animate creatures].

I.   And rabbis?

J.   If the Scripture had stated, "... <u>in</u> a writ...," matters would have been as you claim.
But now that it is written, "... a writ...," the purpose is so as to make known matters
in general.

K.   And as to the language, "... write..." how do rabbis interpret it?

L.   They require that expression to indicate that it is through the act of writing [the bill
of divorce] that a woman is divorced, and it is not through the payment of money
[owing on the occasion of the divorce] that the woman is divorced.

M.   [Why would someone have thought otherwise]? It might have entered your mind to
rule that, since the leaving of the marriage is compared to the establishment of the
marriage, just as the relationship at the outset is established through the payment of
money, so at the end the relationship may be broken off through the payment of
money. Accordingly we are informed that that is not the case.

N.   Now how, for his part, does R. Yose the Galilean attain that same principle, [since
he interprets the language of the verse at hand for another purpose]?

O. He derives that lesson from the language, "a writ of divorce," meaning, "A writ is what cuts the relationship, and no other consideration cuts the relationship."

P. And the other party?

Q. That formulation is required to indicate that the relationship is broken off through something that effectively severs the tie between him and her.

R. For it has been taught on Tannaite authority:

S. [If the husband said], "Lo, here is your writ of divorce, on the condition that you not drink wine, that you not go to your father's house for ever," this is not an act of totally severing the relationship.

T. [If he said,] "... for thirty days...," lo, this is an act of severing the relationship. [The husband cannot impose a permanent condition, for if he could do so, then the relationship will not have been completely and finally severed.]

U. And the other party?

V. He derives the same lesson from the use of the language, "total cutting off" as against merely "cutting off."

W. And the other party?

X. The rabbis do not derive any lesson from the variation in the language at hand.

The operative principle is that one may not make use of a tree or a camel on the festival day (M. Bes. 5:2). The restrictions then are the same as they are on the Sabbath. The contrast between M. 2:3A-B and C-D is therefore quite clear. E-L then form a secondary, and rather extended, expansion of the same point as is made about C. If the sukkah depends upon the tree, then it may not be used on the festival day. If it stands on its own and does not depend on the tree, then it may be used on the festival, as M. 2:3K-L explain. So what we have is a primary statement, in rather trivial terms, and then a secondary development, somewhat overblown, given the obvious point to be made here. Units I and II provide routine clarification for the Mishnah, with the former discovering the authority behind the Mishnah's anonymous rule, the latter clarifying the details of the law. The real action is at unit III, which serves to introduce units IV-VIII. Now we take up the slightly silly possibility that someone uses a beast to form the wall of a sukkah, a conception that the framer of the Mishnah cannot imagine, e.g., at M. 2:3C. The discussion of the issue of not using a beast is really focused upon the operative considerations, and this leads us to identify the authority behind the two distinct criteria. Once we have determined that a given authority espouses one of the two principles, we forthwith investigate whether or not that authority remains consistent through other cases in which the same principle applies. The discussion thus is continuous, protracted, and beautifully composed, even though we can identify a number of distinct subunits. Unit VIII then takes up a matter introduced, to begin with tangentially, in unit IV.

2:4A

A. He who makes his sukkah among trees, and the trees are its sides -- it is valid.

I.

A. Said R. Aha bar Jacob, "Any partition that cannot stand in an ordinary wind is not regarded as a valid partition."

B. We have learned in the Mishnah: He who makes his sukkah among trees, and the trees are its sides -- it is valid [M. 2:4A].

C. And lo, they go back and forth.

D. Here with what do we deal? It is with a strong tree [which does not sway].

E. But lo, there are the branches [which do sway]?

F. We deal with a case in which he wove the branches with shrubbery and bay trees [to make them solid].

G. If that is the case, what purpose is there in stating the rule [since the partition in this case would be entirely valid]?

H. What might you have said? We should make a precautionary decree against such an arrangement, lest someone come and make use of the tree [e.g., to support objects on the festival day, which would be forbidden]?

I. So we are informed [that we make no such decree].

J. Come and take note: If there was a tree, fence or a partition of reeds, these are regarded as equivalent to a corner piece [of boards] [T. Er. 1:15A]. [These partitions would move with the wind, yet are valid].

K. We deal here too with a case where it is valid because the owner has woven the branches with shrubbery and bay trees [to make them solid].

L. Come and take note: A tree which overshadows the ground -- if its foliage was not three handbreadths above the ground, they carry under it [in the theory that it forms a partition and designates a distinct domain thereby] [M. Er. 10:8A-C].

M. Why should that be the case? Lo, the branches move back and forth [with the wind and so should not be regarded as a valid partition]?

N. Here too, it is valid, because the owner has woven the branches with shrubbery and bay trees.

O. If so, then a person should be permitted to carry throughout the area. On what account then did R. Huna, son of R. Joshua, say, "People may carry there [25A] if the partitioned area is only over an area of two seahs"? [Why not permit carrying over the entire partitioned area, if it is a valid partition at all?]

P. It is because here we deal with a fictive abode which is meant to be used in the open air, and in the case of any dwelling which is meant to be used in the open air [that is, lacking fixed roof and walls], people may carry only in an area of two seahs [and no more, despite the provision of valid partitions that ordinarily would allow for a greater area of movement than that].

Q. Come and take note: If one has taken as his place for Sabbath residence a hill that is ten handbreadths high and in extent from four cubits to two seahs, so also in a hole ten handbreadths deep and four cubits to two seahs in extent, or in a harvested area surrounded by areas of corn -- he may walk freely over the entire area and for two thousand cubits beyond.

R.   Now that is the case even though the walls formed of the sheaves of corn sway back and forth [in the wind].

S.   In this case too we deal with his weaving the sheaves with shrubs and bay trees.

The reason for the Mishnah's rule is that the branches form partitions. This leads to Aha's qualification, and then an extensive secondary expansion, proving that that qualification is both valid and also worth stating. The rest allows us to review a sequence of cases to make the same point, with the good result of allowing us to review parallel cases of partitions that serve to set up the walls for the domain for Sabbath carrying.

2:4B-D

B.   Agents engaged in a religious duty are exempt from the requirement of dwelling in a sukkah.

C.   Sick folks and those who serve them are exempt from the requirement of dwelling in a sukkah.

D.   [People] eat and drink in a random manner outside of a sukkah.

I.

A.   How do we know on the basis of Scripture [that the rule at M. 2:4B is correct]?

B.   It is in line with that which he have learned on Tannaite authority:

C.   "When you sit in your house" (Deut. 6:7) serves to exclude one who is engaged in carrying out a religious duty.

D.   "And when you walk by the way" (Deut. 6:7) serves to exclude a newly-married groom [who likewise does not have to carry out the religious duty of reciting the Shema, to which the cited verse refers].

E.   On this basis they have stated: He who marries a virgin is exempt from the requirement to recite the Shema, and he who marries a widow is liable.

F.   What is the sort of evidence that implies the stated distinction?

G.   Said R. Huna, "'... on the way...' -- Just as the [taking of a trip] on the way is an optional matter, so too anything that is an optional matter [would have to be set aside for the saying of the Shema,] thus excluding one who is engaged in the performance of a religious duty.

H.   But does the cited language not refer to one who is going along the way to carry out a religious duty, and lo, the All-Merciful has said that such a one should recite the Shema?

I.   If so, Scripture should have said, "... in sitting... and in going..." What is the sense of "in your sitting... in your going..." [which Scripture does state]? It refers to going on your own business. Under such circumstances you are liable. Lo, if you are going on the purpose of carrying out a religious duty, however, then you will be exempt.

J.   If that is the case, then even he who marries a widow also should be exempt [from the requirement of reciting the Shema].

K.   He who marries a virgin is preoccupied, he who marries a widow is not preoccupied.

L.   Is that to suggest that whenever a person is preoccupied, he also will be exempt from the requirement of reciting the Shema?

M.   Then what about the case of one whose ship is sinking in the ocean, who is surely preoccupied. Is this a case in which one also would be exempt?

N.   And if you wish to say that that indeed is the case, has not R. Abba bar Zabeda said Rab said, "A mourner is liable to carry out all of the religious duties that are stated in the Torah except for the religious duty involved in putting on the phylacteries.

O.   "For lo, in their regard, the word 'beauty' is stated [at Ez. 24:17] [and a mourner should not don something of beauty]."

P.   In the case at hand [involving a virgin] one is preoccupied with the carrying out of a religious duty, while in the other case [where the ship is sinking], he is preoccupied with an optional matter.

II.

A.   Now does the law derive from the cited passage [see I, Deut. 6:7] that he who carries out a religious duty is exempt from the obligations to carry out some other religious duty?

B.   Surely it derives [not from what served above but] from the following proof-text, for it has been taught on Tannaite authority:

C.   "And there were certain men who were unclean on account of a human corpse" (Num. 9:6). [These men were occupied with a religious duty and could not keep the Passover celebrated in Nisan, so they kept it in Iyyar, a month later, and hence observed what was the second Passover. This proves that those occupied in carrying out a religious duty involving the corpse were exempt from the religious duty involving the Passover sacrifice, and the cited generalization follows.]

D.   Who indeed were these men?

E.   "They were the ones who were carrying Joseph's bier," the words of R. Yose the Galilean.

F.   [25B] R. Aqiba says, "They were Mishael and Elzaphan, who were busy taking care of the bodies of Nadab and Abihu."

G.   R. Isaac says, "If they were carrying Joseph's bier, they could have had sufficient time to attain cultic purity [prior to Passover]. If they were Mishael and Elzaphan, they also should have had sufficient time to attain cultic cleanness. [So who were they, and why were they unclean with corpse-uncleanness?]

H.   "But they were people who were busy dealing with a neglected corpse [which religious duty takes priority over all others], and the seventh day [beyond their contracting corpse uncleanness in that connection] coincided with the eve of Passover, as it is said, 'They could not keep the Passover on that day' (Num. 9:6).

I.   "The sense is that that particular day they could not observe, but they could have kept the day following."

J.   [Now that we have shown that there are two distinct texts that prove a person involved in carrying out one religious duty is exempt from having to carry out others, the one regarding the <u>Shema</u> (Deut 6:7), the other regarding Passover (Num. 9:6), we ask why both proof-texts are necessary.] It is necessary [to have both proof-texts]. For had we derived the law only from the latter case [Num. 9:6], [I should have reached the conclusion that the reason is that] the occasion on which the obligation to keep the Passover had not yet come. But in the former case [Deut. 6:7, see I], where the occasion for reciting the <u>Shema</u> has arrived, I might have said that one would not be exempt.

K.   It is necessary [to have both proof-texts (Deut. 6:7 and Num. 9:6)]. And had I derived the proof only from the former case, [namely, the recitation of the <u>Shema</u>], I might have supposed that it is because violation of the requirement is not subject to the penalty of extirpation. But in the latter case [namely, Passover], in which failure to carry out the religious duty of observing the Passover sacrifice is penalized by extirpation, I might have reached the conclusion that the remission of the obligation does not apply.

L.   Accordingly, it was necessary to supply two proof-texts.

III.

A.   [Returning to the] cited [passage from I.N, which is]: Said R. Abba bar Zabeda said Rab, "A mourner is liable to carry out all of the religious duties that are stated in the Torah except for the religious duty involved in putting on the phylacteries.

B.   "For lo, in their regard, the word 'beauty' is stated."

C.   [How so?] Since the All-Merciful said to Ezekiel, "Bind your beauty on you" (Ez. 24:17), [his sense is that] "<u>You</u> are the one who is obligated, but everyone else [who is in mourning] is exempt. [Ezekiel, in particular, is admonished to give up the normal rites of mourning. So he is told to put on his phylacteries. Other mourners are exempt from doing so.]

D.   That rule pertains to the first day [of mourning], since it is written, "And the end thereof as a bitter day" (Amos 8:10). [Slotki, p. 109, n. 20: The beginning of the verse is, "And I will make it as the mourning for an only son." Since "day" in the singular is used, it follows that actual mourning is limited to one day.]

E.   And R. Abba bar Zabeda said Rab said, "A mourner is liable to the religious duty of dwelling in the <u>sukkah</u>."

F.   That fact is self-evident.

G.   What might you have said?

H.   Since R. Abba bar Zabeda said Rab said, "One who is in distress is exempt from the religious duty of dwelling in a <u>sukkah</u>," this one also is in the category of one who is in distress. So we are informed that that is not the case.

I.   The exemption of one who is in distress applies to a person who suffers distress on account of some objective fact, but in this case [that is, the one of the mourner], he is the one who causes distress for himself. He has, therefore, to regain his composure.

J.   And R. Abba bar Zabeda said Rab said, "A groom and the groomsmen and all the members of the wedding are exempt from the religious duty of dwelling in a <u>sukkah</u> all seven days of the Festival."

K. What is the reason for that exemption?

L. Because they have to rejoice [in the marriage].

M. But let them eat their festive meals in the sukkah and rejoice in the sukkah?

N. True rejoicing is only under the marriage canopy.

O. But let them then eat in the sukkah and rejoice under the marriage canopy?

P. True rejoicing takes place only where a meal is eaten.

Q. Then let them set up the marriage canopy in the sukkah?

R. Abayye said, "[They do not do so] because of considerations of privacy. [The sukkah was isolated. Should the groom have to leave, the bride would be left alone and a stranger might enter.]"

S. Raba said, "Because of the anguish of the groom [who will not want to show affection in so public a place, which has, after all, only three walls]."

T. What is the practical issue between the two explanations?

U. At issue is a case in which people routinely go out and come in [to the place at which the sukkah is located].

V. In the view of him who has said that the operative consideration is the possibility of [the bride's being left alone with a stranger], there is no such possibility.

W. In the view of him who has said that the issue is the anguish of the groom, that consideration remains valid.

X. Said R. Zira, "I ate in the sukkah and rejoiced in the marriage canopy, and my heart was all the happier, because I thereby kept two religious duties [at once]."

IV.

A. Our rabbis have taught on Tannaite authority:

B. The groom, the groomsmen, and all the members of the wedding are exempt from the religious duty of [reciting] the Prayer, and the phylacteries, but are liable to recite the Shema.

C. [26A] In the name of R. Shila they said, "The groom is exempt, but the groomsmen and all the members of the wedding are liable."

V.

A. It has been taught on Tannaite authority:

B. Said R. Hanania b. Aqabia, "Those who write scrolls, phylacteries, and parchments for mezuzot -- they, their employees, and employees of their employees,

C. "and all those who are engaged in the work of Heaven --"

D. (this includes those who sell blue --)

E. "are exempt from the religious requirement of reciting the Shema, the Prayer, the phylacteries, and all religious duties that are listed in the Torah."

F. This serves to second the view of R. Yose the Galilean.

G. For R. Yose the Galilean would say, "He who is occupied with one religious duty is exempt from the obligation of carrying out another religious duty."

VI.

A. Our rabbis have taught on Tannaite authority:

B. Wayfarers by day are exempt from the religious duty [of dwelling in the sukkah] by day and liable to carry it out at night.

C. Those who are on a trip by night are exempt from the religious duty of dwelling in a sukkah by night and liable by day.

D. Those who make their journey by day and by night are exempt from the religious duty of dwelling in a sukkah both by day and by night.

E. Those who are going to carry out a religious duty are exempt both by day and by night [cf. T. Suk. 2:3F].

F. This is illustrated by the behavior of R. Hisda and Rabba bar R. Huna. When they went to visit the exilarch's establishment of the Sabbath of the festival [of Sukkot], they would sleep on the river bank at Sura. They said, "Since we are engaged as agents to carry out a religious duty, we are exempt [from the religious duty of sleeping in the sukkah]."

G. Our rabbis have taught on Tannaite authority:

H. City guards by day are exempt from the religious requirement of dwelling in a sukkah by day, but they are liable by night.

I. City guards [cf. M. 2:5B] by night are exempt from the religious requirement of dwelling in a sukkah by night, but they are liable by day.

J. City guards by day and by night are exempt from the religious requirement of dwelling in a sukkah by day and by night...

K. Garden-guards and orchard-guards are exempt by day and by night [T. Suk. 2:3C-G].

L. [As to the case of the last-named,] why not build a sukkah there and dwell in it [out in the fields or orchards]?

M. Said Abayye, "You shall dwell... (Lev. 23:42) as you ordinarily live."

N. Raba said, "The hole in the fence is an invitation to the thief. [Thieves will know where the guards are.]"

O. What is the practical difference between the two explanations?

P. At issue is a case in which the guard is in charge of a pile of fruit. [Abayye still will not approve building a sukkah there, Raba will.]

VII.

A. Sick folk and those who serve them [M. 2:4C]:

B. And [this is the case] not only of one who is seriously ill,

C. but even if someone has a headache or a pain in the eye.

D. Said Rabban Simeon b. Gamaliel, "M'SH W: I had a pain in the eye in Caesarion, and R. Yose b. Rabbi permitted me to sleep, along with my servant, outside of the sukkah" [T. Suk. 2:2B-D, in T.'s version].

E. Rab permitted R. Aha Bardela to sleep in a sukkah in a tester-bed [Slotki, p. 112, n. 11: which is ten handbreadths high and has a roof and is ordinarily forbidden], so as to keep out gnats.

F. Raba permitted R. Aha bar Adda to sleep outside of the shade of the sukkah on account of the stench of the clay.

G. Raba is consistent with views stated elsewhere, for Raba has said, "One who is in anguish is exempt from the religious duty of dwelling in a sukkah."

H. And lo, we have learned in the Mishnah: Sick folk and those who serve them are exempt from the requirement of dwelling in a sukkah [M. 2:4C] -- which bears the implication that the exemption applies to sick folk and not to those who are [merely] distressed!

I. [We may interpret the sense of the passage in this way:] In the case of one who is sick, he and his attendents are exempt, but in the case of one who is in distress, while he is exempt, those who attend him are not.

VIII.

A. People eat and drink in a random manner outside of a sukkah [M. 2:4D]:

B. And what falls into the category of a random meal?

C. Said R. Joseph, "Two or three eggs."

D. Said Abayye to him, "And yet, on many occasions a person finds enough nourishment in such a meal, and it would then fall into the category of a regular meal."

E. Rather, said Abayye, "It is about as much as a snack of a [disciple] of a master's household before he goes into the study-session."

IX.

A. Our rabbis have taught on Tannaite authority:

B. People may eat a random meal outside of a sukkah but they may not take a snooze outside of a sukkah.

C. What is the reason for this distinction?

D. Said R. Ashi, "It is a precautionary decree, so that someone not fall into a deep sleep."

E. Said Abayye to him, "But along these same lines, it has been taught on Tannaite authority: 'A man make take a snooze while wearing his phylacteries but he may not take a regular nap.' [Surely we should take precautions] lest he fall into a deep sleep [in this case too]!"

F. R. Joseph, son of R. Ilai, said, "[It is permitted to snooze while wearing phylacteries] in a case in which one hands over to others responsibility for waking him up out of his sleep. [In that case we need not take precautions of another sort.]"

G. To this explanation R. Mesharshia objected. "Who will watch the watchman?"

H. Rather, said Rabbah bar bar Hana said R. Yohanan, "We deal [in the case of one who may snooze while wearing phylacteries] with one who does so while simply putting his head between his knees."

I. Raba said, "[As to the sukkah], there is no issue of distinguishing regular sleep from a snooze. [Both sorts are not to be done outside of the sukkah.]"

J. One Tannaite teaching holds: A man may take a snooze while wearing his phylacteries, but not fall into deep sleep.

K. A second Tannaite teaching holds: Whether a snooze or deep sleep, [one may do so while wearing phylacteries].

L.   Yet a third: Whether a snooze or a deep sleep, one may not [do so while wearing phylacteries].

M.   There is no contradiction among the three versions of the rule. In the third case, the man holds the phylacteries in his hand, [and if he falls asleep at all, the phylacteries will fall down]. In the first case, he leaves them on his head [in which case we distinguish a snooze from deep sleep]. In the second he spreads a cloth under him [so that, should the phylacteries fall, they will not hit the ground].

N.   What is the length of a snooze [as distinct from deep sleep]?

O.   Rami bar Ezekiel taught on Tannaite authority, "Enough time to walk a hundred cubits."

P.   It has been taught on Tannaite authority along these same lines:

Q.   "He who falls asleep while wearing his phylacteries, and, [when he wakes up,] sees that he has ejaculated [so must remove the phylacteries], takes hold of the strap [of the phylacteries], [26B] but not of the box thereof," the words of R. Jacob.

R.   And sages say, "A man may sleep in his phylacteries only to take a snooze but not to fall into a deep sleep [so such an event will not take place].

S.   "And how long is a snooze?

T.   "Sufficient time to walk a hundred cubits."

U.   Said Rab, "It is forbidden for a person to sleep by day any longer than a horse ever sleeps."

V.   And how long does a horse ever sleep?

W.   For sixty breaths.

X.   Said Abayye, "The length of time that the master [Rabbah] sleeps is the same as the time that Rab sleeps, and Rab sleeps as long as Rabbi, and Rabbi sleeps as long as [King] David, and David sleeps as long as a horse, and a horse sleeps for sixty breaths."

Y.   During the day time Abayye would snooze as long as it takes to go from Pumbedita to Be Kube. In his regard R. Joseph recited this verse: "How long will you sleep, O lazy man, when will you get up?" (Prov. 6:9).

X.

A.   Our rabbis have taught on Tannaite authority:

B.   "He who goes in to sleep by day may, if he wishes, take off his phylacteries, and may, if he wishes, leave them on.

C.   But if he does so by night, he must remove them and may not leave them on," the words of R. Nathan.

D.   R. Yose says, "Youngsters must always remove them and may not leave them on, because they routinely become unclean [when asleep, from nocturnal emissions]."

E.   May we then draw the conclusion that R. Yose takes the view that one who has had a seminal emission is prohibited from putting on phylacteries?

F.   Abayye replied, "In this case we deal with youngsters who go to sleep with their wives, [and we impose a precautionary decree, that the man must remove his phylacteries] lest the couple do what comes naturally [which may not be done while wearing phylacteries]."

G.   Our rabbis have taught on Tannaite authority:

H.   If someone forgot and had sexual relations while wearing his phylacteries, he does
not take hold either of the strap or the box [of the phylacteries] until he washes his
hands. Only then may he remove the phylacteries. The reason is that the hands are
always busy [and may have touched some unclean thing].

The Talmud provides a rather full account of the three topics of the Mishnah-paragraph at hand, following the order as well. Unit I presents a proof for M. 2:4B, unit II
presents a second and then justifies the need for both. Unit III clarifies a passage adduced
in evidence in the foregoing, and this leads us back to the main theme, allowing us to
proceed directly to M. 2:4C -- a fine and artful transition. Unit IV takes up the underlying
principle -- exemption from religious duty in general. At issue now are categories of
persons to which unit III has made reference. Unit V proceeds to the same issues. Unit VI
then turns to Tosefta's complement to the Mishnah-passage at hand. Unit VII cites the
Mishnah -- M. 2:4C -- and moves on to Tosefta's complement. Unit VIII cites M. 2:4D and
provides definitions relevant to the matter. Unit IX then carries forward the exposition
of the rule of M. 2:4D. But the theme now investigated -- the wearing of phylacteries
while one is asleep -- takes over and the Talmud's remaining materials deal with that
secondary question. Overall, therefore, what we have is exposition of the Mishnah, then
secondary expansion of the exposition, carefully organized and in a straight-line from
start to finish.

2:5

A.   M^{C}SH W: They brought Rabban Yohanan b. Zakkai some cooked food to
taste, and to Rabban Gamaliel two dates and a dipper of water.

B.   And they said, "Bring them up to the sukkah."

C.   And when they gave to R. Sadoq food less than an egg's bulk, he took it
in a cloth and ate it outside of the sukkah and said no blessing after it.

I.

A.   Does the precedent [of M. 2:5] mean to contradict the rule [of M. 2:4D]? [We have
just been told that people may eat a casual snack outside of the sukkah. What is the
point of M. 2:5A-B?]

B.   There is a lacuna in the tale, and this is how it should be told:

C.   "If someone wishes to impose upon himself a more strict rule, he may do so, and
there is no element, in his doing so, of self-aggrandisement [or presumptuousness]."

D.   "And M^{C}SH W: They brought Rabban Yohanan b. Zakkai some cooked food to taste,
and to Rabban Gamaliel two dates and a dipper of water, [27A], and they said, 'Bring
them up to the sukkah.'"

II.

A.   And when they gave to R. Sadoq less than an egg's bulk, he took it in a cloth and ate
it outside of the sukkah and said no blessing after it [M. 2:5C]:

B.   Does this then bear the implication that if it had been of the bulk of an egg, he would have had to eat it in the sukkah?

C.   Then this precedent would constitute a refutation of the view of R. Joseph and Abayye [who define a casual meal as two or three eggs, or a student's snack, a bulk of an egg. Here such a meal would appear to belong in a sukkah only, contrary to their view of a random snack.]

D.   No, the point is that food of less than the bulk of an egg does not require the washing of hands and the saying of a blessing, while food of the bulk of an egg would require the washing of the hands and the saying of a blessing.

At unit I the Talmud clarifies the relationship of the case to the law that it is supposed to illustrate, and in unit II the secondary implications of the second precedent are brought into line with an established rule. So the whole constitutes Mishnah-exegesis.

2:6

A.   R. Eliezer says, "Fourteen meals is a person obligated to eat in the sukkah,

B.   "one by day and one by night."

C.   And sages say, "There is no fixed requirement, except for the first two nights of the festival alone."

D.   And further did R. Eliezer say, "He who has not eaten his meal in the Sukkah on the first night of the festival should make up for it on the last night of the festival."

E.   And sages say, "There is no way of making it up.

F.   "Concerning such a case it is said, That which is crooked cannot be made straight, and that which is wanting cannot be reckoned (Qoh. 1:15)."

I.

A.   What is the scriptural basis for the opinion of R. Eliezer?

B.   "You will dwell" (Lev. 23:42) as you usually dwell. Just as in a dwelling a person [eats] one [meal] by day and one by night, so the sukkah must serve both by day and by night [as the setting for a meal].

C.   And sages [concur that the sukkah is] like a dwelling, [drawing a different conclusion from the analogy, namely:]

D.   Just as in the case of a dwelling, if one wants, he eats a meal, and if one wants, he does not eat a meal, so in the case of a sukkah, if one wants, he eats a meal, and if one wants, he does not eat a meal.

E.   If that is the case, then even in the first night of the festival [there should] also [be no obligation to eat in the sukkah, contrary to M. 2:6C].

F.   Said R. Yohanan in the name of R. Simeon b. Yehosedeq, "'The fifteenth' (Lev. 23:39) is stated here [with reference to the festival of Sukkot], and elsewhere it is stated, 'the fifteenth' (Lev. 23:6) with respect to the festival of unleavened bread.

G.   "Just as, in that latter instance, on the first night there is a fixed obligation [to eat unleavened bread], while from that point onward in the holy week, it is an optional matter,

H.   "so here too in the case of the first night it is a fixed obligation [to eat in the sukkah], while from that time onward it is an optional matter."

I.   In the case of Passover, how do we know [that it is a formal obligation to eat unleavened bread on the first night of Passover]?

J.   Scripture states, "In the evening you will eat unleavened bread" (Ex. 12:18).

K.   In this way Scripture imposes a fixed obligation in this regard.

II.

A.   And further did R. Eliezer say [etc.] [M. 2:6D]:

B.   But did R. Eliezer not say, Fourteen meals is a person obligated to eat in the sukkah, one by day and one by night [M. 2:6A-B]? [Slotki, p. 117, n. 13: And since the last day is not subject to the obligation, and any person sitting in the sukkah on that day in fulfillment of the commandment is guilty of adding to the commandments, how can that day compensate for the first?]

C.   Said Bira said R. Ami, "R. Eliezer retracted [that view]."

D.   How does one make up [the meal of the first night, if he misses it]?

E.   If one might propose that he does so with bread, then he thereby eats the meal of the festival day [that he is obligated to eat anyhow, so how can that make up for the day he has missed]?

F.   What then is the sense of "make up"?

G.   One makes up the missing meal with various kinds of desserts.

H.   It has been taught along these lines on Tannaite authority:

I.   If one has made up [a missing meal] with various kinds of desserts, he has carried out his obligation.

III.

A.   The butler of Agrippas the king asked R. Eliezer, "In the case of a person such as I, who am used to eat only a single meal a day, what is the law as to my eating only a single meal in the sukkah and thereby carrying out my obligation?"

B.   He said to him, "Every day you go along and eat various sorts of desserts for your own honor, and now shouldn't you add one additional savory in the honor of your creator?"

C.   And he further asked him, "And what about me, for I have two wives, one in Tiberias and one in Sepphoris, and I have two sukkahs, one in Tiberis and one in Sepphoris. What is the law on my going from one sukkah to the other and thereby carrying out my obligation [even though one is supposed to carry out his obligation to dwell in a sukkah by doing so in a single sukkah during the seven days of the holiday]?"

D.   He said to him, "No, [you may not do so.] For I rule that whoever goes out from one sukkah to another loses out on the religious duty he has performed through the first of the two."

IV.

A.   It has been taught on Tannaite authority:

B.   R. Eliezer says, "[27B] People may not go out from one sukkah to another, and they may not erect a sukkah to begin with on the intermediate days of the festival [but it must be built in advance of the first holy day of the festival week]."

C.   And sages say, "People may go from one sukkah to another, and they may also erect a sukkah on the intermediate days of a festival."

D.   And all parties concur that if the sukkah falls down, the owner may go and rebuild it on the intermediate days of the festival.

E.   What is the scriptural basis for the position of R. Eliezer?

F.   Scripture has said, "You shall keep the fest of Sukkot for seven days" (Deut. 16:13), which is to say, make a sukkah that is suitable for seven days.

G.   And rabbis?

H.   This is the sense of Scripture: "Make a sukkah for the festival" [without specification as to how long it must last].

I.   "And all parties concur that if the sukkah falls down, the owner may go and rebuild it on the intermediate days of the festival."

J.   That is self-evident!

K.   Not so, for what might you have said? This really is another sukkah, and it is not for seven days [and so not acceptable].

L.   So we are informed that [even in Eliezer's view] that is not the case.

V.

A.   It has been taught on Tannaite authority:

B.   R. Eliezer says on the first festival day of the Festival, "Just as a man may not fulfill his obligation to take hold of a lulab by using that of his fellow, for it is written, 'And you shall take hold for yourself on the first day of the fruit of goodly trees, branches of palm trees' (Lev. 23:40), meaning, such as belong to you,

C.   "so on the first festival day of the Festival a man may not carry out his obligation to dwell in the sukkah by doing so in the sukkah of his fellow, for it is written, 'The festival of Sukkot you shall keep for yourself for seven days' (Lev. 23:42), meaning, making use of a sukkah that belongs to you yourself."

D.   And sages say, "Even though they have said, 'On the first festival day of the Festival a man may not fulfill his obligation to take hold of the lulab by using that of his fellow,'

E.   "nonetheless, on the first festival day of the Festival he may carry out his obligation to dwell in the sukkah by doing so in the sukkah of his fellow, for it is written, 'All that are homeborn in Israel shall dwell in sukkahs' (Lev. 23:42), teaching that every Israelite may dwell in a single sukkah. [Obviously it will then be a sukkah that some of them do not own.]"

F.   Now how do rabbis interpret the specific reference, at Lev. 23:42, to "for yourself"?

G.   They require that reference to prove that one may not make use of a stolen sukkah, but, with reference to one that is merely borrowed, they point to the verse of Scripture that speaks of "all that are homeborn" (Lev. 23:42).

H. And as to R. Eliezer, how does he deal with that same reference?

I. He requires it to treat the categories of the proselyte, who converted it in the intervening days [between the first and last days of the Festival], and the minor who reached maturity in the intermediate days, [showing that they too must make a sukkah for themselves, even from the point at which the obligation came to apply to them, in the middle of the festival week].

J. And as to rabbis?

K. Since they have said that people may make a sukkah on the intermediate days of the festival, they take the view that no scriptural proof is needed, [in addition, to indicate that the named categories may build a sukkah for themselves during those days].

VI.

A. Our rabbis have taught on Tannaite authority:

B. There was the precedent involving R. Ilai, who went to greet R. Eliezer, his master, in Lud, on the Festival.

C. He said to him, "Ilai, are you not among those who observe the Festival by remaining at rest?"

D. For R. Eliezer maintained, "I praise those who take their ease and do not leave their homes on the Festival, for it has been written, 'You shall rejoice, you and your household' (Deut. 14:26) [including your wife, hence you must stay home on an occasion of rejoicing]." [T. Suk. 2:1C].

E. Is this the case? And did not R. Isaac say, "How do we know that a man is liable to greet his master on the Festival?

F. "As it is said, 'Why will you go to him today? It is neither the New Moon nor the Sabbath' (2 Kgs. 4:23), which bears the implication that on the New Moon and on the Sabbath one is liable to greet his master" [and hence Ilai did the right thing].

G. There is no contradiction. The one verse [which indicates one is liable to do so] speaks of a trip which one can make in one day, and the other speaks of a trip one cannot make in one day.

H. Our rabbis have taught on Tannaite authority:

I. There was the precedent, in which R. Eliezer spent the Sabbath [during the Festival] in Upper Galilee in the sukkah of Yohanan, son of R. Ilai at Caesarea, and, some say, in Caesarion. The sun came into the sukkah. [Thinking of avoiding the glare], he said to him, "What is the law as to my spreading a sheet over [the sukkah]?"

J. He said to him, "You have no tribe in Israel that did not produce a judge."

K. The sun now shone half the height of the sukkah. He said to him, "What is the law as to my spreading a sheet over it?"

L. He said to him, "You have no tribe in Israel from which prophets did not go forth. The tribe of Judah and Benjamin produced kings on the instructions of prophets."

M. The sun reached the feet of R. Eliezer [as it climbed into the sky]. Yohanan took a sheet and spread it over the sukkah.

N. R. Eliezer threw his cloak over his back and left.

O. It was not because [Eliezer wished to] evade answering the questions, he had said, but because [Eliezer] never made a statement that he had not heard from his master.

P. Now how did [Eliezer] act in this way [going out from his own sukkah to keep the Festival at Yohanan's sukkah]? And did not R. Eliezer say, "One may not go forth from one sukkah to another sukkah"? [So surely he should have stayed home and used his own sukkah the entire time.]

Q. It was on a different festival [not Sukkot, and the purpose of sitting in the sukkah had nothing to do with observing the Festival of Sukkot].

R. But did not R. Eliezer himself say, "**I praise those who take their ease and do not leave their homes on the Festival**"?

S. It was the Sabbath [and not a festival].

T. But he could have inferred the answer to the questions from a ruling that he himself had made, for we have learned in the Mishnah:

U. As to the window-shutter [a stopper of a skylight] -- R. Eliezer says, "When it is tied on and suspended, they shut the window with it, and if not, they do not shut the window with it." And sages say, "One way or the other, they shut the window with it" [M. Shab. 17:7]. [Slotki, p. 122, n. 2: Now since the question was whether spreading the cloth over the sukkah would be regarded as adding to it on the Sabbath, why did not R. Eliezer deduce from this analogous case that the answer was in the affirmative?]

V. [28A] In that other case [involving the shutter, one may not do so,] because [in doing so,] one deprives [the shutter of its distinct identity as an object and so ends up simply adding to the building when he closes the shutter. That is, the shutter is regarded as simply part of the building]. But in the former case [involving a sheet on the sukkah], one does not deprive [the sheet of its identity, because no one can regard it as part of the sukkah itself, and the sheet will be removed. Slotki, p. 122, n. 6: The window-shutter becomes part of the frame, but the cover does not become part of the sukkah.]

VII.

A. There was the story concerning R. Eliezer, who spent the Sabbath in the Upper Galilee. People asked him questions about thirty matters of law concerning the sukkah. In the case of twelve of them he said to them, "I have heard the answer."

B. In the case of eighteen of them, he said to them, "I have not heard the answer."

C. R. Yose b. R. Judah says, "The matters were reversed. In the case of eighteen of them, he said to them, 'I have heard the answer.' In the case of twelve of them, he said to them, 'I have not heard the answer.'"

D. They said to him, "Is it the case that everything you say derives only from what you have heard?"

E. He said to them, "You have tried to make me say something that I did not hear from my masters. In my life, no one ever came to the study house before me, I never slept in the study house, either a real nap or a snooze, I never left anybody behind me when I left, I never engaged in idle chatter, and I never said anything that I did not hear from my master."

F. They said about Rabban Yohanan ben Zakkai: He never engaged in idle chatter, he never went four cubits without words of Torah and without wearing his phylacteries, no one ever got to the study house before him, he never slept in the study house, either a real nap or a snooze, he never reflected upon holy matters while in filthy alleys, he never left anyone behind him in the study house when he went out, no one ever found him sitting and dreaming, but only sitting and repeating traditions, only he himself opened the door of his house for his disciples, he never said anything that he had not heard from his master, and he never said, "Time has come to arise from studying in the study house," except for doing so on the eve of Passover and on the eve of the Day of Atonement.

G. And that is how R. Eliezer, his disciple, conducted himself after him.

VIII.

A. Our rabbis have taught on Tannaite authority:

B. Hillel the Elder had eighty disciples, thirty of whom were worthy that the Presence of God should rest upon them as upon Moses, our master, thirty of whom who were worthy that the sun stand still for them as it did for Joshua b. Nun, and twenty of whom were of middle rank.

C. The greatest among them all was Jonathan b. Uzziel, and the least among them was Rabban Yohanan ben Zakkai.

D. They said concerning Yohanan ben Zakkai that he never in his life left off studying Mishnah, Gemara, laws and lore, details of the Torah, details of the scribes, arguments a minori ad majus, arguments based on analogy, [Slotki:] calendrical computations, gematrias, the speech of the ministering angels, the speech of spirits, the speech of palm-trees, fullers' parables and fox fables, great matters and small matters.

E. "Great matters" refers to the Works of the Chariot.

F. "Small matters" refers to the reflections of Abayye and Raba.

G. This serves to carry out that which is said in Scripture: "That I may cause those who love me to inherit substance and fill their treasuries" (Prov. 8:21).

H. Now since the least of them was this way, how much the more so was the greatest of them!

I. They say concerning Jonathan ben Uzziel that when he was in session and occupied with study of Torah, every bird that flew overhead was burned up.

Unit I provides a scriptural basis for Eliezer's opinion. The inquiry opens the underlying issue of which potential analogy we invoke, with sages comparing the rule of the Festival of Sukkot to that applying to Passover. Unit II goes on to Eliezer's second rule. Unit III augments the foregoing, with a story that makes the same point as the rule. Unit IV introduces a further rule in Eliezer's name, relevant to the topic of the Mishnah-paragraph only in general terms. Unit V contributes yet another dispute on Eliezer's view of a rule for Sukkot, one that signals what will be coming before us at M. 3:1. Unit VI proceeds with yet another item on Eliezer and the Festival. Units VII-VIII conclude with secondary augmentations of unit VI's details. So the entire construction presents a pastiche of materials on Eliezer and the Festival of Sukkot, appropriate in theme even when irrelevant in detail to the Mishnah-paragraph at hand.

2:7-8

A. He whose head and the greater part of whose body are in the sukkah, but whose table is in the house --

B. the House of Shammai declare invalid.

C. And the House of Hillel declare valid.

D. Said the House of Hillel to the House of Shammai, "Was not the precedent so, that the elders of the House of Shammai and the elders of the House of Hillel went along to pay a sick-call on R. Yohanan b. Hahorani, and they found him sitting with his head and the greater part of his body in the sukkah, and his table in the house, and they said nothing at all to him!"

E. Said the House of Shammai to them, "Is there proof from that story? But in point of fact they did say to him, 'If this is how you act, you have never in your whole life fulfilled the religious requirement of dwelling in a sukkah!'"

M. 2:7

A. Women, slaves, and minors are exempt from the religious requirement of dwelling in a sukkah.

B. A minor who can take care of himself is liable to the religious requirement of dwelling in a sukkah.

C. M^CSH W: Shammai the Elder's daughter-in-law gave birth, and he broke away some of the plaster and covered the hole with sukkah-roofing over her bed, on account of the infant.

M. 2:8

I.

A. How do we know on that basis of Scripture [the rule at M. 2:8A]?

B. It is in accord with that which our rabbis have taught:

C. "Homeborn" (Lev. 23:42) by itself [without "the" and "every"] would have included every homeborn [encompassing women and minors].

D. [Since it says,] "The homeborn," it means to exclude women, and "Every..." serves to encompass minors. [That explains M. 2:8A, B].

E. A master has said, "'The homeborn' (Lev. 23:42) serves to exclude women."

F.   Does this then imply that the word, "homeborn" [without the] applies both to women and to men?

G.   And has it not been taught, "The homeborn" (Lev. 16:29) [in regard to observance of the Day of Atonement] serves to encompass homeborn women, indicating that they are liable to undertake the distress [of the fast].

H.   Therefore when the word "homeborn" is used [without the "the"] it means to refer only to males.

I.   Said Rabbah, "[In fact] these are matters of received law, and the purpose of rabbis was simply to find scriptural support for the received law."

J.   Which [of the two laws, the one referring to the sukkah or the one about the fasting on the Day of Atonement then] is based on Scripture and which is a received law?

K.   And further, what need do I have to make reference either to a received law or to Scripture? In the case of the requirement to dwell in a sukkah, that is a religious duty calling for an act of commission and based upon a particular time, and any religious duty calling for an act of commission and based upon a particular time leaves women exempt. [They do not have to keep a law which requires them to do something at a particular time, since they have prior obligations to their families.]

L.   As to the Day of Atonement, it derives from a teaching in accord with that which R. Judah said R. Rab said.

M.   For R. Judah said Rab said, and so too did a Tannaite authority of the house of R. Ishmael state, "Scripture has said, 'Man or woman' (Num. 5:6), [28B] so treating men and women as equal in regard to all those acts subject to penalty that are listed in the Torah." [Accordingly, both matters -- sukkah, Day of Atonement, derive from secondary exegesis of the law. In no way do they depend upon either a received tradition or a primary exegesis or proof text.]

N.   Said Abayye, "Under all circumstances, the sukkah [rule concerning women] is a received law, and it is necessary [to make the matter explicit as a received law].

O.   "[Why so?] I might have thought to argue as follows: 'You shall dwell' (Lev. 23:42) in the manner in which you ordinarily dwell. Just as, in the case of an ordinary dwelling, a man and his wife [live together], so in the case of a sukkah, a man and his wife must live together. [Thus I might have reached the conclusion that a woman is liable to dwell in the sukkah.] So we are informed [that that is not the case.]"

P.   Said Raba, "It indeed was necessary to provide such a proof [but it is different from Abayye's argument in the same regard]. For I might have said that we shall derive the rule governing the fifteenth [of Tishri, that is, Sukkot] from the fifteenth [of Nisan,] that is the festival of unleavened bread.

Q.   "Just as, in the latter case, women are liable [to eat unleavened bread], so in the present case, women are liable [to dwell in a sukkah]. So we are informed [that that is not the case]."

R.   Now that you have maintained that the rule about women's exemption from the sukkah is a received law, what need do I have for a Scriptural proof-text?

S.   It is to encompass proselytes [within the requirement to dwell in a <u>sukkah</u>].

T.   You might have said, "The home born in Israel" (Lev. 23:34) is what the All-Merciful has said, thus excluding proselytes.

U.   So we are informed that that is not the case, [and proselytes come under the obligation].

V.   As to the Day of Atonement, since what R. Judah said what Rab said has provided an adequate proof, [that women must fast on the day of atonement, what need do we have for further proof]?

W.   The proof-text encompasses additional affliction [on the eve of the Day of Atonement, prior to nightfall. The fast begins even before sunset. That additional time is added to the fast, and it applies to women as much as to men.]

X.   You might have thought that since the All-Merciful has excluded the additional affliction from the penalties of punishment and admonition [so that, if one does not observe that additional period of fasting, he is not punished on that account], women are not obligated to observe that additional period at all.

Y.   Accordingly, we are informed [that that is not the case, and women are obligated as much as are men.]

<u>II.</u>

A.   A master has said, "Every" [homeborn] serves to encompass minors."

B.   And have we not learned in the Mishnah:

C.   <u>Women, slaves, and minors are exempt from the religious requirement of dwelling in a sukkah [M. 2:8A]</u>?

D.   There is no contradiction [between the exegesis that proves minors must observe the requirement of living in a <u>sukkah,</u> and the Mishnah that states that they need not do so.]

E.   In the case of the exegesis, we speak of a minor who has reached the age at which he becomes educable, while in the Mishnah's case we speak of a minor who has not reached that age.

F.   But is it not the case that the rule that a minor who has reached the age at which he is educable must dwell in the <u>sukkah</u> derives from the authority only of rabbis?

G.   [True enough, but] the verse of Scripture supplies support for their view.

<u>III.</u>

A.   <u>A minor who can take care of himself... [M. 2:8B]</u>:

B.   What is the definition of a minor who can take care of himself?

C.   Members of the household of R. Yannai said, "It is any child who defecates and does not need to have his mother wipe him."

D.   Rabbi says, "It is any child who wakes up from his sleep without crying for his mother."

E.   But adults may also cry out for their mothers!

F.   Rather, it is any who wakes up from his sleep and does not call, "Mother! mother!"

<u>IV.</u>

A.   M^CSH W: Shammai the Elder's daughter-in-law... [M. 2:8C]:

B.   Does the precedent not contradict the rule [that the minor is exempt (M. 2:8A-B)]?

C.   There is a lacuna in the tale, and this is how it is to be repeated:

D.   "And Shammai imposes a strict rule upon himself.

E.   "And there also was the precedent that Shammai the Elder's daughter-in-law gave birth, and he broke away some of the plaster and covered the hole with sukkah-roofing over her bed on account of the infant [M. 2:8C]."

The Talmud ignores M. 2:7 entirely. Unit I provides an elaborate account of the scriptural basis for M. 2:8A. Unit II works through the same matter. Units III and IV gloss the Mishnah's statements.

2:9

A.   All seven days a person treats his sukkah as his regular dwelling and his house as his sometime dwelling.

B.   [If] it began to rain, at what point is it permitted to empty out [the sukkah]?

C.   From the point at which the porridge will spoil.

D.   They made a parable: To what is the matter comparable?

E.   To a slave who came to mix a cup of wine for his master, and his master threw the flagon into his face.

I.

A.   Our rabbis have taught on Tannaite authority:

B.   All seven days a person treats his sukkah as his regular dwelling and his house as his sometime dwelling [M. 2:9A].

C.   How so?

D.   If he had handsome garments, he brings them up to the sukkah, [if he had] lovely spreads, he brings them up to the sukkah. He eats and drinks and walks about in the sukkah.

E.   What is the Scriptural basis for this rule?

F.   It is in accord with that which our rabbis have taught on Tannaite authority:

G.   "You shall dwell" (Lev. 13:42) in the manner in which you ordinarily dwell.

H.   On this basis, they have said: All seven days a person treats his sukkah as his regular dwelling and his house as his sometime dwelling [M. 2:9A]. How so? If he had handsome garments, he brings them up to the sukkah, lovely spreads, he brings them up to the sukkah. He eats and drinks and walks about in the sukkah.

I.   And he should repeat his traditions in the sukkah.

J.   Is this so? And has not Raba said, "One may recite Scripture and repeat Mishnah-teachings in the sukkah, but he reviews his Talmud-learning [following Rashi] outside of the sukkah.

K. There is no contradiction, the first of the two statements alludes to merely reviewing, the second to deep reflection.

L. [29A] That is in line with what Raba bar Hama did, when he was standing in session before R. Hisda. First they reviewed the Talmud together, and then they went and engaged in deep reflection on it.

II.

A. Said Raba, "Drinking cups are to be in the sukkah, food dishes are to be outside of the sukkah. Earthenware pitchers and wooden pails are to be outside of the sukkah.

B. A lamp may be in the sukkah, and some say, outside of the sukkah.

C. There is no dispute in the two versions, the one speaks of a large sukkah [in which one may keep the lamp], the other, a small sukkah [which should not be crowded by needless objects].

III.

A. If it began to rain... [M. 2:9B]:

B. It was taught on Tannaite authority: [From the point at which a porridge] of beans [will spoil] [M. 2:9C].

C. Abayye was in session before R. Joseph in a sukkah. The wind blew, and chips fell [from the roofing, into their food].

D. R. Joseph said to them, "Clear my dishes out of here."

E. Said to him Abayye, "And lo, we have learned: From the point at which the porridge will spoil [M. 2:9C], [and we are far from that]!

F. He said to him, "So far as I am concerned, since I am sensitive, it is as if the porridge was spoiled."

IV.

A. Our rabbis have taught on Tannaite authority:

B. [If] one was eating in a sukkah, and it rained, and he went and stood somewhere else [cf. M. 2:9B],

C. even though the rain let up,

D. they do not obligate him to go back, until he completes his meal.

E. If he was sleeping in a sukkah and it rained and he got up and went away,

F. even though the rain let up,

G. they do not obligate him to go back, until it is dawn [T. Suk. 2:4].

H. As to the preceding sentence, the question was asked:

I. Do we read the final word's spelling so that it means "until he wakes up" or "until dawn"?

J. Come and take note: "Until dawn and the morning star appears."

K. Why say the same thing twice? Rather, "Until he wakes up, and the morning star appears."

V.

A. They made a parable: To what is the matter comparable [M. 2:9D]:

B. They asked, "Who poured [in line with M. 2:9E] upon whom?"

C. Come and take note, for it has been taught on Tannaite authority:

D.   His master threw the flagon into his face [M. 2:9E] and said to him, "I don't want your service any more."

VI.

A.   Our rabbis have taught on Tannaite authority:

B.   [In T.'s version:] When the lights are in eclipse, it is a bad omen for the whole world.

C.   It is to be compared to a mortal king who built a palace and finished it and arranged a banquet, and then brought in the guests. He got mad at them and said to the servant, "Take away the light from them," so all of them turned out to be sitting in the dark.

D.   It has been taught on Tannaite authority: R. Meir did say, "When the lights of heaven are in eclipse, it is a bad omen for Israel, for they are used to blows.

E.   "It is to be compared to a teacher who came into the school house and said, 'Bring me the strap.' Now who gets worried? The one who is used to being strapped" [T. Suk. 2:6H-D].

VII.

A.   Our rabbis have taught on Tannaite authority:

B.   [In Tosefta's version] When the sun is in eclipse, it is a bad omen for the nations of the world.

C.   [When] the moon is in eclipse, it is a bad omen for Israel,

D.   since the gentiles reckon their calendar by the sun, and Israel by the moon.

E.   When it is in eclipse in the east, it is a bad omen for those who live in the east.

F.   When it is in eclipse in the west, it is a bad omen for those who live in the west.

G.   When it is in eclipse in-between, it is a bad omen for the whole world.

H.   When it turns red, it is a sign that punishment by the sword is coming into the world.

I.   When it is like sack-cloth, it is a sign that punishment by pestilence and famine are coming into the world.

J.   If they are smitten at its entry [into sunset], the punishment will tarry. [When they are smitten] when they rise, the punishment is coming fast.

K.   And some say matters are reversed.

L.   You have no nation in the whole world which is smitten, the god of which is not smitten right along with it,

M.   as it is said, And against all the gods of Egypt I will execute judgments (Ex. 12:12).

N.   When Israel do the will of the Omnipresent, they do not have to worry about all these omens,

O.   as it is said, Thus says the Lord, Do not learn the way of the gentiles, nor be dismayed at the signs of the heavens, for the nations are dismayed at them (Jer. 10:2) [T. Suk. 2:6E-R].

P.   So idolators will be dismayed, but Israelites should not be dismayed.

VIII.

A.   Our rabbis have taught on Tannaite authority:

B.   For four reasons is the sun eclipsed:

C.   Because a head of a court has died and has not been properly mourned,

D.   because a betrothed girl has cried out in a town and none goes to her assistance,

E.   because of pederasty,

F.   and because of two brothers whose blood is spilled simultaneously.

G.   [In Tosefta's version] And because of four reasons are the lights of heaven eclipsed:

H.   because of counterfeiters, perjurers, people who raise small cattle in the land of Israel and people who cut down good trees.

I.   And because of four sorts of bad deeds in the property of Israelite householders handed over to the government:

J.   because of holding on to writs of indebtedness which have already been paid,

K.   because of lending on interest,

L.   [29B] because of pledging funds to charity but not paying up, and

M.   because of having the power to protest and not protesting [wrong-doing] [T. Suk. 2:5].

N.   Said Rab, "For four reasons is the property of householders confiscated for taxes:

O.   "because of those who hold back the wages of a hired hand,

P.   "because of those who oppress a hired hand,

Q.   "because of those who remove the yoke from their shoulders and put it on their fellow,

R.   "and because of arrogance.

S.   "But arrogance outweighs all the others.

T.   "And with reference to humble people, it is written, 'But the humble shall inherit the earth and delight themselves in the abundance of peace' (Ps. 37:11)."

After carefully explaining the law of the Mishnah in units I-IV, the Talmud amplifies the matter of M. 2:9D-E. Since the weather is taken to present a bad omen, the matter of other omens, with special reference to eclipses of the sun, moon, and stars, enters in. This occupies the remainder of the discussion, with abundant materials from Tosefta used to fill the space at hand.

3:1

A. A stolen or dried up palm branch is invalid.

B. And one deriving from an asherah or an apostate town is invalid.

C. [If] its tip was broken off, or [if] its leaves were split, it is invalid.

D. [If] its leaves were spread apart, it is valid.

E. R. Judah says, "Let him tie it up at the end."

F. Thorn-palms of the Iron Mountain are valid.

G. A palm branch which is [only] three handbreadths long,

H. sufficient to shake,

I. is valid.

I.

A. [The authority at hand] declares that there is no difference between the first day of the Festival and the second day of the Festival [in declaring that a dried up palm branch is invalid]. [The obligation on the first day derives from Scripture, on the second, only from the authority of rabbis.]

B. Now that poses no problems with respect to a dried up palm branch, because we require one that is "goodly" (Lev. 23:40), and that trait is absent here.

C. But as regards a stolen one, to be sure, with respect to the first day of the Festival, concerning which it is written, "...for you..." (Lev. 23:40), which implies that it must belong to you. [Obviously, the palm-branch must belong to the one who makes use of it, for the stated reason. There is ample authority for rejecting it.]

D. But with regard to the second day of the Festival [to which the verse of Scripture does not make reference,] why [should a stolen palm branch be unacceptable]?

E. Said R. Yohanan in the name of R. Simeon b. Yohai, "[30A]. It is because what you have in hand is the commission of a religious duty accomplished through the commission of a transgression, [namely, the stealing of the palm-branch].

F. "For it is written, 'And you have brought that which is stolen, the lame and the sick' (Mal. 1:13).

G. "The one that is stolen is compared to the one that is lame. Just as the one that is lame cannot be healed, so the one that is stolen cannot be healed. [What is stolen may not be used.]

H. "And do we make no distinction between the situation prevailing before the owner has despaired of recovering the stolen possession [at which point the title to the property still belongs to the owner] and that prevailing after the owner has

- 153 -

despaired of recovery [at which point the title to the property passes over to the thief]? [Surely there should be a difference.]

I. "Now as to the situation prevailing before the owner has despaired of recovering the animal, there is no problem, for it is written, 'When any one brings an offering of what is yours to the Lord' (Lev. 1:2) and this beast does not belong to him [who brings it].

J. "But after the owners have despaired of recovering the property, lo, the thief has acquired possession of the beast through the owner's despair. [Analogously in the case at hand, the thief acquires possession of the branch, and therefore can use it for the performance of the religious duty.]

K. "Therefore is it not on the count that we deal with a commission of a religious duty carried out through commission of a transgression? [That then is the reason behind the rejection of the stolen palm branch.]"

L. And R. Yohanan said in the name of R. Simeon b. Yohai, "What is the meaning of the following verse of Scripture: 'For I the Lord love justice, I hate robbery with iniquity' (Is. 61:8)?

M. "The matter may be compared to the case of a mortal king who was passing the custom house. He said to his staff, 'Pay the custom-fee to the revenuers.'

N. "They said to him, "But do not all the proceeds of the customs go to you?'

O. "He said to them, 'Let everyone who goes by learn from my example and not try to cheat the customs.'

P. "So the Holy One, blessed be he, said, 'For I the Lord... hate robbery in burnt-offerings' [The word for iniquity and that for burnt-offerings appears in the same consonants.]

Q. "'Let my children learn from me and avoid robbers.'"

R. [Concerning the question at C, on which the preceding, D-Q, has focused,] it has also been stated on Amoraic authority:

S. Said R. Ammi, "A dried up one is invalid, because it does not fall into the category of 'goodly' (Lev. 23:40).

T. "A stolen one is invalid because it involves the commission of a religious duty accomplished through the commission of a transgression."

II.

A. [Now the basic thesis on this matter, rejecting the stolen palm-branch on the second day of the Festival], stands at variance with that which R. Isaac said. For R. Isaac bar Nahmani said Samuel [said], "The rule at hand [M. 3:1A] applies only to the first day of the Festival. But on the second day of the Festival, since one may carry out his obligation with a palm-branch that is borrowed, he also may carry out his obligation with one that is stolen."

B. To this view R. Nahman bar Isaac objected, "A stolen or dried up palm-branch is invalid [M. 3:1A]. implying that a borrowed one is valid. Now at what point would that validity apply? If I say that a borrowed one is valid on the first day of the Festival, lo, '...for yourselves...' is written, meaning, 'one belonging to you yourself,' and this one [that is borrowed] is not the property of the person [who has borrowed it]. Consequently reference must be to the second day of the Festival. Now, it is also specified that a stolen one is invalid. [Is it really possible that a stolen branch be forbidden on the second day?]"

C.   No, [at issue is] practice on the first day of the Festival. The Mishnah passage [cited at B] deals only with the less probable of the two matters, as follows:

D.   It is no issue that one may not make use of a borrowed palm-branch, which does not belong to the person who uses it at all. [Obviously, such a palm-branch would be invalid. Therefore, the Mishnah did not state this explicitly.] But as to a stolen one, I might have said that, under ordinary circumstances of thievery, we have a case in which the owner has despaired or recovering his property, [so that we now impute ownership to the thief]. In such a case the palm-branch might be held to fall into the category of the property of the thief himself. Therefore we are informed [by the Mishnah] that that is not the case.

III.

A.   Said R. Huna to the traders, 'When you buy myrtles from idolators [for use in binding with the palm branch], do not cut them yourself, but let them do the cutting for you and let them then give the myrtle to you.'

B.   "What is the reason for this ruling? Under ordinary circumstances idolators are land-grabbers, [30B] and land may not be acquired [in permanent title] through thievery [since the owner will never despair of recovering his property].

C.   "Therefore let the idolators do the cutting, so that what is in their possession [that is, the cut myrtles] may be subject to the imputed despair of the owner [who will give up hope of compensation for the crop, but not the land], with a change of right of possession in your hands." [Slotki, p. 134, n. 16: He is of the opinion that abandonment of right by the owner is not sufficient to constitute acquirement of title by the possessor unless there was in addition either (a) a change of domain, (b) a change in the nature of the object, or (c) a change in its name. But even if abandonment alone were sufficient, the robbery, if the traders themselves had cut the myrtles, would have been committed by them, and they would have been guilty of performing a precept by means of a transgression.]

D.   But, even if the [Israelite] traders themselves cut the myrtles, why not impute the point at which the owner despairs of getting his property back, at which the point of transfer takes place, to the time at which the myrtles are in the hands of the Israelite traders, and let the transfer of domain take place when the myrtles are in the hands of the purchasers themselves? [Slotki, p. 135, n. 1: Since the purchasers commit no robbery, they might well use the myrtles.] [Why tell the traders to make the idolators do the cutting, when this has no affect up on the purchasers' status vis a vis the myrtles in any event?]

E.   The issue pertains to the myrtle that is for the use of the traders themselves. [If they were to cut the myrtles for themselves, there would be no change in domain, and the ones who used the myrtles -- the same as those who cut them -- would be guilty of robbery.]

F.   Now why not regard the right of possession of the myrtles as having been trans-
     ferred by the change in the character of the myrtles effected through binding the
     myrtles, willows, and palm-branch together? [This would constitute a point at which
     the myrtles would enter a different domain, so meeting the objection posed just
     now.]

G.   [That change in the character of the myrtles would, in fact, be null, for] the framer
     of the rule at hand [Huna takes the position that, in preparing the lulab of the
     several species] for use on Sukkot it is not necessary to bind the species together.

H.   If you prefer, I may offer as the following reason not the fact the the lulab does not
     require binding,] for it does have to be bound. Rather, the consideration is that this
     is a change that can be obviated by restoring the object to its former condition, and
     that is not regarded as a substantive change at all.

I.   Then let the change be so consequential as to allow us to impute ownership [to the
     one who now uses the myrtles] namely, through changing the name of the myrtle
     itself. For, to begin with, it was called myrtle, and now it is called [31A] "Hoshan-
     nah" ["Save, us" in the Psalm chanted with the myrtle, "Save, we beseech you"].

J.   [That reason cannot apply], for a myrtle may be called "Hoshannah" in any event, [so
     there is no real change in the name].

IV.

A.   Our rabbis have taught on Tannaite authority:

B.   A sukkah that has been stolen, and [a sukkah which one has made] by spreading
     sukkah-roofing in public domain --

C.   R. Eliezer declares it invalid.

D.   And sages declare it valid.

E.   Said R. Nahman, "The dispute concerns a case in which one has forcibly ejected his
     fellow from his sukkah, and R. Eliezer is consistent with his position elsewhere.

F.   "For he has said, 'A person may not carry out his obligation to dwell in a sukkah by
     using a sukkah that belongs to his fellow.'

G.   "If, then, if the real estate upon which the sukkah is stolen, then the sukkah is also
     considered stolen. [This sukkah since it was built on public property falls into the
     category of a stolen one.]

H.   "One may also propose that in this case the real estate is not stolen but merely
     borrowed, then the sukkah falls into the category of a borrowed one.

I.   "[Therefore] Rabbis too are consistent with their view, for they hold the position
     that a person may carry out his religious obligation of dwelling in a sukkah by
     making use of a sukkah belonging to his fellow.

J.   "Further, land may not fall into the category of thievery, and the sukkah at hand is
     in the category of a borrowed one. [On that account, rabbis validate use of the
     sukkah that has been stolen]."

K.   If, however, one has stolen wood and spread sukkah-roofing on it, all parties concur
     that the owner of the wood has a claim only for the value of the wood. [The thief
     acquires the wood, and what he does with it is not pertinent to the owner, who is
     simply compensated.]

L. How does [one know this to be the case]? Since it is stated explicitly that we may draw an analogy to the case of public domain, we reason as follows:

M. "Just as in the public domain property that does not belong to the person who has used it, so a sukkah does not fall into the category of the property of the person who has used it. [In the case of stolen wood, the thief changes the use and name of the wood, and the sukkah he has built is not stolen nor borrowed and so is valid, even in Eliezer's view. As to the sukkah in public domain, just as we deal with a sukkah built on land that is not the property of the one who has made it, so in the case of a stolen sukkah, it must be one from which the owner has been thrown out by force.]

V.

A. An old lady came before R. Nahman [a member of the exilarch's staff]. She said to him, "The exilarch and all the rabbis on the exilarch's staff are sitting in a stolen sukkah [since they stole the wood from me]."

B. While she cried out, [R. Nahman paid no attention to her. She said to him, "Does a woman whose father had three hundred eighteen slaves [namely, Abraham] cry out before you, and you pay no mind to her?"

C. R. Nahman said to [the others], "She is a pain, but she has a claim only on the cost of the wood alone."

VI.

A. Said Rabina, "As to a sukkah's main beam which was stolen, [and the removal of which would ruin the sukkah], rabbis have provided a remedy for the problem [which is to pay the owner the cost of the wood.]

B. "This remedy is comparable to the remedy provided in the case of a stolen main beam [used in a house]."

C. That fact is obvious! What difference can there be among various kinds of beams [used in different sorts of dwellings, that we have to be told that the remedy applicable to a stolen main beam of a house applies also to a main beam of a sukkah that is made of stolen wood]?

D. What might you have said? The remedy pertained to wood, which is readily available, [so the original owner can use the money paid in compensation to buy more wood for his needs]. But in the case of this sort of main beam, which is not readily available, I might have said that the remedy does not apply.

E. So we are informed that that is not the case. [We allow the thief to pay compensation for the wood, even when it is not easy to get more wood of the same quality].

F. The ruling at hand applies during the seven days of the Festival, but after the seven days of the Festival, the wood must be restored to its original condition.

G. And if the thief joined the beam with mortar, even after the seven days of the Festival, the thief may pay merely compensation for the wood [and may leave his sukkah standing].

VII.

A. It has been taught on Tannaite authority:

B. A dried up [palm-branch] is invalid.

C.   R. Judah declares it valid.

D.   Raba said, "The dispute pertains only to the palm-branch, for rabbis take the view that we draw an analogy between the palm-branch and the citron. Just as the citron must be 'goodly' (Lev. 23:40), so the palm-branch must be 'goodly.'

E.   "And R. Judah takes the view that we do not draw an analogy between the palm-branch and the citron, [which is why he thinks a dried palm branch is valid].

F.   "But in the case of the citron, all parties concur that we require that it exhibit the trait of being 'goodly.'"

G.   Is it then the case that, for the palm-branch, R. Judah does not insist that it be "goodly"?

H.   And have we not learned in the Mishnah:

I.   R. Judah says, "Let him tie it up at the end" [M. 3:1E].

J.   What is the operative consideration? Is it not because he requires that the palm-branch be "goodly"?

K.   No, it is in accord with the reason that has been taught on Tannaite authority:

L.   R. Judah says in the name of R. Tarfon, "[The phrase], 'Branches of palm-trees' (Lev. 23:40) indicates that the branches must be bound up. If they were separated, one has to bind them up."

M.   Is it the case, then, that R. Judah does not require [that the lulab] to be "goodly"?

N.   And have we not learned in the Mishnah:

O.   "They bind up the lulab [palm-branch, willow-branch, and myrtle branch] only with strands of its own species," the words of R. Judah [M. 3:8A].

P.   What is the operative consideration: Is it not because he requires that the lulab [of the several species] be "goodly"?

Q.   No, for lo, Raba has said, "One may do so even with base, even with the root of a palm tree [which clearly do not enhance the palm branch]."

R.   What then can be the reason for R. Judah's view?

S.   In that case he takes the view that the lulab must be bound up [as one], for if one brings another species [of vegetation, in addition to the species that are bound together in the lulab], he will have five species [and not the requisite number, which is four, listed at Lev. 23:40. One cannot add to what Scripture requires.]

T.   Now [moving on from the lulab,] does R. Judah require that the citron fall into the category of what is "goodly"?

U.   And has it not been taught on Tannaite authority:

V.   As to the four species of the lulab, just as they do not reduce their number [to less than four], so they do not add to their number [bringing more than four].

W.   [If] one does not have a citron, he should not use a pomegranate, a quince, or any other sort of fruit.

X.   [If the four species] were wrinkled, they are valid. [If] they were dried up, they are invalid.

Y.   R. Judah says, "If [the four species] were dried up, they are valid."

Z. Said R. Judah, "M'SH B: [31B] The townsfolk of the villages would leave the lulabs to their children in time of need."

AA. They said to him, "A time of need does not yield proof." [T. Suk, 2:9]

BB. Now the cited story indicates, then, that R. Judah says, "Also if the four species were dried up, they are valid."

CC. Does this not refer to the citron [and indicate that he does not require that the citron fall into the category of "goodly"?

DD. No, he refers to the lulab.

EE. [Reviewing the cited passage as to secondary elements:] The foregoing master has stated: Just as they do not reduce their number, so they do not add to their number

FF. That is self-evident.

GG. [No it is not self evident] for you might have reasoned [as follows]: Since R. Judah has said, "A lulab has to be bound together, "and if one brings binding of another species, [one might have claimed that] that binding will be deemed separate, and the species of the lulab will be deemed separate. Thus we are informed that that is not the case. [The binding must be of one of the species already in use in the lulab].

HH. The master has said, If one does not have a citron, he should not use a pomegranate, quince, or any other sort of fruit.

II. That is self-evident.

JJ. [No it is not self evident.] For you might have reasoned [as follows:] Let him bring [some other sort of similar fruit] so that the basic rule governing the citron will not be forgotten.

KK. So we are informed that that is not the case, for on some occasions confusion might result, since people might be confused [as to which is the valid species].

LL. Come and take note:

MM. An old citron is invalid.

NN. And R. Judah declares it valid.

OO. Is this not a refutation of the view of Raba?

PP. It is a refutation indeed.

QQ. But does not R. Judah require that [the citron] fall into the category of "goodly"?

RR. Have we not learned in the Mishnah:

SS. And as to a citron which is as green as a leek —

TT. R. Meir declares it valid.

UU. And R. Judah declares it invalid [M. 3:61-K].

VV. Is R. Judah's reason not that he requires the citron to fall into the category of what is "goodly"?

WW. No, it is because the fruit is not yet ripe.

XX. Come and take note:

YY. As to a small citron.

ZZ. R. Meir says, "[It must be at least] the size of a nut."

AAA. R. Judah says, "[At least] The size of an egg" [M. 3:7A-C].

BBB. Is R. Judah's reason not that he requires the citron to fall into the category of what is "goodly"?

CCC. No, not at all. The reason is that [if it is smaller than an egg] the fruit is not yet ripe.

DDD. Come and take note:

EEE. And as to the largest acceptable size of a citron:

FFF. "It must be of such size that one can hold two in one hand," the words of R. Judah.

GGG. R. Yose says, "Even one in two hands: [M. 3:7D-F].

HHH. Is R. Judah's reason not that he requires the citron to fall into the category of what is "goodly"?

III. No, it is in line with what Rabbah said, "The lulab is to be in the right hand and the citron in the left hand." Now on some occasions one may switch them, and one of them [the citron] might fall and become invalid. [Slotki, p. 149, n. 7:7 If the citron is too large for him to grasp in his hand together with his lulab, as he is changing over, he will drop it. Hence the ruling that one should be able to hold two in one hand, one of these two representing the space the lulab would occupy during the change.]

JJJ. But, in the view of R. Judah, does Scripture not state, "Goodly" (Lev. 23:40)?

KKK. [Judah interprets this to mean] that [the appropriate fruit, namely the citron], is one that remains on the tree [on which it grows] from one year to the next." [This represents a play on the word HDR, which may be read "goodly" or "that which remains" or "dwells."]

VIII.

A. And one deriving from an asherah or an apostate town [M. 3:1B]:

B. Is one deriving from an asherah invalid? But has Raba not said, "A lulab that has served for the purposes of idolatry one should not take, but if he has taken such a one, it is valid."

C. Here we deal with an asherah from the time of Moses, which is regarded as crushed to less than the minimal size for a lulab. [Since the asherah will be burned, it is regarded as if it has already been burned.]

D. Take note of the language at hand, since we compare the lulab of the asherah to one deriving from a condemned apostate city. [In this latter case, we treat what is going to be burned as if it already had been burned.]

E. That indeed proves the case.

IX.

A. If its tip was broken off [M. 3:1C]:

B. Said R. Huna, "The law is taught only in the case of one that is broken off. But if it is merely split, it is valid."

C. But is what is merely split valid? And has it not been taught on Tannaite authority:

D. A palm-branch that is bent over [32A], thorny, split, or curved like a sickle, is unfit. If a palm-branch has hardened, it is invalid. If it appears to have hardened [but has not actually done so], it is valid [So we see an explicit statement that a split palm-branch is invalid.]

E.   Said R. Pappa, "[Where it is invalid,] it is a case in which the palm-branch is like a prong [naturally split to a considerable extent]."

F.   As to the statement that [it is invalid if it is] curved like a sickle, said Raba, "That statement applies only where it is bent forward, but if it is bent backward, that accords with its nature. [It would then be valid.]"

G.   R. Nahman said, "If it curves to the sides, it is in the category of curving forward."

H.   And some say that it is in the category of curving backward.

I.   And Raba said, "A palm-branch, of which all of the foliage grows on one side, is blemished and invalid."

X.

A.   If its leaves were split [M. 3:1C]:

B.   Said R. Pappa, "'Split' means that the palm-branch leaves are shaped like a broom. 'Separated' means that they were parted from one another [Slotki, p. 140, n. 10: But joined to the rib at their roots]."

C.   R. Pappa raised the question, "What is the law if the central leaf [at the junction of two leaves] was split?"

D.   Come and take note: Said R. Joshua b. Levi, "If the central leaf was removed, the palm-branch is invalid."

E.   Now would not the same rule apply if the central leaf was split?

F.   No, the case of removing it differs, because the leaf then is completely lacking.

G.   There are those who said the same matter in the following version:

H.   Said R. Joshua b. Levi, "If the central leaf was split, it is treated as if the central leaf was removed, and it is invalid."

XI.

A.   [With regard to M. 3:1E] it has been taught on Tannaite authority:

B.   R. Judah says in the name of R. Tarfon, "The statement 'Branches of palm trees' (Lev. 23:40) indicates that the palm-branches must be bound. If, therefore, the leaves were separated, one has to bind them up."

C.   Said Rabina to R. Ashi, "How do we know that the reference to 'branches of palm trees' refers in particular to the palm-branches' [green sprouts, in particular]? Perhaps the reference is to the branches of a hardened palm [Slotki, p. 141, n. 1: a palm which is some years old, whose branches have become hardened like other tree branches, and there must be one central branch and one protruding from each side]?"

D.   [That cannot be the case, for] we require a case of branches that can be bound up, and [that condition is] not [met by hardened ones].

E.   And might I say that it refers to the stalk itself [one without leaves]?

F.   Since the word speaks of "bound," it bears the implication that there is something separated [that must be bound], while this one is permanently joined.

G.   But might I say that it means [Slotki:] the inflorescence of palms [Slotki, p. 141, n. 6: a spike covered with flowers and enveloped by one or more spathes. Being only one or two years old, its leaves can still be bent and bound to the central parts.]

H.   Said Abayye, "'Its ways are ways of pleasantness and all her paths are peace' is what is written. (Prov. 3:17) [Slotki, p. 141, n. 7: It is unpleasant to hold this prickly spike and therefore the Torah could not have referred to it.]"

I.   Said Raba Tosfaah to Rabina, "And might I suggest that the reference is to two palm-branches [and not one containing several sprigs]?"

J.   "It is written, 'Branch of' [defectively, thus in the singular]."

K.   "Might I say then that it refers to only one?"

L.   "Then it would have been written, 'A branch.'"

XII.

A.   Thorn-palms of the Iron Mountain are valid [M. 3:1F]:

B.   Said Abayye, "The rule has been stated that these are valid only in a case in which the head of the one reaches the side of the junction of the next, but if the head of the one does not reach the side of the junction of the next, it is invalid."

C.   It has been taught on Tannaite authority along these same lines:

D.   Thorn-palms of the Iron Mountain are invalid.

E.   Lo, we have learned in the Mishnah that they are valid!

F.   Does this [contradiction] not then bear the implication that the view of Abayye is correct [since his view harmonizes both statements]?

G.   It does indeed bear that implication.

H.   [32B] There are those who present the matter as a contradiction in the following manner:

I.   We have learned in the Mishnah: Thorn-palms of the Iron Mountain are valid [M. 3:1F].

J.   And has it not been taught on Tannaite authority: "They are invalid"?

K.   There is no contradiction between the two versions. In the one case we deal with one in which the head of one reaches the side of the junction of the leaves of the other, and in the other case we deal with one in which the head of the one does not reach the side of the junction of the leaves of the other.

L.   Said R. Marion said R. Joshua b. Levi, and there are those who state that Rabba bar Mari repeated in the name of R. Rabban Yohanan ben Zakkai, "There are two palms in the valley of Hinnom, and a pillar of smoke ascends from between them, and this is the matter in connection with which we [have learned to] repeat: Thorn-palms of the Iron Mountain are valid [M. 3:1F], and this is the very doorway to Gehenna."

XIII.

A.   A palm-branch which is only three handbreadths long [M. 3:1G]:

B.   R. Judah said Samuel said, "The requisite length of the myrtle and the willow is a minimum of three handbreadths, and of the palm-branch is four handbreadths, so that the palm-branch should be a handbreadth higher than the myrtle."

C.   And R. Parnakh said R. Yohanan said, "The stem of the palm-branch [not merely the leaves] should be a handbreadth higher than the myrtle."

D.   Have we not learned in the Mishnah: A palm-branch which is only three handbreadths long, sufficient to shake, is valid [M. 3:1G-I]? [How insist then that it must be at least four handbreadths long, as both Samuel and Yohanan maintain?]

E. I should repeat the matter with an <u>and</u> [thus: three handbreadths long and sufficient to shake, so referring to the part beyond the myrtle and willow, which is not bound and can be waved', and then each authority works matters out according to his view [Slotki, p. 142, n. 6: According to Samuel, a handbreadth including the leaves, according to R. Yohanan, one excluding the leaves].

F. Come and take note: **The required measure of the length of a myrtle branch and a willow branch is three handbreadths, and of a palm branch, four** [T. Suk. 2:8B].

G. Would this not mean, including the leaves [as against Yohanan's view]?

H. No, excluding the leaves.

XIV.

A. Returning to the body of the text just now cited [XIII F]:

B. **The required measure of the length of a myrtle branch and a willow branch is three handbreadths, and of a palm-branch, four.**

C. R. Tarfon says, "**This is measured by a cubit divided into five handbreadths**" [T. Suk. 2:8B-C].

D. Said Raba, "May R. Tarfon's master forgive him. A myrtle three handbreadths long we can scarcely find, so will there be a question of one <u>five</u> handbreadths long?"

E. When R. Dimi came, he said, "[This is the sense of Tarfon's statement]. Take a cubit which has six handbreadths and make it into five. [So the handbreadth now is a fifth of a cubit]. Take off the three for the myrtle, so the remainder is for the palm branch. What is it then in normal handbreadths? Three and three fifths. [Slotki, p. 143, n. 4: Since the three handbreadths of the myrtle are equivalent to $3 \times 1\ 1/5 = 3\ 3/5$ normal handbreadths.]"

F. Now there is a contradiction between two statements made by Samuel.

G. Here Rab Judah said Samuel said, "The requisite length of the myrtle and the willow is a minimum of three handbreadths, and of the palm branch is four handbreadths."

H. Elsewhere R. Huna said Samuel said, "The law accords with the view of R. Tarfon." [Slotki, p. 143, n. 4: Tarfon prescribes 3 3/5 normal handbreadths.]

I. Samuel did not state matters precisely. [He said three handbreadths, but he meant 3 3/5, as Tarfon requires.]

J. Now I might well propose that we invoke the principle that someone is not precise, when imprecision results in a more strict ruling, but do we invoke that principle when it results in a lenient ruling? [Will Samuel accept a shorter than proper palm branch, that is, three rather than 3 3/5th?]

K. When Rabin came, he said, "[Tarfon referred to] a cubit that has five handbreadths. Make a cubit of five into one of six handbreadths. Deduct three of these for the myrtle, and the remainder is for the palm branch. How much [in normal hand-breadths] is it? Two and a half." [Slotki, p. 143, n. 10: The normal cubit of six handbreadths being divided into five, each handbreadth is 5/6th of a normal handbreadth. The three handbreadths of the myrtle, therefore, equal $(3 \times 5/6 = 15/16 =)$ 2 1/2 normal handbreadths, leaving 2 1/2 for the extending portion of the palm-branch.]

L.   Do not two statements of Samuel then contradict each other [since he demands three but also says the law follows Tarfon, who accepts a palm branch of only two and a half handbreadths]?

M.   He did not state matters precisely, and in this case, in not stating matters precisely, he imposed a more strict requirement.

N.   For R. Huna said Samuel said, "The law accords with R. Tarfon."

Unit I takes up M. 3:1A and is continued by unit II. Unit III introduces a secondary issue, raised by the reference to thievery. At exactly what point does ownership of an object pass from the original owner to the thief? The theory is that this is effected by the owner's despair of recovering the object, joined to a change of domain, of the character of the object, or the name or category of the object. The inquiry here is subtle and sophisticated. It did not have to attach to M. 3:1A. Unit IV goes on to another aspect of thievery, now referring not to the stolen palm branch but a stolen sukkah. Unit V continues unit IV. Unit VI raises a distinct question, relevant in a general way, namely, the disposition of stolen wood used in a sukkah. The prevailing law is that a thief may pay compensation, rather than having to return the stolen wood itself. That rule is applied to the matter at hand. Unit VII proceeds to a protracted inquiry into the status of the dried up palm branch, M. 3:1A, with reference to Judah's position on other elements of the rite of the Festival. At what point do we insist that a cultic object fall into the category of "goodly," that is, of the highest quality? The repertoire of relevant items is rich. In constructing the unit, the framer found it possible to link together a broad variety of materials, but he cannot be said to have introduced original or important principles, such as we find in the earlier units. Unit VIII moves us on to M. 3:1B, unit IX to M. 3:1C, X to M. 3:1C, XI to M. 3:1E, XII to M. 3:1F, XIII-XIV to M. 3:1G. So the entire construction has been worked out to align with the sequence of topics of the Mishnah, though the more interesting units introduce their own, autonomous considerations.

3:2

A.   A stolen or dried up myrtle branch is invalid.

B.   And one deriving from an asherah or an apostate town is invalid.

C.   [If] its tip was broken off, [or if] its leaves were split,

D.   or if its berries were more numerous than its leaves,

E.   it is invalid.

F.   But if one then removed some of them, it is valid.

G.   But they do not remove [some of them] on the festival day.

I.

A.   Our rabbis have taught on Tannaite authority:

B.   "Boughs of a thick tree" (Lev. 23:40) [refers to] a tree, the boughs of which cover the trunk. What would such a tree be?

C.   One must say, This refers to the myrtle.

D.   Might I say it refers to an olive?

E.   We require thick [leaves, which form a wreath], and that trait is not present.

F.   And might I say it refers to a plane tree?

G.   We require that the branches cover the trunk, and that trait is not present.

H.   And might I say it refers to an oleander?

I.   Said Abayye, "'Its ways are ways of pleasantness' (Prov. 3:17), a trait lacking [in the oleander]."

J.   Raba said, "Proof that it cannot be the oleander derives from here: 'Therefore love truth and peace' (Zech. 8:19). [Slotki, p. 144: There is in it neither peace, since it stings, nor love, since it is bitter and poisonous.]"

II.

A.   Our rabbis have taught on Tannaite authority:

B.   If the leaves are plaited so as to look like a chain, it is the myrtle.

C.   R. Eliezer b. Jacob says, "'The boughs of a thick tree' (Lev. 23:40) refers to a tree in which the flavor of the wood and the fruit is the same. One must say that this is the myrtle."

III.

A.   It has been taught on Tannaite authority:

B.   A tree with thick leaves is valid, and one that does not have thick leaves is invalid.

C.   What is the definition of having thick leaves?

D.   Said Rab Judah, "It is a case when three leaves grow out of one nest" [Slotki].

E.   R. Kahana said, "Even if they grow in twos or ones."

F.   R. Aha, son of Raba, went looking for one which had leaves in twos and ones. This was on the basis of the statement of R. Kahana.

G.   Said Mar, son of Amemar, to R. Ashi, "Father called that kind of myrtle a wild myrtle."

IV.

A.   Our rabbis have taught on Tannaite authority:

B.   If most of the leaves of a myrtle have fallen off and only the smaller number remains on it, it is valid, so long as its wreath-work [three leaves coming out of each nest of the stem] remains."

C.   Now the statement bears a contradiction. You have said, ""If most of the leaves have fallen off, it remains valid." And then it is taught, "So long as its wreath-work remains."

D.   Now if two of the three leaves have dropped off, where will there be wreath-work at all?

E.   Said Abayye, "You may find such a thing [33A] in an Egyptian myrtle, which has seven leaves in each nest. Thus when four drop off, there still will be three left."

F.   Said Abayye, "The foregoing teaching then implies that an Egyptian myrtle is suitable for use as a hoshannah [a myrtle used in the lulab]."

G.   That fact is perfectly self-evident.

H. [Nonetheless, we have to make it explicit. For] what might you have said? Since that sort of myrtle bears a distinctive name of its own, it is not suitable [for use in the lulab]. So we are informed [that that conclusion is incorrect].

I. And might I say that that indeed is a correct conclusion?

J. The All-Merciful has specified, "Boughs of a thick tree" (Lev. 23:40) — meaning, of any sort whatsoever.

K. Our rabbis have taught on Tannaite authority:

L. If most of the leaves have dried up, and three twigs with fresh leaves remain, it is valid.

M. And R. Hisda said, "That is the case if the fresh leaves are at the tip of its sprig."

V.

A. If its tip was broken off [M. 3:2C]:

B. Ulla bar Hinena taught on Tannaite authority, "If its tip was broken off but a berry grew on the detached myrtle, it is valid."

C. R. Jeremiah raised the question: "If its tip was broken off on the eve of the festival, and a berry grew up on the myrtle on the festival, what is the law? Do we apply to the things used for the performance of religious duties the principle, 'once disqualified, always useless,' or do we not apply that principle [that pertains to sacrificial animals? That is, once a beast designated for a sacrifice is blemished, it remains so, even though the blemish later disappears or is removed.]"

D. You may find the answer from the following rule, which we have learned in the Mishnah:

E. If one covered up the blood [of a slaughtered beast, as one is supposed to do, and the blood became uncovered, the man is exempt from having to cover it up again. But if the wind blew and covered up the blood, the man is liable, nonetheless, to cover it up [M. Hul. 6:4].

F. And Rabbah bar bar Hana said R. Yohanan [said], "That statement applies only to a case in which the blood was once again uncovered. But if the blood was not once again uncovered, the man is exempt from having to cover up blood, [that the wind has covered with dirt]."

G. Now we reflected on this matter: Why, when the blood is once more uncovered, is one liable to cover it up? Once [the blood] has been dealt with improperly, [that should close the question and leave it] unfit, [so why should the man have to cover it up again]?

H. And R. Papa said, "That is to say that we do not apply to the performance of things used for religious duties the principle, 'once disqualified, always useless'!"

I. [No, that is no solution to Jeremiah's problem. For it begs the question, since] what [Jeremiah] asked is hardly going on its own to supply the answer!

J. At issue in his mind is whether the principle, 'once disqualified, always unfit,' pertains to the performance of religious duties without distinction as to whether the result is a lenient or strict ruling, or whether it pertains to a doubt in the case only of a strict ruling but not a lenient ruling.

K.   [We have to say that the question must] stand.

L.   May one say that at issue between the following Tannaite authorities is the same principle?

M.   "[If one has a myrtle in which the berries were more numerous than the leaves, M. 3:2D, and one] went and picked off [the berries], the myrtle remains invalid," the words of R. Eleazar b. Sadoq.

N.   And sages declare it valid.

O.   Now the premise of what follows is that all parties to the dispute concur that a lulab does not have to be bound together, and, even if you should wish to take the view that it does have to be bound, we nonetheless do not derive the law of the lulab from the law of the sukkah, concerning which it is written, "You will make" -- and not what is ready-made [Slotki, p. 147, n. 1: So that the disqualification of the lulab (on account of the myrtle that has been doctored) cannot be due to the fact that, when the myrtle became fit, the lulab had already been made]. [These two premises will recur presently.]

P.   It would then follow, would it not, that this is at the core of the dispute at hand:

Q.   He who holds that the myrtle is unfit takes the view that we do apply to the performance of the various religious duties the principle, "once disqualified, always unfit."

R.   And the one who declares it fit takes the position that we do not invoke the principle that what is once disqualified is always unfit in the case of things used in the performance of religious duties.

S.   No, it does not at all follow. All parties maintain that we do not invoke the principle that, in the performance of the religious duties, what is once disqualified is always unfit.

T.   At issue here is the separate question of whether we derive the rules governing the lulab from those that pertain to the making of the sukkah.

U.   One authority holds that we do derive the rules of the lulab from those governing the sukkah [in which case the lulab must be ready and suitable in advance of the festival].

V.   And the other authority takes the view that we do not derive the rules of the lulab from those governing the sukkah.

W.   If you wish, I shall propose that, if we all concur that the lulab does require binding, all parties would also concur that the rules of the lulab do derive from those governing the sukkah. Here at issue, however, is whether in fact the lulab requires binding. The parties then dispute about what is at issue between the following Tannaite authorities.

X.   For it has been taught on Tannaite authority:

Y.   A lulab [palm-branch, willow-branch, myrtle branch] whether bound up or not bound up is valid.

Z.   R. Judah says, "One which is bound up is valid, and one which is not bound up is invalid" [T. Suk. 2:10A-B].

AA. What is the scriptural basis for the view of R. Judah?

BB. He derives the meaning of the word "take" occurring in two different and related contexts [and draws an analogy from the one to the other], with special reference to the word "take" used in regard to the binding of the hyssop.

CC. It is written here, "And you shall take for yourself on the first day" (Lev. 23:40), and with reference to hyssop it is written, "And you shall take a bundle of hyssop" (Ex. 12:22).

DD. Just as, in that latter instance, we speak of a bundle when we use the word "take," so here we speak of a bundle where we use the word "take."

EE. And as to rabbis? They do not draw on analogy from the use of the word "take" in the one case for the meaning of the usage in the other.

FF. Who is the Tannaite authority behind that which our rabbis have taught on Tannaite authority:

GG. As to the lulab [myrtle, palm branch, willow], the religious duty is that one bind it together, but if one has not bound it together, it is nonetheless valid.

HH. Now who can stand behind this statement?

II. Surely it cannot be R. Judah, for if one has not bound the species together, why would the lulab be valid?

JJ. And it cannot be the view of rabbis, for what religious duty does not carry out if one binds the species together, seeing that they do not require one to do so at all.

KK. No, it indeed is the view of rabbis, and the religious duty of binding the species is solely on the count of the verse, "This is my God, and I shall glorify him" (Ex. 15:2), [bearing the implication that one should make the lulab look nicer by binding the species together, but there is no requirement that one actually do so.]

VI.

A. Or if its berries were more numerous [M. 3:2D]:

B. Said R. Hisda, "This matter did our greater master [Rab] (the Omnipresent be his support!) state, 'The rule of our Mishnah has been stated only with reference to [a myrtle which had all of its berries] in a single place, but if they were in two or three places, the myrtle is valid.'"

C. Said Raba, "[33B] If the berries were spread about in two or three places, it would look spotty and so would be invalid."

D. Rather, if the statement imputed to Rab was made at all, this is how it was made:

E. Or if its berries were more numerous than its leaves, it is invalid [M. 3:2D]:

F. Said R. Hisda, "This matter did our great master [Rab] (the Omnipresent be his support!) state, 'The rule of our Mishnah has been stated only in the case of a myrtle with black berries, but if the berries were green, they are a species of myrtle and valid.'"

G. Said R. Papa, "Those that are red fall into the category of those that are black.

H. "For R. Hanina said, 'Black blood is really red blood that has deteriorated.'"

VII.

A. But if one then removed some of them, it is valid [M. 3:2F]:

B. When did he remove them? If I say that it was before he bound the species together, that is self-evident [since the myrtle was valid from the moment at which it was bound, and that is obvious].

C. Rather, it must be after one has bound the species together.

D. Then you have a case in which, to begin with, what is used for the performance of a religious duty is disqualified [but one has thereafter rendered the object suitable].

E. From that fact you may solve the problem and conclude that what is unsuitable to disqualified to begin with is not permanently unsuitable.

F. No, it was indeed after the man bound the species together that he removed the berries. But he is of the view that the act of binding the species, represents merely a designation of the object, for its actual use and mere advance designation of the object has no standing whatsoever. [Slotki, p. 149: "The binding is merely a designation for its purpose, and a mere designation is of no consequence." N. 1: The plants do not thereby assume the full character of a lulab.]

VIII.

A. But they do not remove some of them on the festival day [M. 3:2G]:

B. Now if one transgressed and did remove the excess berries, what is the law?

C. Is it valid? But then [referring back to VI E] when did the berries become black?

D. If I say that the berries turned black on the preceding day, then we have a case in which, to begin with, the object was disqualified, and one may properly draw the conclusion that, if an object is at once disqualified, it is not permanently unsuitable.

E. Rather it is a case in which the berries turned black on the festival day.

F. Then we have a case in which the object was suitable and then became disqualified. So one may draw the inference that what was once suitable and then becomes disqualified may then become suitable again.

G. No, we may not draw that inference at all. We deal with a case in which the berries turned black to begin with, in which case it indeed follows that what was disqualified to begin with does not remain unfit.

H. But you may not deduce from this case the principle that what was to begin with suitable and then became unsuitable does not once more become suitable.

IX.

A. Our rabbis have taught on Tannaite authority: But they do not remove some of them on the festival day [M. 3:2G].

B. In the name of R. Eliezer b. R. Simeon they have said, "They do remove some of them."

C. But lo, [by doing so] does he not repair [and make ready] an object on the festival day itself? [Surely an object has to be prepared prior to the Festival. Only preparation of food may take place on the festival day itself.]

D. Said R. Ashi, "We deal with a case in which one cut the myrtle for the purpose of eating [and then changed his mind and used it for the lulab. In this case one may improve the myrtle, in line with the original definition of what it was to be used for, namely, eating.]"

E.   And R. Eliezer b. R. Simeon takes the view of the matter that his father did, who
      said that something that one does not intend as a forbidden act of labor is permitted
      [on the festival day. The original intent was a valid one.]

F.   But lo, Abayye and Raba both have maintained that R. Simeon concurs that "if one
      has cut off his own head, one does not leave him to die" [meaning that if one has not
      had the intention of bringing about a certain result, it is nevertheless an inevitable
      consequence (Slotki, p. 149, n. 12)], in which case it is forbidden [and the validity of
      the myrtle is the inevitable consequence of the plucking of the berries (Slotki, p.
      149, n. 13)].

G.   Here with what situation do we deal?

H.   We deal with a case in which the man has another hoshannah [myrtle for use on the
      festival]. [Slotki, p. 149, n. 14: Being independent of the one with the berries the
      removal of the latter cannot be regarded as the improvement of an object.] [That is
      to say, in Eliezer's view we do not have a purposeful act of labor here, because the
      man does not need the myrtle he is improving. He has another one. That is why one
      may fix the myrtle up on the festival day.]

X.

A.   Our rabbis have taught on Tannaite authority:

B.   If the binding of the lulab became loose on the festival day, one may bind it up in
      the manner in which vegetables are bound up. [Such a binding involves not knot, and
      one inserts the loose end of the string between the winding and the plants.]

C.   But why [not make a proper binding, rather than the makeshift one just now
      described]? Should one not make a proper loop [which not being a knot, is permitted
      on the Festival (Slotki)]?

D.   Who stands as the authority for this statement [to the contrary]? It is R. Judah, who
      has said that a loop constitutes a valid knot in all regards.

E.   If that is the view of R. Judah, then he would require exactly such a proper knot [so
      why permit it at all]?

F.   The Tannaite authority at hand concurs with R. Judah on one matter and differs
      with him on another. [Judah requires a proper binding, and he regards the loop as a
      proper knot. The Tanna at hand concurs that the lulab must be bound, but he does
      not see the loop as a proper knot, which is why he permits tying it on the festival
      day itself.]

Unit I provides a proof text to show that a myrtle branch is required for the lulab.
That is not the issue of M. 3:2, but, of course, it is the premise. Unit II carries forward
the inquiry of unit I into the definition of what is required by Lev. 23:40, and unit III does
the same. Only unit IV brings us to the rule at hand, now with clear reference to M.
3:2D. Unit V takes up M. 3:2C. But its issue is not the exegesis of the Mishnah. Rather
we begin the secondary inquiry into the implications of the rule at hand for the principle
that what is once disqualified remains perpetually unfit. That principle is subjected to a
close reading in most of the units that follow. As we see, the rules of the sukkah and

lulab are then turned into evidence for the analysis of the general principle. Unit VI then treats M. 3:2D in a more limited framework. Units VII, VIII proceed to units M. 3:2F, G, with a clear effort at both to renew discourse on the general principle taken up at unit V. So the entire sequence has to be regarded as a unitary discussion, and the principal focus of analysis is not the Mishnah-passage before us, but its relevance to an issue selected without special interest in the facts at hand. Unit IX introduces a dispute on the law given in the Mishnah, M. 3:2G. Unit X is autonomous of the Mishnah-passage and also does not introduce an encompassing principle, to which the Mishnah-passage is relevant. But the issue cannot be said to be out of place; it is, rather, an extension of M. 3:2G's reference to what may or may not be done on the festival day itself.

3:3

A.   A stolen or dried up willow branch is invalid.

B.   And one deriving from an asherah or an apostate town is invalid.

C.   [If] its tip was broken off, [if] its leaves split, or [if it was] a moun-
      tain-willow,

D.   it is invalid.

E.   [If] it was shriveled, or [if] some of the leaves dropped off,

F.   or [if it came] from a [naturally watered] field [and did not grow by a
      brook],

G.   it is valid.

I.

A.   Our rabbis have taught on Tannaite authority:

B.   "Willows of the brook" (Lev. 23:40) [refers to those willows] that grow by a brook.

C.   Another consideration: "Willows of the brook" -- that the leaves are drawn out
      [elongated] like a brook [not round].

II.

A.   A further Tannaite teaching:

B.   "Willows of the brook" (Lev. 23:40): I know only that [acceptable are] willows that
      grow by a brook. How do I know the rule that those that grow in an irrigated field
      or in mountains are valid?

C.   Scripture states, "Willows [in the plural] of the brook," thus encompassing those that
      derive from any location.

D.   [34A] Abba Saul says, "When the verse speaks in the plural of 'willows of,' it refers
      to two, one for use in the lulab, the other for use in the sanctuary [and hence the use
      of the plural does not mean what B-C have alleged]."

E.   And as to rabbis [behind B-C], whence do they know that the law at hand covers the
      willow used for the sanctuary?

F.   They derive it as a received law, for R. Assi said R. Yohanan said, "The rule
      governing the ten plants [that constitute a tree planted field, which one may plough

right down to the New Year of the Sabbatical Year, rather than ceasing cultivation well in advance of the Sabbatical Year, as one must do in ordinary fields not planted in trees], the rule about the willow, and the rule about the water-offering, constitute law revealed to Moses from Sinai."

III.

A. Our rabbis have taught on Tannaite authority:

B. "Willows of the brook" (Lev. 23:40) [refers to those that grow by a brook],

C. thus excluding a mountain-willow [M. 3:3C], which grows in the mountains.

D. Said R. Zira, "What is the scriptural basis at hand? 'He placed it beside many waters, he set it as a mountain willow' (Ez. 17:5) [SPSPH, the same word for mountain-willow as is used in the Mishnah]. [Thus one set beside water is deemed distinct from one set in the mountains.]'

E. Said to him Abayye, "But perhaps the latter clause ['He set it...'] serves to explain the former clause, that is, 'He placed it beside many waters,' and what would that mean? 'He set it as a mountain willow.'"

F. If so, what is the sense of "he set it"?

G. Said R. Abbahu, "Said the Holy One, blessed be he, 'I had the plan of having Israel before me as something 'set beside many waters,' and what might that mean? It means like a willow. But they set themselves like a mountain-willow.'"

H. There are those who repeat the preceding verse of Scripture with reference to the following teaching on Tannaite authority [so that Zira objects to the proof, rather than adducing it, thus:]

I. "He placed it beside many waters, he set it as a mountain willow" (Ez. 17:5).

J. To this [reading of the verse as a proof text for M. 3:3C's prohibition of the mountain willow], R. Zira objected, "But perhaps the latter clause serves to explain the former clause? That is, 'He placed it beside many waters,' and what would that mean? 'He set it as a mountain willow.'"

K. If so, what is the sense of "he set it"?

L. Said R. Abbahu, "Said the Holy One, blessed be he, 'I had the plan of having Israel before me as something 'set beside many waters,' and what might that mean? It means a willow. But they set themselves like a mountain-willow.'"

IV.

A. Our rabbis have taught on Tannaite authority:

B. What is a willow, and what is a mountain willow?

C. As to a willow, its stem is red, it has a long leaf, and a smooth edge. A mountain willow has a white stem, a round leaf, and an edge serrated like a sickle [T. Suk. 2:7H-I].

D. But has it not been taught on Tannaite authority:

E. If it is like a sickle, it is valid, but if it is like a saw, it is invalid? [Slotki, p. 152, n. 1: A sickle-like edge has all the teeth pointing in a slanting direction towards the handle; a saw-like edge has upright teeth.]

F. Said Abayye, "[The statement that it is valid if it has sickle-like teeth] has been taught with respect to a rounded willow [Slotki, p. 152, n. 3: One with rounded leaves]."

G. Said Abayye, "It follows from the cited teaching that one rounded willow is valid for use as a hoshannah [willow for a lulab]."

H. That is self-evident.

I. It has, nonetheless, to be made explicit, for, otherwise, what might have you [falsely] concluded? Since it has a distinctive name, it will not be valid. Accordingly we are told that that is not the case.

J. And might I say that indeed is the case?

K. "Willows of the brook" (Lev. 23:40) is what the All-Merciful has said, thus accepting them, whatever their source.

V.

A. Said R. Hisda, "As to these three things, their names have been changed since the destruction of the Temple:

B. "What used to be called hilpeta is now called arabta and vice versa. [These are types of willow, and the hilpeta is a mountain willow and invalid, the arabta is a suitable willow].

C. "What difference does it make? It has to do with what may be validly used in a lulab.

D. "A ram's horn is now called a trumpet and a trumpet a ram's horn.

E. "What practical difference does it make? It has to do with what may be validly used for a ram's horn for the New Year.

F. "What used to be called a large table now is called by the word for a small table, and vice versa.

G. "What practical difference does it make? It has to do with trade. [If one sells an object under one name, he must provide that object in accord with the referent of the currently used name and may not appeal to the former usage in providing, in fulfillment of his contract, something other than the required object.]"

H. Said Abayye, "I too may point out that what was once called the second stomach of the ruminant is now called the first, and vice versa.

I. "What practical difference does it make? It has to do with the case of a needle found in the thick wall of the second stomach. [Slotki, p. 152, n. 13: If a needle is found in the first stomach, provided it does not perforate it, the animal remains ritually fit. If it is found in the second stomach the animal is ritually unfit.]"

J. Said Raba bar Joseph, "I too point out that what used to be called Babylon is now called Borsif, and vice versa.

K. "What [34B] practical difference does it make?

L. "It has to do with writing writs of divorce for women [which have to bear the correct title]." [Slotki, p. 152, n. 2: A bill of divorcement executed in the original Borsif and carried to another place is invalid unless the bearer made the declaration: 'In my presence it was written, and in my presence it was signed, "while one brought from Babylon required no such declaration."]

Since earlier units have dealt with the issues of M. 3:3A, B, and most of C, the Talmud now turns directly to what is distinctive in the new paragraph, which is the issue of the mountain willow, units I, II, III, IV. Only unit V proceeds to a fresh subject and leaves the narrow framework of Mishnah-exegesis.

3:4

A. R. Ishmael says, "Three myrtle-branches, two willow-branches, one palm-branch, and one citron [are required],

B. "even if two [of the myrtle-branches] have their tips broken off, and only one does not have its tip broken off."

C. R. Tarfon says, "Even if all three of them have their tips broken off, [they are valid]."

D. R. 'Aqiba says, "Just as one palm-branch and one citron [are required], so one myrtle-branch and one willow-branch [are required]."

I.

A. It has been taught on Tannaite authority:

B. R. Ishmael says, "'The fruit of a goodly tree' (Lev. 23:40) indicates that one [citron] is required, 'Branches of palm trees' (Lev. 23:40) imposes the requirement that there be one [branch] [for the word is written in the singular], 'boughs of thick trees' (Lev. 23:40) means three [myrtle branches] are required [since the Hebrew has three words], and 'willows of the brook' (Lev. 23:40) means that two [willow-branches] are necessary, and even if two of the myrtle branches have their tips broken off, and only one does not have its tip broken off [M. 3:4B], [it is valid]."

C. R. Tarfon says, "three are necessary even if all three have their tips broken off."

D. R. Aqiba says, "Just as one palm-branch and one citron are required, so one myrtle-branch and one willow-branch are required" [M. 3:4D].

II.

A. Said R. Eliezer [omitting "to him"], "Is it possible that the citron should be bound together with the [other species, the palm branch, willow, and myrtle]?

B. "Thus you may say to the contrary: Is it stated, 'The fruit of a goodly tree and branches of palm trees' [with the end signifying that the fruit and the branches are to be bound together]?

C. "It says only, 'The fruit of a goodly tree, branches of palm-trees.'"

D. How do we know that the absence of any one of them invalidates the entire group?

E. Scripture states, "... and you shall take..." (Lev. 23:40), meaning, Your act of taking should be complete [with all four species together].

III.

A. And R. Ishmael [who at M. 3:4B accepts broken off branches]? How will he attain a consistent position? If he requires that myrtle branches be perfect, then all of them should be perfect. If he does not require them to be perfect, then even one of them need not be perfect!

B.   Said Biraah said R. Ammi, "R. Ishmael retracted."

IV.

A.   Said R. Judah said Samuel, "The decided law accords with the position of R. Tarfon."

B.   And Samuel is consistent with his other rulings, for Samuel said to those who sell myrtle, 'Sell at the regular price [despite the increased demand of the season], and if you do not do so, I shall expound the law applying to you in accord with the view of R. Tarfon [who accepts broken myrtles, hence the supply of acceptable myrtle-branches will be much larger]."

C.   What is the basis for his position?

D.   If you wish to say that he wished to apply a lenient ruling to them [people at the holiday season], then let him expound the rule in accord with R. Aqiba, who takes up a still more lenient position [since Tarfon requires three, but Aqiba only one, myrtle-branch].

E.   Three myrtles with a broken tip are commonplace, but one that is not broken is not commonplace [so Tarfon's ruling is the more lenient].

F.   It seems to met that units I and III are continuous, since both of them take up the issues of M. 3:4A. Why unit II is inserted I cannot say; its issue is not relevant here. Unit IV then completes the matter with a statement of decided law. My guess is that unit II is carried in the web of units I, III, but only by the allegation that Eliezer said "to him."

3:5-7

A.   A stolen or dried up citron is invalid.

B.   And one deriving from an asherah or from an apostate town is invalid.

C.   [If it derived from] 'orlah-fruit, it is invalid.

D.   [If it derived from] unclean heave-offering, it is invalid.

E.   [If it derived from] clean heave-offering, one should not take it up. But if he took it up, it is valid.

F.   One which is in the status of doubtfully tithed produce --

G.   the House of Shammai declare invalid.

H.   And the House of Hillel declare valid.

I.   And one in the status of second tithe in Jerusalem one should not carry. But if he carried it, it is valid.

M. 3:5

A.   (1) [If] scars covered the greater part of it,

B.   (2) [if] its nipple was removed,

C.   (3) [if] it was peeled, split, had a hole and so lacked any part whatsoever, it is invalid.

D.   (1) [If] scars covered the lesser part of it,

E. (2) [if] its stalk was removed,

F. (3) [if] it had a hole but lacked no part whatsoever,

G. it is valid.

H. A dark-colored citron is invalid.

I. And one which is green like a leek --

J. R. Meir declares valid.

K. And R. Judah declares invalid.

M. 3:6

A. The measure of the smallest [acceptable] citron --

B. R. Meir says, "The size of a nut."

C. R. Judah says, "The size of an egg."

D. And as to the largest [acceptable size] --

E. "It must be of such a size that one can hold two in one hand," the words of R. Judah.

F. R. Yosé says, "Even one in two hands."

M. 3:7

I.

A. Our rabbis have taught on Tannaite authority:

B. "The fruit of a goodly tree" (Lev. 23:40) refers to a tree, the taste of whose wood and of whose produce is the same. That must be the citron [etrog].

C. And might I say it is a pepper-tree?

D. That would accord with the following teaching on Tannaite authority:

E. R. Meir would say, "On the basis of that which is said, 'And you have planted every kind of tree [for food, then you shall count their fruit as forbidden'], (Lev. 19:23), do I not know that it is a tree for food?

F. "Why then does Scripture say, 'A tree for food'?

G. "You must conclude that it is a tree, the taste of whose wood and of whose produce is the same. One must say that that is a pepper [tree].

H. "This serves, then, to teach you that pepper trees are liable to the prohibitions of fruit from trees in the fourth year after their planting ['orlah],

I. and [in addition] that the Land of Israel lacks nothing [but has every kind of needed produce], for it is written, 'You shall lack nothing in it' (Deut. 8:9)."

J. There [with reference to Lev. 23:40] the statement is because it is not possible [to use pepper for the stated purpose, in the lulab].

K. [Why not?] For how should one do it? If one should take only one [pepper seed], it will not be discernible when it is taken up.

L. If we should take two or three, [that would not do,] for Scripture has specified that one takes up "one" and not two or three pieces of produce.

M.   Therefore [pepper is excluded] because it is not possible [to carry out the obligation with pepper, and that leaves only the citron (etrog)].

II.

A.   Rabbi says, "Do not read 'goodly' (HDR) but stable (HDYR). Just as a stable has large and small [beasts], perfect and blemished ones, so [among citrons] there are large and small ones, perfect and blemished ones. [That proves that the necessary fruit is the citron]."

B.   Is it the case, then, that among other sorts of produce we do not find large and small, perfect and blemished?

C.   But this is the sense of his statement: Before the small ones [of the current crop] come out, the large ones [of last year's crop] remain [a trait that applies only to the citron].

D.   R. Abbahu said, "Do not read 'goodly' (HDR) but 'that which dwells' (HDR), that is to say, something that remains on its tree from one year to the next. [And that is the citron]."

E.   Ben Azzai says, "Do not read 'goodly' but 'water' (HDR/HWDR), [the latter representing the Greek word for water], for in the Greek language they call water hudor.

F.   "What is one that grows beside water? One must say that it is the citron."

III.

A.   And one deriving from an asherah or from an apostate town is invalid [M. Suk. 3:5B]:

B.   What is the reason?

C.   Since [the citron] is going to be burned, it is as if its bits and pieces already have been crushed [and are null].

IV.

A.   If it derived from orlah-fruit it is invalid [M. 3:5C]:

B.   What is the reason for this ruling?

C.   R. Hiyya bar Abin and R. Assi differed on this matter.

D.   One said, "It is because it is never going to be available [permitted] for eating. [The orlah-fruit cannot be used, therefore cannot be called 'yours' as Lev. 23:40 specifies.]"

E.   The other said, "Because it is not subject to monetary value at all [being of no use whatsoever]."

F.   [Now since each authority explains the prohibition in his own way,] the premise at hand must be that the one who requires that [a citron, for use, must ultimately become] available for eating does not require that it possess monetary value,

G.   while the one who requires that the citron have monetary value does not require that it be ultimately available for eating. [On the basis of the premise at hand, which isolates the two requirements and treats one as sufficient without the other, for qualifying, or disqualifying, the citron, we proceed to analyze the problem in light of further relevant rulings.]

H. We have learned in the Mishnah: **If it derived from unclean heàve-offering, it is invalid [M. 3:5D].**

I. Now in line with the thesis of the one who says that the sufficient reason [for excluding the citron in the status of _orlah_] is that it will never become available for eating, this further ruling poses no problems [since the same trait characterizes unclean heave-offering, which may never be eaten but must be burned].

J. But in the view of him who says that the sufficient reason [for excluding the citron in the status of _orlah_] is that it has no monetary value, why [should the citron which is unclean heave-offering be rejected]? One can, after all, [by burning the citron] use it for a fire for his cooking pot. [So the citron can be sold for fuel.]

K. It must follow that all parties concur that we require that a citron be ultimately available for eating [even though at a given moment it may not be permitted to eat a citron in the status at hand].

L. Where there is a dispute, it must have to do with the matter of whether the citron bears monetary value or not.

M. One authority takes the view that we require the possibility at some point of eating the citron but we do not require that it possess monetary value, while the other party takes the view that we also require that the citron possess monetary value.

N. What practical difference does it make?

O. At issue is use of produce in the status of second tithe which is located in Jerusalem [where it may be eaten. Such produce may not be eaten outside of Jerusalem. At issue then is whether or not such produce falls into the category of property one may sell.]

P. The dispute, further, is in accord with the basic principle attributed to R. Meir.

Q. In accord with him who has said that the reason [governing the exclusion of a citron in the status of _orlah_-fruit] is that it will never become available for eating. But in the case of produce in the status of second tithe, it does become available for eating [in Jerusalem itself].

R. But in the view of him who has said that the operative criterion is that the citron does not possess monetary value, produce in the status of second tithe belongs to the Most High. [It does not belong to the farmer but to God, who decrees how it is to be dealt with. So it does not qualify by this criterion.]

S. May you, furthermore, draw the conclusion that it is R. Assi who has said that the decisive criterion is that the citron at hand does not possess monetary value?

T. For R. Assi has said, "A citron in the status of second tithe in the view of R. Meir may not serve for a person to fulfill his obligation on the festival day, and in the view of sages, such a citron may serve for a person to fulfill his obligation on the festival."

U. You may indeed draw that conclusion.

V.

A. As to the body of the text just now cited:

B.   R. Assi said, "A citron in the status of second tithe, in the view of R. Meir, may not serve for a person to fulfill his obligation on the festival day, and, in the view of sages, such a citron may serve for a person to fulfill his obligation on the festival.

C.   "As to unleavened bread in the status of second tithe, in the view of R. Meir, it may not serve for a person to fulfill his obligation on Passover, and, in the view of sages, such unleavened bread may serve for a person to fulfill his obligation on the festival.

D.   "As to dough in the status of second tithe, in the view of R. Meir it is not liable to the separation of dough-offering, and in the view of sages it is liable to the separation of dough-offering."

E.   To this statement R. Papa objected, "Now with respect to the dough, [there is no problem], for it is written, 'Of the first of your dough' (Num. 15:21). [Dough in the status of second tithe is not 'yours' but belongs to the Most High.]

F.   "Likewise with reference to the citron, [there is no problem], for it is written, '... For yourself' (Lev. 23:40), meaning, it must be yours.

G.   "But with respect to unleavened bread, where is it written '<u>Your</u> unleavened bread' [that the unleavened bread must belong wholly to the person who eats it]?! [Such a provision does not appear.]"

H.   Said Rabba bar Samuel, and some say it in the name of R. Yemar bar Shelamiah, "We derive the rule by analogy with regard to the use of the word 'bread.'

I.   "Where it is written, 'Bread of affliction' (Deut. 16:3), and there [in regard to the dough from which bread-offering is to be separated], it is written, [35B] 'When you shall eat of the bread of the land' (Num. 15:19).

J.   "Just as in that latter case, the 'bread' must belong to you, and therefore may not be in the status of tithe, so here, the 'bread' must belong to you and may not be in the status of tithe."

K.   May I propose that the following supports the view that just now stated:

L.   "Dough in the status of second tithe is exempt from the requirement of separating dough-offering," the words of R. Meir.

M.   And sages say, "It is liable to the separation of dough-offering."

N.   May I say that what has just been cited gives support?

O.   That is possible, since it is exactly the same statement as is given above!

P.   No, what is meant is that, just as in the one case, there is a dispute, so in the other there is a dispute [in which case the principle at hand is the same, and Assi's thesis is reinforced].

Q.   Or perhaps the case of dough-offering is distinct from the others, for in that case Scripture has made use of the word "Your dough" two times (Num. 15:20, 21). [Slotki, p. 158, n. 15: In this case alone perhaps, where the fact that it must be one person's property is emphasized, does R. Meir exempt it, but not in the case of the citron or unleavened bread, where Scripture laid no such emphasis.]

<u>VI.</u>

A.   <u>If it derived from unclean heave-offering, it is invalid [M. 3:5D]</u>:

B.   The reason is that it never becomes available for eating [but remains prohibited].

VII.

A. If it derived from clean heave-offering, one should not carry it [for purposes of the
    lulab] [M. 3:5E]:

B. There is a dispute about this matter between R. Ammi and R. Assi.

C. One said, "It is because [in taking it up, one usually wets it so as to keep it fresh,
    and this] renders it susceptible to uncleanness [which one should not do to food in
    the status of heave-offering. One must protect the cultic cleanness of such food,
    which serves as priestly rations.]"

D. The other said, "It is because one causes it to be worth less [by using it and so
    damaging the peel, and one may not diminish the value of heave-offering, which is
    holy and must be protected]."

E. What would be the practical difference between these two views?

F. It would be a case in which one designated as heave-offering the entire citron,
    except for its outer skin.

G. In the view of the one who said that the operative consideration is that one renders
    the fruit susceptible to uncleanness, that same consideration applies here.

H. But in the view of the one who says that he causes loss to the value of what is in the
    status of heave-offering, that consideration is absent. [The peel, which is damaged,
    is not in the status of heave-offering.]

VIII.

A. But if he took it up, it is valid [M. 3:5E]:

B. From the viewpoint of him who has invoked the criterion that [in the case of the
    citron] it does not become available for eating at any point in the future, lo, to the
    citron at hand, it does become available for eating in the future,

C. and in the view of him who has said that the operative criterion is that it is not
    subject to monetary value, lo, this produce [clean heave-offering] most certainly
    does have monetary value.

IX.

A. One which is in the status of doubtfully tithed produce [M. 3:5F]:

B. [Since one may not eat fruit in the status of doubtfully tithed produce], what is the
    reason that the House of Hillel [declare it valid]?

C. Since, if the farmer wants, he may declare all of his property ownerless, in which
    case he would be in the status of a poor man, and such a citron would be suitable for
    him in that status, now too we regard the produce as falling into the classification
    of what is "yours" [for potentially it could gain that status].

D. For we have learned in the Mishnah: People may give to the poor or to billeted
    troops doubtfully tithed produce to eat [M. Dem. 3:1P].

E. But the House of Shammai take the view that a poor man is not permitted to eat
    doubtfully tithed produce.

F. For we have learned in the Mishnah: People may give to the poor or to billeted
    troops doubtfully tithed produce to eat [M. Dem. 3:1], in which connection R. Huna
    said, "It has been taught on Tannaite authority: 'The House of Shammai say, "They
    do not give to the poor or to billeted troops doubtfully tithed produce to eat."

G.   "'And the House of Hillel say, "They do give to the poor or to billeted troops doubtfully tithed produce to eat."'"

X.

A.   And one in the status of second tithe in Jerusalem [M. 3:5I]:

B.   In the view of him who has said that the operative consideration is that, in using the citron, one renders it susceptible to uncleanness, in the present instance that consideration applies.

C.   And in the view of him who has said that one lowers the value of the produce by using it, that consideration applies here too.

XI.

A.   But if he carried it, it is valid [M. 3:5I]:

B.   According to him who has said that the operative consideration is that the produce does not ultimately become available for eating, this represents the view of all parties [to the dispute cited earlier].

C.   In the view of him who has said that the operative consideration is that the citron at hand is not subject to monetary value, in accord with whose view is the present rule given?

D.   It accords only with the position of rabbis.

XII.

A.   If scars covered the greater part of it [M. 3:6A]:

B.   Said R. Hisda, "This teaching was stated by our great master [Rab], (and the omnipresent be his support!), 'The statement at hand applies only if the scars were located in a single place, but if they were located in two or three places, it is valid.'"

C.   Said Raba to him, "To the contrary, if the scars were located in two or three cases, it would look spotted and hence would be unfit."

D.   But if the statement was made, it was made with reference to the latter clause of the passage at hand, If scars covered the lesser part of it [M. 3:6D] [as follows:]

E.   Said R. Hisda, "This teaching was stated by our great master [Rab] (and the Omnipresent be his support!) 'The statement at hand applies only if the scars were located in a single place, but if they were located in two or three places, it would look spotted and hence would be unfit.'"

F.   Said Raba, "If the spots were on the [Slotki:] oblate part [the part of the citron which slopes towards the nipple], even if it is of the slightest extent, the citron also is not suitable."

XIII.

A.   If its nipple was removed [M. 3:6B]:

B.   R. Isaac b. Eleazar taught on Tannaite authority, "If its peduncle was removed" [So Slotki].

XIV.

A.   If it was peeled [M. 3:6C]:

B.   Said Raba, "A citron which was peeled back like a red date is valid."

C.   And lo, we have learned in the Mishnah, If it was peeled, it is invalid [M. 3:6C]?

D. There is no problem. [36A] The former statement deals with one which has been entirely peeled, the latter to one which has been only partially peeled. [The latter is regarded as spotty.]

XV.

A. If it was split, had a hole... [M. 3:6C]:

B. Ulla bar Hanina taught on Tannaite authority [on the statement, ... had a hole and so lacked any part whatsoever, it is invalid], "If the hole goes through completely, it is invalid whatever the size of the hole.

C. "But if it does not go through completely, then it is invalid only if the hole is the size of an issar-coin."

XVI.

A. Raba raised this question, "If symptoms that would in the case of a beast render the beast terefah appeared in a citron, what is the law?

B. What issue, in fact, does he raise?

C. If the issue is the rule in a case in which the citron was peeled, we have learned in the Mishnah-passage at hand [that it is invalid] [M. 3:6C].

D. If the issue is whether the citron was split, we have learned in the Mishnah-passage at hand [that it is invalid] [M. 3:6C].

E. If the issue is whether the citron had a hole in it, we have learned in the Mishnah-passage at hand [that it is invalid] [M. 3:6C].

F. When he raises the question, it deals with that which Ulla said R. Yohanan [said], "A lung, [the contents of which] pour out as from a ladle [Slotki] -- [the beast] is suitable."

G. And Raba, "That rule pertains when the arteries are viable. Lo, if the arteries are not viable, it is in the status of terefah."

H. As to the present matter [of the citron], what is the rule? [Slotki, p. 161, n. 11: The seed kernels are regarded as corresponding with the arteries of the lungs.]

I. Perhaps in the case of the beast, in which the air cannot reach [the lung-arteries], the beast could return to health. But here, in which the air can reach [the innards of the citron], that is not the case, for the citron will rot.

J. Or, on the other hand, perhaps there is no distinction between the two cases.

K. Come and take note: A citron that is swollen, rotted, pickled, boiled, Ethiopian [dark], white, or spotty, is invalid. One that is round as a ball is invalid, and some say, "Also twin[s, that have grown together]."

L. As to a citron that is half-ripe, R. Aqiba declares it invalid. And sages declare it valid.

M. If the farmer grew it in a frame and made it look like some other species, it is invalid.

N. Accordingly, it has been taught that one that is swollen, rotted [is invalid, and that would settle the question just raised].

O. Would that not refer to one that is swollen on the outside and rotted on the inside?

P.   No, both traits are exhibited on the outside. There is no contradiction, for the one speaks of a citron that is swollen even though it is not rotted, and the other speaks of one that is rotted even though it is not swollen.

Q.   [Reverting to the cited passage], a master said: An Ethiopian citron that is dark is invalid.

R.   And has it not been taught on Tannaite authority, "An Ethiopian citron is valid. One that is _like_ an Ethiopian one [but not grown there] is invalid."

S.   Said Abayye, "We too have learned on Tannaite authority the same teaching: 'One that is _like_ an Ethiopian one.'"

T.   Said Raba, "There is no contradiction, one speaks of us, the other of them." [Slotki, p. 161, n. 4: In Palestine Ethiopian citrons are unknown and therefore they are declared invalid. In Babylonia Ethiopian citrons were common and valid.]

U.   [Reverting to the cited passage once more: As to a citron that is half ripe,] R. Aqiba declares it invalid, and sages declare it valid.

V.   Said Rabbah, "R. Aqiba and R. Simeon say the same thing. R. Aqiba is represented by the passage we have just now cited.

W.   "What is the matter of R. Simeon?

X.   "It is in accord with that which we have learned in the Mishnah:

Y.   "R. Simeon declares exempt [from tithes] citrons when they are small [M. Ma. 1:4]."

Z.   Said Abayye to him, "Perhaps that is not the case. R. Aqiba may take the view he does in the present case [of the citron] because we require that the citron be 'goodly,' and that trait is absent [in a half-ripe citron]. But in the case of the matter of tithes, he would accord with rabbis [who hold that a half-ripe citron would be liable to tithing].

AA. "Or one may maintain the contrary is true, namely, that R. Simeon takes the view he does [of the liability of half-ripe citrons to tithing] only because it is written, 'You shall surely tithe all the increase of your seed' (Deut. 14:22), [so applying the tithe to produce such as] people bring forth for sowing [that is, ripe fruit]. But in the matter of the citron used for the Festival, he may well accord with rabbis.

BB. [36B] "And he might go no further than that."

CC. [Reverting again to the cited passage:] If a farmer grew it in a frame and made it look like some other species, it is invalid.

DD. Said Raba, "That statement pertains only to one that is made to grow into the shape of another species, but if it retained its own natural shape, it remains valid."

EE. That is self-evident. The cited passage is explicit in referring to its taking the shape of another species!

FF. It was, nonetheless, required to make such a statement [as Raba's] to speak of a case in which the citron was formed into the shape of planks joined together [which Raba regarded as a shape natural to the citron].

XVII.

A.   It has been stated on Amoraic authority:

B.   A citron that mice have gnawed --

C. Said Rab, "Such as that would not fall into the category of 'goodly.'"

D. Is that really the case?

E. But lo, R. Hanina [Slotki:] tasted part of it, and thereby carried out with it his obligation to make use of the citron.

F. In that case, the cited Mishnah [... lacked any part whatsoever, it is invalid (M. 3:6C)] presents a problem to R. Hanina.

G. Indeed, the cited passage of the Mishnah poses no problem to R. Hanina. In the one case [in which a citron lacking any part is invalid], we refer to [use of a gnawed citron] on the first day of the festival, in the other [in which it is acceptable], we refer to the second day. [The second day is subject only to rabbinical authority, therefore the requirements are less strict.]

H. But to Rab we discern a difficulty [in the conflicting rulings].

I. Rab would say to you, "The case of mice is different [so that even on the second day of the festival, such a citron would not be acceptable], for mice are disgusting."

J. [In a different version of the foregoing], others say, "Rab said, 'Such a citron indeed falls into the category of goodly.'

K. "And lo, R. Hanina tasted part of it and thereby carried out with it his obligation to make use of the citron.

L. "But does the Mishnah at hand not present a problem to R. Hanina?

M. "[No,] for in the one case [in which such a citron is unacceptable], it is the first day of the Festival, in the other, it is the second."

XVIII.

A. The measure of the smallest acceptable citron [M. 3:7A]:

B. Said Rifram bar Papa, "Parallel to the dispute in the present passage is the dispute concerning rounded pebbles."

C. For it has been taught on Tannaite authority:

D. On the Sabbath it is permitted to take along three rounded pebbles into the privy. [Such a privy has no walls, and ordinarily one could not carry an object into it.]

E. What is the minimum size?

F. R. Meir says, "The size of a nut."

G. R. Judah says, "The size of an egg."

XIX.

A. And as to the largest acceptable size [M. 3:7E]:

B. It has been taught on Tannaite authority:

C. Said R. Yose, "There was a precedent involving R. Aqiba, who came to the synagogue with his citron on his shoulder."

D. Said R. Judah to him, "There is no proof from that precedent. For even there, people said to him, 'This does not fall into the category of 'goodly.'"

Commencing with the established formal-formulary pattern, M. 3:5A-B, the unit on the citron (etrog) proceeds in a quite different direction. It makes the point that the citron must be available for eating, and, it follows, what may not be eaten, M. 3:5C, D, also will not serve. Doubtfully-tithed produce must be properly tithed; since, when taken up, they may not be eaten because they require further preparation, the House of Shammai invalidate them. Since they nonetheless can be made suitable for eating, the House of Hillel validate them. Second tithe in Jerusalem may be eaten, but falls under the rule of E. The triplet of contrast, M. 3:6A-C, D-G, is clear as given. (C3 must match D3). The three appended disputes, M. 3:6-7, deal with problems of definition. The sequence of the Talmud's units is in accord with the sentences of the Mishnah-paragraph. Unit I simply provides that the fruit to which Lev. 23:40 refers is the citron (etrog). Unit II carries forward the exegesis of the same verse, with the same purpose. Unit III moves on to M. 3:5B, unit IV, 3:5C with unit IV continued at unit V, then unit VI attends to M. 3:5D, VII to M. 3:5E, VIII to M. 3:5E, IX to M. 3:5F, X and XI to M. 3:5I, XII to M. 3:6A, XIII to M. 3:6B, XIV, XV, and XVII to M. 3:6C, with M. 3:6C also richly complemented at XVI. Units XVIII and XIX deal with M. 3:7A, E. So only unit XVI serves a purpose other than a close reading of the language and sense of the Mishnah's sentences, and there the relevance is self-evident.

3:8

A.   "They bind up the lulab [now: palm-branch, willow-branch, and myrtle-branch] only with [strands of] its own species," the words of R. Judah.

B.   R. Meir says, "Even with a rope [it is permitted to] bind up [the lulab]."

C.   Said R. Meir, "M'SH B: The townsfolk of Jerusalem bound up their palm-branches with gold threads."

D.   They said to him, "But underneath they [in fact had] tied it up with [strands of] its own species."

I.

A.   Said Raba, "[People may bind up the palm-branch, willow-branch, and myrtle branch into the lulab] even with bast, even with strips of the roots of a date-palm."

B.   And Raba said, "What is the reason for R. Judah's view [at M. 3:8A]? He takes the position that the lulab must be bound up, and if one makes use of some other species [besides those in the lulab itself], you would come out with five, and not [only the] four, [required] species."

C.   And Raba said, "How do I know that even bast or the root of a palm tree constitute species of the palm-tree [and hence may be used]?

D.   "For it has been taught on Tannaite authority: '"You shall dwell in sukkah [tabernacles]" (Lev. 23:42), meaning, a sukkah made of any sort of material,' the words of R. Meir.

E.   "R. Judah says, 'A sukkah is customarily [made] only of the four species that are used in the lulab.

F. "'And logic presents the following argument. If the lulab, use of which is not required by night as by day, is customarily made up only of the four species, a sukkah, which is applicable by night as by day, surely should be made up only of the four species.'

G. "They said to him, 'Any argument a fortiori which you may prove, so that at the outset the result is a more strict ruling emerges but at the end a more lenient ruling, is no logical argument. [The upshot of the argument at hand is to produce a lenient ruling, as will now be explained.]

H. [37A] "'If one did not find the four species, he may sit and do nothing [and make no sukkah at all]. Yet the Torah has stated, "You shall dwell in sukkah," which must mean, made of anything whatsoever.'

I. "'And so Ezra says, "Go out to the mountain and get olive branches and branches of wild olive and myrtle branches and palm branches and branches of thick trees to make sukkot as it has been written" (Neh. 8:15).'"

J. What does R. Judah say about this verse?

K. He takes it to speak [with reference to other than the four species] of the sukkah [not the roofing], while the references to "myrtle branches, palm branches, and branches of thick trees" alone refer to the sukkah-roofing.

L. But have we not learned in the Mishnah: "People may make sukkah-roofing out of boards," the words of R. Judah [M. Suk. 1:6].

M. [Slotki, p. 165, n. 8: Since only that which is valid for the lulab is valid for the sukkah,] it surely follows that bast and palm-tree roots fall into the category of species that serve for the lulab.

N. It does indeed follow.

O. But does R. Judah take the view that the four species may serve [for sukkah-roofing] and no other species may be used?

P. And has it not been taught on Tannaite authority:

Q. If one has made a sukkah-roofing with boards of cedar wood, if they are four handbreadths, all parties concur that the roofing is invalid.

R. If there are not four handbreadths,

S. R. Meir declares the roofing invalid, and R. Judah declares it valid. And R. Meir concludes that if there is a space between each board of the breadth of a board, one may put laths between the boards and the roofing is valid. [Cedar is not one of the four species, yet Judah accepts it for the sukkah-roofing, so he does not hold that only the four species may be used].

T. What is the meaning of "cedar"? It means "myrtle."

U. And that accords with Rabbah bar R. Huna, for Rabbah bar R. Huna said, "In the house of Rab [the ruling is] that there are ten species of cedars, as it is said, 'I will plant in the wilderness cedar, the acacia tree, the myrtle,' etc. (Is. 41:19). [So the myrtle also may fall into the category of the cedar.]"

II.

A. R. Meir says, "Even with a rope it is permitted to bind up the lulab [M. 3:8B]:

B.   Said R. Meir, "M'SH B: The nobility of Jerusalem bound up their palm-branches with gold threads."

C.   They said to him, "From that precedent there is no proof. Underneath they in fact had tied it up with strands of its own species" [T. Suk. 2:10F-G].

III.

A.   Said Rabbah to those who bind the hoshannah [the lulab in its entirety] for the establishment of the exilarch, "When you bind up the hoshannah for use in the establishment of the exilarch, leave a handle, so that there should not be any interposition [between the hand of the one who holds it and the lulab itself]." [Slotki, p. 166, n. 8: Rabbah holds that according to Pentateuchal law, the binding is unnecessary. Hence it would form an interposition between one's hand and the wreath.]

B.   Raba said, "Whatever serves to adorn the lulab does not constitute an interposition [that would disqualify a person from holding and using that lulab. Such an exposed handle is unnecessary.]"

C.   And Rabbah said, "A person should not take hold of a hoshannah by means of a scarf, because we require an unblemished act of taking [that is, direct control without interposition] and that is lacking [if one uses a scarf]."

D.   And Raba said, "If one takes hold of something by means of an intervening object, that nonetheless is regarded as a valid act of taking."

E.   Raba said, "On what basis do I maintain that if one takes hold of something by means of an intervening object, that is regarded as a valid act of taking?

F.   "It is on the basis of the following teaching, which we have learned in the Mishnah: A hyssop which is too short -- one makes it suffice with a thread and with a spindle and immerses it and brings it up and holds on to the hyssop itself and sprinkles [with it] [M. Par. 12:1].

G.   "Why so? Has not the All-Merciful said, 'And he shall take.. and immerse...' (Num. 19:18)? Thus it is inferred that if one takes hold of something by means of an intervening object, that is regarded as a valid act of taking."

H.   But why so? Perhaps in that case, the rule differs, since one has tied one object to the other, and [the handle] is therefore regarded as part of the body of the object to which it is tied.

I.   Rather, proof derives from here: If the ash fell from the reed to the trough, it is unfit [M. Par. 6:1F].

J.   [37B]. Lo, [it follows] if one threw the ashes into the water the ashes remain valid. [Slotki, p. 167, ns. 5-6: The ashes of the red cow were carried in tubes from which they emptied into a stone trough containing the water [for mixing]. If the ashes fall into the water of their own accord, they became invalid, since the putting into the water must be done with intention. Though, as in the case when they fell of their own accord, the man did not hold the ashes themselves, but only the tube which contained them, if the man threw the ashes into the water, the ashes remain valid.]

K.   Why so? "And they shall take of the ashes... and he shall put..." (Num. 19:17). Does it not follow, then, that if one takes hold of something by means of an intervening object, that is regarded as an act of taking?

L.   And Rabbah said, "One should not poke the lulab into the bound willow and myrtle [hoshannah], lest some of the leaves fall off and constitute interposing matter."

M.   And Raba said, "In the case of one species together with the same species, there is no problem of interposition."

N.   And Rabbah said, "A person should not sheer the palm branch while it is in the willow and myrtle [hoshannah], lest loose leaves remain and constitute interposing matter."

O.   And Raba said, "In the case of one species together with the same species, there is no problem of interposition."

P.   And Rabbah said, "As to a myrtle branch used to carry out the religious duty [of taking the myrtle branch], it is forbidden to sniff it, while as to the citron used for the same purpose, it is permitted to do so.

Q.   "What is the reason for this ruling? As to the myrtle, since it is used for its scent, when one sets it aside, it is for its scent that one sets it aside [and hence it cannot be used for other than its designated purpose, which is the carrying out of the religious duty. Now sniffing it merely for the scent is to use it for a secular purpose instead of its sacred purpose.]

R.   "But as to the citron, which is used for eating, when one sets it aside, it is for eating that one sets it aside [and smelling it has no bearing upon the sacred purpose for which it has been designated]."

S.   And Rabbah said, "When a myrtle is attached [to the bush] [on the Sabbath], it is permitted to sniff it, and when a citron is attached to the tree, it is forbidden to sniff it.

T.   "What is the reason behind this distinction? Since the myrtle is used for smelling, if you permit one to smell it, he will not come to cut it down. But a citron is for eating. If you permit one to smell it, one will come and cut it down [to eat it, and this is something one may not do on the Sabbath]. [To avoid that transgression, one may not even smell it. No transgression will be likely to follow sniffing the myrtle, since one will not be tempted to cut it down.]"

U.   And Rabbah said, "A lulab is to be held in the right hand, and a citron in the left.

V.   "What is the reason? The former stands for the commission of three religious duties, the latter, only one."

W.   Said R. Jeremiah to R. Beriqa, "What is the reason that a people say a blessing only 'over the taking of the lulab' [without referring to the other species]?

X.   "It is because it is higher than the others."

Y.   Then why not lift up the citron and say a blessing over that too?

Z.   He said to him, "The reason is that as a species it [the palm tree] is higher than the others."

The construction as a whole -- units I, III -- is framed around a variety of sayings pertinent to the theme of the Festival in general, and the citron and lulab in particular. Unit II in fact serves as a prologue for unit III. The whole set derives from Rabbah and Raba, framed in a clear pattern. The insertion of the whole construction is on account of the opening discussion, directly relevant to the Mishnah-paragraph at hand. The construction clearly follows its own interests and has been put together to stand quite independent of the passage at hand. But the component that commences so clearly addresses the exegesis of the Mishnah that the entire, unitary construction must be seen as an effort to build a miniature, running "Talmud."

3:9A-D

A. And at what point [in the Hallel-psalms, 113-118] did they shake [the lulab]?

B. "At 'O give thanks unto the Lord' (Ps. 118), beginning and end; and at, 'Save now, we beseech thee O Lord' (Ps. 118:25)," the words of the House of Hillel.

C. And the House of Shammai say, "Also: At, 'O Lord, we beseech, thee, send now prosperity' (Ps. 118:25)."

D. Said R. Aqiba, "I was watching Rabban Gamaliel and R. Joshua, for all the people waved their palm-branches, but they waved their palm-branches only at, 'Save now, we beseech thee, O Lord' (Ps. 118:25)."

I.

A. Who mentioned the issue of waving the lulab [that the Mishnah raises that issue at all]?

B. It pertains to that earlier passage: "Any lulab that is three handbreadths [in length], sufficient for waving, is valid."

C. And, at the present point, the statement then is made: At what point... did they shake the lulab [M. 3:9A].

II.

A. There was have learned in the Mishnah:

B. As to the two loaves of show-bread and the two lambs of the Festival of Weeks, how does one carry out the rite?

C. He puts the two loaves of bread on top of the two lambs and places his two hands below and swings them forward and backward and upward and downward, as it is written, "Which is waved and which is raised up" (Ex. 29:27) [M. Men. 5:6I-L].

D. Said R. Yohanan, "One swings forward and backward, to Him who owns all four winds, upward and downward to Him who owns heaven and earth."

E. In the West the matter was repeated in this way:

F. Said R. Hama bar Uqba said R. Yose b. R. Hanina, "One swings forward and backward to hold back destructive winds, upward and downward to hold back destructive dews."

G.   Said R. Yose bar Abin, and some say R. Yose bar Zabila, "That is to say [38A] that
      doing even trivial parts of a religious duty serves to hold back punishment.

H.   "For lo, the act of waving is nothing more than a trivial aspect of the religious duty,
      and yet it holds back destructive winds and dew."

I.   And Raba said, "And so is the case with the lulab."

J.   R. Aha bar Jacob would wave the lulab and say, "This is an arrow in the eyes of
      satan."

K.   But this is not a good thing, because it may lead [satan] to be provoked against him
      [who does it].

Unit I is a propos, but unit II serves M. Men. 5:6. It is relevant here only because of
the statement of Raba that the rule applies also to waving the lulab. Hence unit II was
framed to serve M. Men. 5:6 and transferred here.

3:9E-H

E.   He who was on a trip and had no lulab [with which] to carry [out his
      religious duty] --

F.   when he reaches home, should carry the lulab at his own table.

G.   [If] he did not carry his lulab in the morning, he should carry it at dusk,

H.   for the entire day is a suitable time for the palm-branch.

I.

A.   You have stated: He should carry the lulab at his own table [M. 3:9F].

B.   That bears the implication that one interrupts [his meal to do so].

C.   The following was raised as an objection: [A man should not sit down before the
      barber close to the afternoon prayer unless he already has prayed, nor at that time
      should a man go into a bath house or into a tannery, nor to eat, nor to enter into
      judgment.] But if they began, they do not break off what they were doing [M. Shab.
      1:2A-E]. [In principle, then, people do not interrupt what they were doing.]

D.   Said R. Safra, "There is no contradiction. In the one case we deal with a period
      during which there is yet time during the day [to complete what one was doing and
      also the religious duties], in the other we deal with a case in which there is no time
      to complete the religious duty by day."

E.   Said Raba, "What contradiction can there be? In the one case we deal with what is
      done on the authority of the Torah, in the other, what is done in the authority of
      rabbis [and for the former, one interrupts what one is doing in order to carry out the
      religious duty, in the latter, one does not.]"

F.   Rather, said Raba, "If there is a problem, this is the problem: When he reaches
      home, he should carry the lulab at his own table [M. 3:9F]. That bears the implica-
      tion that one interrupts [the meal for that purpose]. But then it teaches: If he did
      not carry his lulab in the morning, he should carry it at dusk [M. 3:9G]. That bears

the implication that one does not interrupt [what he is doing in order to carry out the deed of taking up the lulab]."

G. Said R. Safra, "There is no contradiction between the two statements of the Mishnah-paragraph at hand. In the one case we deal with a period during which there is yet time during the day, in the other we deal with a case in which there is no time to complete the action by day."

H. Said R. Zira, "What contradiction do we have after all? Perhaps it is the case that it is a religious obligation to interrupt [the meal to take the lulab], but if one has not done so, then: If he did not carry his lulab in the morning, he should carry it at dusk, for the entire day is a suitable time for the palm-branch [M. 3:9G-H]."

I. Rather, said R. Zira, "In point of fact, matters are just as we said to begin with. And as to your argument that the one rule pertains to a religious duty resting on the authority of the Torah, the other on the authority of rabbis, in the present case we deal with the second day of the festival, observance of which, to begin with, rests only on the authorities of rabbis.

J. "You may find evidence by a close reading of that which we have learned in the Mishnah: He who was on a trip and had no lulab to carry [M. 3:9E].

K. "Does anyone imagine that on the first day of the festival it would be permitted [to make such a trip to begin with? Hence the passage can only speak of the second day of the festival anyhow]."

The Talmud's sustained discussion aims at resolving the implicit contradiction between M. 3:9F and G. This is accomplished through making matters explicit at M. Shab. 1:2, and then proceeding to apply what has been discovered to the issue at hand. The dispute is thoroughly worked out.

3:10-11 A-D

A. He for whom a slave, woman, or minor read answers after them by saying what they say.

B. But it is a curse to him.

C. If an adult-male read for him, he answers after him [only] "Halleluyah."

M. 3:10

A. Where they are accustomed to repeat [the last nine verses of Ps. 118], let one repeat.

B. [Where it is the custom] to say them only once, let one say them only once.

C. [Where it is the custom] to say a blessing after it, let one say a blessing after it.

D.   Everything follows the custom of the locality.

M. 3:11A-D

I.

A.   Our rabbis have taught on Tannaite authority:

B.   While [sages] have said, "A son may say a blessing for his father, a slave for his master, a woman for her husband," nonetheless, sages have said, "May a curse come upon a man whose wife or children say blessings for him [because of his ignorance]."

II.

A.   Said Raba, "[38B] Important rules are to be derived from the customs relating to the recitation of the Hallel-psalms:

B.   "The prayer-leader says, 'Halleluyah,' and the people say, 'Halleluyah.' On the basis of that statement we learn that it is a religious duty to respond to the word 'Halleluyah' by repeating it.

C.   "The prayer-leader says, 'Praise Him, you servants of the Lord' (Ps. 113:1) and the people say, 'Halleluyah.' On the basis of that statement we learn that if an adult recites the prayer, one responds with the word 'Halleluyah,' to what he has said.

D.   "The prayer-leader says, 'Give thanks to the Lord' (Ps. 118:1), and the people respond, 'Give thanks to the Lord.' On the basis of that statement we learn that it is a religious duty to respond at the start of the several segments [of the Hallel-Psalms]."

E.   It has been stated, in addition, on Amoraic authority:

F.   Said R. Hanan bar Raba, "It is a religious duty to respond at the start of the several segments of the Hallel-Psalms."

G.   [Reverting to Raba's statement, we proceed:] "The prayer-leader says, 'Save now, we beseech you, O Lord' (Ps. 118:25), and the people answer, 'Save now, we beseech you, O Lord.' On the basis of that statement we learn that if a minor was reciting the Hallel-psalms, the people respond by repeating what he says after him.

H.   "The prayer-leader says, 'O Lord, we beseech you, send now prosperity' (Ps. 118:25), and the people respond, 'O Lord, we beseech you, send now prosperity.' On the basis of that statement we learn: Where they are accustomed to repeat [what has been said], let one repeat [M. 3:11A].

I.   "The prayer-leader says, 'Blessed is he who comes' (Ps. 118:26), and the people reply, 'In the name of the Lord' (Ps. 118:26). On the basis of that statement we learn that one who merely hears [a statement with approval] is in the status of one who has actually made the statement himself [Since the person is not obligated to repeat the words, he clearly fulfills his duty merely by hearing them]."

III.

A.   R. Hiyya bar Abba was asked, "If one has heard [the cited phrase] but did not respond to it, what is the law?"

B. He said to them, "Sages, scribes, heads of the people, and exegetes have ruled: 'If one has heard [the passage] but not responded, he nonetheless has carried out his obligation.'"

C. Along these same lines it has been stated on Amoraic authority:

D. Said R. Simeon b. Pazzi said R. Joshua b. Levi in the name of Bar Qappara, "How do we know that the one who hears [a passage] is in the same status as one who responds to it?

E. "Since it is written, '... even all the words of the book which the King of Judah has read aloud' (2 Kgs. 22:16).

F. "Now did Josiah read them? Was it not Shaphan who read them aloud, as it is written, 'And Shaphan read it before the king' (2 Kgs. 22:10)?

G. "On the basis of the passage at hand, therefore, we conclude that the one who hears a passage is in the same status as one who responds to it."

H. But perhaps, in the discourse at hand, after Shaphan read the passage aloud, Josiah read it aloud too?

I. Said R. Aha bar Jacob, "Don't let such a thought enter your mind.

J. "For it is written, 'Because your heart was tender and you humbled yourself before the Lord when you heard what I spoke' (2 Kgs. 22:19). That is, 'When you heard,' not 'when you read.'"

IV.

A. Said Raba, "A person should not say, 'Blessed he is who comes' (Ps. 118:26) and then, after a pause, go and say, 'In the name of the Lord.' Rather, he should say, 'Blessed is he who comes in the name of the Lord' [as a] complete [sentence, without interruption]."

B. [39A] Said Raba, "A person should not say, 'May the great name...,' and then, after a pause, say, 'be blessed.' Rather: 'Let the great name be blessed' [as a] complete [sentence, without interruption]."

C. Said R. Safra to him, "By Moses! Did you give the rule correctly? [Surely not!] But in both passages it is the completion of the clause, and we have no reason to object to a pause."

V.

A. Where it is the custom to repeat [M. 3:11A]:

B. It has been taught on Tannaite authority:

C. Rabbi repeats certain words in the passage.

D. R. Eleazar b. Parta adds some words.

E. What does he add?

F. Said Abayye, "He adds the practice of repeating the words starting at, 'I will give thanks to you' (Ps. 118:21) to the end of the Psalm."

VI.

A. Where it is the custom to say a blessing after it, let one say a blessing after it [M. 3:11C]:

B. Said Abayye, "That rule pertains only to saying a blessing after the Hallel-psalms. But as to reciting a blessing before repeating them, it is one's religious duty to say such a blessing."

C. For R. Judah said Samuel said, "In the case of carrying out all religious duties, one says a blessing prior (^{C}WBR) [to doing] them and then goes on to carry them out."

D. And how do we know that the word (^{C}WBR) means "prior"?

E. It is in line with that which R. Nahman bar Isaac has said, "It is written, 'Then Ahimaaz ran by the way of the plain and he overtook (L^{C}BR) the Cushite' (2 Sam. 18:23) [meaning that he got ahead of him, hence attained priority]."

F. Said Abayye, "It is from the usage of the word at hand in the following verse, 'And he himself went before them' (Gen. 33:3)."

G. And if you wish, you may derive the same meaning implicit in the verse from the following usage: "And their king has gone ahead in front of them, and the Lord is at the head of them" (Mic. 2:13).

Unit I complements M. 3:10A-B. Unit II proceeds to an extended set of conclusions supplied by Raba, pertinent to M. 3:10C, also to M. 3:11A, which is cited. The essay, however, is not composed as an exegesis of the passage at hand. Unit III then supplements the passage by dealing with one who did not respond to hearing a passage of prayer or psalms. Unit IV provides yet another supplement. Units V and VI then gloss M. 3:11A, C, as indicated. So we have a mixture of exegetical complements to the Mishnah-passage and secondary supplements on the themes at hand.

3:11E-F

E. He who buys a lulab [palm-branch, myrtle-branch, willow-branch] from his fellow in the Seventh Year — [the seller] gives him a citron as a gift.

F. For one is not permitted to buy [the citron] in the Seventh Year. [Transactions in certain produce may not be carried on in the Seventh Year, so the citron cannot be sold or bought. The restrictions do not affect the other components of the lulab.]

I.

A. What is the law [if the seller] is not willing to give over [the citron] as a gift?

B. Said R. Huna, "The purchaser should cover the money paid for the citron with that paid for the lulab [paying what covers all four items but declaring that he is giving the price for three]."

C. But why not simply hand it over to him directly [paying the money for the citron without further ado]?

D. It is because people may not hand over the price of produce grown in the Seventh Year to an am ha'ares [who cannot be relied upon to observe the restrictions of the Seventh Year].

E.   For it has been taught on Tannaite authority:

F.   They do not hand over an am ha'ares money received in exchange for produce of the Seventh Year in more than the amount of what is needed to buy food for three meals. If one has handed money over [in excess of that amount,] he must say, "Lo, these coins are to be deconsecrated in exchange for produce that I have in my house" [39B], and [the seller] then comes [to the man's house] and eats the designated food in accord with the restrictions affecting the sanctification of produce in the Seventh Year.

G.   Under what circumstances [does the foregoing rule apply]? To the case of one who purchases produce that derives from ownerless property [to begin with], but if one purchases produce that has been held as private property [that is, that has been guarded], it is forbidden to give to the seller even so much as a half-issar [since one may not trade in produce grown in the Seventh Year that one has kept as his own in violation of the law]. [In the former case, we impute to the am ha'ares the intent of keeping the law, in the latter we assume he will trade with the money received in exchange for the produce, and that money is now subject to the restrictions of the Seventh Year.] [The question of C has now been answered.]

H.   R. Sheshet objected, "Is it indeed permitted to pay over funds sufficient for three meals [and no larger sum of money] only in the case of the purchase of produce from what is in fact ownerless property?

I.   But the following represents an objection [to that distinction]: Rue, goosefoot, purslane, hill-coriander, water-parsley, and meadow-eruca are exempt from the separation of tithes and may be bought during the Sabbatical Year from anyone [even one suspected of violating the laws of the Sabbatical Year], because produce of their type is not cultivated [but grows wild] [M. Sheb. 9:1A-B, Newman, p. 180]. [There is no restriction as to the volume of the purchase or the price that may be paid.]"

J.   [Sheshet] introduced the objection and he also resolved it: "They taught the foregoing rule to apply only to a purchase price sufficient to provide one's food [for three meals.]"

K.   So did Rabbah bar bar Hana say R. Yohanan said, "They taught the foregoing rule to apply only to a purchase price sufficient to provide one's food [for three meals]."

L.   How do we know that the phrase used to indicate "food sufficient to provide one's food [for three meals]" [the word mana] refers to food? As it is written, "And the king provides food (YMAN) for them as a daily portion of the king's food" (Dan. 1:5).

M.   [Reverting to the point at hand, we now ask:] If [we may pay over only enough money as may be used to purchase food for three meals], the same rule should apply also to the lulab? [Why should money used for the purchase of a lulab not be restricted as the money paid for the citron is restricted?]

N.   [The restrictions of the Sabbatical Year do not apply to the lulab,] for the lulab [used in the Sabbatical Year] has in fact grown in the sixth year prior to the Seventh Year [with the bulk of the growing season prior to the Seventh Year. The result is that the restrictions on produce grown in the Seventh Year do not apply].

O.   If so, is not the citron also the product of growth in the sixth year, which has merely come to completion in the Seventh Year?

P.   In the case of determining the status of the citron, we follow the criterion provided by the point at which the citron is harvested [rather than the point at which the bulk of its growth has been completed, and the citron is harvested in the Seventh Year for use on the Festival. Hence it is regarded as produce of the Seventh Year and subject to the restrictions of that year.]

Q.   But in point of fact [that is not the case], for, both Rabban Gamaliel and R. Eliezer concur that, so far as the issue of the Seventh Year is concerned, the citron's status is governed by the point at which it blossomed [and that is in the sixth year, and hence the foregoing statement cannot be correct. We shall now introduce the evidence for the proposition at hand.]

R.   We have learned in the Mishnah: "A citron is in the status of a tree in three respects and in the status of a vegetable in one. It is in the status of a tree in regards to the laws of orlah, produce of the fourth year [which must be eaten in Jerusalem], and produce of the seventh Year. And it is in the status of a vegetable in one aspect, that, at the season [40A] of its harvest, one has to set aside the tithes to be derived from it," the words of Rabban Gamaliel. R. Eliezer says, "It is in the status of a tree in all respects" [M. Bik. 2:6, Wenig, pp. 79-80]. [All parties concur then that the status of the citron is governed by when its fruit is harvested, when no authority at hand will concur with that view.]

S.   [Answering this objection:] The authority [who takes the position, that the status of the citron is dictated by the point at which its fruit is harvested], accords with the following Tanna.

T.   For it has been taught on Tannaite authority:

U.   Said R. Yose, "Abtolemos affirmed in the name of five elders that a citron is subject to the separation of the tithes required in the year in which it is picked. And in Usha our rabbis voted concerning this matter, and ruled that a citron is subject to the separation of tithes and to the restrictions of the Seventh Year in accord with the year in which it is picked" [T. Sheb. 4:21C-D, Newman, p. 133].

V.   But who mentioned the Sabbatical Year at all [that that issue should be suddenly introduced in the end of foregoing statement but not at the beginning]?

W.   The cited text contains a lacuna, and this is how it should be repeated:

X.   A citron is subject to the separation of tithes required in the year in which it is picked, and to the restrictions of the Sabbatical Year as these apply to the year in which it blossomed. And in Usha our rabbis voted concerning this matter and ruled that a citron is subject to the separation of tithes and to the restrictions of the Seventh Year in accord with the year in which it is picked.

II.

A.   The operative consideration, then, is that the lulab at hand is assigned to the sixth year that leads into the Seventh. Lo, had it been subjected to the rules of the Seventh Year, it is taken for granted in the foregoing discussion that the lulab would be regarded as sanctified [in accord with the rules governing the Seventh Year].

B. But why should this be the case at all? Lo, the lulab is [made up merely of] wood, and wood is not subject to the restrictions of the sanctity of produce grown in the Seventh Year.

C. For it has been taught on Tannaite authority:

D. As to leaves of reeds and of vines which one piled up as a cover on a field, if one then gathered them in order to eat them, they are subject to the rules of sanctity affecting produce of the Seventh Year. If he gathered them for use as wood, they are not subject to the rules of sanctity affecting produce of the Seventh Year. [So what is used only as wood is not subject to the taboos of the Seventh Year.]

E. [The case involving use of wood for firewood] is to be distinguished [since Scripture itself has made a distinction in respect to the applicability of the taboos of the Seventh Year], for Scripture has stated, "... for you for food" (Lev. 25:6).

F. In this way Scripture establishes an analogy between what is "for you" and what is "for food."

G. The restriction governing the Sabbath Year produce applies to that which both imparts benefit and also is consumed at the same moment, thus eliminating wood, which imparts benefit only after it is consumed [and turned into coals]. [Slotki, p. 178, n. 14: A lulab, however, whose main use is for sweeping a floor, is used up or consumed at the same time that the benefit is derived from it.]

H. But there is the case of pine wood, which imparts benefit at the same moment at which it is consumed [since it is used for torches].

I. Said Raba, "Wood under ordinary conditions is meant for burning." [We do not take account of exceptional instances. The norm generates the law.]"

III.

A. As to the use of wood for heating, there is a dispute among Tannaite authorities.

B. For it has been taught on Tannaite authority:

C. Produce of the Seventh Year may not be used either for steeping or for washing, [since it is meant to be eaten].

D. R. Yose says, "People may use it for that purpose."

E. What is the Scriptural basis for the rule of the first of the two Tannaite authorities?

F. It is that Scripture has said, "... for eating" (Lev. 25:6) -- and not for steeping or washing.

G. What is the Scriptural basis for the position of R. Yose?

H. It is that Scripture has said, "For you," meaning for all your needs, even steeping and washing.

I. And the first of the two Tannaite authorities has also to note that it is written, "For you."

J. That use of the word "for you" is meant to establish the analogy between what is "for you" and what is "for eating," yielding the principle that that which both imparts its benefit and also is consumed at the same moment [may define a permitted utilization of produce of the Seventh Year], then excluding the labor of steeping and washing, in which case the benefit that the produce imparts comes after the consumption of the produce. [Slotki, p. 179, n. 8: If flax, for instance, is steeped in wine of the Sabbatical Year in the process of its preparation, the wine is already spoiled by the time the flax is ready for us.]

K. And as to R. Yose, is it not written, "For eating"?

L. He requires that reference to yield a different point entirely, namely, "For eating" -- and not for an ointment. [One may not use as an ointment produce of the Seventh Year, e.g., olive oil.]

M. For it has been taught on Tannaite authority:

N. "For food" (Lev. 25:6) — and not for an ointment.

O. You maintain that the sense is, "'For food' and not for an anointment." But perhaps it means only, -- and not for laundering [clothes].

P. When the passage states, "For you," lo, that encompasses the matter of using produce of the Seventh Year in connection with laundry.

Q. Lo, how, then, shall I interpret the reference, "For food"?

R. It must mean, "For food" -- and not for an ointment.

S. On what basis, however, do you wish to include [using produce of the Seventh Year] for laundering and to exclude anointing [with that same produce]?

T. [40B] I include laundering, which applies equally to everybody, and I exclude anointing, which does not apply to everybody. [Everybody eats, everybody washes, but not everybody uses ointments.]

U. Who stands behind this statement, which our rabbis have taught on Tannaite authority:

V. "For food" (Lev. 25:6) and not for an ointment.

W. "For food" and not for perfume,

X. "For food" and not for an emetic?

Y. In accord with which Tannaite authority? It accords with the view of R. Yose.

Z. For it cannot be in accord with rabbis, for if it were, there also are the matters of steeping and washing [which they would explicitly exclude].

IX.

A. Said R. Eleazar, "Produce of the Seventh Year is deconsecrated only through sale. [Slotki, p. 180, n. 5: Only if it is sold to a second party, not by exchanging the one for the other while the owner retains the produce for himself, as in the case of holy things.]"

B. And R. Yohanan said, "It may be deconsecrated both through sale and through exchange [with the declaration, 'This produce is exchanged for that money']." [Eleazar takes the view that the produce must be sold to a second party, not exchanged for other produce. In the case of Holy Things, the owner retains the produce to be consecrated for himself, simply by substituting other produce for it (Slotki).]

C. What is the scriptural basis for the position of R. Eleazar?

D. Since it is written, "And in this year of the Jubilee you shall return" (Lev. 25:13). [Jubilee rules pertain, also, to the Seventh Year, of course.] And nearby it is written, "And if you sell anything to your neighbor" (Lev. 25:14). Thus it is by means of sale [that what is subject to the rules of the Seventh Year is to be transferred], and not through the means of deconsecration [that would be the case for Holy Things, which may be removed from the status of sanctification not only through sale but also through substitution.]

E. What is the scriptural basis for the view of R. Yohanan?

F. Since it is written, "For it is a Jubilee, it shall be holy" (Lev. 25:14), [so establishing an analogy to Holy Things].

G. Just as Holy Things may be deconsecrated through both sale and exchange, so produce subject to the restrictions of the Seventh Year may be deconsecrated through both sale and exchange.

H. And as to R. Yohanan, how does he interpret this reference to "And if you sell anything to your neighbor" (Lev. 25:14)?

I. He requires it for proof of the proposition attributed to R. Yose b. R. Hanina. For it has been taught on Tannaite authority:

J. Said R. Yose bar Hanina, "Come and see how difficult are agricultural occupations even indirectly related to those forbidden in the Seventh Year. How so? If a man does work on produce of the Seventh Year, he begins to sell his movables, as it is said, 'In this year of Jubilee each of you shall return to his property. And if you sell to your neighbor...' (Lev. 25:13-14)" [T. Ar. 5:9A-C].

K. And as to R. Eleazar, how does he deal with the proof-text adduced in behalf of the view of R. Yohanan?

L. He requires it for proof for the following teaching on Tannaite authority: "For it is a jubilee, it shall be holy unto you' (Lev. 25:12).

M. Just as sanctification takes effect for money that is paid in exchange for what is sanctified, also the taboos of the Seventh Year take effect for money paid in exchange for produce of the Seventh Year.

N. There is a Tannaite teaching in accord with the view of R. Eleazar, and there is a Tannaite teaching in accord with the view of R. Yohanan.

O. The Tannaite teaching in accord with the view of R. Eleazar is as follows:

P. The restrictions applicable to the Seventh Year take effect for funds paid over for such produce, as it is said, "For it is a jubilee, it shall be holy unto you" (Lev. 25:12).

Q. Just as sanctification takes effect for money that is paid for what is sanctified, so that the money is subject to prohibition, also the taboos of the Seventh Year take effect for money paid for produce of the Seventh Year, so that the produce is subject to the same prohibitions.

R. If one might wish to propose, "Just as the status of sanctification takes effect for money paid for what is Holy Things so that the object that had been sanctified then goes forth to the status of deconsecration [and is now profane and not holy], so the status of sanctification takes effect for money paid for what is in the status of the Seventh Year so that the produce that had been in the status of the Seventh Year now goes forth to deconsecration [and is no longer subject to the restrictions of the Seventh Year],"

S. the following verse of Scripture prevents one's reaching such a conclusion: "... it shall be..." (Lev. 25:12), meaning, it shall remain exactly in the state of being that it had before, [that is, holy.]

T. How so?

U. If with produce subject to the restrictions of the Seventh Year one bought meat, both the produce and the meat must be removed at the time in the Seventh Year at which one is liable to remove from one's house, and make available as free and ownerless property, produce that is subject to the restrictions of the Seventh Year.

V. If [in the aftermath of the same transaction] one purchased fish with the meat, the meat has now been dropped from the matter and the fish enters in its place.

W. If with the fish one bought wine, the fish leave the chain and the wine joins it.

X. If with the wine one bought oil, the wine leaves and the oil enters.

Y. How so? [In the case of one who sold produce of the Seventh Year, used the money received to purchase some other produce, and then exchanged this produce, in turn, for still other produce,] the very last produce obtained in this manner is subjected to the laws of the Seventh Year, and the produce itself [i.e., the original produce of the Seventh Year remains] forbidden [that is, subject to the restrictions of the Seventh Year] [M. Sheb. 8:7D-E, Newman, p. 171].

Z. [This accords with the view of R. Eleazar,] for, since the Tannaite teaching is phrased repeatedly in terms of "purchase" [and not exchange as well], it follows that it is only through sale, and not through exchange, that produce of the Seventh Year is deconsecrated.

AA. It has been taught on Tannaite authority in accord with the view of R. Yohanan:

BB. "The same rule applies to both produce subject to the restrictions of the Seventh Year and produce in the status of second tithe:

CC. "Both of them may be given secular status and so deconsecrated in exchange for a domesticated beast [of equivalent value], a wild beast, and fowl, whether living or slaughtered," the words of R. Meir.

DD. And sages say, "It may be in exchange for those that have been properly slaughtered, but not in exchange for those that are yet alive. That is a precautionary decree, lest a farmer raise flocks from them [and the flocks would retain their consecrated status, but the farmer might not impute to the offspring of the consecrated beasts that same status, and hence would commit sacrilege]."

EE. Said Raba, "The cited dispute concerns the male beasts, but as to the female beasts, all parties concur that in exchange for properly slaughtered beasts such an exchange may take place, but in exchange for living ones, it may not take place, as a precautionary decree, lest a farmer raise flocks from them."

FF. Said R. Ashi, "The dispute concerns the original produce [that itself was subject to the sanctified status as either produce subject to the restrictions of the Seventh Year or produce in the status of second tithe].

GG. "But as to produce received in a subsequent exchange, all parties concur that the deconsecration may be effected through either sale or exchange.

HH. "And as to the repeated reference to purchase, since the word purchase is used in the opening clause, the word purchase is repeated also in the later ones."

II. Rabina objected to this view of R. Ashi on the basis of a cited teaching, "He who has a sela-coin subject to the restrictions of the Seventh Year [in which case, whatever is purchased with that money must be used up in the Seventh Year itself] and wants to buy a shirt with that money [and the shirt will outlast the year], how does he proceed?

JJ. "Let him go to a storekeeper whom he ordinarily patronizes and say to him, 'For this sela give me produce.' He then gives him the sela and then goes and says to the storekeeper, 'Lo, these pieces of fruit are given over to you as a gift.' The storekeeper then replies to him, Lo, this sela is given to you as a gift.' The man then goes and buys anything he wants with the money [because the coin now is no longer subject to the restrictions of the Seventh Year. The original coin was exchanged for the produce. The coin the man now receives is merely a gift from the storekeeper.]

KK. "Now in the present case, the produce in question is that which has been received in a subsequent exchange [and is not the original produce that itself had been subject to the sanctified status of produce of the Seventh Year, since that original produce had been exchanged for the coin prior to the transaction we have just now witnessed.] And yet, the framer of the passage teaches that the transaction is carried on as a purchase but not as an exchange."

LL. Rather [revising the attempted theory], said R. Ashi, "The dispute at hand pertains to produce that has entered the process at a later point but is not the original produce that had been subject to the restrictions of the Seventh Year.

MM. "But as to the original produce, all parties [Eleazar, Yohanan] concur that it may be given secular status and relieved of its sanctification only through purchase and not through exchange."

NN. And lo, it has been taught [in support of Yohanan's view]: The same rule applies to both produce subject to the restrictions of the Seventh Year and produce in the status of second tithe [and the latter surely may be deconsecrated through exchange, not only through purchase]!

OO. What is the sense of the word "Seventh Year" in the cited teaching? The meaning is "money received for produce of the Seventh Year."

PP. For if you wish to maintain that at hand is actual produce which is in the status of tithe [and not money exchanged for that produce], lo, it is written, "You shall bind the money in your hand" (Deut. 14:25). [The exchange thus can be made only for money, since Scripture takes for granted that the produce in the status of second tithe has been exchanged for money, with the actual produce left home and the money brought to Jerusalem.]

QQ. Here too we speak only of money that has been given in exchange for produce subject to the restrictions of the Seventh Year.

In the Seventh Year one may not purchase produce grown in that year. The citron, picked that year, alone falls under the rule. Hence the citron is to be given as a gift, while the other items may be bought and sold. The other items are wood, not food, and may be bought and sold. Since the topic of produce in the Seventh Year is introduced, the Talmud pursues that subject, opening with attention to the Mishnah's statements, then moving on to other principles relevant to the theme but not to what the Mishnah has specifically alleged. Yet, as we see, the theme, in unit IV, is important, because it deals with transactions in produce of the Seventh Year, to which M. 3:11F makes reference. So the theme is scaled down to conform to the points of interest of the Mishnah-paragraph at hand. Unit I raises an important question generated by the rule of the Mishnah. Unit II continues the interests of unit I, and unit III, of unit II. So units I-III form a singular, protracted exercise. Then unit IV raises its own very interesting question, which it works out in a thorough way. The entire construction is a model of secondary speculation on a topic on which, in primary terms, the framers of the Talmud have very little to say, yet which, as is clear in unit I, they wish to discuss.

3:12

A.   At first the lulab was carried in the Temple for seven days, and in the provinces, for one day.

B.   When the Temple was destroyed, Rabban Yohanan b. Zakkai ordained that the lulab should be carried in the provinces seven days,

C.   as a memorial to the Temple;

D.   and that the whole of the day on which the sheaf of first fruits is waved should be forbidden [for the use of new produce, which may be used only from the waving of the 'omer and thereafter; this had formerly been offered at noon].

M. 3:12

I.

A.   How do we know on the basis of Scripture that we establish a memorial to the destroyed sanctuary?

B.   Said R. Yohanan, "Scripture has said, 'For I will restore health to you, and I will heal you of your wounds, says the Lord, because they have called you an outcast. She is Zion, there is none that seeks for her' (Jer. 30:17).

C.   "'There is none that seeks for her' [stated as a criticism] implies that a quest [for her welfare] is called for."

II.

A.   And that the whole of the day on which the sheaf of first fruits is waved [M. 3:12D]:

B.   What is the reason for that ordinance?

C.   Quickly may the sanctuary be rebuilt, so [without such an ordinance] people may say, "Last year we did not consume new produce [of the current crop, rather than from last year's] from the time of first light in the east? Now too we should eat [new produce from dawn]." But people will not know that in that last year, when there was no house of the sanctuary, it was the advent of dawn on the fifteenth of Nisan that, by itself marked the point at which it was permitted to eat produce of the new crop. But now, when there is a Temple once more, it is the waving of the sheaf of first fruits in the Temple rite [not merely dawn] that serves to permit the consumption of the new crop.

D.   Now at what point does the foregoing statement take for granted the new Temple will be rebuilt?

E.   If we should propose that it will be rebuilt on the sixteenth, then it is a simple fact that the eating of the new crop of produce is permitted solely by the dawn [on the sixteenth, since there is no rite in the Temple to be expected on that day. In point of fact the Temple will not be rebuilt in time to make a difference.]

F.   Accordingly, it must follow that [the premise is that] the Temple will be rebuilt on [or before] the fifteenth of Nisan, in which case the eating of the new crop should be permitted [on the sixteenth] only from midday onward.

G.   For lo, we have learned in the Mishnah: Those who live a distance from Jerusalem are permitted [to eat new produce] from noon onward, since the court [of the Temple, responsible for the waving of the sheaf of new produce which permits the use of the new crop] is not likely to be slovenly about [carrying out the rite] [M. Men. 10:5]. [The rite would be done by noon on the sixteenth of Nisan, so people in different places could rely on it.]

H.   It was necessary, nonetheless, [to ordain the rule assigned to Yohanan ben Zakkai that it is forbidden to eat new produce for the entire day on which, when the Temple stood, the sheaf of first fruits was waved] to take account of the possibility that the Temple might be rebuilt by night or near sunset [of the fifteenth of Nisan, in which case the waving of the sheaf of first fruits would have to await noon on the sixteenth of Nisan. Dawn by itself would not matter, and people would err, as at E-F].

I.   [Said] R. Nahman bar Isaac said, "[That is not the principal consideration at all. Rather], Rabban Yohanan ben Zakkai followed the theory of R. Judah, who said, 'On the strength of the authority of the Torah-law, the entire day of the sixteenth of Nisan [that is, the day on which the sheaf of first fruits is waved] is forbidden as to the consumption of the new crop.

J.   "For it is written, [41B] 'Until this self-same day' (Lev. 23:14), meaning, until the very day, and he further takes the view that the word 'until' is inclusive [meaning that the prohibition remains in effect until the very end of the time named, that is, until the end of the day]."

K.   But does [Judah] concur with the view of [Yohanan ben Zakkai]?

L.   And lo, [Judah] differs [with views assigned to Yohanan], for it has been taught on Tannaite authority:

M.   When the Temple was destroyed, Rabban Yohanan ben Zakkai made an ordinance that eating new produce would be forbidden for the entire day on which the sheaf of first fruits was to be waved.

N.   Said R. Judah to him, "But is it not the case that, on the basis of the law of the Torah, that entire day is prohibited in any event, since it is written, 'Until this self-same day' (Lev. 23:14), meaning, until the very day [at the end of that day]. [So there is no need for such an ordinance.]"

O.   R. Judah is the one who erred. He thought that [Yohanan] had made his ruling in the view that the prohibition of eating the new crop derived only from the authority of rabbis [and was not based on the authority of the Torah], but that is not the case, for [Yohanan] took the position that the prohibition rested on the authority of the Torah.

P.   What then is the sense of "ordained" [since surely rabbis cannot effect an ordinance based on their own authority and so set aside a rule based on the authority of the Torah. Indeed, an ordinance based on rabbis' authority alone would have no bearing.]

Q.   "What is the sense of "ordained"?] It is that he made an exegesis of the Torah and on <u>that</u> basis [and not on the strength of rabbinical authority alone] he made his ordinance.

The two ordinances take account of the destruction of the Temple. The sheaf of first fruits was offered on the sixteenth of Nisan, so from the afternoon onward, it had been permitted to eat produce harvested in the present growing cycle. But Yohanan permitted use of the new produce for the whole of the sixteenth of Nisan, as a memorial to the Temple. Unit I explains the basic thesis at hand, and unit II explores the foundation for Yohanan's ruling. This is in two parts. At first we explain the ordinance about the eating of new produce on the basis of an anticipated miracle. Then we proceed to a second and more theoretical legal explanation of the same matter.

3:13-14

A.   [If] the first festival day of the Festival [of Sukkot] coincides with the Sabbath, all the people bring their lulabs to the synagogue [on the day before].

B.   On the next day they get up and come along. Each one finds his own and takes it.

C.   For sages have said, "A person does not fulfill his obligation [to wave the lulab] on the first day of the Festival by using the lulab of his fellow.

D.   "And on all other days of the Festival, one does fulfill his obligation [to wave the lulab] by using the lulab of his fellow."

M. 3:13

A. R. Yose says, "[If] the first day of the Festival [of Sukkot] coincides with the Sabbath, [if] one forgot and brought his lulab out into the public domain, he is exempt [from the obligation to bring a sin-offering],

B. "because he brought it out [intending to do what is] permitted."

M. 3:14

I.

A. Whence on the basis of Scripture do we know [that a person must use his own lulab on the first day of the Festival]?

B. It is in accord with that which our rabbis have taught on Tannaite authority:

C. "And you shall take" (Lev. 23:40) means that each person is responsible for an act of taking [the lulab and citron].

D. "For yourself" means that [what you take] must belong to you personally, thus excluding one that is borrowed or stolen.

E. On the basis of the foregoing exegesis, sages have stated the following [in T.'s version:]

F. On the first day of the festival a person does not fulfill his obligation [to wave the lulab] by using the lulab of his fellow [M. 3:13C],

G. unless he gives it over to him as an unconditional gift.

H. M^CSH B: Rabban Gamaliel, R. Joshua, R. Eleazar b. Azariah, and R. Aqiba were traveling in a boat and had no lulab with them. Rabban Gamaliel bought a lulab for a thousand zuz. Once he had fulfilled his obligation with it, he gave it to his fellow, and his fellow to his fellow, so that all of them fulfilled their obligation. Afterward they returned it to him. [T. Suk. 2:11A-C].

I. Why was it necessary to add the detail that they returned it to him?

J. It is to provide a rule quite tangential to the main point, which is that a gift made on the stipulation that what is given be returned nonetheless falls into the category of a gift.

K. That accords, also, with what Raba said, "'Here is this citron [as a gift to you] on condition that you return it to me' -- if one has taken it and carried out his obligation and returned it to the other, he has carried out his obligation, but if he did not return it, he did not carry out his obligation."

L. Why was it necessary to add the detail that he paid a thousand zuz for it?

M. It was to let you know how much [the rabbis at hand] prized the carrying out of the commandments.

II.

A. Said Mar bar Amemar to R. Ashi, "Father would say his prayers while [holding] it."

B. They objected: A person should not hold phylacteries in his hand, or a scroll of the Torah in his arms, and say his prayers, nor should he urinate while holding them or sleep in them either on a regular basis or even for a quick nap. In this connection Samuel said, "In the same category fall a knife, dish, bread, and money." [H could Mar bar Amemar's father have held the lulab while saying his prayers?

C.   In the cases at hand, in holding the listed objects in his hand the man is not in the
        process of carrying out a religious duty, so he may well be disturbed about them [and
        worry not to drop them], but here [in the case of the lulab] he is in the process of
        performing a religious duty by holding on to that object, and, accordingly, he will
        not be disturbed about the matter.

III.

A.   It has been taught on Tannaite authority [in T.'s version]:

B.   Said R. Eleazar b. R. Sadoq, "It was the practice of the townsfolk of Jerusalem to do
        things thus: One would enter the synagogue carrying the lulab in his hand.

C.   "He would arise to read the translation [of the Scripture] or to take his place before
        the ark, with his lulab in his hand.

D.   "[If] he arose to read in the Torah or to raise his hands [in the priestly benediction of
        the congregation], he would put it down on the ground.

E.   "When he went out of the synagogue, his lulab was in his hand.

F.   "When he went in to visit the sick and to comfort mourners, his lulab was in his hand.

G.   "But when he entered the study-house, he would give it to his son or his messenger
        and return it to his house" [T. Suk. 2:10H].

H.   What does the cited passage teach us?

I.   It shows how conscientious the people were in carrying out religious duties.

IV.

A.   R. Yose says, "If the first day of the Festival..." [M. 3:14A]:

B.   Said Abayye, [42A] "The stated rule applies only in a case in which the man had not
        carried out his obligation with [the lulab prior to leaving his house. In that case, he
        is not culpable for taking it out into public domain.] But if he had carried out his
        obligation with that lulab, he is liable [for violating the Sabbath by carrying the
        lulab into public domain. Now he has no exculpation since he need not carry out a
        religious duty.]"

C.   Lo, at the moment that a man took up the lulab [in his house] he carried out his
        obligation with it [so how can we find a case in which Abayye's condition is met,
        that is, in which the man has not already carried out his obligation with the lulab
        prior to leaving his house]?

D.   Said Abayye, "We deal [in the Mishnah's rule] with a case in which the man had
        turned the lulab upside down [in which case he had not fulfilled his obligation to take
        it up, so that, when he left the house, the intention to carry out his religious duty
        still mattered]."

E.   Raba said, "Even if you say that he had not turned it over [the rule of the Mishnah
        pertains]. In the present case, with what situation do we deal? It is with a case in
        which the man carried the lulab out of his house in a utensil. [In that case we
        cannot say the man has taken up the lulab and carried out his obligation with it.]"

F.   But it is Raba himself who has said, "Taking something up by means of an inter-
        vening object falls into the category of taking up [and one would carry out his

obligation to take up the <u>lulab</u> even if he had the <u>lulab</u> in an intervening object, such as a vase]."

G.   That position [of Raba] pertains to a case in which one took up an object in a respectful way, but if he took it up in a disgraceful way, Raba's principle would not apply. [Slotki, p. 89, n. 8: If one takes it with a scarf one wears out of respect, it is valid, but if one carries it out in a vessel, thus showing lack of respect, it is not valid.]

<u>V.</u>

A.   [Dealing with the principle of M. 3:14B:] said R. Huna, "R. Yose would say, 'In the case of a burnt-offering of fowl which was found among other birds [Slotki, p. 189: at the southwestern side of the altar, where, in addition to burnt-offerings of fowl, sin-offerings of fowl were also sometimes offered], and in which the priest thought that the fowl at hand had been offered as a sin-offering [in which case the bird may be eaten by the priest, while, had it been offered as a burnt-offering, it could not be eaten by the priest but had to be wholly burned up], [the priest is] exempt from liability [for eating the bird].'"

B.   Now precisely what did R. Yose propose to tell us? Is it that if one has made an error in carrying out a matter involving a commission of a religious duty, he is exempt?

C.   But this is exactly what we have at hand [at M. 3:14B]!

D.   [It was, nonetheless, necessary to make the present rule explicit], for what might you have maintained [otherwise]? In that case [of the <u>lulab</u>] in which the man has made an error in carrying out a religious duty, he is exempt, because he was in process of performing a religious duty.

E.   But here [in the case of the error at the altar] while the man has erred in carrying out a religious duty, he himself was not doing a religious duty [in eating the fowl]. In such a case, then, I might have supposed that we do not invoke the principle [of M. 3:14B]. Accordingly, we are informed that that is not the case, [and we do invoke the cited principle].

F.   The following objection was raised: R. Yose says, "He who on the Sabbath slaughters for the daily whole offering a beast that had not been properly examined [for blemishes] is liable to a sin-offering [for violating the Sabbath, since the beast that had not been examined may not be used for the daily whole-offering], and he also has to bring another beast for the daily whole-offering." [This would contradict Huna's thesis, since it shows that the priest has erred while carrying out a religious obligation and also has not performed his religious obligation, and he is indeed culpable. So the conditions that are proposed at B-C+D have been met.

G.   [Differentiating the case of the daily whole-offering], he said to him, "That case is excluded, for in that regard it has been stated on Amoraic authority:

H.   "'Said R. Samuel bar Hattai said R. Hamnuna the Elder said R. Isaac bar Asian said R. Huna said Rab, "This is the rule in a case in which the priests brought the beast for the daily whole-offering from the corral of the beasts which had not yet been inspected for blemishes."'" [Slotki, p. 190, n. 8: The man had no right at all to take an animal from an unexamined supply, and his act, therefore, is not a mistake committed when under the anxiety of performing a religious duty but almost a willful transgression.]

M. 3:12 now is shown to serve as a prologue to the final unit of the chapter, since the taking of the lulab all seven days means that the prohibitions of the Sabbath must now be introduced. Taking the lulab on the first day of the festival coinciding with the Sabbath overrides the restrictions of the Sabbath (a concept made explicit at M. 4:2). We now provide for that contingency. There is no need to carry the lulab to the synagogue; it is left there overnight. What can be done in advance must be (M. Shab. 19:1). The explanation of the detail at B about finding one's own lulab, C-D, is the first of several appended rules. Yose's, which is clear as stated and bears its own gloss, is the second. Unit I provides a basis for M. 3:13C. Unit II complements I M. Unit III makes the same point as I M. Unit IV goes on to M. 3:14A and solves a niggling problem, and unit V is continuous with the foregoing.

3:15

A.   A woman receives the lulab from her son or husband and puts it back into water on the Sabbath.

B.   R. Judah says, "(1) On the Sabbath they put it back into [the same water], (2) on the festival-day they add water, and (3) on the intermediate days of the festival they change the water."

C.   A minor who knows how to wave the lulab is liable to the requirement of waving the lulab.

I.

A.   [The rule of M. 3:15A] is self-evident [and did not have to be stated].

B.   [No, it had to be made explicit, for] what might you have said? Since a woman is not subject to the obligation [to carry the lulab], I might have said that she also should not receive it [on grounds of handling, on the Sabbath, an object that is useless to her (Slotki, p. 190, n. 10)].

C.   So I am informed that that is not the case [and she may handle the lulab on the Sabbath, even though a woman is not obligated to carry out that religious duty].

II.

A.   It has been taught on Tannaite authority:

B.   A minor who knows how to shake an object is liable to observe the commandment of the lulab. If he knows how to cloak himself, he is liable for the commandment of show-fringes. If he knows how to speak, his father teaches him Torah and how to recite the Shema [T. Hag. 1:2D-F].

C.   What, in this context, is the definition of Torah?

D.   Said R. Hamnuna, "'Moses commanded the Torah to us, as an inheritance for the congregation of Jacob' (Deut. 33:4)."

E.   What in context is the definition of the <u>Shema</u>?

F.   The first verse thereof.

G.   If a child knows how to keep his body cultically clean, people eat food prepared according to the rules of cultic cleanness relying upon the cleanness of his body. If he knows that how to keep his hands clean, people eat food prepared in conditions of cultic cleanness relying upon the cleanness of his hands.

H.   If he has intelligence to be consulted about his condition, a matter of doubt concerning him in private domain is resolved in favor of uncleanness, in the public domain, it is resolved in favor of cleanness [T. Toh. 3:10A-C, 3:9E].

I.   If a child [of priestly caste] knows how to spread his hands [and deliver the priestly benediction], they give him a share of the priestly offerings at harvest time.

J.   If a child knows how properly to slaughter a beast, people may eat meat from a beast that he has slaughtered [T. Hag. 1:2/0].

K.   Said R. Huna, "But that rules applies only if an adult is supervising him."

L.   If he knows how to eat an olive's bulk of grain, they dispose of his excrement and urine at a distance of four cubits from a settlement [T. Hag. 1:2P].

M.   Said R. Hisda, "But that rule applies only to a minor who can eat such a volume of food in as much time as it takes to eat a piece half-loaf of bread."

N.   Said R. Hiyya, son of R. Yeba, "And in the case of an adult, even though he cannot eat that volume of food in as much time as it takes to eat a half-loaf of bread, [the same rule applies].

O.   "For it is written, 'He who increases knowledge increases sorrow' (Qoh. 1:18). [Slotki, p. 192, n. 11: The older a man is, the more offensive his excrement.]"

P.   If he can eat an olive's bulk of roast meat, they include him in the slaughter of a Passover-sacrifice, as it is said, "According to the amount that every man eats" (Ex. 12:4).

Q.   R. Judah says, "Under no circumstances do they slaughter a Passover-sacrifice on his account unless he knows how to distinguish good food from bad. How so? If they give him a stone, he throws it away, and if they give him a nut, he takes it" [T. Hag. 1:2P-T].

M. 3:15A permits the woman to handle the <u>lulab</u> on the Sabbath, even though she is not obligated to wave it. This triggers the addition of B and C, two further rules relevant to M. 3:15A, first, on changing the water, second, on who else is obligated to take up the <u>lulab</u>. Unit I provides a minor clarification of M. 3:15A. Unit II supplements the reference to the minor, M. 3:15C, with an extensive passage of Toseftan materials on the same theme, which are glossed.

BAVLI SUKKAH CHAPTER FOUR

A.   [The rites of] the lulab and the willow-branch [carried by the priests around the altar, M. 5:5] are for six or seven [days].
B.   The recitation of the Hallel-Psalms and the rejoicing are for eight [days].
C.   [The requirement of dwelling in the] sukkah and the water libation are for seven days.
D.   And the flute-playing is for five or six.

M. 4:1

A.   The lulab is for seven days: How so?
B.   [If] the first festival day of the Festival coincided with the Sabbath, the lulab is for seven days.
C.   But [if it coincided] with any other day, it is for six days.

M. 4:2

A.   The willow-branch [rite] is for seven days: How so?
B.   [If] the seventh day of the willow-branch coincided with the Sabbath, the willow-branch [rite] is for seven days.
C.   But [if it coincided] with any other day, it is for six days.

M. 4:3

A.   The religious requirement of the lulab [on the Sabbath]: How so?
B.   [If] the first festival day of the Festival coincided with the Sabbath, they bring their lulabs to the Temple mount.
C.   And the attendants take them from them and arrange them on the roof of the portico.
D.   But the elders leave theirs in a special room.
E.   They teach them to make the following statement: "To whomever my lulab comes, lo, it is given to him as a gift."
F.   On the next day they get up and come along.
G.   And the attendants toss them before them.
H.   They grab at lulabs and hit one another.
I.   Now when the court saw that this was leading to a dangerous situation,

they ordained that each and every one should take his lulab in his own
home.

M. 4:4

I.

A. But why [would it be forbidden to carry the lulab on the Sabbath if that does not
coincide with the first day of the Festival (M. 4:2B-C)]? After all, it is merely an
act of moving the object, and it should override the restrictions of the Sabbath
[without the imposition of such a strict rule as is indicated by the law].

B. Said Rabbah, "It is indeed a precautionary decree, lest a person take the lulab in
hand and go to an expert [in the laws governing the rite] so as to learn [what is to be
done] [43A], and, in so doing, carry the lulab for four or more cubits in the public
domain [which must not be done].

C. "That accounts also for the rule pertaining to the shofar [which is not to be carried
or blown on the Sabbath] and the scroll of Esther [which id not to be carried or read
on the Sabbath]."

D. If that is the operative consideration, then even when the first day [of the Festival
coincides with the Sabbath], the prohibition likewise [should apply].

E. As to the first day, lo, rabbis have made an ordinance covering it, requiring that the
rite be performed at home [M. 4:41] [and the possibility of law-violation then does
not exist].

F. That solves the problem, to be sure, for the period after the ordinance [to which M.
4:41 refers] had been laid down, but what is there to say about the situation prior to
that ordinance?

G. As to conduct on the first day of the Festival, which is governed by the authority of
the Torah-law so that even in the outlying areas [not in the Temple], taking the lulab
is done on the authority of the Torah, rabbis made no such decree.

H. But as to the other days, on which taking the lulab in the outlying areas is not done
on the authority of the law of the Torah, the rabbis made their precautionary decree
[even pertaining to the Temple].

I. If that is the operative consideration, then at the present time also [the law should
be the same]. [Slotki, p. 195, n. 8: The command to take the lulab should override
on the first day the Sabbath even now when the Temple is no longer in existence.]

J. We [in Babylonia] are not able precisely to establish the lunar calendar [and so do
not know for sure that, in taking up the lulab on the Sabbath day, we are not
violating the sanctity of the Sabbath without proper justification].

K. If that is the case, then, since they [in the Land] are precise in setting the lunar
calendar, for them [in the Land of Israel] the taking of the lulab should surely
override the restrictions on the Sabbath.

L. That is indeed the case, for we learn in the Mishnah: If the first festival day of the
Festival coincided with the Sabbath, all the people bring their lulabs to the Temple
mount [M. 4:4B].

M.   A further version of the matter on Tannaite authority states: "to the synagogue."

N.   That would then produce the inference that in the one case we speak of the age in which the Temple stood [that is, at M. 4:4B], while in the other case [M] we speak of the age in which the Temple is no longer standing.

O.   That inference indeed emerges.

II.

A.   How do we know that taking the lulab on the Sabbath in the outlying districts is done on the authority of the Torah?

B.   It is in accord with that which is taught on Tannaite authority:

C.   "And you shall take" (Lev. 23:40) -- indicating that the act of taking should be carried out by each and every one.

D.   "For yourselves" -- something that belongs to you, excluding one that is borrowed or stolen.

E.   "On the day" (Lev. 23:40) — even if it is the Sabbath.

F.   "First" -- even in the outlying districts.

G.   "The first" -- This teaches that doing so overrides the restrictions of the Sabbath only on the first festival day of the Festival alone.

III.

A.   A master has said, "'On the day ...'" -- even if it is the Sabbath.'

B.   "But it is merely an act of moving the object [and it should override the restrictions of the Sabbath]. Is a verse of Scripture really required to permit carrying on that occasion?"

C.   Said Raba, "It is necessary to produce such a verse only with respect to carrying, in addition, the things that are used in connection with the carrying of the lulab [but not the lulab itself].

D.   "And the proof text is required in accord with the view of the Tannaite authority who stands behind the following teaching of Tannaite origin:

E.   "'Carrying not only the lulab but also whatever is needed in connection with it overrides the restrictions of the Sabbath,' the words of R. Eliezer."

F.   What is the scriptural basis for the position of R. Eliezer?

G.   Scripture has said, "On the day ..." even if it is the Sabbath.

H.   And as to rabbis [who reject Eliezer's position], how do they deal with the phrase, "On the day ..."?

I.   They require that phrase to prove the proposition:

J.   "By day" -- and not by night. [The lulab is taken by day but not by night.]

K.   And how does R. Eliezer prove the same point?

L.   He derives the same proposition from the end of the verse at hand, as follows:

M.   "And you shall rejoice before the Lord your God for seven days" (Lev. 23:40) -- days, not nights.

N.   And as to rabbis?

O.   If the proof derived from that verse, I might have reached the false conclusion that I should derive the sense of the word "days" from the use of the word "days" in connection with dwelling in the sukkah itself.

P.   Just as the use of the word "days" in that latter connection means that even the nights are involved, so the word "days" used in the present connection likewise means that the nights are involved. [To avoid reaching that incorrect conclusion, rabbis will not invoke the proof-text at hand to demonstrate the point they wish to make.]

IV.

A.   And as to the sukkah itself, how do we know [that the word "days" encompasses even the nights, so that one must dwell in the sukkah both by day and by night]?

B.   It is in line with that which rabbis have taught on Tannaite authority:

C.   "You shall dwell in sukkot for seven days" (Lev. 23;42) -- "days" means, "and even nights."

D.   You say that days means, "And even nights." But perhaps the sense is "days and not nights."

E.   It [D] is a matter of logic. Here the word "days" is used, and the word "days" is used in connection with the lulab.

F.   Just as in that latter context, the sense is that the lulab is to be carried by day but not by night, so here too the sense should be that people must dwell in sukkot by day and not by night.

G.   Or take the following route: Here it is stated, "Days." In connection with [the seven days of] consecrating [the priesthood] the word "days" is used.

H.   Just as in that latter case, when [at Lev. 8A:35] the word "days" appears, it means, "even the nights," so here too the word "days" means "and even the nights."

I.   Let us then see which analogy applies.

J.   We should reason concerning a matter the religious requirement of which applies all day long, from another matter the religious requirement of which applies all day long, but let not proof derive from a matter the religious requirement of which applies for only a single hour [namely, the lulab, which is properly dealt with in a brief span of time. People do not have to carry the lulab around all day long.]

K.   Alternatively let us derive the analogy from something the religious requirement of which applies for all generations [that is, the taking of the lulab, the dwelling in the sukkah] from another matter the religious requirement of which applies for all generations. But let not the rite of consecration of the priesthood provide the governing analogy, for that rite does not apply for all generations [but only for the very first act of consecrating the priestly caste, in the time of Aaron].

L.   Scripture twice states, [43B] "You shall dwell" (Lev. 23:42) so as to provide grounds for constructing an analogy.

M.   Here "You shall dwell" is stated, and with regard to the rite of consecration of the priesthood, "You shall dwell" is used [at Lev. 8:33, 35].

N.   Just as in that latter case, when the word "days" is used, it encompasses even the nights, so here too, when the word "days" is used, it encompasses even the nights.

V.

A.   The willow-branch rite is for seven days: How so [M. 4:2A]:

B. As to conducting the rite of the willow-branch on the Sabbath if that day coincides with the seventh day of the Festival why should the rite on that day override the restrictions of the Sabbath?

C. Said R. Yohanan, "It serves to make it public that the rite derives from the authority of the Torah [and so is carried out when the seventh day of the Festival coincides with the Sabbath. Thus overriding the rules of the Sabbath constitutes a demonstration that the rite itself rests upon scriptural authority]."

D. If that is the case, why not carry the lulab on the Sabbath even when the first day of the Festival does not coincide with the Sabbath, as a means of publicizing the fact that carrying the lulab is done on the authority of the Torah?

E. The lulab is not carried on the intermediate days when they coincide with the Sabbath on account of the present precautionary decree made for the reasons given by Rabbah [I B].

F. If that is the case, should we not make an equivalent decree governing the rite of the willow-branch?

G. In the case of the rite of the willow-branch, agents of the court are the ones who bring the necessary willow-branches [and they will not make an error], while, as to the lulab, the task of bringing it is given over to everyone [and the concern of Rabbah is well justified in such a situation].

H. If it is the case [that the willow is taken all seven days of the Festival on the authority of the Torah], then let the willow-rite override the Sabbath, whatever day it falls [and not only on the seventh occasion of performing the rite, as M. 4:3B has specified].

I. [If such favor were shown to the willow-rite] then people would imagine that the basis for carrying the lulab [not accorded similar recognition] was dubious.

J. But [at least] let the willow-rite override the restrictions of the Sabbath on the first day of the Festival [as is the case with the lulab that overrides the restrictions of the Sabbath, [and the willow is there only because it is part of the lulab, not because of the willow-rite itself].

L. But why then should the willow-rite not override the restrictions of the Sabbath on any of the other days [apart from the seventh? Why should we rule that the willow-rite overrides the restrictions of the Sabbath only when the seventh time the rite is done and the Sabbath coincide?]

M. Once you have removed the rite from the first day [of the festival, should it coincide with the Sabbath], you might as well reset it at the seventh occasion for doing the rite [even if it should coincide with the Sabbath].

N. If that is the operative consideration, then at the present time, why should [the willow-rite] not override the restrictions of the Sabbath [when the seventh occasion of the rite coincides with the Sabbath]?

O. The reason is that we are not able precisely to establish the lunar calendar [as above].

P. If that is the case, then since they [in the Land of Israel] are precise in setting the lunar calendar, the rite should override the restrictions of the Sabbath.

Q. When Bar Hadeh came, he said, "It never happened. [Slotki, p. 199, n. 3: The date of the beginning of the month was so arranged that the seventh day of the Festival never coincided with the Sabbath. This was effected by adding a day to the previous month or to any other of the preceding months.]"

R. When Rabin and all those who go down [from the Land of Israel] came, they said, "It did actually happen, and [the rite of the willow] did not override the restrictions of the Sabbath."

S. Then is there not a question [as proposed just now at L]?

T. Said R. Joseph, "Who will tell us that the rite of the willow-branch is done by taking it up [which would involve overriding the restrictions of the Sabbath]? Perhaps it is done by setting up [the willow along the sides of the altar, and that can be done in advance of the Sabbath]."

U. Abayye objected to this explanation, "The rites of the lulab and the willow-branch are for six or seven days [M. 4:1A].

V. "Does this not yield the comparison of the rite of the willow branch to that of the lulab? Just as the rite of the lulab is carried out by taking the lulab in hand [which then means the rite must override the restrictions of the Sabbath], so the rite of the willow branch must be carried out by taking the willow branch in hand [not just setting it up by the altar]?"

W. What makes you say so? This rite is done in accord with its rule, and that one in accord with its rule.

X. Abayye objected, "Every day they walk around the altar one time ... and on that day [the seventh day of the willow-branch] they walk around the altar seven times [M. 4:5D, F].

Y. "Is this not done while carrying the willow-branch?

Z. No, it is done while carrying the lulab.

AA. And lo, R. Nahman said Rabbah bar Abbahu said, "It is with the willow-branch."

BB. He said to him, "He may have told you that it is done with the willow-branch, but I maintain that it is done with the lulab."

CC. It has been stated on Amoraic authority:

DD. R. Eleazar says, "It is done carrying the lulab."

EE. R. Samuel bar Nathan said R. Hanina [said], "It is done with the willow branch."

FF. And so R. Nahman said Rab bar bar Abbuhah said, "It is done with the willow branch."

GG. Said Raba to R. Isaac, son of Rabbah bar bar Hanan, "True son of Torah, come and let me tell you a lovely teaching that your father said:

HH. "Lo, as to that which we have learned in the Mishnah: Every day they walk around the altar one time and on that day they walk around the altar seven times [M. 4:5D, F], this is what your father said in the name of R. Eleazar, 'It is done with the lulab.'"

II.   It was objected:

JJ.   The rite of the lulab overrides the prohibitions of the Sabbath at the beginning of
       the Festival of Sukkot [that is, when the Sabbath coincides with the first festival
       day of Sukkot], and the rite of the willow branch at the end [when the rite of the
       willow branch carried out for the seventh time is supposed to be done on the
       Sabbath].

KK.   One time the seventh occasion for the rite of the willow branch coincided with the
       Sabbath, so people brought on the eve of the Sabbath willow saplings and left them
       in the courtyard.

LL.   The Boethusians found out about them and took them and hid them under boulders.

MM.   The next day the common folk found out about the matter and dragged the branches
       out from under the stones and the priests brought them, and they set them up around
       the altar.

NN.   The Boethusians did this because they did not concede that the rite of beating the
       willow branches against the altar overrides the restrictions of the Sabbath [T. Suk.
       3:1A-E].

OO.   What follows from this passage is that the rite of the willow branch is carried out by
       taking the willow branch itself.

PP.   That refutes the proposition under discussion.

QQ.   Why, then should taking the willow on the seventh day of the Festival not override
       the Sabbath [in the Land of Israel, where the lunar calendar is accurately reported]?

RR.   Since we [in Babylonia] do not overlook the restrictions of the Sabbath in connection
       with that rite they too will not overlook those restrictions.

SS.   But what about the first day of the Festival, on which, for us, we do not overlook
       the restrictions of the Sabbath [for we do not take up the lulab on that day], while
       they do overlook the restrictions of the Sabbath and take up the lulab?

TT.   [44A] One may say: For them [in the Land of Israel] the restrictions of the Sabbath
       should not be set aside.

UU.   But then these two Tannaite teachings contradict one another.

VV.   One maintains the wording, All the people bring their lulabs to the Temple Mount
       [M. 4:4B] and the other phrases matters, " ... to the synagogue."

WW.   Now we replied, "The one speaks of the time in which the house of the sanctuary
       stood, the other when it is no longer standing."

XX.   That is not the case. Both passages refer to the time that the house of the
       sanctuary was standing, but, nonetheless, there is still no contradiction. One speaks
       of the sanctuary, the other of how matters are done in outlying districts.

VI.

A.   Said Abayye to Raba, "How is it the case that, in respect to the lulab, we do carry
       out the rite for seven days as a memorial to the Temple, while in the case of the
       willow-rite, we do not carry out the rite for seven days as a memorial to the
       sanctuary [since the willow rite is carried out nowadays for only one day]?"

B. He said to him, "It is because a man fulfills his obligation by means of the willow-branch that is contained in the lulab in any event [so there is no need for a
further such commemoration with the willow-branch]."

C. He said to him, "But that is done on account of the lulab itself [and not for the
express purpose of making use of the willow-branch in commemoration of the
destruction of the Temple].

D. "And if you should maintain that one lifts up the lulab one time [in regard to the
lulab] and yet another time [in regard to the willow-branch], but lo, there are
occasions every day on which we do not do things that way."

E. [Replying to the original question,] said R. Zebid in the name of Raba, "As to the
lulab, which is carried on the authority of the Torah, we make use of the object for
seven days as a memorial to the sanctuary.

F. "As to the willow-branch, which rests only upon the authority of rabbis, we do not
carry out the rite for seven days as a memorial to the sanctuary."

VII.

A. In accord with whom [is the view that the authority of the rite of the willow-branch
is only rabbinical and not derived from the Torah]?

B. Of one should propose that it accords with Abba Saul, has he not said, the following:

C. "'Willows of the brook' (Lev. 23:40 [in the plural] indicates that there are two, one
to be used in the lulab, the other to be used in the rite of the sanctuary [and both,
then, deriving from the authority of Scripture]."

D. Nor could it be in accord with the view of rabbis, for, in their view, it is a law
transmitted [from Sinai, and hence enjoying the same standing as Torah-law].

E. For R. Assi said R. Yohanan said in the name of R. Nehunia of the Plain of Bet
Hawartan, "The laws governing the ten plants the willow-branch and the water-offering [of the rite of the Festival] constitute laws revealed to Moses from Sinai [as
explained above, 34A]."

F. But, said R. Zebid in the name of Raba, "In the case of the lulab, which enjoys a
foundation in the authority of the Torah for its utilization on the first day of the
Festival which coincides with the Sabbath even in the outlying districts, we carry it
for seven days as a memorial to the sanctuary.

G. "In the case of the willow-branch, which does not enjoy a foundation in the authority
of the Torah for its utilization in the outlying districts, we do not carry it for seven
days as a memorial to the sanctuary."

VIII.

A. Said R. Simeon b. Laqish, "Blemished priests [who may not ordinarily serve] may
enter the area between the hall [leading to the interior of the Temple (Slotki)] and
the altar so as to carry out the religious duty of the willow-branch."

B. "Said R. Yohanan to him, "Who said this?"

C. 'Who said it? He is the very one who said it, for R. Assi said R. Yohanan said in the
name of R. Nehunia of the Plain of Bet Hawartan, "The laws governing the ten
plants, the willow-branch, and the water-offering [of the rite of the Festival]
constitute laws revealed to Moses from Sinai."

D. But [the issue is], who said that this is done by actually taking up the willow? Perhaps it is done by standing them up [by the altar].

E. Who has made this statement with reference, in particular, to blemished priests? Perhaps it applies to unblemished ones alone.

IX.

A. It has been stated on Amoraic authority:

B. Yohanan and R. Joshua b. Levi --

C. One of them said, "The rite of the willow-branch is an institution established by the prophets."

D. The other said, "The rite of the willow-branch is a mere custom carried on by the prophets."

E. You may conclude that it is R. Yohanan who has said that the rite of the willow branch is an institution established by the prophets.

F. For R. Abbahu said R. Yohanan said, "The rite of the willow-branch is an institution established by the prophets."

G. You may indeed reach that conclusion.

H. Said R. Zira to R. Abbahu, "Did R. Yohanan make such a statement at all?

I. "And has not R. Yohanan said in the name of R. Nehunia of the Plain of Bet Hawartan, 'The laws governing the ten plants, the willow-branch, and the water offering [of the rite of the Festival] constitute laws revealed to Moses from Sinai.'"

J. He was struck dumb for a moment, and then he said, "The laws were forgotten and the prophets came along and reestablished them."

K. But did R. Yohanan maintains that [laws were forgotten during the exile in Babylonia]?

L. And did not R. Yohanan say, "As to what is yours that I have reported, in fact it belongs to them. [Slotki, p. 203, n. 12: The knowledge of the Law which he first thought was the possession of the Palestinians was in fact in the hands of the Babylonians. How then could it be said that he held that the Torah was forgotten during the Babylonian exile?]"

M. There is no contradiction. [44B]In the one case we speak of the rite carried on in the sanctuary [and that is a law Moses received at Sinai], in the other, the practice of the rite in the outlying districts [and that is what only the prophets instituted].

X.

A. Said R. Ammi, "As to the willow-branch, it is subject to a minimum measure.

B. "It may be taken only by itself.

C. "A person does not carry out his obligation [to take up the willow branch] by doing so with the willow-branch that is in the lulab."

D. Since the cited authority [Ammi] has said that it may be taken only by itself [and not in conjunction with other species], is it not self-evident that a person does not carry out his obligation by doing so with the willow-branch that is in the lulab?

E. What might you have said? The former rule applies only to a case in which the householder did not lift up the lulab, containing the willow-branch, and then go and lift it up a second time [thus once for the lulab, inclusive of the willow-branch, the other time for the willow-branch on its own]. But in a case in which one has lifted up the lulab and then gone and done so a second time, I might have said that that is not the case.

F.   So we are informed that we make no such supposition.

G.   And R. Hisda said R. Isaac [said], "A person does carry out his obligation [to take up the willow-branch] by doing so with the willow-branch that is in the lulab."

H.   And what is the minimum measure for the lulab [A]?

I.   Said R. Nahman, "It must have three twigs with fresh leaves."

J.   And R. Sheshet said, "Even one leaf and one twig."

K.   "One leaf and one twig?!" How can you think so?

L.   Rather, I should phrase matters, "Even one leaf on one twig."

XI.

A.   Said Aibu, "I was standing before R. Eleazar b. R. Sadoq, and someone brought a willow-branch to him. He took it and shook it and did so again, but did not say a blessing.

B.   "He took the position that the matter is simply a custom that the prophets introduced."

C.   Aibu and Hezekiah, sons of the daughter of Rab, brought a willow-branch before Rab. He beat it and did so again, but he did not say a blessing over it.

D.   He took the position that the matter is simply a custom that the prophets introduced.

E.   Said Aibu, "I was standing before R. Eleazar b. R. Sadoq, and someone came to him and said to him, 'I own villages, vineyards, and olive groves. The villagers come and hoe in the vineyards, and [as payment] they eat the olives [and this is done in the Seventh Year, when the land is treated as if it is ownerless.]

F.   "Is this proper or improper [for them to take as payment for hoeing the vineyards the olives that they eat]?'

G.   "He said to him, 'It is not proper.'

H.   "As the man was leaving, [Eleazar] said, 'I have been living in this land for forty years, and I have never seen a man walking in the right paths the way this one does.'

I.   "The man came back and said to him, 'What should I do?'

J.   "He said to him, 'Declare the olives to be ownerless property for those in need, and pay money for those who do the hoeing.'"

K.   Now it is permitted to hoe [in the Seventh Year]?

L.   And has it not been taught on Tannaite authority:

M.   "But the seventh year you shall let [the land] rest and lie still" (Ex. 23:11).

N.   "You shall let it rest" from hoeing,

O.   "and lie still" from having stones removed.

P.   Said R. Uqba bar Hama, "There are two kinds of hoeing. In one kind one closes up the holes [around the roots of a tree], and in the other, he aerates the soil [around the roots of a tree].

Q.   "Aerating the soil is forbidden, closing up the holes is permitted [since the former serves the roots of the tree, the latter merely protects the tree (Slotki)]."

R.   Said Aibu in the name of R. Eleazar bar Sadok, "A person should not walk on the eve of the Sabbath [Friday] more than three parasangs [for fear he may not reach his destination prior to the Sabbath]."

S.   Said R. Kahana, "The statement at hand applies only to someone going home [where people might have food ready for him, if he is not expected]. But as to going to his inn, he depends upon what he has in hand [for food, so there is no problem]."

T.   There are those who report matters as follows:

U.   Said R. Kahana, "The statement at hand was necessary only to apply even to one who was going to his home."

V.   Said R. Kahana, "Such an incident happened to me, and [at home] I did not find even a fish-pie [because I came in unexpectedly]."

XII.

A.   The religious requirement of the lulab on the Sabbath: how so [M. 4:4A]:

B.   A Tannaite teacher repeated the following Tannaite teaching before R. Nahman: They arrange them on the roof of the portico [M. 4:4C].

C.   He said to him, [45A] "But do they have to dry them out [that they should be arranged up there? [If they dry out, the lulabs are invalid.]"

D.   But say, " ... on the portico."

E.   Said Rahba said R. Judah, "The Temple Mountain had a double colonnade, one within the other."

M. 4:2 and M. 4:3 take up the items of M. 4:1A and explain why they may be done either on six or on seven days. Only if the first festival day of the Festival coincides with the Sabbath are these rites carried out on the Sabbath. If the first festival day of the Festival is on any other day, then for the Sabbath which falls in the intermediate days of the festival these rites are suspended (compare M. 3:12). That is the point repeated at M. 4:2 and M. 4:3. It will not be relevant to M. 4:1B or C, since there is no problem with the Sabbath for these rites, or to M. 4:1D, because there is no basis for permitting the flute-playing to override the restrictions of the Sabbath in any event. The supplement at M. 4:4, to M. 4:2 goes over the ground of M. 3:12-13. The narrative is complete at B-F +G. H-I are jarring, just as the consideration of E is surprising in light of the certainty of M. 3:13 on a quite different theory. In all, this is an odd item, contradicting M. 3:12 at I and M. 3:13 at E-F. Unit I proceeds directly to the issue of not carrying the lulab on the Sabbath when the Sabbath and the first day of the Festival do not coincide, that is, the premise of the entire construction. Unit II is continuous with the foregoing, I G. Unit III still goes over the same issue, and unit IV is continuous with the foregoing, supplementing and completing its discussion. Unit V moves us to M. 4:2 and seeks the needed proof for the law. The issue of the basis for the rite of the willow-branch, and its relationship to the rite of the lulab, persists to the end. Unit VI reverts back to the issue of the memorial to the destroyed sanctuary, accomplished with the latter and not the former, and explains why that is the case. Unit VII proceeds to the issue of the scriptural basis once more. Because of VII E, VIII, IX are appended, though the latter is in place. Unit X introduces fresh material, relevant to the theme at hand. The issue of the basis for the willow-rite recurs at XI, now in quite novel materials. Since Aibu-Eleazar b. R. Sadoq stands at the head of the lot, other materials, not relevant to the opening issue, are gathered together, which indicated that the materials were formed as a unit around the name of the authority at hand, not the Mishnah-paragraph under discussion. Unit XI then proceeds to M. 4:4A.

4:5-7

A. The religious requirement of the willow-branch: How so?

B. There was a place below Jerusalem, called Mosa. [People] go down there and gather young willow-branches. They come and throw them up along the sides of the altar, with their heads bent over the altar.

C. They blew on the shofar a sustained, a quavering, and a sustained note.

D. Every day they walk around the altar one time and say, "save now, we beseech thee, O Lord! We beseech thee, O Lord, send now prosperity (Ps. 118:25)."

E. R. Judah says, "[They say], 'Ani waho, save us we pray! Ani waho, save us we pray!'"

F. And on that day [the seventh day of the willow-branch] they walk around the altar seven times.

G. When they leave, what do they say?

H. "Homage to you, O altar! Homage to you, O altar!"

I. R. Eliezer says, "For the Lord and for you, O altar! For the Lord and for you, O altar!"

M. 4:5

A. As the rite concerning it [is performed] on an ordinary day, so the rite concerning it [is performed] on the Sabbath.

B. But they would gather [the willow-branches] on Friday and leave them in the gilded troughs [of water], so that they will not wither.

C. R. Yohanan b. Beroqah says, "They would bring palm tufts and beat them on the ground at the side of the altar,

D. "and that day was called the 'day of beating palm tufts.'"

M. 4:6

A. They take their lulabs from the children's hands and eat their citrons.

M. 4:7

I.

A.   It has been taught on Tannaite authority:

B.   [The place named at M. 4:5B] was Kolonia.

C.   As to the Tannaite authority at hand, why does he call it Mosa?

D.   Since it was exempt from the royal tax, he calls it Mosa [removed, that is, removed from the tax rolls].

II.

A.   They come and set them up along the sides of the altar [M. 4:5B]:

B.   It was taught on Tannaite authority: They [willows] were sizable and long, eleven cubits high, so that they would bend over the altar by one cubit.

C.   Said Maremar in the name of Mar Zutra, "That statement implies that people would leave them at the base of the altar [but not on the ground].

D.   "For if you should imagine that they left them on ground, [take note of the following]: [The altar] rose by one cubit and drew in by one cubit [on every side]. This is the foundation ... It rose by five cubits and drew in by one cubit. This is the circuit [M. Mid. 3:1B-F]. It rose three cubits, and this was the place of the horns [Cf. M. Mid. 3:1H].

E.   "Now how then can the willows have bent over the altar [if they were set on the ground? [Slotki, p. 208, n. 6: The willow-branch, placed in a slanting position against the altar nine cubits in height and removed sufficiently from its base to allow for the horizontal distance of two cubits from the side of the base to the top of the altar would not project at all beyond the top of the altar. What then would remain for bending over?]

F.   "Does this not imply that the people placed them at the base of the altar [and not on the ground]?"

G.   It does indeed bear that implication.

H.   Said R. Abbahu, "What verse of Scripture makes that same point [that the boughs bent over the altar]? It is as it is said, 'Order the festival procession with boughs, even unto the horns of the altar' (Ps. 118:27). [Slotki, p. 208, n. 9: The height of the horns was one cubit above the top of the altar, and boughs that reached to the top of the horns naturally bent one cubit over the altar top.]"

III.

A.   Said R. Abbahu said R. Eleazar, "Whoever takes up a lulab with its binding and a willow-branch with its wreath is regarded by Scripture as if he had built an altar and sacrificed an offering on it.

B.   "For it is said [45B] 'Order the festival procession with boughs, even unto the horns of the altar' (Ps. 118:27)."

C.   Said R. Jeremiah in the name of R. Simeon b. Yohai, and R. Yohanan in the name of R. Simeon of Mahoz in the name of R. Yohanan of Makkut, "Whoever makes an addition [Slotki] to the festival by eating and drinking is regarded by Scripture as if he had built an altar and sacrificed an offering on it.

D.   "For it is said, 'Order the festival procession with boughs, even unto the horns of the altar' (ps. 118:27)."

IV.

A.   Said Hezekiah said R. Jeremiah in the name R. Simeon b. Yohai, "In the case of things used in carrying out all religious duties, a person is able to fulfill his obligation only by using those objects in the manner in which they grow [with the natural bottom at the bottom, the natural top of the top],

B.   "as it is said, 'Acacia wood standing up,' (Ex. 26:15)."

C.   It has been taught along these same lines on Tannaite authority:

D.   "Acacia wood standing up" (Ex. 26:15) means that the wood is arranged so that it stands up in the manner in which it grows [with the grain perpendicular to the ground].

E.   Another interpretation: "Standing" in the sense that they had up[right] the golden plating [that is affixed to them].

F.   Another interpretation of "Standing:"

G.   Should you say, "Their hope is lost, their prospects null," Scripture to the contrary says, "Acaia wood standing up" (Ex. 26:15), meaning that they stand for ever and ever.

H.   And Hezekiah said R. Jeremiah said in the name of R. Simeon b. Yohai, "[Because of the troubles I have known], I can free the entire world from punishment from the day on which I was born to this very moment, and were my son, Eliezer with me, it would be from the day on which the world was made to this moment, and were Yotam b. Uzziah with us, it would be from the day on which the world was made to its very end."

I.   And Hezekiah said R. Jeremiah said in the name of R. Simeon b. Yohai, "I have myself seen the inhabitants of the upper world, and they are only a few. If they are a thousand, my son and I are among their number. If they are only a hundred, my son and I are among their number. If they are only two, they are only my son and I."

J.   But are they so few in number? And lo, Raba said, "The row [of the righteous] before the Holy One, blessed be he, is made up of eighteen thousand,

K.   "as it is said, 'There shall be eighteen thousand round about' (Ez. 48:35)."

L.   There is [few] no contradiction [between the two views]. The former number refers to those [few] who see Him through a bright mirror, the latter [larger] number, through a dirty mirror.

M.   But are those who see him through a bright mirror so few? And has not Abayye said, "There are in the world never fewer than thirty-six righteous men who look upon the face of the Presence of God every day.

N.   "For it is said, 'Happy are those who wait for him' (Is. 30:18), and the numerical value of the letters in the word 'for him' is thirty-six"?

O.   There is no contradiction. The latter number [thirty-six] speaks of the ones who may come in with permission, the former [two, Simeon and his son] are the ones who may come in without even asking for permission].

V.

A.   When they leave, what do they say [M. 4:5G]:

B.   And lo, [in saying, "For the Lord and for you, O altar" [M. 4:5I], they will be joining the Name of heaven and something else.

C.   And it has been taught on Tannaite authority: Whoever [in seeking salvation] joins the Name of heaven and something else will be uprooted from the world,

D.   as it is said, "Except for the Lord entirely by himself" (Ex. 22:19).

E.   This is the sense of the statement: "To the Lord we give thanks and to you we give praise, to the Lord we give thanks, and to you we give hommage."

VI.

A.   As the rite concerning it is performed on an ordinary day, so the rite concerning it is performed on the Sabbath [M. 4:6A-B]:

B.   Said R. Huna, "What is the scriptural basis for the rule as framed by [involving a distinct rite of the lulab performed at the altar] R. Yohanan b. Beroqah [M. 4:6C-D]

C.   "It is because the word for branches is written in the plural [at Lev. 23:40], thus indicating that there are to be willows, one for the lulab and the other for use in beating on the altar [as at M. 4:6C].

D.   "But rabbis point out that the word is written defectively [without the customary signification of the plural, hence only a single one is involved]."

E.   R. Levi says, "The matter is compared to a date-palm. Just as a date palm has only one heart, so Israel has only one heart -- for their Father in heaven."

VII.

A.   Said R. Judah said Samuel, "[A blessing is said over] the lulab for seven days but for the sukkah only one [the first day of the festival].

B.   "What is the reason for this distinction?

C.   "In the case of the lulab, the nights [on which the lulab is not taken up] break up the days, so that taking up the lulab each day constitutes the commission of a distinct religious duty.

D.   "But in case of the sukkah, in which the nights do not form divisions between the days [since the sukkah is to be used by night as much as by day], all seven days are regarded as a single protracted interval of one day."

E.   And Rabbah bar bar Hana said R. Yohanan said, "The sukkah is to be given a blessing seven days, but the lulab only one.

F.   "What is the reason for this distinction?

G.   "The sukkah derives use of the sukkah for seven days derives from the authority of the Torah.

H.   "But use of the lulab for the other days of the Festival derives only from the authority of a rabbis, so saying a blessing only on the first day is entirely sufficient."

I.   When Rabin came, he said R. Yohanan [said], "The same rule applies to both this and that: the blessing is to be said all seven days."

J.   Said R. Joseph, "Select the position stated by Rabbah bar bar Hana, for all the Amoraic authorities stand with him in respect to the sukkah [and insist that a blessing be said all seven days]."

K. The following objection was raised:

L. [46A]One who makes a lulab for himself says, "Praised [be Thou, O Lord ...], who gave us life and preserved us and brought us to this occasion."

M. When he takes it [in hand] to carry out his obligation, he says, "Praised [be Thou, O Lord ...] who has sanctified us through his commandments and commanded us concerning the taking of the lulab."

N. And though he has said a blessing on the first day, he just recite the benediction over [the lulab] all seven [days of the festival].

O. [B. omits:] One who performs any of the commandments must recite a benediction over them.

P. One who makes a sukkah for himself says, "Praised [be Thou, O Lord ...] who has brought us to this occasion."

Q. [One who] enters to dwell in it says, "Praised [be Thou, O Lord ... [who has sanctified us through his commandments and commanded us to dwell in the sukkah."

R. Once he recites a benediction over it on the first day, he need not recite the benediction again [or remaining days of the festival] [T. Ber. 6:10, 6:9, trans. T. Zahavy].

S. There is a contradiction between one statement and another on the lulab [for Rabbah b. b. Hana wants the benediction for the lulab only on the first day, not all seven] and likewise between the two statements on the sukkah [since Rabbah b. b. Hana requires a blessing over the sukkah all seven days and the cited passage of Tosefta has the blessing only on the first day].

T. Now indeed there really is no contradiction between the two statements concerning the lulab, since the one [requiring a daily blessing] refers to the time in which the house of the sanctuary was standing, the other to the time when the house of the sanctuary was no longer standing.

U. But there really is a disagreement between the two statements concerning the sukkah.

V. It in fact represents a point under dispute among Tannaite authorities.

W. For it has been taught on Tannaite authority:

X. "As to the phylacteries, every time one puts them on, he must say a blessing over them," the words of Rabbi.

Y. And sages say, "One says a blessing only when he puts them on in the morning alone. [Later on in the day he need not do so]."

Z. It has been stated on Amoraic authority:

AA. Abayye says, "The decided law accords with the view of Rabbi."

BB. And Raba said, "The decided law accords with the view of rabbis."

CC. Said R. Mari, son of the daughter of Samuel, "I saw that Raba did not in fact act in accord with his own tradition [that one says the blessing only once]. Rather, he would get up early and go into the privy, then come out and wash his hands, and only then put on his phylacteries, and say the requisite blessing.

DD.   "But if he should need to make use of the privy again during the day, he would go into the privy and come out and wash his hands and put on his phylacteries and say another blessing.

EE.   "And we too act in accord with the view of Rabbi and say a blessing [for the sukkah] all seven days."

FF.   Said Mar Zutra, "I saw R. Papi, who would say a blessing every time he put on his phylacteries."

GG.   Rabbis of the household of R. Ashi, whenever they touched them, would say a blessing for them.

VIII.

A.   Said R. Judah said Samuel, "The religious duty of taking the lulab applies all seven days."

B.   And R. Joshua b. Levi said, "On the first day it is a religious duty to take up the lulab. From that point forth, it is a religious requirement imposed only by the elders."

C.   And R. Isaac said, "On every day of the festival, it is merely a religious requirement imposed by elders, and that applies even to the first day."

D.   But lo, we have it as an established fact that the first day's [observance of the rite] is based upon the authority of the Torah.

E.   Then I should formulate the statement, "Exclusive of the first day."

F.   If so, then, that [E] is just what R. Joshua b. Levi has said [B].

G.   Then I should formulate the matter, "And so has R. Isaac said."

H.   And Rab also takes the view that the religious duty of carrying the lulab applies for all seven days of the Festival.

I.   For R. Hiyya bar Ashi said Rab said, "he who lights the Hanukkah light has to say a blessing." [Since the lighting of the Hanukkah lamp is only on the authority of rabbis, it must follow that Rab will concur likewise in the case of the lulab, carried on the last six of the seven days solely on the authority of the rabbis, also requires a blessing, and the rest follows].

J.   R. Jeremiah said, "He who says the Hanukkah light has to say a blessing."

K.   What blessings does he say,"?

L.   Said R. Judah, "On the first day, the one who lights the flame says three blessings and the one who sees it says two. From that night onward, the one who lights the light says two blessings, and the one who sees it says only one blessing."

M.   What blessing does one say?

N.   "Blessed ... who has sanctified us by his commandments and commanded us to light the Hanukkah light."

O.   And where did he so command us?

P.   [The commandment concerning Hanukkah, a rabbinically ordained rite, derives from the verse,] "You shall not turn aside" (Deut. 17:11). [Even what rabbis require enjoys the authority of the Torah.]

Q. And R. Nahman bar Isaac said, "'Ask your father and he will tell you' (Deut. 32.7).
    [The point is the same.]

R. R. Nahman bar Isaac repeated this matter explicitly, "Rab said, 'All seven days it is
    a religious duty to carry the lulab.'"

IX.

A. Our rabbis have taught on Tannaite authority:

B. **He who makes a sukkah for himself says, "Praised who has kept us in life ..." One
    who enters to dwell in it says, "Praised ... who has sanctified us ..." [T. Ber. 6:9].**

C. If the sukkah was ready-made and available, if the householder can do something
    new to it, he still says a blessing. But if not, when he goes in to dwell there, he says
    two blessings.

D. Said R. Ashi, "I saw that R. Kahana said all of the blessings [for the sukkah] over the
    cup of wine used for the sanctification."

E. Our rabbis have taught on Tannaite authority: He who has to carry out many
    religious duties says, "Blessed ... who has sanctified us by his commandments and
    commanded us concerning the religious duties [in general]."

F. R. Judah says, "He says an individual blessing for each one" [cf. T. Ber. 6:9].

G. Said R. Zira, and some say it in the name of R. Hanina bar Papa, "The decided law
    accords with the view of R. Judah."

H. And R. Zira, and some say it in the name of R. Hanina bar Para, "What is the
    scriptural basis for the view of R. Judah?

I. "It is because it is written, 'Blessed be the Lord day by day' (Ps. 68:20).

J. "Now do people say a blessing for him by day, but by night they do not as say a
    blessing for him? [Surely not.]

K. "But the verse comes to tell you that, day by day, one must give back to him
    appropriate blessings.

L. "Here to, for each and every matter one should give back to him a blessing that is
    appropriate to that deed."

M. And R. Zira said, and some say it was R. Hanina bar Papa, "Come and see that the
    trait of the Holy One, blessed be he, is not like the trait of mortal man.

N. "In the case of mortal man, an empty vessel [46B] holds something, but a full vessel
    does not.

O. "But the trait of the Holy One, blessed be he, [is not like that.] A full utensil will
    hold [something], but an empty one will not hold something.

P. "For it is said, 'And it shall come to pass, if you will listen diligently' (Deut. 28:1).
    [One has to learn much and if he does, he will retain his knowledge.]

Q. "The sense is, If you will listen, you will go on listening, and if not, you will not go
    on listening.

R. "Another matter: If you hear concerning what is already in hand, you will also hear
    what is new.

S. "'But if your heart turns away' (Deut. 30:17), you will not hear anything again."

X.

A. They take their lulabs from the children's hands [M. 4:7A]:

B. Said R. Yohanan, "A citron [that has been used for its religious purpose] may not [be eaten] on the seventh day [of the festival], but on the eighth, it may [be eaten].

C. "But as to the sukkah, even on the eighth day it may not [be used for fuel]. [People may not burn up the wood that has been used in the sukkah, even after the seven days of use of the sukkah are over. They must wait until after the Eighth Day of Assembly.]"

D. And R. Simeon b. Laqish said, "as to the citron, even on the seventh day it also may [be eaten, once it is no longer needed for its religious purpose]."

E. What is at issue between the two authorities?

F. One party holds that it was specifically for carrying out a religious duty that the citron was set aside. [Once that has been carried out, even on the seventh day, it may be eaten, thus Simeon b. Laqish.]

G. And the other party takes the view that it was set aside for the entire day [on which it is required for the performance of a religious duty, and not only for the religious purpose for which it is needed. Hence it may not be eaten on the whole of the seventh day, even after it has served its religious purpose, thus Yohanan.]

H. R. Simeon b. Laqish objected to R. Yohanan [by citing the Mishnah-passage at hand]: "They take their lulabs from the children's hands and eat their citrons [M. 4:7].

I. "Now would it not then be the case that the same rule applies to adults [which would support the view that people may eat the citron even on the seventh day of the Festival]?"

J. No, the rule applies only to children.

K. There are those who state matters in this way:

L. R. Yohanan objected to R. Simeon b. Laqish: "They take their lulabs from the children's hands and eat their citrons [M. 4:7].

M. "That rule then applies indeed to the children, but not to the adults [and that would support the view that people may not eat the citron on the seventh day of the Festival]."

N. No, the rule applies both to children and to adults. The reason that the passage refers specifically to children is that this is how things generally are.

O. Said R. Papa to Abayye, "In the view of R. Yohanan, what is the difference between the sukkah and the citron [that he objects to using the wood in the sukkah for fuel even on the eighth day]?"

P. He said to him, "[The sukkah may be needed until the very last moment of the seventh day and into the eighth. [For] the sukkah may well serve at twilight [at the end of the seventh day], since if the householder was eating a meal there, he would want to sit in the sukkah and eat there [right past sunset]. In this case the use of the sukkah was originally planned for twilight. Since the sukkah had been designated for use at twilight, it also was designated for use for the entirety of the eighth day.

Q.   "But the citron, which serves no purpose at twilight [at the end of the seventh day of the Festival] has not then been designated for use at twilight, and, in consequence, likewise has not been designated for use of the whole of the eighth day either."

R.   [Reverting to the issue raised at B], Levi said, "Even on the eighth day it is forbidden to eat the citron."

S.   And the father of Samuel said, "On the seventh day it is forbidden to eat the citron, but on the eighth day it is permitted."

T.   But the father of Samuel adopted the thesis of Levi. R. Zira adopted the thesis of the Father of Samuel.

U.   For R. Zira said, "It is forbidden to eat a citron that has been invalidated for all seven days of the Festival, [but one _may_ do so on the eighth day]."

XI.

A.   Said R. Zira, "A person should not acquire possession for a child of a _lulab_ on the first festival day of the Festival.

B.   "What is the reason? It is that a child has the power to acquire possession [of an object] but not the power to impart the right of possession to another party, with the result that the man would end up carrying out his obligation to make use of the _lulab_ with a _lulab_ that does not belong to him [which, we know, is not permitted]."

C.   And R. Zira said, "Someone should not say to a child 'I'm going to give you something,' and then not give it to him.

D.   "The reason is that the child will come to learn how to lie,

E.   "for it is said, 'They have taught their tongues to speak lies' (Jer. 9:4)."

XII.

A.   [Reverting to the issue of unit IX:] Now in the dispute between R. Yohanan and R. Simeon b. Laqish [we have the following parallel debate]:

B.   It has been stated on Amoraic authority:

C.   If one has set aside seven citrons for use [in carrying out his religious obligation] on the seven successive days of the Festival:

D.   Said Rab, "With each one of them, in succession, he carries out his religious obligation, and then he eats that one forthwith."

E.   But R. Assi said, "With each one of them, in succession, he carries out his religious obligation, but then only on the following day does he eat the citron that he has used."

F.   What is at issue here?

G.   One party holds that it was specifically for carrying out a religious duty with it that that citron was set aside. [Once that has been carried out, it may be eaten even on the same day, so Rab.]

H.   The other party takes the view that it was set aside for the entire day [on which it is required for the performance of a religious duty, and not only for the religious purpose for which it is needed. Hence it may not be eaten on the selfsame day, even after it has served its religious purpose, so Assi.]

XIII.

A.   Now how are we, who keep two days of the Festival, to do things?

B.   Said Abayye, "As to the eighth day which might be the ninth day of the festival, it is forbidden [to eat the citron]. As to the ninth day, which might be the eighth day, it is permitted [to eat the citron]."

C.   Maremar said, "Even on the eighth day which may be the seventh, it is permitted [to eat it]."

D.   In Sura people act in accord with Maremar's position.

E.   R. Shisha, son of R. Idi, acted in accord with Abayye's position.

F.   And the decided law accords with Abayye's position.

XIV.

A.   Said R. Judah, son of R. Samuel bar Shilat, in the name of Rab, "On the eighth day which may be the seventh, we treat it as the seventh day so far as use of the sukkah is concerned, and the eighth day so far as the requisite blessing is concerned. [One makes use of the sukkah, but does not say a blessing in that connection when one says the daily prayers, the grace after meals, and the sanctification over wine]."

B.   And R. Yohanan said, "It is deemed equivalent to the eighth day for all purposes."

C.   As to dwelling in the sukkah, all parties concur that people must dwell there on that day.

D.   Where there is a dispute [47A] it concerns saying blessings [in connection with doing so, that is, "Praised ... who has commanded us to dwell in the sukkah"].

E.   In the view of him who has said that day is regarded as the seventh day so far as the sukkah is concerned, people also must say the requisite blessing.

F.   As to him who says, "It is treated as the eighth day for all purposes," people do not say the cited blessing.

G.   Said R. Joseph, "Stick with the view of R. Yohanan.

H.   "For R. Huna bar Bizna and all the great sages of the generation happened to come to a sukkah on the eighth day that may have been the seventh. They sat down in the sukkah but said no blessing. [That then accords with Yohanan's view of matters.]"

I.   But perhaps they were in accord with the view of him who has said, "Once one says a blessing for sitting in the sukkah on the first festival day of the Festival, one does not have to say a blessing in that regard any more."?

J.   There is a tradition in connection with this story that the sages had just then come in from the fields [and so had not yet sat in a sukkah during the entire festival, so that possibility cannot be invoked in explaining away the precedent at hand].

K.   There are those who report that all parties concur [as against D] that one does not say the blessing in connection with sitting in the sukkah. Where there is a dispute, it is whether or not to begin with one has to sit in the sukkah at all on that day.

L.   In the view of one who maintains that the day in doubt as is treated as the seventh day as regards the sukkah, one does have to sit in the sukkah.

M.   In the view of him who maintains that the day in doubt is treated as to the eighth day for all purposes, one does not have to sit in the sukkah on the day that is subject to doubt.

N. Said R. Joseph, "Stick with the view of R. Yohanan."

O. "For who is the authority behind the statement [in the name of Rab]? It is R. Judah, son of R. Samuel bar Shilat, and on the eighth day which might be the seventh, he sat outside of a sukkah [contrary to the law as he cited it. So he himself did not believe the rule as he reported it.]"

P. The decided law is that people do sit in the sukkah on that day but do not say the requisite blessing in that connection.

XV.

A. Said R. Yohanan, "On the eighth day of the Festival "the Eighth Day of Solemn Assembly] people say the blessing of 'the season' [who has kept us in life and sustained us and brought us to this season"] but they do not say that blessing on the seventh day of Passover."

B. And R. Levi bar Hama, and some say, R. Hama bar Hanina, said, "You may know that that is the case [that the eighth day of the Festival is treated as a distinct festival, so requiring the distinct blessing of 'season,' as specified just now].

C. "For lo, it is distinct [from the preceding days of the Festival] in three aspects: in use of the sukkah, in waving the lulab, and in making the water-offering."

D. In the view of R. Judah, who has held that one would make the water offering with a log of water on all eight days, the eighth day of the Festival is distinct from the preceding seven days in two aspects [and not three]."

E. If that is the principal consideration, then as to the seventh day of Passover, lo, it too is distinct from the preceding days, in regard, in particular, to the matter of the religious requirement of eating unleavened bread.

F. For a master has said, "On the first night of Passover it is a religious duty [to eat unleavened bread] and from that point onward it is an optional, but not an obligatory, matter."

G. How now! In that case [Passover] it is distinct from the first night only, but it is hardly distinct from the remaining days. But in the present case [of the eighth day of the Festival] the holy day is distinct even from the other days.

H. Said Rabina, "This one [namely, the eighth day of the Festival is distinct from the preceding day [and all the others], while that one [the seventh day of Passover] is distinct from the days preceding the day before.

I. [Slotki, p. 220, n. 6: The next three statements point out that in the section dealing with the sacrifices of the Festival, Num. 29:12-39, there are differences between the first seven days of the Festival of Sukkot and the eighth day, either in respect of the laws of the sacrifices or the expressions used in connection with them, proving that the latter is a separate festival. These differences are that (a) on each of the seven days a number of bullocks were sacrificed, while on the Eighth Day only one was offered [Num. 29:36]; (b) the descriptions of the sacrifices of the second to the seventh day begin with the word, and, suggesting continuity, while that of the Eighth Day commences, 'On the eighth day,' omitting the and; (c) on the seventh day it says, "According to their ordinance, "connecting it with the previous days, whereas the Eighth Day, has, "according to the ordinance."]

J. R. Nahman bar Isaac said, "Here [on the eighth day] it is written only, 'On the day,' while there it is written, 'And on the day.'"

K. R. Ashi said, "Here [concerning the eighth day] it is written, 'In accord with the ordinance,' while there [in the case of the seventh day] it is written, 'according to their ordinance.'"

L. May we say that the following passage supports the view of R. Yohanan [at A, that the blessing, "who has brought us to this season" is said on the Eighth Day of the Festival]:

M. The bullocks, rams, and lambs [offered on the Festival] impair one another [so that if one is not offered properly, the entire group of animals is invalidated and a new group must be offered up properly].

N. And R. Judah says, "They do not impair one another, for lo, they grow fewer in number as the days pass." [Slotki, p. 221, n. 1: As the number is in any case steadily diminished, the additional omission of one or more cannot affect the remainder.]

O. They said to him, "But is it not the case that all of them [including rams and lambs] are reduced in number on the eighth day [which thus should be regarded as a separate entity]?"

P. He said to them, "The Eighth Day [of Solemn Assembly] is an entity unto itself. For just as the seven days of the Festival require an offering, song, blessing, and lodging overnight in Jerusalem."

Q. [47B] Now does not the reference to "a blessing" in the foregoing passage not allude to that covering the season [as Yohanan has claimed. This then explicitly supports that view.]

R. No, it speaks of a separate reference, to the Eighth Day of Solemn Assembly, in the Grace after Meals and in the Prayer.

S. That conclusion, moreover, is reasonable, for if you think that reference here is made to the blessing for the season, is the blessing for the season stated at all on all seven days of the Festival? [No, it is not. So the sense of the allusion to "a blessing" cannot bear that meaning at all. It can only be what R. has said.]

T. No, there is no difficulty after all. For if someone did not say a blessing for the season on one day, he says it on the next day or on the day after that [with the result that the reference to "blessing" may well be to the blessing for the season, against A and Q.]

U. In any event, we require that the blessing over the season be recited over a cup of wine, [and people do not have a cup of wine on the intermediate days of the festival, so the problem indeed recurs].

V. [If then we assume that "blessing" in the cited passage refers to the blessing of the season, would this not] support the view of R. Nahman, for R. Nahman said, "As to the blessing of the season, one says it even in the market place [and not necessarily over a cup of wine]"?

W. Now if you maintain that we require a cup of wine in that connection, is there a requirement for a blessing over a cup of wine every day [of the Festival]? [Surely not!]

X.   Perhaps we deal with a case in which a cup of wine came to hand only later on.

Y.   [Reverting to the clarification of the cited passage, P, we ask:] Does R. Judah then take the view that the Eighth Day of Solemn Assembly imposes the requirement of lodging overnight of Jerusalem?

Z.   And has it not been taught on Tannaite authority:

AA.   R. Judah says, "How on the basis of Scripture do we know that as to the second Passover [in Iyyar, not Nisan], it is not necessary to stay overnight in Jerusalem? As it is said, 'And you shall turn in the morning and go into your tents' (Deut. 16:7) and, forthwith thereafter, it is written, 'Six days you shall eat unleavened bread' (Deut. 16:8).

BB.   "What follows from the juxtaposition of these two verses is simple. In the case of the Passover that requires a six day observance of unleavened bread there also is the requirement of lodging overnight, and in the case of the Passover that does not require a six day observance of the rite of unleavened bread also does not require lodging overnight in Jerusalem."

CC.   What then is excluded? Is it not to exclude, in addition, the Eighth Day of the Festival?

DD.   No, it serves only to eliminate the second Passover, which is similar to [the First Passover. Other festivals are not under discussion.]

EE.   That indeed is a reasonable conclusion, for we have learned in the following passage of the Mishnah:

FF.   The offering of the first fruits requires a sacrifice, song, waving of the produce, and lodging overnight in Jerusalem [M. Bil. 2:4].

GG.   Who then takes the view that the offering of the the first fruits requires an act of waving? It is R. Judah.

HH.   And he also takes the view that lodging overnight in Jerusalem is required.

II.   For it has been taught on Tannaite authority:

JJ.   R. Judah says, "'And you shall set [the basket of first fruits] down' (Deut. 26:10).

KK.   "This refers to waving the basket.

LL.   "You say it refers to waving the basket, but perhaps the sense is that it is literally set down.

MM.   "Since further on, it says, 'And set it down' (Deut. 26:4), that takes care of that action.

NN.   "To what, then, does the cited verse, 'And you shall set ... down ...' refer? It can only refer to waving."

OO.   But perhaps the cited passage of the Mishnah accords with the view of R. Eliezer b. Jacob [Slotki, p. 223, n. 4: and not with R. Judah, who may maintain that whatever rite lasts for less than six days requires neither the one nor the other.]

PP.   For it has been taught on Tannaite authority:

QQ.   "'And the priest shall take the basket out of your hand' (Deut. 26:4) teaches that the basket of first fruits has to be waved," the words of R. Eliezer b. Jacob.

RR.   What is the reason for the view of R. Eliezer b. Jacob?

SS. There is an analogy drawn between the use of the word "hand" here and the use of the same word in connection with peace-offerings.

TT. Here it is written, "And the priest shall take the basket out of your hand" (Deut. 6 26:4), and there [with reference to the peace-offering] it is written, "His own hands shall bring the offering to the Lord (Lev. 7:30).

UU. Just as in the present case it is the priest who does the work, so there it is the priest who does it.

VV. Just as in that other passage, it is the owner who participates, so here too the owner participates.

WW. How is this possible [for both to be involved]? The priest puts his hand underneath the hand of the owner and waves [the basket of first fruits, just as he would do in the case of the animal brought as a sacrifice in the category of peace-offerings].

XX. What, at any rate, is the upshot of the issue?

YY. R. Nahman said, "People say the blessing for the season on the Eighth Day of the Festival."

AAA. The decided law is that people do say the blessing for the season on the Eighth Day of the Festival.

BBB. It has been taught on Tannaite authority in accord with the view of R. Nahman:

CCC. The Eighth Day [48A] of Solemn Assembly constitutes a festival unto itself for the matters of balloting to see which priest does what job, for the saying of the blessing for the season, for the character of the holiday as distinct from the Festival of Sukkot [so the sukkah is not used], the sacrifice, the psalm, and the benediction. [In all these aspects it is a completely distinct holy day and not a continuation of the Festival of Sukkot].

The most interesting aspect of the construction before us does not pertain to the Mishnah-paragraph, but to the relationship between the seven days of the Festival of Sukkot and the Eighth Day of Solemn Assembly, with which the Festival concludes. Is this part of the Festival or a distinct holy day on its own? My own inclination is to suppose that the protracted discussion -- unit XV -- would better serve M. 4:8A-B, which follows. But it clearly is meant to continue the units that come before it. These, after all, persistently refer to the eighth day, specifically to the doubts concerning the designation, in the Exilic communities, of the eighth day. So, overall, the construction appears to follow a rather subtle program. Units I and II gloss the cited clauses of the Mishnah. I take it unit III is inserted because it is joined through Abbahu's name to the foregoing, and unit IV because of Jeremiah-Simeon b. Yohai. Unit V then reverts to M., as indicated, along with unit VI. Unit VII opens a secondary issue, the blessings said over the lulab and the sukkah and the comparison between the two distinct rites. This leads directly to the issue of how we treat religious rites repeated from day to day. Are they of the same status, or is the important act only the first one, so unit VIII? The same issue is worked out in unit IX. Unit X then directs attention to M. 4:7A. But the issue of the relationship between two of the rites of the Festival, on the one side, and successive days of the festival -- particularly the seventh, then the eighth (the Eighth Day of Solemn Assembly) is raised. That issue thus extends unit VII's basic premise. Unit XI is inserted whole but plays no role; unit XII continues unit X. Unit XIII forms a separate unit but ties in closely with the foregoing. Unit XIV reverts to the established issue, the matter of doubt about the eighth day of the Festival and its status. Then unit XV presents a massive and well-composed discussion of the same issue. So, in all, units VIII-XV in the balance appear to be continuous, an impressive feat of sustained argument.

4:8A-B

A.   The Hallel-Psalms and the rejoicing are for eight days: How so?

B.   This rule teaches that a person is obligated for the Hallel-Psalms, for the rejoicing, and for the honoring of the festival day, on the last festival day of the Festival, just as he is on all the other days of the Festival.

I.

A.   How on the basis of Scripture do we know this rule?

B.   It accords with that which our rabbis have taught on Tannaite authority:

C.   "And you shall be altogether joyful" (Deut. 16:15) serves to encompass the last nights of the festival.

D.   Perhaps it refers only to the first Festival day.

E.   When Scripture says, "Altogether," the word serves to distinguish [one set of Festival days from the other].

F.   Why then encompass the last nights of the Festival and exclude the first ones?

G.   I encompass the last nights of the Festival, [on the days] before which there is an aspect of rejoicing, and exclude the first nights of the festival, [on the days] before which there is no aspect of rejoicing.

The Talmud provides a scriptural basis for the Mishnah's rules. The larger issues of the required conduct on the Eighth Day of Solemn Assembly have already been worked out in the preceding.

4:8C-F

C.   The obligation to dwell in the sukkah for seven days: How so?

D.   [If] one has finished eating [the last meal of the festival], he should not untie his sukkah right away.

E.   But he brings down the utensils [only] from twilight onward --

F.   on account of the honor due to the last festival day of the Festival.

M. 4:8

I.

A. [In line with M. 4:8E], if someone has no utensils to bring down, what is the law?

B. If he had no utensils?! Then what did he use [in the sukkah]?

C. Rather, the question is to be phrased as follows:

D. If the householder had no place to which to bring down his utensils, what is the law? [What if he had nowhere else to eat?]

E. R. Hiyya bar Ashi said, "He removes four handbreadths [of the roof of the sukkah itself, thus removing the sukkah from valid use]."

F. R. Joshua b. Levi said, "He lights a lamp in it [which is not to be done in a valid sukkah. That indicates that the sukkah is no longer in use in connection with the Festival.]"

G. And there is no difference between the two authorities, one referring to how we do things [here in Babylonia], and the other to how they do things there [in the Land of Israel]. [In Babylonia, the eighth day may be the seventh, so one cannot remove the sukkah-roofing, and kindling the lamp is the only reasonable procedure.]

H. [Lighting a lamp] is suitable in the case of a small sukkah [where one may not bring a lamp], what is there to say?

I. One may bring into the sukkah dishes for eating.

J. For Raba said, "Dishes for eating are to be kept outside of the sukkah, dishes for drinking are to be kept in the sukkah." [Thus bringing the dishes into the sukkah indicates that the sukkah now is no longer preserved for sacred purposes.]

The Talmud clarifies a minor aspect of the rule, M. 4:8E.

4:9-10

A. The water-libation: How so?

B. A golden flask, holding three logs in volume, did one fill with water from Siloam.

C. [When] they reached the Water Gate, they blow a sustained, a quavering, and a sustained blast on the shofar.

D. [The priest] went up on the ramp [at the south] and turned to his left [southwest].

E. There were two silver bowls there.

F. R. Judah says, "They were of plaster, but they had darkened because of the wine."

G. They were perforated [48B] with holes like a narrow snout,

H. one wide, one narrow,

I. so that both of them would be emptied together [one of its wine, flowing slowly, the other of its water, flowing quickly].

J. The one on the west was for water, the one on the east was for wine.

K. [If] he emptied the flask of water into the bowl for wine, and the flask of wine into the bowl for water, he has nonetheless carried out the rite.

L. R. Judah says "A log [of water] would one pour out as the water libation all eight days."

M. And to the one who pours out the water libation they say, "Lift up your hand [so that we can see the water pouring out]."

N. For one time one [priest] poured out the water on his feet.

O. And all the people stoned him with their citrons.

M. 4:9

A. As the rite concerning it [was carried out] on an ordinary day, so was the rite [carried out] on the Sabbath.

B. But on the eve of Sabbath one would fill with water from Siloam a gold jug, which was not sanctified,

C. and he would leave it in a chamber [in the Temple].

D. [If] it was poured out or left uncovered, one would fill the jug from the laver [in the courtyard].

E. For wine and water which have been left uncovered are invalid for the altar.

M. 4:10

I.

A. What is the scriptural source for the rule [at M. 4:9C about sounding the ram's horn]?

B. Said R. Ina, "It is that Scripture has said, 'Therefore with joy you shall draw water from the wells of salvation' (Is. 12:3).

II.

A. There were two heretics, one called Joy, the other, Gladness.

B. Said Joy to Gladness, "I am better than you, for it is said, 'They shall obtain Joy and Gladness' (Is. 35:10)."

C. Said Gladness to Joy, "I am better than you, for it is written, 'Gladness and Joy go to the Jews' (Est. 8:17)."

D. Said Joy to Gladness, "Some day they will take you and make you a courier, since it is said, 'For with gladness they shall go forth' (Is. 55:12)."

E. Said Gladness to Joy, "One day they will take you and fill you with water, as it is written, 'Therefore with joy you shall draw water' (Is. 12:3)."

III.

A. A heretic named Joy said to R. Abbahu, "You are destined to draw water for me in the world to come, for it is written, 'Therefore with joy you shall draw water' (Is. 12:3)."

B. He said to him, "If it were written, 'For joy,' matters would have you been as you maintain. But since it is written, 'With joy,' the sense is that with the skin of that man [you] people will make a water-bucket and will draw water with it."

IV.

A. The priest went up on the ramp at the south and turned to his left, southwestward [M. 4:9D]:

B. Our rabbis have taught on Tannaite authority:

C. All who go up to the altar go up on the right, that is, to the east, and walk around the altar and go down on the left, that is, of the west

D. except for those who go up for these three purposes, who go up on the left and turn around [going up at the west and going down at the west]:

E. those who go up for the water-offering, for the wine-offering, and for the burnt offering of fowl when the east side of the altar is too busy [T. Zeb. 7:7].

V.

A. ...but they had darkened... [M. 4:9F]:

B. Now there is no problem regarding the one for wine, which will darken, but why should the one for water darken?

C. Since the authority at hand has said, If he emptied the flask of water into the bowl for wine, and the flask of wine into the bowl for water [M. 4:9K],

D. it turns out that the one for water may darkened as well.

VI.

A. They were perforated with holes like a narrrow snout [M. 4:9G]:

B. May we conclude that the Mishnah's statement accords with the view of R. Judah and not that of rabbis?

C. For we have learned in the Mishnah:

D. R. Judah says, "A log of water would one pour out as the water libation all eight days" [M. 4:9L].

E. But it cannot accord with rabbis, for, from their viewpoint, why should the water and wine not pour out together? [In Judah's view the wine was, in volume, three logs, so a larger hole would be needed for the wine flask than for the water. So far as rabbis are concerned, each was three logs in volume.]

F. No, that is not a valid surmise. You may maintain that the passage accords even with the view of rabbis. Wine is thick, water is thin.

G. That view is a reasonable one, for so far as R. Judah is concerned, the language he should prefer would be "broad" and "narrow."

H. For it has been taught on Tannaite authority:

I. R. Judah says, "Two bowls were there, one for water, one for wine. The mouth of the one for wine was broad, the mouth of the one for water was narrow, so that both of them would be emptied together [cf. M. 4:9G-I]. [The Tannaite teaching thus assigns M. 4:9G-I to the authority of Judah].

J. That is conclusive proof [for the proposition of F-G].

VII.

A.   The one on the west was for water [M. 4:9J]:

B.   Our rabbis have taught on Tannaite authority:

C.   For there was the case of the Boethusian who poured out the water on his feet, and all the people stoned him with their citrons [M. 4:9N-O].

D.   And the horn of the altar was damaged that day [so the sacred service was annulled for that day], until they brought a lump of salt and put it on it, not because the altar was once more validated, but so that the altar should not appear to be damaged.

E.   [49A] For any altar lacking a horn, ramp, or foundation is invalid.

F.   R. Yose b. R. Judah says, "Also the rim" [T. Suk. 3:16D-F].

VIII.

A.   Said Rabbah bar bar Hanan said R. Yohanan, "The pits [under the altar, to which the wine of the libation offering flowed] had been created in the six days of creation,

B.   "for it is said, 'The roundings of your thighs are like the links of a chain, the work of the hands of a skilled workman' (Song 7:2).

C.   "'The roundings of your thighs' — these are the pits.

D.   "'Like the links of a chain' indicates that their cavity goes down to the abyss.

E.   "'The work of the hands of a skilled workman' — this refers to the skillful handiwork of the Holy One, blessed be he."

IX.

A.   A Tannaite authority of the house of R. Ishmael: "'In the beginning' (Gen. 1:1) is not to be read 'in the beginning,' but rather, 'he created the pit [of the altar].'"

X.

A.   It has been taught on Tannaite authority:

B.   R. Yose says, "The cavity of the pits descended to the abyss, as it is said, Let me sing of my well-beloved, a song of my beloved touching his vineyard. My well-beloved had a vineyard on a very fruitful hill. And he digged it and cleared it of stones and planted it with the choicest vine and built a tower in the midst of it and also hewed out a vat therein (Is. 5:1-2).

C.   "And he built a tower in the midst of it — this is the sanctuary.

D.   "And [also] hewed out a vat therein — this is the altar.

E.   "And also hewed out a vat therein — this is the pits."

F.   R. Eliezer b. R. Sadoq says, "There was a small passage-way between the ascent and the altar at the west side of the ramp.

G.   "Once every seventy years the young priests would go down there and gather up the congealed wine, which looked like circles of pressed figs, and they burned it in a state of sanctity, as it is said, In the holy place shall you pour out a drink-offering of strong drink unto the Lord (Num. 28:7).

H.   [49B] "Just as the pouring out must be in a state of sanctity, thus the burning of it must be in a state of sanctity" [T. Suk. 3:15C-I].

I.   What evidence is there [for the statement of H]?

J.   Said Rabina, "There is an analogy to be drawn between two uses of the word 'Holy.'"

K. "Here it is written, 'In the Holy Place shall you pour out a drink-offering of strong drink to the Lord' (Num. 28:7), and it is written elsewhere, 'Then you shall burn the remainder with fire, it shall not be eaten, because it is holy' (Ex. 29:34)."

L. In accord with whose view does the following accord, as has been taught on Tannaite authority:

M. As to drink-offerings, at the outset the laws of sacrilege apply to them. Once they have poured down into the pits, the law of sacrilege do not apply to them.

N. May I maintain that it must be R. Eleazar bar Sadoq [Slotki, p. 231, n. 8: who holds that the pits reached only to the floor of the court and that the wine poured into them was retrievable]?

O. For it cannot be rabbis, who take the view that the pits descended to the abyss. [Slotki, p. 231, n. 9: No law, surely, is required for an object that is for ever lost in the abyss.]

P. You may take the view that it accords even with rabbis' position. We deal with the place where the wine was collected.

Q. There are those who repeat the matter in the following version:

R. May we say that it accords with rabbis and not R. Eleazar bar Sadoq?

S. For if the rule accorded with R. Eleazar, do the remnants not remain in their condition of sanctification?

T. You may maintain that the rule accords even with R. Eleazar.

U. You have nothing which has already served for the fulfillment of the religious duty concerning it and yet which remains subject to the laws of sacrilege.

XI.

A. Said R. Simeon b. Laqish, "When the priests pour wine out on the altar, they stop up the pits.

B. "This serves to carry out that which is said: 'In holiness you shall pour out a drink-offering of strong drink to the Lord' (Num. 28:7)."

C. What is the sense of the passage?

D. Said R. Papa, "'Strong drink' refers to drinking, satisfaction, and plenty."

E. Said R. Papa, "That then bears the implication that when a man has had enough wine, it is because his throat has had its fill."

F. Said Raba, "A young disciple of rabbis, who does not have much wine, should drink it in large mouthfuls [Slotki: since thereby he has the same satisfaction as if he drank much wine]."

G. Raba would swallow the wine of the cup of benediction in a big gulp.

XII.

A. Raba interpreted [Scripture as follows], "What is the sense of what is written, 'How beautiful are your steps in sandals, O prince's daughter' (Song 7:2)?

B. "How beautiful are the steps of Israel when they come up for a festal pilgrimage.

C. "'Prince's daughter' -- daughter of Abraham, our father, who was called a prince, as it is said, 'The princes of the peoples are gathered together, the people of the God of Abraham' (Ps. 47:10).

D.   "'The God of Abraham' and not the God of Isaac and Jacob?

E.   "The sense is, 'The God of Abraham, who was first of the converts [to God].'"

XIII.

A.   A Tannaite authority of the house of R. Anan taught, "What is the sense of Scripture's statement, 'The roundings of your thighs' (Song 7:2)?

B.   "Why are the teachings of Torah compared to the thigh?

C.   "It is to teach you that, just as the thigh is kept hidden, so teachings of Torah are to be kept hidden."

D.   That is in line with what R. Eleazar said, "What is the sense of the verse of Scripture, 'It has been told you, O man, what is good, and what the Lord requires of you: only to do justly, to love mercy, and to walk humbly with your God' (Mic. 6:8)?

E.   "'To do justly' refers to justice.

F.   "'To love mercy' refers to doing deeds of loving kindness.

G.   "'And to walk humbly with your God' refers to taking out a corpse for burial and bringing the bride in to the marriage-canopy.

H.   "And is it not a matter of argument a fortiori:

I.   "Now if, as to matters which are ordinarily done in public, the Torah has said, 'To walk humbly,' matters which are normally done in private, all the more so [must they be done humbly and in secret, that is, the giving of charity is done secretly]."

J.   Said R. Eleazar, "Greater is the one who carries out an act of charity more than one who offers all the sacrifices.

K.   "For it is said, 'To do charity and justice is more desired by the Lord than sacrifice' (Prov. 21:3)."

L.   And R. Eleazar said, "An act of loving kindness is greater than an act of charity.

M.   "For it is said, 'Sow to yourselves according to your charity, but reap according to your loving kindness' (Hos. 10:12).

N.   "If a man sows seed, it is a matter of doubt whether he will eat a crop or not. But if a man harvests the crop, he most certainly will eat it."

O.   And R. Eleazar said, "An act of charity is rewarded only in accord with the lovingkindness that is connected with it.

P.   "For it is said, 'Sow to yourselves according to your charity, but reap according to your loving kindness' (Hos. 10:12)."

XIV.

A.   Our rabbis have taught on Tannaite authority:

B.   In three aspects are acts of loving kindness greater than an act of charity.

C.   An act of charity is done only with money, but an act of loving kindness someone carries out either with his own person or with his money.

D.   An act of charity is done only for the poor, while an act of loving kindness may be done either for the poor or for the rich.

E.   An act of charity is done only for the living. An act of loving kindness may be done either for the living or for the dead.

XV.

A. And R. Eleazar has said, "Whoever does an act of charity and justice is as if he has filled the entire world with mercy.

B. "For it is said, 'He loves charity and justice, the earth is full of the loving kindness of the Lord' (Ps. 33:5).

C. "Now you might wish to say that whoever comes to jump may take a leap [Slotki: whoever wishes to do good succeeds without difficulty].

D. "Scripture accordingly states, 'How precious is your loving kindness, O God' (Ps. 36:8). [Slotki, p. 233, n. 11: The opportunity of doing real, well deserved charity and dispensing it in a judicious manner is rare].

E. "Now you might wish to say that the same is the case for fear of Heaven [so that one who fears Heaven nonetheless has trouble in carrying out charity and justice].

F. "Scripture accordingly states, 'But the loving kindness of the Lord is from everlasting to everlasting upon them that fear him' (Ps. 103:17)."

G. Said R. Hama bar Papa, "Every man who enjoys grace is assuredly a God-fearer.

H. "For it is said, 'But the loving kindness of the Lord is from everlasting to everlasting upon them that fear him' (Ps. 103:17)."

I. And R. Eleazar said, "What is the sense of the following verse of Scripture: 'She opens her mouth with wisdom, and the Torah of loving kindness is on her tongue' (Prov. 31:26)?

J. "Now is there such a thing as a Torah that is one of loving kindness and a Torah that is not one of loving kindness?

K. "But rather the study of Torah done for its own sake falls into the category of Torah of loving kindness, and Torah not studied for its own sake falls into the category of Torah that is not of loving kindness."

L. There are those who say, "Study of Torah in order to teach it is Torah of loving kindness, while Torah learned not so as to teach it is Torah that is not of loving kindness."

XVI.

A. As the rite concerning it was carried out on an ordinary day, so was the rite carried out on the Sabbath [M. 4:10A]:

B. But why [bring the water in a jug that was not sanctified] [M. 4:10B]?

C. Said Zeiri, "The framer of the passage takes the view that there is no minimum volume for the water offering, while utensils of the Temple service serve to sanctify their contents even without the prior intent [of the one who uses them].

D. [50A] "Now if the priest should bring the water in a jug that had been sanctified, the water [being sanctified] will be made unfit through being left to stand over night. [There is nothing the priest can do to prevent the sanctification of the water, and what has been sanctified is subject to the prohibition against being left overnight. So the only solution is not to bring the water in a sanctified utensil to begin with.]"

E. Said Hezekiah, "Utensils of service sanctify their contents only with prior intent [of the one who uses them. So the issue raised by Zeiri is of no bearing. But it is a precautionary decree, so that people will not think that the water was deliberately sanctified [and then left overnight]."

F.   Said R. Yannai said R. Zira, "Even if you say that there is a minimum volume of water that is required for the water-offering, and, further, that utensils of service sanctify what is put in them only with the prior intention of the one who uses them, nonetheless the rule would be the same. [Why?]

G.   "It is a precautionary decree lest people say that the priest filled the utensil for the purpose of sanctifying [through washing] the hands and feet. [Slotki, p. 235, n. 2: Such water must first be hallowed, and however large its quantity, it might still be regarded as intended to be used for this purpose. If the water were allowed to be used on the next day, wrong conclusions might be drawn.]"

XVII.

A.   If it was poured out or left uncovered [M. 4:10D]:

B.   Why [was the water not used]? One should simply pour the water through a strainer.

C.   May I then say that the Mishnah-passage does not accord with the view of R. Nehemiah?

D.   For it has been taught on Tannaite authority:

E.   Water that has been passed through a strainer nonetheless is subject to the consideration that it has been left uncovered.

F.   Said R. Nehemiah, "When is this the case? It is when the receptacle on the bottom has been left uncovered. But if the receptacle on the bottom has been covered, then even though the one on top [from which the fluid will pour out to be strained] has been left uncovered, there is no consideration of danger on account of the utensil's fluid being left uncovered.

G.   "The reason is that the venom of a snake is like a fungus that floats to the surface and stands there [Slotki: in the strainer]."

H.   You may say that the Mishnah-rule at hand [which does not take account of the possibility of straining the water that has been left uncovered] follows even the view of R. Nehemiah.

I.   R. Nehemiah would make such a rule when the liquid that has been left uncovered is for ordinary use, but for use for the Most High, would he make the same rule?

J.   For does not R. Nehemiah maintain the view: "Present it now to your governor, will he be pleased with you? Or will he accept your person?" (Mal. 1:8). [What is used for the divine service must be unblemished.]

Unit I provides a minor gloss to M. 4:9C, and units II, III are appended as an anthology of materials on the cited proof-text. Unit IV proceeds to M. 4:9D, V to M. 4:9F, VI to M. 4:9G, VII to M. 4:9J. Once the subject of the pits under the altar is raised, it is pursued in its own terms at units VIII, IX, X, XI. Since Raba occurs in XI, XII, which provides a further pertinent statement of his, is appended. Then the exposition of Song 7:2 at XII A accounts for the inclusion of XIII, on the same verse, a kind of running amplification, as something in one item triggers the inclusion of the next. The same consideration accounts for all that follows to the end of XV. Then units XVI-XVII go on to complete the exposition of the Mishnah-passage. So there are two principles of ag-glomeration: (1) exposition of the Mishnah, and (2) amplification of materials used in the exposition of the Mishnah.

5:1A-C [50A-50B]

A. Flute-playing is for five or six [days]:

B. This refers to the flute-playing at the place of the water-drawing,

C. which overrides the restrictions neither of the Sabbath nor of a festival-day.

I.

A. [50B] It has been stated on Amoraic authority:

B. R. Judah and R. Ina --

C. One repeats [the word for the place of the water drawing] as shoebah, and the other repeats it as hashobah.

D. Said Mar Zutra, "The one who repeats [the word] as shoebah does not make a mistake, and the one who repeats it as hashobah does not make a mistake.

E. "The one who repeats it as shoebah does not make a mistake, for it is written, 'And you shall draw [sheabtem] water with joy' (Is. 12:3).

F. "The one who repeats it as hashobah does not make a mistake. For R. Nahman said, 'It is an important religious duty (hashubah), deriving from the six days of creation [Slotki, p. 236, n. 6: when the pits were created to receive the libations].'"

II.

A. Our rabbis have taught on Tannaite authority:

B. "Flute playing overrides the restrictions of the Sabbath," the words of R. Yose b. R. Judah.

C. And sages say, "It does not override the restrictions even of the festival day" [T. 4:14] [accounting for the rule of M. 5:1C].

D. Said R. Joseph, "The dispute at hand relates only to the song for the sacrificial rite [of the daily whole offering, along with the wine-libation]. For R. Yose reasons that the principal aspect of the song is the [playing of the] instrument, which then forms part of the cultic rite and so overrides the restrictions of the Sabbath along with the other rites.

E. "Rabbis reason that the principal aspect of the song is its vocal expression, so that [the flute] does not form part of the cultic rites and does not override the restrictions of the Sabbath.

F. "But as to the song at the festival of water drawing, all parties concur that it is merely an expression of rejoicing and does not override the restrictions of the

Sabbath [so that Yose b. R. Judah may concur with the rule at hand at M. 5:1]."

G.   Said R. Joseph, "Whence shall I bring evidence that this is what is at issue?

H.   "As has been taught on Tannaite authority:

I.   "As to utensils of cultic service which one made out of wood, Rabbi declares them invalid, and R. Yose bar Judah declares them valid.

J.   "Is it not in the principle at hand that they differ? The one who declares them valid reasons that the principal aspect of the song is the playing of the instrument, on which basis it is validated by analogy with the reed-flute that Moses played [that was made of wood. Hence musical instruments for the cult may be made of wood. The one at hand is valid, by analogy with the instrument of Moses, and further serves as essential to the cult.]

K.   "The one who declares them invalid reasons that the principal aspect of the song is its vocal expression, and does not draw on the analogy with the reed-flute that Moses played."

L.   No, all parties concur that the principal aspect of the song is the playing of the instrument.

M.   At issue in the cited dispute is [whether we may draw an analogy from] what is impossible to what is possible. [Slotki: What it is possible to manufacture from another material from that which it is impossible to manufacture from another material. P. 237, n. 6: It was impossible to make the best of pipes of anything but reeds. All other vessels, however, can be made from metal.]

N.   The one who declares [wooden utensils] valid takes the view that we may draw an analogy from what is impossible to what is possible [Slotki, p. 237, n. 7: Hence he allows all vessels to be made from wood as was the reed-pipe of Moses].

O.   The one who declares [wooden utensils] invalid takes the view that we may not draw an analogy from what is impossible to what is possible [Slotki, p. 237, n. 8: Hence it is only the pipe, which cannot be satisfactorily made of other materials, that may be made of wood, but not any other vessels, which can well be made of metal].

P.   If you wish, however, I may propose that all parties concur that the principal aspect of the song is the vocal expression of it, and, moreover, we may not draw an analogy from what is impossible to what is possible.

Q.   At issue here is [something entirely other, namely,] when we draw analogies based on the candlestick [of the Temple, which provides the generative analogy for rules on the utensils of the Temple,] which of two exegetical principles, the one known as "generalization followed by specification," or the one called "extension and limitation" [as will now be spelled out] do we apply?

R.   Rabbi applies the exegetical principle of "generalization followed by specification" [in which the generalization includes only the elements expressed in the specific example, thus permitting only a very narrow reading of the proposed analogy.]

S.   R. Yose b. R. Judah applies the exegetical principle of "extension and limitation" [in which the generalization is treated as encompassing, and a single item is excluded therefrom, thus permitting a much broader reading of the analogy].

T.   Rabbi applies the exegetical principle of "generalization followed by specification:"

U.   [Citing the verse, "And you shall make a candlestick of pure gold, of beaten work shall the candlestick be made" (Ex. 25:31),]

V.   "And you shall make a candlestick..." [represents] a generalization, "of pure gold" [constitutes] a specification [limiting the foregoing], "of beaten work shall the candlestick be made" [then supplies] a further generalization.

W.   [Accordingly, we have in hand] a generalization, a specification [which limits the foregoing], and a further generalization. You may then draw an analogy only in accord with the limitations of the specification.

X.   Just as, in the specification, it is explicitly stated that the candlestick must be made of metal, so any [utensil of the cult] must be made of metal. [That is why Rabbi declares invalid utensils of cultic service that are made out of wood.]

Y.   R. Yose b. R. Judah, [by contrast,] applies the exegetical principle of "extension and limitation."

AA. "And you shall make a candlestick..." represents an extension [or, an encompassing statement], "... of pure gold," constitutes a limitation on the foregoing. Then the framer of the passage went and made yet another extension by the encompassing statement, "of beaten work shall the candlestick be made."

BB. [Accordingly, we have in hand] an extension, a limitation, and a further extension. The second extension then encompasses everything.

CC. And what is subject to the encompassing statement? It serves to encompass [all sorts of objects, of whatever substance. Any sort of substance, including wood, may be used to manufacture utensils for the Temple.

DD. What then is the force of the limitation ["of pure gold"]?

EE. It has the force of excluding the use of earthenware.

FF. Said R. Papa, "[51A] The following Tannaite dispute [concerns the] same [matter, namely, whether the voice or the instrument is what counts in the sacrificial rite].

GG. "['Those who played the musical instruments in the Temple] were servants of the priests,' the words of R. Meir.

HH. "R. Yose says, 'They were of the families of Bet Happegarim and of Bet Sipperay-yah. They came from Emmaus. They married their daughters into the priesthood.'

II. "R. Hananiah b. Antigonos says, 'They were Levites' [M. Ar. 2:4].

JJ. [Now, R. Papa continues:] "Is this not what is at issue?

KK. "The one who holds that they were servants reasons that the vocal expression is the principal aspect of the song for the sacrificial rite [and Levites did the singing, so the priests could use slaves merely to play the instruments].

LL. "The one who holds that they were Levites reasons that the principal aspect of the song is the instrument [and hence Levites were the ones who played the instruments]."

MM. And do you take such a view? If so, how do you explain the position of R. Yose!?

NN. If he reasons that the principal aspect the song is the vocal expression, then he should agree that even slaves can play the instruments.

OO. If he reasons that the principal aspect of the song is the instrument, then Levites [should be required, and Israelites should not be acceptable, [but the people he lists were in fact of pure Israelite genealogy].

PP. But, all parties to the dispute at hand surely concur that the principal aspect of the song for the sacrificial rite is its vocal expression.

QQ. The issue at hand then is this:

RR. One authority thinks things were actually done in the way he claims, and the other authority thinks that things were actually done in the way he claims. [So at issue is mere historical fact.]

SS. Then what difference does it make [if it does not settle the theoretical principle at hand]?

TT. What is at issue is whether, because a man has appeared on the platform [and engaged in singing psalms with the Levites, we later draw conclusions as to issues of] genealogy and rights to tithe [of that man's descendants].

UU. He who maintains that [the instrumentalists] were slaves reasons that, [merely because a person has appeared] on the platform, people will not promote his descendants genealogy and rights to tithe. [Slaves may take part, because this will make no difference anyhow as to the genealogical status or rights to tithe accorded to his descendants.]

VV. He who maintains that they were Israelites reasons that [later on] people may promote the genealogy of [his descendants] on the basis of [his appearance on] the platform. [This would indicate that the man had a carefully-inspected family tree, containing no inappropriate or disqualifying unions]. But that would not apply to the rights of his descendants to tithe.

WW. He who maintains that they were Levites reasons that people will promote [his descendants, on the basis of [the ancestor's appearance on] the platform, both as to their genealogy and as to their tithe rights..

XX. R. Jeremiah bar Abba said, "The dispute [of Yose b. Judah and Rabbis, II B-D] concerns the song of the rite of drawing the water [that is, the instrument playing].

YY. "R. Yose bar Judah maintains that [the rites expressing] an additional moment of rejoicing also override the restrictions of the Sabbath [Slotki, p. 240, n. 5: even though it is not an integral part of the service].

ZZ. "And rabbis maintain that [the rites expressing] an additional moment of rejoicing do not override the restrictions of the Sabbath.

AAA. "But as to the song that accompanies the sacrificial rite, all parties concur that this is [integral to] the act of service and does override the restrictions of the Sabbath."

BBB. The following objection was raised [to what Joseph proposed]:

CCC. "The song for the rite of water-drawing overrides the restrictions of the Sabbath," the words of R. Yose bar Judah.

DDD. And sages say, "It does not override even the restrictions of the festival day."

EEE. Does this not refute R. Joseph's position [that Yose concurs that the song at the rite of water-drawing does not override the Sabbath]?

FFF. It assuredly does refute his position.

GGG. May I then say that it is with respect to the song for the rite of the water-drawing that the parties differ, but as to the song for the sacrificial rite, all parties concur that it does override the restrictions of the Sabbath? [Indeed so.]

HHH. This would then constitute a refutation of R. Joseph's views on two matters [both on the water-drawing and on the sacrifices. Joseph takes the view that Yose holds that the song does not override the Sabbath. But here it is shown that Yose <u>says</u> it does override the Sabbath. Joseph further proposes that sages say the song does not override the Sabbath, but in the present reading it would indicate that they do think the song overrides the Sabbath.]

III. R. Joseph may reply to you as follows:

JJJ. The parties differ on the song for the rite of the water-drawing, and that is the same rule that applies to the song for the sacrifices.

KKK. [And as to the fact that there is a difference of opinion expressed] with respect to the song of the water-drawing, it serves to show you how far R. Yose bar Judah will go in maintaining his view.

LLL. For [he holds that] even with respect to the rite of water-drawing, the song overrides the restrictions of the Sabbath.

MMM. But lo, it has been taught on Tannaite authority:

NNN. <u>This refers to the flute-playing at the place of the water-drawing, which overrides the restrictions of neither the Sabbath nor of a festival day [M. 5:1B-C]</u>?

OOO. May we not then infer, this is the song that does not override [the restrictions of the Sabbath], but the song that accompanies the sacrifice does override [the restrictions of the Sabbath]?

PPP. Now from whose principle [does that inference follow]? If we say it is R. Yose bar Judah, has he not said that the song for the rite of water-drawing also overrides [the restrictions of the Sabbath, so why not the song at hand]?

QQQ. Is it not then the position of rabbis, thus representing a refutation of the views of R. Joseph on two matters?

RRR. It indeed constitutes a decisive refutation.

III.

A. What is the Scriptural basis for the position of him who maintains that the principal aspect of the song is the playing of the instrument?

B. It is in line with that which is written, "And Hezekiah commanded to offer the burnt-offering upon the altar. And when the burnt-offering began, the song of the Lord began also, and the trumpets together with the instruments of David, king of Israel" (2 Chr. 29:27). [Slotki, p. 241, n. 5: Thus the other instruments, no less than the trumpets sounded at the time of sacrifice, make "the song of the Lord."]

C. What is the scriptural basis for the position of him who maintains that the principal aspect of the song is its vocal expression?

D.   It is in line with that which is written: "It came even to pass, when the trumpeters
     and the singers were as one to make one sound to be heard" (2 Chr. 5:13). [Slotki, p.
     241, n. 6: No instrumental music is mentioned. "The trumpeters" refers not to the
     players of the instruments that accompanied the singing, but to those who sounded
     the trumpets at the time of sacrifice. Hence it was "the singers" alone who made
     the music here.]

E.   And as to the other party [who maintains the position at hand, that the vocal singing
     is the main thing], is it not written, "And Hezekiah commanded..."?

F.   This is the sense of the verse: "The song of the Lord began also" -- vocally.

G.   "Together with the instruments of David, king of Israel -- which served to sweeten
     the sound of the voice.

H.   And as to the other party [who maintains that the instrument is the main thing], is it
     not written, "When the trumpeters and the singers were as one"?

I.   This is the sense of the verse: The singers are comparable to the trumpeters.

J.   [How so?] Just as the trumpeters [played] with instruments, so the singers [played]
     with instruments.

The conclusion of the exposition of M. 4:1 is at M. 5:1A-C. Since the celebration
herein referred to does not override the prohibitions of the Sabbath, if the first day of the
Festival does not coincide with the Sabbath, then the Sabbath comes on an intermediate
day of the Festival, leaving five days for the flute-playing; but if the first day of the
Festival coincides with the Sabbath, then there will be six ordinary days on which the
celebration may take place. Unit I provides a minor gloss on the reading of M. 5:1A. Unit
II then consists of a vast and brilliant exposition of a set of distinct principles, all of them
shown to bear upon the issue at hand. It would be difficult to point to a more suitable
example of Bavli's power of sustained argument and protracted inquiry into principles.
The basic issue -- whether the principal and important aspect of the song is the instrument or the voice -- is intertwined with a number of distinct, but mutually cogent cases
and problems, including the materials at hand. But there can be no doubt that the
construction as a whole was accomplished without reference to the narrow exegetical
needs of M. 5:1. Joseph, Papa, and Jeremiah all participate in a single, common
construction, which is why I cannot propose that we divide their respective proposals into
distinct units. II EEE makes this clear, since it jumps back to Joseph's views, ignoring
Jeremiah's. Unit III is a secondary complement to the foregoing. I may say quite simply
that the Talmud of the Land of Israel has no counterpart to this construction.

                                   5:1D-5:4

D.   They said: Anyone who has not seen the rejoicing at the place of the
     water-drawing in his life has never seen rejoicing."

                                   M. 5:1

A. At the end of the first festival day of the Festival [the priests and Levites] went down to the woman's courtyard.

B. And they made a major enactment [by putting men below and women above].

C. And there were golden candle-holders there, with four gold bowls on their tops, and four ladders for each candle stick.

D. And four young priests with jars of oil containing a hundred and twenty logs, [would climb up the ladders and] pour [the oil] into each bowl.

M. 5:2

A. Out of the worn-out undergarments and girdles of the priests they made wicks,

B. and with them they lit the candles.

C. And there was not a courtyard in Jerusalem which was not lit up from the light of bet hashsho'ebah.

M. 5:3

A. The pious men and wonder-workers would dance before them [51B], with flaming torches in their hand,

B. and they would sing before them songs and praises.

C. And the Levites played on harps, lyres, cymbals, trumpets, and [other] musical instruments beyond counting,

D. [standing, as they played] on the fifteen steps which go down from the Israelites' court to the women's court.

E. corresponding to the fifteen Songs of Ascents which are in the Book of Psalms --

F. on these the Levites stand with their instrument and sing their song.

G. And two priests stood at the upper gate which goes down from the Israelites' court to the women's court, with two trumpets in their hands.

H. [When] the cock crowed, they sounded a sustained, a quavering, and a sustained blast on the shofar.

I. [When] they got to the tenth step, they sounded a sustained, a quavering, and a sustained blast on the shofar.

J. [When] they reached the courtyard, they sounded a sustained, a quavering, and a sustained blast on the shofar.

K. They went on sounding the shofar in a sustained blast until they reached the gate which leads out to the east.

L. [When] they reached the gate which goes out toward the east, they turned around toward the west,

M.   and they said, "Our fathers who were in this place turned with their backs toward the Temple of the Lord and their faces toward the east, and they worshipped the sun toward the east (Ez. 8:16).

N.   "But as to us, our eyes are toward the Lord."

O.   R. Judah says, "They said it a second time, 'We belong to the Lord, our eyes are toward the Lord.'"

M. 5:4

I.

A.   Our rabbis have taught on Tannaite authority:

B.   Anyone who has not seen the rejoicing at the place of the water-drawing in his life has never seen rejoicing [M. 5:1D].

C.   Someone who has not seen the beauty of Jerusalem has never seen a lovely city.

D.   Someone who has not seen the house of the sanctuary when it stood has never seen a lovely building.

E.   Which [Temple]?

F.   Said Abayye, and some say R. Hisda, "This refers to the building of Herod."

G.   Of what material was it built?

H.   Said Rabbah, "Of yellow and white marble."

I.   There are those who say, "Yellow, blue, and white marble."

J.   It went out by a ledge and in by a ledge [so it rose in tiers], so as to hold the plaster.

K.   [Herod] planned to cover it with gold.

L.   Rabbis said to him, "Let it be. It is lovelier as is, since it looks like a wave rising out of the sea."

II.

A.   It has been taught on Tannaite authority:

B.   Said R. Judah, "Whoever has never seen the double colonnade [the basilica-synagogue] of Alexandria in Egypt has never seen Israel's glory.

C.   "They said it was a kind of large basilica, with one colonnade inside another.

D.   "Sometimes there were twice as many people there as those who went forth from Egypt.

E.   "Now there were seventy-one golden thrones set up there, one for each of the seventy-one elders of the Great Sanhedrin, each one worth twenty-one talents of gold, with a wooden platform in the middle.

F.   "The minister of the synagogue stands on it, with flags in his hand. When [one began to read, and] it came time to answer, 'Amen,' the other would wave the flags so the people would answer, 'Amen,' for each and every blessing. Then that one would wave the flags, and they would answer, 'Amen.'

G.   "They did not sit in a jumble, but the goldsmiths sat by themselves, the silversmiths by themselves, the weavers by themselves, the bronze-workers by themselves, and the blacksmiths by themselves.

H.   "All this why? So that when a poor traveller came along, he could find his fellow craftsmen, and on that basis he could gain a living for himself and his family" [T. Suk. 4:6A-G].

I.   Said Abayye, "And all of them did Alexander of Macedon kill.

J.   "What is the reason for which they were punished? It was because they transgressed the following verse of Scripture: 'You shall henceforth return no more that way [to Egypt]' (Deut. 17:16).

K.   "But they went back.

L.   "When [Alexander] came and found them reading from the Scripture, 'The Lord will bring a nation against you from afar' (Deut. 28:49), he said, 'Now since that man [I] ought to have arrived in my ships in ten days, but the wind blew so the ships arrived in five days, [and so he assumed Scripture spoke about him], so he fell on them and killed them."

III.

A.   At the end of the first festival day of the Festival... [M. 5:2A]:

B.   What was the major enactment [to which M. 5:2B refers]?

C.   Said R. Eleazar, "It accords with that which we have learned in the Mishnah: [The women's court] at first was smooth [with no attachments to the walls], but they surrounded it with a gallery, so that the women look on from above, with the men below, so that they should not mingle [M. Mid. 2:5P].

IV.

A.   Our rabbis have taught on Tannaite authority:

B.   At first the women were inside and the men outside, but the people turned to silliness.

C.   [The court] ordained that the women should sit outside and the men inside.

D.   But they still came to silliness.

E.   [The court] ordained that the women should sit above and the men below [Cf. T. Suk. 4:13].

F.   And how could the court have done so? Is it not written, "All this do I give you in writing as the Lord has made me wise by his hand upon me" (1 Chr. 28:19). [Since God himself had revealed the layout of the Temple, how could the court have made changes in the design?]

G.   Said Rab, "They found a pertinent verse of Scripture and expounded it: [52A] 'And the land shall mourn, every family apart; the family of the house of David apart, and their wives apart' (Zech. 12:12).

H.   "They said, 'Now is it not an argument a fortiori: If, in the future age, when the people will be engaged in mourning so that the evil inclination [to sexual activity] will have no power over them, the Torah has said that the men and the women must be separated, now, when the people are engaged in rejoicing, and the evil inclination does have power over them, it is all the more so [that the men and women should be separated from one another]."

I.   What was the reason for the mourning [to which reference is made in Zechariah's statement]?

J.   R. Dosa and rabbis differed on this matter.

K.   One said, "It is on account of the Messiah, the son of Joseph, who was killed, and the other said, "It is on account of the evil inclination, which was killed."

L.   Now in the view of him who said, "It is on account of the Messiah, the son of Joseph, who was killed," we can make sense of the following verse of Scripture: "And they shall look on me because they have thrust him through, and they shall mourn for him as one mourns for his only son" (Zech. 12:10).

M.   But in the view of him who has said, "It is on account of the evil inclination, which was killed," should this be an occasion for mourning? It should be an occasion for rejoicing. Why then should [the people] have wept?

N.   [The answer] is in accord with the exposition of R. Judah: "In the time to come, the Holy One, blessed be he, will bring the evil inclination and slay it before the righteous and before the wicked.

O.   "To the righteous the evil inclination will look like a high hill, and to the wicked it will appear like a hair thin thread.

P.   "These will weep, and those will weep.

Q.   "The righteous will weep, saying, 'How could we ever have overcome a hill so high as this one!'

R.   "The wicked will weep, saying, 'How could we not have overcome a hair-thin thread like this one!'

S.   "And so too the Holy One, blessed be he, will share their amazement, as it is said, "'Thus says the Lord of Hosts. If it be marvelous in the eyes of the remnant of this people in those days, it shall also be marvelous in my eyes' (Zech. 8:6)."

V.

A.   Said R. Assi, "The inclination to do evil to begin with is like a spider's thread and in the end like cart ropes.

B.   "For it is said, 'Woe to them who draw iniquity with cords of vanity and sin as with cart ropes' (Is. 5:18)."

VI.

A.   Our rabbis have taught on Tannaite authority:

B.   To the Messiah, son of David, who is destined to be revealed -- speedily, in our days! -- the Holy One, blessed be he, will say, "Ask something from me, and I shall give it to you."

C.   So it is said, "I will tell of the decree... this day have I begotten you, ask of me and I will give the nations for your inheritance" (Ps. 2:7-8).

D.   When [the Messiah, son of David] sees the Messiah, son of Joseph, killed, he will say before [God], "Lord of the Age, I ask of you only life."

E.   He will say to him, "Life? Before you spoke of it, David your father had already prophesied about you, as it is said, 'He asked life of you, you gave it to him, [even length of days forever and ever'] (Ps. 21:5)."

VII.

A.   R. Avira expounded -- and some say it was R. Joshua b. Levi, "The evil inclination has seven names.

B.   "The Holy One, blessed be he, called it 'evil,' as it is said, 'For the inclination of man's heart is evil from his youth' (Gen. 8:21).

C.   "Moses called it 'uncircumcised,' as it is said, "Circumcise therefore the foreskin of your heart' (Deut. 10:16).

D.   "David called it 'unclean,' as it is said, 'Create in me a clean heart, O Lord' (Ps. 51:12), bearing the implication that there is an unclean one.

E.   "Solomon called it, 'the enemy,' as it is said, 'If your enemy is hungry, give him bread [Torah] to eat, and if he is thirsty, give him water [Torah] to drink. For you will heap coals of fire upon his head, and the Lord will reward you' (Prov. 25:21-22).

F.   "Do not read, 'will reward you' but 'will make him stay at peace with you.'

G.   "Isaiah called it 'stumbling block,' as it is said, 'Cast you up, cast you up, clear the way, take up the stumbling block out of the way of my people' (Is. 57:14).

H.   "Ezekiel called it, 'stone,' as it is said, 'And I will take away the heart of stone out of your flesh, and I will give you a heart of flesh' (Ez. 36:26).

I.   "Joel called it, 'the hidden,' as it is said, 'But I will remove far away from you the hidden one' (Joel 2:20)."

VIII.

A.   Our rabbis have taught on Tannaite authority:

B.   "But I will remove far away from you the hidden one" (Joel 2:20) speaks of the impulse to do evil, which is ready and hidden away in a man's heart.

C.   "And I will drive it into a land barren and desolate" (Joel 2:20) speaks of a place in which are found no men against whom it may make an attack.

D.   "With his face toward the eastern sea" (Joel 2:20): For it set its eyes against the first sanctuary and destroyed it and killed the disciples of sages who were there.

E.   "And his hind part toward the western sea" (Joel 2:20): For it set its eyes against the second sanctuary and destroyed it and killed the disciples of sages who were there.

F.   "That its foulness may come up and its ill-savor may come up" (Joel 2:20): For he neglects the nations of the world and attacks only the enemies of Israel.

IX.

A.   "For it has done great things" (Joel 2:20): Said Abayye, "And against disciples of sages more than against all the others."

B.   [The power of the inclination to do evil over disciples of sages is] illustrated by the case of Abayye. He heard a man say to a woman, "Come on, let's walk along the path."

C.   He said, "I'll go and keep them from violating any prohibitions."

D.   He followed them for three parasangs over a meadow.

E.   When they were parting from one another, he heard them say to one another, "Our path is long, though our company is sweet."

F.   Said Abayye, "If I ["the one who hates me"] had been there, I should not have been
     able to overcome myself."

G.   He went and leaned on a door post, most distressed. A certain old man came along
     and repeated to him the following tradition on Tannaite authority: "Whoever is
     greater than his fellow also possesses a greater inclination to do evil."

X.

A.   Said R. Isaac, "A man's inclination [to do evil] overcomes him every day.

B.   "For it is said, 'Only [52B] evil all day long' (Gen. 6:5)."

C.   Said R. Simeon b. Laqish, "A man's inclination [to do evil] prevails over him every
     day and seeks to kill him.

D.   "For it is said, 'The wicked watches the righteous and seeks to slay him' (Ps. 37:32).

E.   "And if the Holy One, blessed be he, were not there to help him, he could not
     withstand it.

F.   "For it is said, 'The Lord will not leave him in his hand nor suffer him to be
     condemned when he is judged' (Ps. 37:32)."

XI.

A.   It was taught on Tannaite authority in the house of R. Ishmael, "If that vile one
     meets you, drag it to the house of study.

B.   "If it is a stone, it will dissolve. If it is iron, it will be pulverized."

C.   "If it is a stone, it will dissolve," as it is written, "Ho, everyone who is thirsty, come
     to water" (Is. 55:1). And it is written, "The water wears down stones" (Job. 14:19).

D.   "If it is iron, it will be pulverized," as it is written, "Is not my word like fire, says
     the Lord, and like a hammer that breaks the rock into pieces" (Jer. 23:29).

XII.

A.   Said R. Samuel bar Nahmani said R. Jonathan, "The evil inclination entices a man in
     this world and then gives testimony against him in the world to come.

B.   "For it is said, 'He who indulges his servant as a child will have him as a manon in
     the end,' (Prov. 29:21), and, in accord with the alphabet-system of R. Hiyya [Slotki,
     p. 249, n. 12: a form of arrangement of the letters of the alphabet in groups of two,
     each group corresponding to the numerical value of ten or a hundred], a witness is
     called a manon."

XIII.

A.   R. Huna contrasted the following verses of Scripture: "It is written, 'For the spirit
     of harlotry has caused them to err' (Hos. 4:12) [thus the cause is external to the
     person].

B.   "But it also is written, '[For the spirit of harlotry] is within them' (Hos. 5:4).

C.   "In the beginning, it caused them to err, but in the end, it is within them."

D.   Said Raba, "In the beginning one calls it a passer-by, then a guest, and finally, a man
     [of the household].

E.   "For it is said, 'And there came a passer-by to the rich man, and he spared to take
     of his own flock and of his own herd, to dress for the guest [no longer passer-by],'
     and [at the end] the verse states, 'But he took, the poor man's lamb and dressed it
     for the man [now a household member] who had come to him' (2 Sam. 12:4)."

XIV.

A. Said R. Yohanan, "There is in man a small organ, which makes him feel hungry when he is sated,

B. "and makes him feel sated when he is hungry,

C. "as it is said, 'When they were starved, they became full' (Hos. 13:6)."

XV.

A. Said R. Hana bar Aha, "In the school house they say, There are four things that the Holy One, blessed be he, regrets he created, and these are they:

B. "'Exile, the Chaldeans, the Ishmaelites, and the inclination to do evil.'

C. "'Exile,' as it is written, 'Now, therefore, what am I doing here says the Lord, since my people is taken away for nothing' (Is. 52:5).

D. "'The Chaldeans,' as it is written, 'Behold the land of the Chaldeans, this is the people that was not' (Is. 23:13).

E. "'The Ishmaelites,' as it is written, 'The tents of the robbers prosper, and they who provoke God are secure since God has brought them with his hand' (Job 12:6).

F. "'The inclination to do evil,' as it is written, '[And I will gather her that is driven away] and her that I have afflicted' (Mic. 4:6)."

XVI.

A. Said R. Yohanan, "Were it not for the following three verses of Scripture, the feet of (those who hate) Israel would have sunk.

B. "One, as it is written, 'And her that I have afflicted' (Mic. 4:6) [in creating the impulse to do evil].

C. "The second, as it is written, 'Behold, as the clay in the hand of the potter, so are you [in my hand, O House of Israel]' (Jer. 18:6).

D. "The third, as it is written, 'And I will take away the heart of stone out of your flesh and I will give you a heart of flesh' (Ez. 36:26)."

E. R. Papa said, "Likewise the following: 'And I will put my spirit into you' (Ez. 36:27)."

XVII.

A. "And the Lord showed me four craftsmen" (Zech. 2:3):

B. Who were the four craftsmen?

C. Said R. Hana bar Bizna said R. Simeon Hasida, "The Messiah, son of David, and the Messiah, son of Joseph, and Elijah, and the righteous priest."

D. R. Sheshet objected, "If so, then what about the verse of Scripture, 'And he said to me, These are the horns which scattered Judah' (Zech. 2:4). These [horns] are the ones who had come to restore [Israel's condition, and not to afflict them]!"

E. He said to him, "Go on to the end of the verse, 'These then are come to frighten them, to cast down the horns of the nations, which lifted up their horn against the Land of Judah, to scatter it' (Zech. 2:4). [Slotki, p. 251, n. 11: This shows that the 'horns' refer to the enemies of Israel and not to the craftsmen.]'

F. He said to him, "What do I need to get involved with Hana in matters of [interpretation] of scriptural lore!"

XVIII.

A.   "And this shall be peace: when the Assyrian shall come into our land, and when he shall tread in our palaces, then shall we raise up against him seven shepherds and eight princes among men" (Mic. 5:4).

B.   Who are the seven shepherds?

C.   David in the middle, Adam, Seth and Methusalah on his right, Abraham, Jacob and Moses, on his left.

D.   And who are the eight princes among men?

E.   Jesse, Saul, Samuel, Amos, Zephaniah, Zedekiah, the Messiah, and Elijah.

XIX.

A.   Four ladders [M. 5:2C]:

B.   It was taught on Tannaite authority:

C.   The height of a candlestick was fifty cubits.

XX.

A.   And four young priests with jars of oil containing a hundred and twenty logs [M. 5:2D]:

B.   The following question was raised: Was the total volume a hundred and twenty logs in all, or did each one contain [the volume of one hundred twenty logs]?

C.   Come and take note: With jars of oil in their hands, each containing thirty logs, one hundred twenty logs in all.

XXI.

A.   It was taught on Tannaite authority:

B.   And [the young priests] were better developed in strength than the son of Martha, daughter of Boethus.

C.   They say that the son of Martha, daughter of Boethus, could take two sides of a large ox which cost one thousand zuz and walk with them, heel to toe, and bring them up onto the altar [T. Yoma 1:14].

D.   But his brothers, the other priests, would not allow him to do so, on the principle: "In the multitude of the people is the king's glory" (Prov. 14:28). [Twenty-four priests had to do the work, as a gesture of respect to the rite.]

E.   What is the sense of "better developed"?

F.   If you say that it was on account of weight, do not [the two sides of the ox] weigh more?

G.   But in the case [of Martha's son], there was a rise every four [cubits, a step of only one cubits], so that the weight did not have to be carried up a perpendicular incline.

H.   But here we deal with ladders and a perpendicular rise.

XXII.

A.   And there was not a courtyard in Jerusalem [M. 5:3C]:

B.   It has been taught on Tannaite authority:

C.   [53A] Women would sift wheat by the light [of the fire] at the place of the water drawing.

XXIII.

A. The pious men and wonder workers [M. 5:4A]:

B. It has been taught on Tannaite authority:

C. [In T.'s version:] Pious men and wonder workers would dance before them with flaming torches in their hand, and they would sing before them songs of praise [M. 5:4A-B].

D. What did they sing?

E. "Happy is he who has not sinned. But all who have sinned will He forgive."

F. And some of them say, "Fortunate is my youth, which did not bring my old age into shame" — these [who say this song] are the wonder-workers.

G. And some of them say, "Fortunate are you, O years of my old age, for you will atone for the years of my youth" — these [who say this song] are the penitents [T. Suk. 4:2].

XXIV.

A. It has been taught on Tannaite authority:

B. They said concerning Hillel, the elder, that, when he was celebrated at the rejoicing at the place of the water-drawing, he would say this: "If I am here, everyone is here, and if I am not here, who is here?"

C. He would say, "To the place which my heart craves, there do my feet lead me.

D. "If you will come to my house, I shall come to your house.

E. "If you will not come to my house, I shall not come to your house,

F. "as it is said, In every place where I cause my name to be remembered I will come to you and bless you (Ex. 20:24)."

G. So too: He saw a skull floating on the water. He said to it, "Because you drowned others, others drowned you, and those who drowned you will be drowned [in their turn]."

XXV.

A. Said R. Yohanan, "A man's feet are his pledges.

B. "To the place where he is wanted, they take him."

C. There were two Ethiopians who stood before Solomon, Elihoreph and Ahyah, sons of Sisha, scribes of Solomon" (1 Kgs. 4:3).

D. One day [Solomon] saw that the angel of death was sad.

E. He said to him, "Why are you sad?"

F. He said to him, "It is because they want from me these two Ethiopian [scribes] who are in session now."

G. [Solomon] put them [scribes] in charge of the spirits and sent them to the province of Luz [which the angel of death cannot enter].

H. When they came to the province of Luz, they died.

I. The next day Solomon saw that the angel of death was happy. He said to him, "Why are you so cheerful?"

J. He said to him, "You sent them to the very place where they were expected from me. [That is where I was supposed to go to fetch them.]"

K. Solomon cited the following saying, "A man's feet are his pledges. To the place where he is wanted, they take him."

XXVI.

A. It has been taught on Tannaite authority:

B. **They said concerning Rabban Simeon b. Gamaliel that when he was rejoicing at the celebration of the place of the water-drawing, he would take eight flaming torches and juggle them, and they never touched one another.**

C. **When he would prostrate himself, he would dig his two thumbs into the ground and prostrate himself and kiss the ground, and then he would straighten up, and no one else can do such a thing [T. Suk. 4:4].**

D. This is called the bowing [mentioned at Ex. 4:31]. [Slotki, p. 254, n. 4: The feat consisted in the leverage of the body without bending or using the hands.]

E. Levi showed that form of prostration before Rabbi, and he was lamed [by dislocating his thigh].

F. But is this what caused [his limp]?

G. And did not R. Eleazar say, "A person should never reproach Heaven, for lo, a great man reproached Heaven and he was crippled. And who was it? It was Levi."

H. Both this and that caused Levi's limp.

I. Levi juggled before Rabbi with eight knives.

J. Samuel juggled before Shupar the King with eight glasses of wine.

K. Abayye juggled before Rabbah with eight eggs, or, some say, four.

XXVII.

A. It has been taught on Tannaite authority:

B. **Said R. Joshua b. Hananiah, "Whenever we rejoiced at the celebrations of the place of the water-drawing, we never saw [a moment's] sleep. How so?**

C. **We would get up in time for the morning daily whole-offering.**

D. [In T.'s version] **"From there we would go to the synagogue, from there to the additional offerings [in the Temple], from there to eating and drinking, from there to the study house, from there to the Temple to see the evening daily whole-offering, from there to the celebration of the rejoicing of bet hashsho'ebah"** [T. Suk. 4:5].

E. Is this so? And did not R. Yohanan say, "If someone took an oath, saying, 'By an oath, I shall not sleep for three days,' they flog him forthwith [for taking an oath that he could never keep], and he may go to sleep right away." [So how could Joshua have claimed that he stayed awake on the several days that the celebration encompassed?]

F. This is the sense of his statement: "We never got a real sleep," because they napped on one another's shoulders.

XXVIII.

A. Fifteen steps [M. 5:4D].

B. [As to the statement, <u>Corresponding to the fifteen Songs of Ascents which are in the book of Psalms</u> (M. 5:4E)], Said R. Hisda to one of the rabbis who in his presence was laying out matters of lore, "Have you heard, when David made up his fifteen Songs of Ascent, what he had in mind in composing them?"

C.   He said to him, "This is what R. Yohanan said:

D.   "'When David dug the pits [under the altar, which, in fact, had not been made in the six days of creation as others claim,] the waters of the deep welled up and were going to flood the world.

E.   "'David said the fifteen Songs of Ascent and brought the water back down.'"

F.   If that were the case, then they should have been called the Songs of <u>Descent</u> [and not of Ascent]!

G.   He said to him, "Since you call the matter to mind, this in fact is what has been said about it:

H.   "When David dug the pits, the waters of the deep welled up and were going to flood the world.

I.   "David said, 'Is there anyone who knows whether or not it is permitted to write the divine name [53B] on a piece of pottery and to toss it down into the deep so that the water will subside?'

J.   "No one was around to tell him.

K.   "Said David, 'Whoever knows how to rule but does not state [the rule], will be strangled by the throat.'

L.   "Ahitophel reasoned <u>a fortiori</u> on his own [not from tradition] as follows: 'Now if in order to make peace between a man and his wife, the Torah has said, "My name, which is written in a state of sanctification, may be blotted out by water," so as to make peace for the entire world, how much more so [may the divine name be written down and blotted out]!'

M.   "[Ahitophel] said to [David], 'It is permitted [to do so].'

N.   "[David] wrote the divine name on a piece of pottery and tossed it into the deep, and the waters subsided by sixteen thousand cubits.

O.   "When David saw how much the water had subsided, he said, 'The nearer it is, the more it will water the earth.'

P.   "Thereupon he said fifteen songs of ascent, so the waters of the deep came back up by fifteen thousand cubits, and they now remain a thousand cubits below [the surface of the earth]."

Q.   Said Ulla, "That yields the inference that the thickness of the crust of the earth is a thousand cubits."

R.   Yet do we not see that if someone digs down only a little, water comes up?

S.   Said R. Mesharsheia, "That results from the high level of the Euphrates['s source]."

XXIX.

A.   <u>And... priests stood at the upper gate which goes down</u> [M. 5:4G]:

B.   R. Jeremiah asked, "As to the statement, <u>When they got to the tenth step</u> (M. 5:4I), [what is the meaning of this reference to the tenth step]?"

C.   "Is it that they went down five steps and stood on the tenth, or that they went down ten steps and stood on the fifth?"

D.   The question stands unresolved.

XXX.

A.   Our rabbis have taught on Tannaite authority:

B.   Since it is said, "And their faces toward the east" (Ez. 8:16, M. 5:4N), do I not know
     that "their backs were turned toward the Temple of the Lord"?

C.   What then does Scripture mean to say by specifying, "their backs were toward the
     Temple of the Lord"?

D.   It-teaches that they stripped and relieved themselves downward [in the direction of
     the Temple].

XXXI.

A.   We belong to the Lord, our eyes are toward the Lord [M. 5:4P].

B.   Is it so [that Judah proposed the phrase "to the Lord" be repeated twice]?

C.   Did not R. Zira say, "Whoever says, 'Hear, hear' [two times] is as if he said, 'We give
     thanks, we give thanks,' [which one may not do in prayer, since this is a mark of
     heresy implying the existence of more than one God]"?

D.   But this is the sense of the statement: "They worshipped the sun toward the east"
     (Ez. 8:16), but for our part "We belong to the Lord, our eyes are toward the Lord"
     [M. 5:4P] in hope.

To understand the exegetical program of the framers of the protracted Talmudic
passage before us, let us first specify the points at which the exegesis of the Mishnah is at
hand. These are as follows: Units I (with Tosefta's complement at unit II), III (with the
same at IV), XIX, XX (complemented by Tosefta at XXI), XXII, XXIII (with Tosefta's
amplification at XXIV, XXVI, XXVII), and XXVIII-XXXI. The only substantial materials
not serving the purpose of Mishnah-exegesis then are found at V-XVIII. These form a long,
connected but not continuous, essay on the theme of the inclination to do evil, seen
mainly as lust. If that long discourse had not been inserted (with the obvious intent of
clarifying the reason for separating men from women, M. 5:2B), the passage before us
would have conformed to the familiar one, in which the framers of the Talmud say
whatever they wish mainly in the setting of Mishnah-exegesis and amplification.

5:5

A.   They sound no fewer than twenty-one notes in the Temple, and they do
     not sound more than forty-eight.

B.   Every day there were twenty-one blasts on the shofar in the Temple:

C.   three at the opening of the gates, nine at the offering of the daily
     whole-offering of the morning, and nine at the offering of the daily
     whole-offering of the evening.

D.   And on [days on which] an additional offering [is made], they would add
     nine more.

E.   And on the eve of the Sabbath they would add six more:

F.   three to make people stop working, and three to mark the border between the holy day and the ordinary day.

G.   On an eve of the Sabbath which came during the festival there were forty-eight in all:

H.   three for the opening of the gates, three for the upper gate and three for the lower gate, three for the drawing of the water, three for the pouring of the water on the altar, nine for the offering of the daily whole-offering in the morning, nine for the offering of the daily whole-offering of the evening, nine for the additional offerings, three to make the people stop work, and three to mark the border between the holy day and the ordinary day.

I.

A.   The rule of the Mishnah-paragraph does not accord with the view of R. Judah.

B.   For it has been taught on Tannaite authority:

C.   R. Judah says, "They do not sound fewer than seven nor more than sixteen [notes on the shofar]" [T. Suk. 4:10C] [vs. M. 5:5A].

D.   What is at issue between the two authorities?

E.   R. Judah reasons that the drawn out sound, the wavering note, and the drawn out sound, all together add up to one blast [thus seven to sixteen].

F.   The authority of the Mishnah passage [at M. 5:5A] reasons that each drawn out sound or each wavering sound counts for a single blast [hence twenty-one to forty-eight].

G.   What is the scriptural basis behind the position of R. Judah?

H.   Scripture has said, "And you shall sound a drawn out note, a wavering note" (Num. 10:5) [thus treating each as a part of a larger group].

I.   And rabbis? They take that verse to indicate that there must be a drawn out sound before and after [a wavering one].

J.   What is the scriptural basis for the position of rabbis?

K.   It is in accord with that which is written, "When the congregation is to be gathered together, you shall sound a drawn out note, but you shall not sound a wavering note" (Num. 10:7).

L.   Now if you suppose that the drawn out note and the wavering note form a single sound, would the All-Merciful specify that one should carry out only half of a required religious duty, and not carry out the other half of it? [Surely not!]

M.   And R. Judah? That verse refers to a mere signal [and not to the execution of a religious duty].

N.   And rabbis? True enough, it is a signal, but the All-Merciful has treated it as a religious duty.

O.   In accord with which of the two authorities is that which R. Kahana has stated, "There may not be any interval at all between the sounding of the drawn-out note and the sounding of the wavering note"?

P. In accord with whom? Surely it must accord with R. Judah [who treats the two as a single drawn-out note].

Q. That fact is self-evident!

R. [54A] What might you have supposed [had it not been made explicit]?

S. [Kahana's statement] might accord also with the view of rabbis, and it would then serve to exclude the opinion of R. Yohanan, who has said, "If one has sounded nine drawn out sounds over a period of nine hours during the day, he has carried out his obligation [to do so on the New Year]."

T. Accordingly we are told [that Kahana stressed there must be no interval at all, so as to exclude the possibility that rabbis might concur with Yohanan's view. Only Judah may serve as Yohanan's precedent.]

U. And might it really be the case [for Kahana]? [Slotki, p. 259, n. 6: Kahana's statement agrees also with the view of the rabbis and excludes only that of R. Yohanan?]

V. If so, what is [the point of his stressing that] "there may be no interval at all"? [Clearly, Kahana could not have taken the proposed position.]

II.

A. On an eve of the Sabbath which came during the festival [M. 5:5G]:

B. Now the framer of the passage does not mention standing on the tenth step [as specified above, M. 5:4I].

C. In accord with which authority is the Mishnah-paragraph at hand?

D. It is in line with the view of R. Eliezer b. Jacob.

E. For it has been taught on Tannaite authority:

F. Three blasts on the tenth step.

G. R. Eliezer b. Jacob says, "Three at the altar."

H. He who maintains [that they blow the shofar] on the tenth step does not maintain [that they blow the shofar] before the altar.

I. He who maintains [that they blow the shofar] before the altar does not maintain [that they blow the shofar] on the tenth step [T. Suk. 4:10G-I].

J. What is the reason for the view of R. Eliezer b. Jacob [that the shofar is sounded at the altar]?

K. Since the shofar has been sounded at the opening of the gates, what need is there to do so again on the tenth step? Is this [step] not [part of the] gate? [It is indeed.] Therefore it is better to do so at the altar.

L. And rabbis reason that, since the shofar is sounded at the water-drawing, why do it at the altar? Therefore it is better to do it on the tenth step. [The shofar is sounded in connection with the rejoicing at the water-drawing. If the shofar is sounded at the altar, it will appear that it is for the willow-ceremony (Slotki).]

III.

A. When R. Aha bar Hanina came from the south, he brought in hand a Tannaite teaching, as follows:

B. "'And the sons of Aaron, the priests, shall blow with trumpets' (Num. 10:8).

C.   "Now there is no call to say, '... shall blow...,' for it has already been stated, 'You shall blow with trumpets over your burnt-offerings and over the sacrifices of your peace-offerings' (Num. 10:1-0).

D.   "Why then did Scripture stress, '... shall blow...'?

E.   "[It is to indicate] that it is in accord with the additional offerings that they sound the shofar."

F.   [Aha] repeated the Tannaite tradition just now given, and he explained its sense: "It is to say that people sound the shofar at the occasion of each additional offering." [Slotki, p. 260, n. 5: If the day is both a Sabbath and a Festival, the prescribed number of nine blasts must be sounded for each of the two additional offerings.]

G.   We have learned in the Mishnah: On the eve of the Sabbath which came during the festival there were forty-eight in all [M. 5:5G].

H.   Now if [what Aha said] were so, the passage would have specified that on the Sabbath that came during the Festival, there were fifty-one in all [since the shofar would be sounded for each additional offering. That is, there would be three more soundings than on the Sabbath eve, to serve for the second additional offering (Slotki)].

I.   Said R. Zira, "It is because on the Sabbath they do not sound the shofar at the opening of the gates. [Thus three are omitted, accounting for the final count of forty-eight.]"

J.   Said Raba, "Who is this, who pays no mind to the flour he produces [but makes things up as he goes along]!

K.   "First of all, we learn in the Mishnah: Every day [M. 5:5B, thus encompassing the sounding of the shofar at the opening of the gates on the Sabbath as well as on weekdays, as M. 5:5B-C make explicit]!

L.   "Secondly, even if there were [the same number of shofar blasts on Friday and on Saturday, that is, forty-eight], the framer of the passage should still have made it explicit: 'On the Sabbath that comes during the Festival, there were forty-eight blasts.' This would then have produced two inferences.

M.   "It would have produced the inference of R. Eliezer b. Jacob [II K], and it would have produced the inference of R. Aha bar Hanina, [in the former case, the point is that the sounding of the shofar occurs at the altar; in the latter, that the shofar is sounded for each additional offering, that is, at the one for the Sabbath, and at the one for the festival]."

N.   Rather, said Raba, "The reason [that the Sabbath is not explicitly mentioned] is that on the Sabbath they do not sound the shofar for the water-drawing rite [the water being drawn on Friday], so the number [of soundings of the shofar] was substantially reduced." [On the Sabbath the shofar is not sounded for the upper gates, the lower gates, the altar, to call people to stop working, or to mark the point at which holy time commenced -- a substantial reduction.]"

IV.

A.   [Continuing the discussion of Aha's claim that the shofar is sounded for each additional offering, we ask]: The framer of the passage should also have made mention of the new year celebration that coincided with the Sabbath, on which there are <u>three</u> additional offerings, that of the new year, the new month, and the Sabbath.

B.   The intent of the framer of the passage was served by his framing matters so as to accord with the view of R. Eliezer b. Jacob [that no sounding of the <u>shofar</u> took place on the tenth step].

C.   Did anyone ask why teach this <u>instead</u> of that? The question is why not teach <u>both</u> this point <u>and</u> also that point!

D.   The framer of the passage took note of one matter and omitted other matters. [The catalogue is by no means complete, so framing the issue in terms of an omitted item is beside the point.]

E.   If so, what else did he leave out?

F.   He left out the case of the eve of Passover. [Slotki, p. 261, n. 10: The sacrifice of the Paschal Lamb was performed by three groups of the people, each one reading the <u>Hallel</u>-psalms -- 113-118 -- three times and sounding three blasts on the trumpet each time, making a total of twenty-seven blasts, which, added to the twenty-one blasts sounded daily, amounts to forty-eight.]

G.   [54B] If [the explanation of the omission at hand is] that he also omitted the case of the soundings of the <u>shofar</u> on the eve of Passover, that in fact is not a significant claim. For lo, in accord with whom is the present passage expressed? It accords with the view of R. Judah, who has said, <u>In all the days of the third group, they never even reached the verse, I love the Lord because he has heard my voice (Ps. 116:1), because its numbers were so small</u> [M. Pes. 5:7G-H]." [In this case, therefore, there were in any event no more than three blasts on the <u>shofar</u>. The Mishnah at hand is so framed as to accommodate such a case.]

H.   But have we not already established that the first phrase of the Mishnah-passage at hand cannot accord with R. Judah [I C, above]?

I.   The Tannaite authority of the passage accords with him in one detail [the one at hand], and differs from him in another detail [the one specified at I B-C].

J.   [Reverting to the original challenge:] what other omissions can you specify, along with the alleged omission at hand?

K.   He left out to the case of the eve of the Passover festival [on which the Pascal Lamb is offered], which coincides with a Friday, on which we omit six blasts [the ones for the third group, as Judah has said], but we add six others [three for signaling the end of work, three to mark the beginning of holy time].

<u>V.</u>

A.   <u>They do not sound more than forty-eight notes [in the Temple] [M. 5:5A]:</u>

B.   No? But there is the case of the day on which the eve of Passover coincides with the Sabbath, on which, in accord with R. Judah, there will be fifty-one blasts [as specified at M. Pes. 5:7], and, in accord with sages [vis à vis Judah] there will be fifty-seven.

C.   When the framer of the passage made his statement, he was referring to something that happens every year, thus omitting reference to the occasion on which the eve of Passover coincides with the Sabbath, which does not take place every year.

D.   But does it happen every year that the eve of the Sabbath will fall within the intermediate days of the festival [since that item is listed at M. 5:5G]? There are times at which it does not occur.

E.   For example, there is this occasion: when the first day of the Festival coincides with a Friday [in which case the Sabbath beyond will be the Eighth Day of Solemn Assembly. The water-drawing will not override the first day of the Festival if it is a Sabbath, and the water-drawing does not take place on the Eighth Day of Solemn Assembly. Accordingly, here is a case in which the eve of the Sabbath does not fall within the intermediate days of the Festival.]

F.   When the first festival day of the Festival occurs on a Friday, we postpone it [by one day, by adding to the month of Ellul thirty days instead of twenty nine]. Why so? Because if the first festival day of the Festival were to come on a Friday, then on what day would the Day of Atonement fall? It would occur on a Sunday [prior to the first festival day]. That is why it is postponed. [Slotki, p. 263, n. 4: The Day of Atonement was not allowed to fall on a Sunday on account of the difficulties involved.]

G.   But do we in fact postpone it [so that the Day of Atonement will not come on a Sunday]? And have we not learned in the Mishnah: The fat produced by offerings sacrificed on the Sabbath [that is, the fat of the daily whole-offering done at twilight] may be burned up on the Day of Atonement [beginning immediately at sundown] [M. Shab. 15:5]. [The daily whole-offering of twilight on a Saturday produces fat to be burned on the altar. Even though the following day, Sunday, which begins at nightfall on Saturday, is the Day of Atonement, these fats nonetheless may be burned on the altar. The days run into one another, because both are holy, and we do not differentiate one holy day from the next. So why would we ever postpone matters so that the Day of Atonement would not occur on a Sunday?]

H.   And R. Zira, furthermore, said, "When we were at school in Babylonia, we used to say the following Tannaite teaching: 'On the Day of Atonement that coincided with a Friday, they did not sound the shofar, and if it coincided with the day after the Sabbath, they did not perform the rite of distinguishing [between the holy Sabbath day and the following day], in the opinion of all parties. [This would prove that the Day of Atonement may fall on a Sunday, there being no distinction between the holiness of the Sabbath and the holiness of the Day of Atonement, just as M. Shab. 15:5 maintains].

I.   "Now, when I came there [to the Land of Israel], I came across R. Judah, son of R. Simeon b. Pazzi, in session and he was stating, 'That represents the view of R. Aqiba.'" [The point remains as just now stated, that there is no distinction between the Sabbath and the Day of Atonement. There is, therefore, no reason that the Day of Atonement cannot coincide with a Sunday.]

J.   Then there is no difficulty. [Why not?] One statement [the Mishnah at hand, which, in omitting reference to the Sabbath that falls on an intermediate day of the Festival, implies that such a coincidence does not take place every year], accords with rabbis [who would postpone the first day of the Festival so as to prevent the Day of Atonement from coinciding with a Sunday], and the other version [which allows the Day of Atonement to occur on a Sunday] accords with "others say" in the following passage:

K.   Others say, "There are between one Pentecost and the next [in the year beyond] or between one New Year and the next intervals of no more than four days of the week, or, in the case of a prolonged year, five [days] [T. Ar. 1:11C]. [Slotki, p. 264, n. 1: If in one year the New Year falls on a Sunday, in the next it must fall on a Thursday, since the twelve months consist of 29 and 30 days alternately or 6 x (29 + 30) = 354 days = 354/7 weeks = 50 weeks and 4 days.] [Now, reverting to the case at hand, the view that the Day of Atonement can fall on a Sunday accords with "others", as against the position of the opposed side, which maintains that no extra day may be added to a month, and no postponement can take place. That position is represented at T. Ar. 1:11A-B, details of which may be omitted here.]

VI.

A.   Further objection was raised [to III A-F, that the shofar is sounded separately to mark each additional offering on a day on which there are several such offerings:] On the festival of a new moon which coincided with the Sabbath, the song in commemoration of the festival of the new moon overrides that said for the Sabbath.

B.   Now if [what Aha says] were so, then one should say the song for the Sabbath and also say the song for the new moon.

C.   Said R. Safra, "Is the sense of 'override' as you maintain [that one replaces the other, which would then imply a principle contrary to Aha's]? What 'override' means is merely, 'takes precedence.' [The one is said before the other, but both are recited.]"

D.   And why is that the case? The established principle is that when what is done all the time coincides with something that is not done all the time, what is done all the time takes precedence [in which case the Sabbath should take precedence over the New Moon, likewise the song commemorating the Sabbath should come before the song commemorating the new moon.]

E.   Said R. Yohanan, "In the present case, [by reversing the accepted order], it is made clear that the new moon has been accurately reckoned at its proper time. [The issue of C-D is irrelevant.]"

F.   Do we act thus reverse the usual order so as to publicize [that that is the case? In point of fact we publicize the accurate reckoning of the new moon in quite a different manner, for we have learned: [The fats of] the daily whole-offering are set down on the altar ramp, on the lower half, at the east side, and those of the additional offerings are set down on the lower half of the ramp, on the west side, and those of the offerings for the new moons are set down on the rim of the altar, above [M. Sheq. 8:8A-C].

G.   And in this connection [55A] said R. Yohanan, "This is done [with the fats from the offering for the new moon] to make certain that people realize that the new moon has been reckoned accurately, at the proper time." [So Yohanan's explanation in the matter of the order of the songs surely is not à propos.]

H.   In point of fact, two quite distinct actions are taken to publicize the same fact, one appropriate to the one circumstance [in the Temple], the other appropriate to the other [in the synagogue worship].

VII

A.   The following objection was raised [to Aha's claim that the shofar is sounded in recognition of each additional offering on a day on which there are several such offerings]:

B.   Raba bar Samuel taught on Tannaite authority, "One might [have reached the conclusion] that, just as the people sound the shofar for the Sabbath by itself [when it is not also the occasion of some festival], and for the new moon by itself [when it does not coincide with a festival or Sabbath], so people should sound the shofar for each additional offering by itself [as Aha has claimed].

C.   "That is why Scripture states, 'And on your new moons' (Num. 10:10)."

D.   Does this not explicitly refute the position of R. Aha?

E.   It does indeed refute his position.

F.   But how does the cited passage do so?

G.   Said Abayye, "Scripture has said, 'And on your new moons' (Num. 10:10), thus establishing a common analogy for all the new moons [and treating them alike]." [Slotki, p. 265, n. 10: Whatever festivals the day of the new moon may have, the number of trumpet blasts is always to be the same, i.e., they are to be sounded for one additional offering only.]

H.   R. Ashi said, "It is written, 'Your month' (Num. 10:10), and it is written, 'On the beginnings of...' (Num. 10:10). [Thus there is a reference to two beginnings for one month.] What month is there that has two beginnings? One has to say that this refers to the New Year [which marks the beginning of the month of Tishri and also the beginning of the year.

I.   "Yet Scripture explicitly says, 'Your month.' The sense, then, is that it is a single occasion, [and even though there is more than one additional offering, the shofar is sounded only once, to mark the one day that serves for two distinct occasions]."

VIII.

A.   In further [refutation of Aha's view], it has been taught on Tannaite authority:

B.   [What psalms did they recite] on the intermediate days of the festival?

C.   On the first day what did they say? "Ascribe to the Lord, you sons of might" (Ps. 29:1).

D.   On the second day what did they recite? "But to the wicked, God says" (Ps. 50:16).

E.   On the third day what did they recite? "Who will rise up for me against the evil-doers? (Ps. 94:16).

F.   On the fourth day? "Consider, you brutish among the people" (Ps. 94:6).

G.   On the fifth day? "I removed his shoulder from the burden" (Ps. 81:7).

H.   On the sixth day? "All the foundations of the earth are moved" (Ps. 82:5).

I.   And if the Sabbath coincided with any of these days [on which Ps. 92 had to be read], "... are moved..." (Ps. 82) is to be replaced [and read on Sunday, and so to the end, with the psalm for the last day omitted entirely]. [This would surely refute the principle behind Aha's statement.]

J.   R. Safra provided a mnemonic for the cited passages, which is <u>Humhabi</u>.

K.   R. Papa provided a mnemonic for the cited passages, which is <u>Humhabi</u>, and you may use as a mnemonic, "the escort of the scribes" [Slotki].

L.   Does the cited passage not serve to refute the view of R. Aha bar Hanina? It does indeed refute it.

IX.

A.   But did not R. Aha bar Hanina not adduce in evidence for his view both a verse of Scripture and also a Tannaite teaching?

B.   Said Rabina, "The sense of the Tannaite teaching [at III A-F] is that people should draw out the sound of the <u>shofar</u>." [Slotki, p. 266, n. 14: The passage merely says that "they sound according to the additional offerings." The explanation that it means separate blasts for each additional offering is R. Aha's alone, and his own interpretation might well be refuted.]

C.   Rabbis of Caesarea in the name of R. Aha say, "It serves to indicate that they add to the number of those who sound the <u>shofar</u>."

X.

A.   Now what do we do, who keep two days [for the festival]?

B.   Abayye said, "[This is how we deal with the paragraphs of the sacrifices in Num. 28, which are to be read on the respective days, when, in the Exile, we omit one of the intermediate days and treat it as an extension of the first festival day of the Festival:] We omit the paragraph for the second day [and the others then follow the normal order]."

C.   Raba said, "We omit the one for the seventh day [with the paragraph referring to the second day moved to the third, and so on throughout.]"

D.   A Tannaite teaching accords with the principle of Raba: If the Sabbath coincides with one of them, "... are moved..." is omitted [as given above].

E.   Amemar made an ordinance in Nehardea that people should go back and repeat the previous portions [Slotki]. [Slotki, p. 267, n. 6: On the first day of the intermediate days, concerning which there is doubt whether it is the second or the third day of the festival, the paragraphs relating to both the second and the third (Num. 29:17-22) are recited; on the second day which might be the third or the fourth, the paragraphs relating to the third and the fourth (Num. 29:20-25) are recited, and so on. None of the paragraphs is omitted.]

The construction at hand must be viewed as yet another triumph of the philosophical powers of the framers of Bavli. The entire, protracted discussion follows a single line of inquiry; every detail belongs. The opening two units appear to serve as mere exegesis of the Mishnah-passage at hand, and, indeed, that is precisely what they contribute, unit I telling us the authority of the rule, unit II doing the same. But, in point of fact, both serve as a prologue for unit III, Aha's interesting thesis, its exposition, analysis, refutation, since, in later stages of the discussion, units I and II recur and prove integral to what follows. Unit III then lays down the challenge. On the surface, his view is merely on a formal issue of how many times they sound the shofar. But in the depths, the view expresses the principle that, if a given day commemorates more than a single sacred event, all of the relevant events must be noted in the rites of the day. We distinguish among aspects of sanctification. That is why -- in the concrete terms at hand -- the shofar is sounded for each additional offering, on a day commemorating several occasions celebrated by additional offerings. When we reflect on the issue of the relationship of the Eighth Day of Solemn Assembly to the prior festival days of Sukkot and the interest in whether the Eighth Day is treated as a festival by itself -- a holy day distinct from others -- or a continuation of the foregoing, we realize that, at hand, we have nothing more than the opposite side of the same coin. That is, the deep issue running through the bulk of the Bavli for our chapter is coherent. How do we deal with a holy day that stands in contiguous relationship with other holy days, on the one side? How do we deal with a holy day that derives its sanctity from a number of diverse sources of sanctification, on the other side? It is a truly amazing feat of framing issues of utter and total abstraction -- the interplay of diverse kinds of sanctification -- in terms sufficiently concrete to join together with the Mishnah-rules at hand. In any event there can be no doubt that the entire passage of the Talmud attached to M. 5:5 is a unitary composition, one of extraordinary power of exposition of the abstract in workaday terms.

5:6

A. [55B] On the first festival day of the Festival there were thirteen bullocks, two rams, and one goat [Num. 29:13, 16].

B. There remained fourteen lambs for the eight priestly watches.

C. On the first day, six offer two each, and the remaining two, one each.

D. On the second day, five offer two each, and the rest, one each.

E. On the third day, four offer two each, and the rest, one each.

F. On the fourth day, three offer two each, and the rest offer one each.

G. On the fifth day, two offer two each, and the rest offer one each.

H. On the sixth day, one offers two, and the rest offer one each.

I. On the seventh, all of them are equal.

J. On the eighth, they go back to drawing lots, as on the [other] festivals.

K. They ruled: "Whoever offered a bullock one day should not offer one the next day.

L. "But they offer them in rotation."

M. 5:6

I.

A. [When the Mishnah-passage states at M. 5:6J that the priests go back and draw lots], may we say that the Mishnah at hand accords with the view of Rabbi and not of rabbis [vis à vis Rabbi]?

B. For it has been taught on Tannaite authority:

C. "As to the bullock that is offered on the Eighth Day [of Solemn Assembly], the priests cast lots [to see who carries out the rites and enjoys the benefice] as at the first, [so that all twenty-four priestly groups cast lots, just as they do when the Festival begins. Involved in the lottery are all clans, not only the priestly clans who had had only two turns on the bullocks (Slotki)]," the words of Rabbi.

D. And sages say, "One of the two priestly clans which did not have a third turn carries out that rite [since the proceeding on the Eighth Day is continuous with the foregoing]."

E. You may even maintain that rabbis [stand behind the cited passage, M. 5:6J].

F. For clearly the two priestly clans are required to cast lots [and that is precisely what M. 5:6J states, without reference to whether the other twenty-two clans do so].

G. In accord with what authority is the following statement, taught on Tannaite authority:

H. **All of the priestly courses repeat the offering of a bullock during the seven days of the Festival a second and a third time, except for the last two, which repeat but do not do it a third time [cf. M. 5:6K-L] [T. Suk. 4:15A].**

I. May I propose that it is Rabbi and not rabbis [since the latter take the view that only one priestly clan misses the chance to offer a sacrifice yet a third time]?

J. You may maintain that even rabbis maintain the present view. What is the sense of **do not do it a third time?** [It makes reference] to the bullocks of the Festival [but not to the bullock that is offered on the Eighth Day, after the Festival has ended].

K. What, then, does the cited passage serve to teach us?

L. It informs us: Whoever offered a bullock one day should not offer one the next day, but they offer them in rotation [M. 5:6K-L].

II.

A. Said R. Eleazar, "What do these seventy bullocks stand for?

B. "They stand for the seventy nations.

C. "What does the single bullock [of the Eighth Day] stand for? It stands for the singular nation.

D. "The matter may be compared to the case of a mortal king, who said to his servants, 'Make a great banquet for me,' but, at the last minute, he said to his best friend, 'Make a little snack for me, so I'll really enjoy something of yours.'"

E. Said R. Yohanan, "It's too bad for the idolators who suffer loss and don't know what they have lost.

F. "When the house of the sanctuary [i.e., the Temple] was standing, the altar would make atonement for them.

G.   "And now who makes atonement for them?"

We deal with the priests' assignments in offering up the various public offerings for the Festival. There were twenty-four priestly watches, all of them allowed to share in the sacrifices. Sixteen of these were occupied with the sixteen beasts (M. 5:6A). Eight were left over for turns on the remainder of the Festival, B. C-I then spell out the consequences. On the first day six of the eight watches offer two sacrifices apiece, and two watches offer one, and so on down, in line with Num. 29:17-32. The point of K-L is that twenty-two priestly watches offer bullocks three times and two have only two turns. Unit I clarifies M. 5:6J and draws it into relationship, with parallel Tannaite statements, thus uncovering the underlying sense of the passage. Unit II deals with the final offering, the one for the Eighth Day of Solemn Assembly.

5:7A-D

A.   Three times a year all the priestly watches shared equally in the offerings of the feasts and in the division of the Show Bread.

B.   At Pentecost they would say to him, "Here you have unleavened bread, here is leavened bread for you."

C.   The priestly watch whose time of service is scheduled [for that week] is the one which offers the daily whole-offerings, offerings brought by reason of vows, freewill offerings, and other public offerings.

D.   And it offers everything.

I.

A.   But the offerings of the feasts [M. 5:7A] belong to the Most High [and not to the priesthood, so why state that they are equally shared]?

B.   Said R. Hisda, "The sense is, 'that which is assigned on the festivals.'"

II.

A.   Our rabbis have taught on Tannaite authority:

B.   How on the basis of Scripture do we know that all the priestly watches shared equally in the offerings of the feasts [M. 5:7A]?

C.   Scripture states, "And come with all the desire of his soul... and minister" (Deut. 18:6, 7). [The Levite to which the verse makes reference is understood as a priest.]

D.   Is it possible [to suppose] that [the same rule applies] also on the rest of the days of the year?

E.   Scripture states, "From one of your gates" (Deut. 18:6).

F.   [The sense is,] "I have made the foregoing statement only to apply to an occasion on which all Israelites enter through a single gate [that is, on a pilgrim festival]."

III.

A.   And in the division of the showbread [M. 5:7A]:

B.   Our rabbis have taught on Tannaite authority:

C. How on the basis of Scripture do we know; all the priestly watches' shared equally in the division of the show bread [M. 5:7A]?

D. [56A] Scripture states, "They shall have portion according to portion to eat" (Deut. 18:8).

E. Just as each has a share in the work [of making the sacrifice], so each has a share in eating the priestly portions.

F. Now what sort of "eating" is at hand?

G. If one should propose [that the allusion is to the eating of the priestly share of] the offerings themselves, that fact derives from another available verse of Scripture, "It shall belong to the priest who offers it" (Lev. 7:9). [This proves that the priest who carries out the sacrifice of an animal keeps the portions of the animal reserved for the priesthood. So Deut. 18:8 cannot be required to make that point.]

H. Therefore [the cited proof text must refer to] the Show-Bread.

I. Is it possible [to suppose] that the same rule applies to obligatory offerings that are sacrificed on the festival but are not in commemoration of the festival itself [such as vow-offerings or sin-offerings that the householder has to offer and that he brings on the occasion of the festival when he makes his pilgrimage]?

J. Scripture states, "Except for that which is sold according to the fathers' houses" (Deut. 18:8).

K. What is it that the fathers have sold to one another?

L. [It is the week of service at the altar that is assigned to each priestly clan, with the statement,] "I shall do it in my week, and you in your week."

IV.

A. At Pentecost they would say to him, "Here you have... [M. 5:7B]:

B. It has been stated on Amoraic authority:

C. Rab said, "[One says] the blessing for the sukkah ['... who has commanded us to dwell in the sukkah'] and afterward the blessing for the season ['who has kept us in life and... brought us to this season']."

D. Rabbah bar bar Hana said, "One says the blessing for the season and afterward for the sukkah."

E. Rab said, "[First] for the sukkah, then for the season, because the obligation pertaining to the day at hand takes precedence."

F. Rabbah bar bar Hana said, "For the season, then for the sukkah, for when one deals with something done frequently and something not frequently, what is done frequently takes precedence, [and the blessing for the season is said at all seasons, while the blessing for the sukkah is said only on the Festival]."

G. May we propose that Rab and Rabbah bar bar Hana carry forward the debate of the House of Shammai and the House of Hillel?

H. For our rabbis have taught on Tannaite authority:

I. Things that are at issue between the House of Shammai and the House of Hillel in regard to the [Sabbath] meal:

J.   The House of Shammai say, "One says a blessing over the Sabbath-day and afterward one says a blessing over the wine."

K.   And the House of Hillel say, "One says a blessing over the wine and afterward one says a blessing over the Sabbath-day" (M. Ber. 8:1).

L.   The House of Shammai say, "One says a blessing over the Sabbath day and afterward one says a blessing over the wine, for the day causes the wine to come, and the day is already sanctified, but the wine has not yet come."

M.   The House of Hillel say, "One says a blessing over the wine and afterward says a blessing over the Sabbath-day, for the wine causes the sanctification of the day to be recited.

N.   "Another consideration: The blessing over the wine is frequent [always being required when wine is used], and the blessing over the day is not frequent [but is said only on certain days]" [T. Ber. 5:51].

O.   When there is something that is done frequently and something that is not done frequently, what is done frequently takes precedence over what is not done frequently.

P.   Now may we then propose that Rab accords with the position of the House of Shammai, and Rabbah bar bar Hana accords with the position of the House of Hillel [as just now explained]?

Q.   Rab may say to you, "I rule even in accord with the principle of the House of Hillel [agreeing with them]. The House of Hillel make the ruling that they did in the cited case only because the wine causes the sanctification to be said. But here, if we do not say the blessing for the season, would we not in any event say the blessing for the sukkah? [We assuredly would!]"

R.   And Rabbah bar bar Hana may say to you, "I rule even in accord with the position of the House of Shammai. In the case at hand [with regard to wine and the Sabbath] the House of Shammai make the ruling that they do only because it is the day that causes the wine to be brought.

S.   "But here, even if we do not say the blessing for the sukkah, do we not in any event say the blessing for the season? [We assuredly do! Since the season is more frequent, it takes precedence.]"

T.   We have learned in the Mishnah: At Pentecost they would say to him, "Here you have unleavened bread, here is leavened bread for you" [M. 5:7B].

U.   Now here we have a case in which the leavened bread is the main thing and the unleavened bread is not essential [for the leavened bread is part of the ritual of the day, so Lev. 23:17 (Slotki), while the unleavened bread is merely the ordinary show-bread of the previous Sabbath (Slotki, p. 273, ns. 2-3)], and the framer of the passage [gives precedence to the unleavened bread and then the leavened, when he provides the formula:] "Here you have unleavened bread, here is leavened bread for you [M. 5:7B].

V.   Would that passage not then provide a refutation of the position of Rab [who holds that the obligation of the day at hand takes precedence? Here it is just the opposite].

W.   In point of fact it is a dispute among Tannaite authorities about the proper framing of the statement at hand.

X.   For it has been taught on Tannaite authority:

Y.   "Here is unleavened bread for you. Here is leavened bread for you."

Z.   Abba Saul says, "Here is leavened bread for you, here is unleavened bread for you" [that is, in the order that Rab would require].

AA. R. Nahman bar Hisda expounded, "It is not in accord with the opinion of Rab, who has said that the blessing for the sukkah is said and afterward the blessing for the season; but the blessing for the season is said and afterward the blessing for the sukkah."

BB. And R. Sheshet, son of R. Idi, said, "The blessing for the sukkah is said and afterward the blessing for the season."

CC. And the decided law is the blessing for the sukkah is said, and afterward the blessing for the season.

V.

A.   The priestly watch whose time of service is scheduled... and the other public offerings [M. 5:7C]:

B.   What does the latter clause serve to include?

C.   It includes the bullock required on account of a transgression caused by the inadvertence of the community and also he-goats brought as atonement for idolatry [that may have been committed during the festival].

VI.

A.   And it offers everything [M. 5:7D]:

B.   What does this phrase serve to include?

C.   It includes offerings brought to keep the altar busy [when otherwise there would be no sacrificial activity there. There would be free will offerings paid for by public funds.]

The reference, M. 5:6J, to other festivals, generates the inclusion of M. 5:7, the shares of the priestly watches on other festivals. The principal interest is in the division of the Show Bread, M. 5:7A-B, E, M. 5:8. Units I-III provide light glosses for the Mishnah's language or proof-texts for its rule. Unit IV is inserted because it adduces in evidence a citation of the Mishnah-paragraph at hand, but the passage -- a rather elegant one -- has not been constructed with the present Mishnah-paragraph in mind. Units V, VI then complete the task of Mishnah-exegesis of a narrow sort.

5:7E - 5:8

E.   On a festival day which comes next to a Sabbath, whether before or after it, all of the priestly watches were equal in the division of the Show-Bread.

M. 5:7

A. [If] a day intervened [between a festival-day and a Sabbath], the priestly watch which was scheduled for that time took ten loaves, and the one that stayed back [in the Temple] took two.

B. And on all other days of the year, the entering priestly watch took six, and the one going off duty took six.

C. R. Judah says, "The one coming on duty takes seven, and the one going off duty takes five."

D. The ones going on duty divide at the north, and the ones going off duty divide at the south.

E. [The priestly watch of] Bilgah always divided it in the south, and their ring was fixed, and their wall-niche was blocked up.

M. 5:8

I.

A. What is the meaning of before or after it? If we propose that "before" refers to the Sabbath before the first festival day of the Festival, and "after" refers to the final festival day of the Festival, then we have nothing other than the Sabbath that falls within the Festival itself. [If the first day of the Festival came on a Friday, or the last on a Sunday, we have a Sabbath of the Festival.]

B. Rather, "before" refers to the last festival day of the Festival, and "after" refers to the first festival day of the Festival.

C. Why then [does the outgoing priestly clan get a share in the Show-Bread [as M. 5:7E specifies]?

D. Since one group has to come early [before the Sabbath] and the other has to stay on [after the Sabbath], rabbis made a provision for them to eat their meals together.

II.

A. If a day intervened... [M. 5:8A]:

B. [56B] [With respect to M. 5:8C, Judah's provision of two extra loaves for the clan coming on duty], why provide these two?

C. Said R. Isaac, "They are an extra salary for the closing of the doors [left open by the outgoing clan]."

D. And why not [have the outgoing group say], "Deduct one now and take one more later" ["Less for less," that is, (Slotki, p. 275, n. 8:) "You take one less now, and when it is your turn to go out, the next incoming course will in its turn be one less"]?

E. Said Abayye, "A young pumpkin is better than a fully-grown one."

III.

A. Said R. Judah, "And [in like manner] they divided the additional offerings [just as they divided the Show-Bread]."

B. The following objection was raised:

C. **The outgoing priestly watch offers the morning daily whole-offering and the additional offerings.**

D. The incoming one then offers the evening daily whole-offering and the incense [T. Suk. 4:24-25A].

E. Now the framer of this passage says nothing about their sharing the additional offerings [as Judah has claimed is the case].

F. The framer of that passage was not dealing with the subject of sharing the additional offerings [and that is why he did not mention it].

G. Said Raba, "And lo, the Tannaite authority of the house of Samuel, who dealt with the division of the sacrifices, does not make mention of the division of the additional offerings in the same context."

H. For the Tannaite authority of the house of Samuel stated, "The outgoing priestly watch offers the morning daily whole offering and the additional offerings, and the incoming priestly watch prepares the evening daily whole-offering and the incense. Four priests go in, two from the outgoing watch, two from the incoming one, and they divide up the Show-Bread."

I. Now we note that he makes no mention at all of their dividing the additional offerings.

J. This then constitutes a refutation of the view of R. Judah, does it not?

K. It does indeed refute his thesis.

IV.

A. The ones going on duty divide at the north [M. 5:8D]:

B. Our rabbis have taught on Tannaite authority:

C. The ones going on duty divide at the north so that it should be publicly visible that they are the incoming group.

D. And the ones who are going off duty divide at the south so that it should be publicly visible that they are going off duty.

V.

A. [The priestly watch of] Bilgah always divided in the south [M. 5:8E]:

B. Our rabbis have taught on Tannaite authority:

C. [The priestly watch of] Bilgah always divided in the south, and their ring was fixed, and their wall niche was blocked up [M. 5:8E],

D. because of Miriam, daughter of Bilgah, who apostasized.

E. She went off and married an officer of the Greek royal house.

F. And when the Greeks went into the sanctuary, she came along and stamped on the top of the altar, screaming at it, "Wolf, wolf! You have wiped out the fortune of Israel, and you [still] did not then stand up for them in the time of their trouble."

G. Now when sages heard this, they made her [course's] ring immovable, and they blocked up their wall-niche.

H. And some say it was because [the priestly watch of Bilgah] delayed in observing its priestly watch.

I. [In T.'s version]: So the watch of Yeshebab went in and served in its stead.

J. Therefore Bilgah always appears to be among the outgoing priestly watches [at the south], and Yeshebab always appears to be among the incoming priestly watches [at the north].

K.   Neighbors of the wicked normally receive no reward,

L.   except for Yeshebab,

M.   neighbor to Bilgah, who received a reward [T. Suk. 4:28].

N.   Now there is no difficulty in the matter from the viewpoint of him who has said that the reason was that the priestly watch of Bilgah delayed in observing its priestly watch. That is [a perfectly reasonable explanation for] why the entire priestly watch-clan was punished.

O.   But from the viewpoint of him who has said [that the reason was that] Miriam, daughter of Bilgah, had apostasized, do we impose a penalty on someone because of what his daughter has done?

P.   Said Abayye, "Indeed so. It is like what people say, 'What the child says in the market place is either the father's or the mother's [talk].'"

Q.   But then we must ask, on account of [the disgrace of] the father and the mother, shall we penalize the entire priestly watch-clan?

R.   Said Abayye, "Woe for the wicked, woe for his neighbor. Good for the righteous, good for his neighbor,'

S.   "as it is said, 'Say to you of the righteous that it shall be well with him, for they shall eat the fruit of their doings' (Is. 3:10)."

We recall (Holy Things II, pp. 159-161) that the Show Bread is removed from the table and replaced on the Sabbath. What is taken away is given out to the priests. Now, if all the priests are available, who gets it? All divide it, if all are present, M. 5:7E. But if there is an intervening day, e.g., if the festival fell on Thursday, then the priestly watch in charge for the following Sabbath took ten loaves. What about the watch which served the preceding week but remained in the Temple over the Sabbath, since it came so close to the festival? That watch took two. The dispute of B-C, D + E, provides some further information in line with B and completes the triplet, M. 5:7E, M. 5:8A, and M. 5:8B. Unit I clarifies the sense of M. 5:7E, unit II, M. 5:8C. Unit III proposes a secondary expansion of M. 5:8, that is, applying the rule at hand to a matter not made explicit in the Mishnah. Unit IV then proceeds to M. 5:8D, and unit V, M. 5:8E.

BROWN JUDAIC STUDIES SERIES

Continued from back cover